International and National Politics

About the Author

Professor B. Vivekanandan is former Chairman of the Centre for American and West European Studies, School of International Studies, Jawaharlal Nehru University, New Delhi. He was Assistant Professor, Associate Professor and Professor at the School of International Studies, JNU, for 29 years. Also, he founded the Jayaprakash Foundation and was its President for 24 years.

Professor Vivekanandan has to his credit many books including *International Concerns of European Social Democrats; Welfare States and the Future; Pathfinders : Social Democrats of Scandinavia; The Shrinking Circle: The Commonwealth in British Foreign Policy, 1945-1974; In Retrospect: Reflections on Select Issues in World Politics, 1975-2000; Issues of Our Times; India Looks Ahead: Jayaprakash Narayan Memorial Lectures; Building on Solidarity: Social Democracy and the New Millennium; As the Mind Unfolds; Echoes in Parliament; Contemporary Europe and South Asia*; and *Why Social Democracy?* Besides, he has published a large number of research papers in several national and international journals of repute.

He was Visiting Professor at Helsinki University, Finland, and at Carleton University, Canada, and was Visiting Fellow at the University of Constanz, Germany, Bruno Kreisky Archiv Foundation and Renner Institute, Austria, and at the Swedish Institute, Sweden. He was a Distinguished Visitor of the Jean Jaures Foundation, Paris.

International and National Politics

Some Selected Essays

by

Prof. B. VIVEKANANDAN

Former Chairman

Centre for American & West European Studies

School of International Studies

Jawaharlal Nehru University

New Delhi

CONCEPT PUBLISHING COMPANY, NEW DELHI-110059

Cataloging in Publication Data—DK
Courtesy: D.K. Agencies (P) Ltd. <docinfo@dkagencies.com>

Vivekanandan, B. (Bhagavathi Panicker), 1939-
International and national politics : some selected essays / by B. Vivekanandan.
p. cm.
With reference to India.
Includes bibliographical references.
Includes index.
ISBN 13: 9788180695964
ISBN 10: 8180695964

1. World politics—1945-1989. 2. World politics—1989- 3. Socialism. 4. India—Politics and government—1947- 5. India—Foreign relations. I. Title.

DDC 320.904 5 22

ISBN-13: 978-81-8069-596-4
ISBN-10: 81-8069-596-4

First Published 2009

Published and Printed by
Ashok Kumar Mittal
Concept Publishing Company
A/15-16, Commercial Block, Mohan Garden
New Delhi-110059 (India)

Phones : 25351460, 25351794
Fax : 091-11-25357109
Email : publishing@conceptpub.com

To

Prof. Madhu Dandavate

Outstanding Socialist Leader and
A Crystal in Indian Politics
Who is No More

Preface and Acknowledgements

The Spectrum is a collection of thirteen significant essays which I have written – a majority of them have been written recently, and others earlier. But all of them are of contemporary value. Each one of them has its own distinction. The themes dealt with in them include: the theoretical and practical aspects of social democracy as a valid system for the societal reconstruction in the new millennium; the position of European Union in the emerging global system; India-Austria relations; the British role in the recent Iraq invasion; prospects of the UN Reforms; Globalization; Welfare States; Tibet's freedom; inter-relationship between peace and power; Common Security doctrine; debilitating features of India's public sector in the 1960s; India's language problem; and an evaluation of India's progress during its silver jubilee celebrations. All these essays have been articulated after making extensive study and research on each subject dealt with.

To explain the context, the essay 'Why Social Democracy?' is the text of three lectures I delivered at the School of International Relations of the Jadavpur University, Calcutta, in March 2005. The essay 'European Union and the Emerging Global System' has been written after extensive research carried on in important EU countries like Britain, France, Germany, Italy and Belgium. It is the finding of a research project on the subject, sponsored by the European Commission, under the JNU-EUSP Project at the Jawaharlal Nehru University, New Delhi. The essay 'Austria Viewed From India' has been written after extensive research I have undertaken in Austria under the programme of the Austrian Academic Exchange Service, with the support of the Bruno

Kreisky Archiv Foundation and Dr. Karl Renner Institute, Vienna. Besides many discussions I had with Austrian official and non-official experts on the subject, the documents I studied for the purpose included the personal papers of the former Austrian Chancellor Dr. Bruno Kreisky. The essay has been published in 2002 as a chapter in the *International Perspectives of Austria* volume, of the *Official History of Austria*, edited by Prof. Oliver Rathkolb, Prof. Otto M. Maschkel, and Dr. Stefan August Lütgenau. The essay 'Britain and the Iraq Invasion' is a paper which I presented at a national seminar at the Centre for International Strategic and Development Studies (CISDS), held in Bombay, in April 2004. Similarly, the essay 'UN Reforms in Perspective' is a paper I presented at an international seminar at CISDS, held in Bombay on the subject, in October 2005. The essay 'Globalization and the Developing Countries' is the lecture I delivered at the Labour Institute for Economic Research in Helsinki, Finland, in September 2001. The essay 'Nordic Welfare States: Viewed From India' is the Plenary Speech I delivered at the Fifth International European Sociology Association Congress, held in Helsinki, Finland, in August 2001. The essay 'Freedom of Tibet' is the paper which I presented at a seminar on the subject, held in Dharamsala, Himachal Pradesh, in 1993. The issue is still a live one. Three other essays — 'Peace Through Power', 'India's Public Sector,' and 'Whither India?' – are papers which have been published earlier in the Bombay journal, *Janata*, where as the essay 'India's Language Question' has been published in the New Delhi journal, *Mainstream*. The essay 'Common Security' is a paper I presented at a Seminar at Jadavpur University, Calcutta, in 1999.

During the course of writing these essays, I had to consult a lot of material from various institutions and libraries in India and abroad. In addition, I held discussions and interviews also with many experts abroad. The institutions and libraries which I would like to thank in this context are:

Jawaharlal Nehru University, New Delhi; Indian Council of World Affairs, New Delhi; Royal Institute of International Affairs, London; London School of Economics and Political Science, London; International Institute of Strategic Studies, London, Jean Jaures Foundation, Paris; Institute for Security Studies (WEU), Paris; Institute Francais de Relations Internationals (IFRI), Paris; Department of Political Studies, University of Rome; Institute of International Affairs, Rome; Department of Social Policy, Free University, Berlin; Cergy-Pontois University, Cergy, France; Friedrich Ebert Stiftung, Bonn; Department of Social Policy, University of Helsinki, Finland; Vienna Institute for Development and Cooperation, Vienna; Bruno Kreisky Archiv Foundation; Vienna; Karl Renner Institute, Vienna; Olof Palme International Centre, Stockholm; and the European Institute for Asian Studies, Brussels. I am thankful to the staff of all these institutions and their libraries for their cooperation.

The scholars whom I would like to thank in this context for the fruitful discussions and interwiews I had with them are: Dr. Bruno Kreisky, Former Chancellor of Austria; Prof. Oliver Rathkolb and Dr. Stefan August Lütgenau of Bruno Kreisky Archiv Foundation, Vienna; Ms Margit Schmidt, Secretary General, Kreisky Forum for International Dialogue, Vienna; Dr. Wolfgang Petritsch and Dr. Georg Lennkh of the Austrian Ministry of Foreign Affairs; Dr. Frederik Reiter, former Chief of Cabinet of Chancellor Bruno Kreisky, Vienna; Dr. Arne Haselbach, former Director, Vienna Institute for Development and Cooperation; Mr. Erwin Lanc, Director, International Institute for Peace, Vienna; Dr. Heinz Fischer, President, Austrian Parliament; Dr. Peter Kreisky, Economic Adviser to Chamber of Labour, Vienna; Dr. Wolfgang Schallenberg, former Secretary General, Austrian Ministry of Foreign Affairs; Dr. Ferdinand Lacina, former Austrian Finance Minister; Dr. Erich Andrlik, Director, Vienna Institute for Development and Cooperation; Dr. Erich Fröschl, Director, Karl Renner Institute, Vienna; Dr. Sourabh

Sanatani, Vienna; Prof. Hartmut Elsenhans, University of Leipzig, Germany; Prof. Martin Kohli, Free University, Berlin; Mr. Malcolm Subhan and Mr. Dick Guppwell, European Institute for Asian Studies, Brussels; Dr. Peter Wilson, British Foreign and Commonwealth Office, London; Dr. Dana Allin, International Institute of Strategic Studies, London; Mr James Gilbert, Principal Administrator, European Commission, Brussels; Dr. Antonio Missiroli, Institute for Security Studies (WEU), Paris; Dr. Guillaume Parmentier, IFRI, Paris; Prof. Chrisopher Hill, Prof. Paul Taylor, Prof. William Wallace and Dr. Karen E. Smith of the London School of Economics and Political Science, London; Dr. Detlef Weigel, Dr. Christoph Jessen and Dr. Ernst Reichel of the German Foreign Office, Berlin; Prof. Fulco Lanchester and Prof. Vinzenzo Nazo of the University of Rome; Prof. Gianni Bonvicini, Institute of International Affairs, Rome; Mr Axel Queval, Jean Jaures Foundation, Paris; Prof. Thomas Meyer, Dortmund University, Germany; Dr Ernst Ulrich von Weizacker, Member of Parliament, Germany; Prof. Jean-Paul Chagnollaud and Dr Sophie Nadal, Cergy-Pontois University, France; Prof. J.P. Roos, University of Helsinki; Dr Jukka Pekkarinen, Director, Labour Institute for Economic Research, Helsinki; and Dr Angathevar Baskaran, Middlesex University Business School, London.

I am thankful to the European Commission for meeting the cost of my field research for the study of 'European Union and the Emerging Global System', under the JNU-EUSP Project of the Jawaharlal Nehru University, New Delhi. Similarly, I am thankful to Dr Bruno Kreisky Archiv Foundation, Dr Karl Renner Institute and the Austrian Academic Exchange Service, all in Vienna, for the support they have extended for my study on Austria.

Finally, words fail to adequately express my thanks to my wife, Vimala, daughters Nimmi and Jayashree and son-in-law Benny for their unfailing support and assistance all through the preparation of this volume.

This volume is dedicated to late Prof. Madhu Dandavate, an outstanding socialist and a beacon of value-based politics in India, with whom I had a three-and-a-half decades unbroken and warm friendship as a comrade-in-arms in the Indian socialist movement.

B. Vivekanandan

Contents

1

Why Social Democracy?

I

Philosophical Foundations

When the Soviet communist system, and the Stalinist dictatorial structures the Russian Revolution had produced, collapsed in the early 1990s, eminent, but ill-informed, rightwing scholars rushed to instantly pronounce that socialism had failed and capitalism had won the race When that euphoria was in full swing, an American diplomat came to the School of International Studies at the Jawaharlal Nehru University, New Delhi, and gave a seminar, waxing eloquence to this line of argument, and made a sweeping observation that the collapse of the Soviet Union marked the failure of socialism. I was present at that seminar. When that American diplomat completed his presentation, I asked him whether his sweeping statement that socialism had failed applied to social democracies practiced in the Scandinavian countries like Sweden, Denmark, Norway and Finland also. Caught unaware, he instantly made a quick retreat and conceded that the Scandinavian social democracies are great democracies, and that they belonged to a different successful category. The point is that, not only that American diplomat was forced to retreat from his sweeping statement that the collapse of the Soviet Union represented the failure of socialism, but also that he was forced to draw a distinction between the Soviet Communism and the Scandinavian Social Democracy.

However, historically, the socialist movement was born with an agenda of securing enduring remedies to the miseries of poor people, as most of these miseries are largely man-made, and remain mainly due to the maldistribution of the fruits of growth in our economy and society. The movement has a history of about two centuries. Born in the context of the Industrial Revolution in Europe, the initial impetus of the socialist movement came from questions like how to end poverty and exploitation and how to promote equality and distributive justice in society. Since then a large number of eminent thinkers and philosophers have spent many years of their lives to refine the movement's goals and methods to promote equality and distributive justice in society.

Socialist Philosophers

The philosophical foundation of social democracy was laid on the ideas propounded by eminent socialist thinkers like St. Simon, Charles Fourier, Robert Owen, Louis Blanc, Edward Bernstein, Ferdinand Lassalle, Joseph Proudhon, Karl Marx, Friedrich Engels, Bernard Shaw, Harold J. Laski and so on. These philosophers were men with deep social commitments, who reacted sharply and strongly against various acts of injustices, oppression and exploitation in society, which shook their conscience and came out with valid propositions to end these maladies. Indeed, each one of them had made a distinct contribution to nourish the socialist movement in the light of their understanding of various problems. However, all these philosophers were moved with a conviction that socialism held the key to achieve equality and justice in society. Following them, a large number of people across the world joined the movement and enriched it.

In this context, I would like to draw your attention to certain pertinent contributions of some of these great socialist thinkers. While doing so, it is important to keep in mind the time and space in which these great philosophers have crystalized their ideas. We must remember that two of the earliest socialist thinkers – St. Simon and Charles Fourier – were children of the Industrial Revolution in Europe. St. Simon (1760-1825) was the first socialist thinker who stressed the need to organize society efficiently. The new socialist society he envisaged was the one that was built on a cooperative relationship based on the model of a workshop. The quintessence of his thought was that people should organize the society in a manner 'most advantageous to the largest number'. His dream was to transform the world into a land of plenty and prosperity and wanted that science and technology and industry should be attuned to achieve this objective. He stressed the need to generate large scale employment opportunities through planned public works. He envisaged a new society in which the proletariat would be abolished and all wage-earners would be made associates in the process of production, an attempt which is now being made in some Scandinavian countries.

While St. Simon focused on the inefficiency of organization in society, Charles Fourier (1772-1837) focused attention on maldistribution and other injustices in the economic system. Fourier was averse to the promotion of large-scale industries and wanted that production should be organized directly for consumption in a decentralized manner. He believed that people's situations should be changed by organizing society on the principle of 'association'. He stressed that people should maintain their contact with soil in order to attain fulfilment in life. Fourier held that commodities should be produced not for trade nor for profit but for consumption and that there should be a close inter-relationship between production and distribution.

Robert Owen

I would like to focus on the contributions of a few other socialists who made outstanding contributions to the movement for social democracy. One is Robert Owen, the father of British Socialism. Owen is a colourful star in the galaxy of great socialists. He was an industrialist who became a socialist. He made his father-in-law's textile mill at New Lanark, in England, as the laboratory of his socialist experiments. He was the founder of the first trade union in the world and was also the founder of the first consumer cooperative society in the world. I had the opportunity to visit this cradle of British socialism at New Lanark a few years ago and I was amazed at the vision Robert Owen had displayed while conducting his socialist experiments there more than a century and-a-half ago. Owen believed that basically the nature of man is good and that it would remain good if he is provided with the right lead and right environment. He set an example by building up a community life revolving around his textile mill at New Lanark.

Robert Owen was the first entrepreneur to abolish the child labour. Pertinently, when Owen assumed the management of the textile mill at New Lanark, he found that 25 per cent of the mill's 2000 employees were poor children, aged between 5 and 10 years. Instantly, he stopped the practice of employing child labour in his mill. In order to provide workers with more leisure time, he cut down the working hours in his factory. He enhanced the wages of the workers of his factory and provided them with good houses and other benefits like sickness benefits, old age insurance, educational facilities, healthy environment, provision of food items at cost price, and so on. He gave key importance to education in the entire exercise of his community building. Owen had shown that better treatment of, and humane relations with, employees would produce better results, and that the best solution to many problems in enterprises would be the establishment of an associative labour.

When the workers of his textile mill faced unemployment due to the shortage of cotton, generally due to late arrival of the shipments from far off countries like Egypt, he gave them alternative employment in the neighbouring agricultural land. The idea was that in case of unemployment, the unemployed should be given occupational re-orientation, so that they could be productively employed elsewhere within a broad framework of an industrial-cum-agricultural society, based on unity and cooperation. Therefore, Owen envisaged a balanced growth of both industry and agriculture, in which agriculture would grow simultaneously as an appendage of industry, by promoting cooperative farming.

He encouraged the building workers, architects, masons, carpenters, plumbers, painters, bricklayers and so on to establish their own cooperative set-up to be free from the clutches of the exploitative private contractors. As a result, in 1833 the building workers in Britain had established 'The Grand National Guild of Builders'. Similarly, Owen promoted the establishment of consumer cooperatives and encouraged the direct exchange of products produced by craftsmen and cooperative producers as a measure to eliminate the middleman's exploitation. In 1844, he pioneered the establishment of the famous Rochdale Society, at New Lanark, and provided the inspiration for the launching of consumer cooperative movements all over Europe, and impressed people by explaining the rationale behind it — the ending of middleman's exploitation.

Owen was emphatic that social revolution should be carried out without bloodshed and violence and that this should be harnessed through a process of ever enlarging cooperative ventures. Equality based on shared privileges, in a decentralized community structure, was his ideal. In New Lanark, he ventured to build a self-sufficient community.

Louis Blanc (1811-1882) was the first exponent of evolutionary socialism. He argued that the state should be attuned to play a key role in the transformation of society, particularly in the organization of the economic development and public welfare. He said that this change in the role of the state could be brought about through the introduction of universal suffrage and through the institutionalization of democratic control over the state apparatus. He believed in reforms and promoted the concept of social solidarity. He was the champion of right to work, trade unions, and of consumers and producers cooperative societies. He wanted to organize society on a community basis. Besides, he was an exponent of the full-employment policy.

Another philosopher who was a champion of evolutionary socialism was Edward Bernstein. He argued that instead of destroying the present society in order to establish a new society of the working class only, the socialists should work for the elevation of workers to the social position of the bourgeoisie, and thus universalize bourgeoisie everywhere in the society. He said that this could be achieved through a constitutional and democratic reform process, by increasing the state control over the means of production, and by improving the conditions of workers and by strengthening the middle classes. He said that by extending franchise, the state power can be captured through the ballot box. He favoured the method of parliamentary democratic reform to establish a socialist society.

Ferdinand Lassalle (1825-1864) was another socialist thinker who held the view that the state should be made an instrument of emancipation of the proletariat. He said that universal suffrage would provide the key to push forward social reforms in a peaceful and democratic manner. He viewed that getting power interlocked with the rule of law is the only civilized way to effect meaningful and enduring social change.

Another 19th century socialist philosopher, Joseph Proudhon (1809-1865), said that 'property is theft', therefore, it should be shared by all. He said that small-scale economic activities, like self-employed peasant families and small-scale production units, would constitute an ideal system than large-scale production units, which were the cause and effect of economic and social inequality. For him, mutuality, expressed through democratic and decentralized small associations, endlessly proliferating and federally associating, constituted an ideal society.

Perception on Marx Needs Change

Karl Marx was another socialist philosopher who made a significant contribution to the development of social democracy. It is not my intention here to explain what young Marx prescribed in his *Communist Manifesto* in 1848 to end exploitation in society. I presume that most of you are familiar with the methodology of revolution and class struggle he had prescribed in it to establish a classless society. On the basis of the *Communist Manifesto* of 1848, and on the basis of what he wrote up to 1871, Marx has been depicted as an undiluted philosopher of violent Revolution. Many so-called Marxists stop studying Marx there. They do not want to go beyond 1871 to examine the thinking of Marx as a mature person, enriched by new experiences. But, on balance, I am fully convinced that in order to do justice to him we have to change our prevalent perception of Marx. He was an outstanding humanist and a democratic socialist.

It may be noted that when Karl Marx wrote the *Communist Manifesto* in 1848 for the Communist League, he was only 29 years old. And Friedrich Engels was only 27. That was a time when Europe was reeling under the heels of despots. There existed neither universal suffrage nor rule of the ballot box in most parts of Europe. Marx's own country, Germany, was no exception. He and his friend Engels were victims of those despots who chased them out of their homeland. Therefore, situations in Germany and Europe at that time dominated the thinking of young Marx when he advocated revolution in the *Communist Manifesto*. This despotic environment in Europe in 1848 led Marx to advocate revolution as the means to end exploitation.

But a big change took place in Marx after the lessons he learnt from the rise and fall of the Paris Commune in 1871. It may be noted that the rise of Paris Commune took place at a time when France was engaged in the Franco-Prussian War of 1870-71. That was the right time, according to Marxian prescriptions, for workers to rise in revolt and capture power and establish a Workers' Commune in Paris. Indeed, Marx was deeply involved in the planning of the rise of the Paris Commune. Therefore, with the blessings of Marx, workers of Paris rose in revolt and successfully captured power and established the Paris Commune in 1871. Though workers successfully captured power in Paris, they could not sustain it for long. After getting defeated in the Franco-Prussian War, the French army retuned to Paris and recaptured power from the Communards and destroyed the Paris Commune. In the process, 20,000 Communards were executed and about 140,000 of them were imprisoned. Two years ago I had visited this spot in Paris where these executions were carried out. The rise of the Paris Commune ended as a big failure in 1871 itself.

Marx in Deep Introspection

The failure of Paris Commune in 1871 drove Marx into a deep introspection, which brought a remarkable change in his perception, and produced a new vision in him which led to a revision in his perception to use revolution as a methodology of regime change. A mature Marx, at the age of 52, made a room for peaceful methods to usher in socialist societies. In a historic speech made in 1872 in Amsterdam, a mature Marx, enriched by the experience of the rise and fall of the Paris Commune, revised his earlier formulation regarding the path of revolution to usher in a socialist society. He said: "We do not claim that the means necessary for bringing about this aim [emancipation of labour] will be the same everywhere. We know that we must take account of the institutions, customs and traditions of various countries, such as United States and Great Britain -

and if I know your institutions better, I should perhaps add Holland — where the workers will be able to achieve their aims by peaceful means. But this will not be the case in all countries".

Three years later, in 1875, in his *Critique of the Gotha Programme* of the German Social Democratic Party, he had underlined the relevance of waging class struggle through a democratic republic. He said: "Freedom consists in the transformation of the state from an organ dominant over society into an organ subordinate to society". He amplified this new outlook further again just three years before his death in 1883. In a letter to a British socialist, H. M. Hyndman, Marx wrote in 1880: "If you say that you do not share the views of my party for England I can only reply that party considers an English revolution unnecessary, but according to historical precedents possible. If the unavoidable evolution turns into revolution it would not only be the fault of the ruling class but also of the working class".

Engels also modified his stance on the path of revolution and showed his faith in the parliamentary democracy. In a letter to the German Social Democratic Party in 1891, eight years after the death of Marx, Engels wrote: "If anything is certain it is that the Party and the working class can triumph only in the form of a democratic republic". He urged the German SPD that its programme must include "the representative assembly of the people". He recognized the significance of universal suffrage as a weapon of emancipation. He wrote in 1895: "With the successful utilization of universal suffrage an entirely new mode of proletarian struggle came into force.... The bourgeoisie and the government came to be much more afraid of the legal rather than the illegal actions of the Workers' Party and the results of elections rather than those of rebellion." He wrote: "The irony of world history turns everything upside down. We, the revolutionaries, the 'Rebels', we are thriving far better on legal methods, than on illegal methods and revolts. The parties of order ... are perishing under the legal conditions created by themselves.... We, under this legality, get firm muscles ... and if we are not so crazy as to let ourselves be driven into street fighting, in order to please them, then nothing else is finally left to them but themselves to break through this legality so faithful to them." He wrote further: "The time is past for revolutions to be carried through by small minorities at the head of unconscious masses".

These mature evaluations of two titans of 'scientific socialism' assume special importance for democratic socialists as well as for true Marxists, as both of them have, in the evening of their lives, endorsed peaceful democratic approach for societal transformation.

I have given these details of the mature thinkings of Marx and Engels to underline the point that there is need to seriously change our perception of Marx and Engels as philosophers of violent revolution. As the evidence I have presented shows, in the ultimate analysis, Marx and Engels had subscribed to the ideas of social democracy, wherever possible. They had shown great respect for democracy and representative form of government wherever they had existed at that time. As a famous British socialist, Harold J. Laski, said, the ideal state Marx had envisaged was democracy.

Therefore, true Marxists need not fight shy of joining the fold of social democrats to bring about progressive reforms in society. The distortions introduced in the Marxian thinking by Lenin, Stalin and Mao should be viewed as distortions only.

Fabian Socialists

Fabian socialists have also made a notable contribution to the development of social democracy. Leading Fabian socialists were Sydney Webb, Beatrice Webb, Bernard Shaw, G.D.H. Cole, Harold J. Laski, R. H. Tawney, and so on. They argued that a democratic state, with an impulse for social reform, cannot be attuned towards revolution and class struggle. Therefore, they supported an evolutionary reformist approach to bring about social transformation, and adopted the path of peaceful evolution of a socialist society. In the early 20th century the attention of Fabians had turned more towards the questions of poverty, distribution of wealth, and equality of income in society.

George Bernard Shaw (1856-1960), a leading Fabian socialist, began his famous book, *The Intelligent Woman's Guide to Socialism and Capitalism*, with an opening sentence which said: "It would be easy, dear madam, to refer you to many books on socialism. But, I strongly advice you not to read a line of them until you and your friends have discussed for yourselves how wealth should be distributed in a respectable civilized country, and arrived at the best conclusion you can". Shaw had championed the cause of equality of income in society. In the same book, *The Intelligent Woman's Guide….*, Shaw wrote: "What the socialists say is that none of these plans will work well, and the only satisfactory plan is to give everybody an equal share no matter what sort of a person she is, or how old she is, or what sort of work she does, or who, or what her father was." Thus the main thrust of Fabians was for economic equality and distributive justice. Their main focus was on equal distribution of the social product.

Indian Socialists

In this line of great social democratic thinkers, I would like to add the names of four outstanding Indian socialists – Jayaprakash Narayan, Acharya Narendra Dev, Ram Manohar Lohia, and Asoka Mehta. They have made significant contributions to develop a socialist vision for India, keeping in view the peculiarities of the Indian situation. Ideologically, the Indian socialists imbibed the social democratic ideas propounded by great European socialists, including by Karl Marx. But the Indian socialists like Jayaprakash Narayan provided greater clarity to the question of why socialists should follow a peaceful non-violent method to usher in a socialist society. He focused attention on the inadequacy of the violent means to achieve a socialist society. He said that in Russia violent revolution did not produce the society Lenin had envisaged. Instead, it produced dictators like Stalin. It failed to produce decent, fraternal and civilized human beings. Moreover, he said, a violent revolution would not result in power going to the people and that it was bound to end in the betrayal of people by failing to keep the promises made to them prior to the revolution. He had a clear perception of the interlocking nature of the character and effects of revolutions. In a brilliant analysis, Jayaprakash Narayan explained: "A social revolution has two parts: destruction of the old order of society and construction of the new. In a successful violent revolution, success lies in the destruction of the old order from the roots. That indeed is a great achievement. But, at that point something vital happens which nearly strangles the succeeding process. During the revolution there is widespread unorganized revolutionary violence. When that violence, assisted by other factors into which one need not go here, has succeeded in destroying the old power structure, it becomes necessary to cry halt to the unorganized mass violence and create out of it an organized means of violence to protect and defend the revolution. Thus a new instrument of power is created, and whosoever among the revolutionaries succeeds in capturing this instrument, they and their party or faction become the new rulers. They become the masters of the new state, and power passes from the hands of the people to them. There is always a struggle for power at the top, and heads roll and blood flows, victory going in the end to the most determined and the most ruthless, the best organized. It is not that the violent revolutionaries deceive and betray: it is just the logic of violence working itself out. It cannot be otherwise." This conviction made the Indian socialists to reject violent means to bring about social transformation in India.

In addition, the Indian socialists have pointed out that in view of the peculiar features of the Indian society, social factors assumed equal importance to economic factors because in India caste and class overlapped in a big way. Therefore, they argued that in India social and economic upliftment of the people will have to go hand in hand along with the principles of equality and distributive justice. It was further enriched by the ideas of Mahatma Gandhi. Unlike in Europe where people's inequality could be measured in economic terms, mainly by dividing them into classes, in India inequality is also measured in social terms due to the existence of castes in Indian society. Therefore, the Indian socialists had to modify the European model of social democracy, and add to it India's peculiar socio-economic situation, while striving for social democratic solutions to India's socio-economic problems.

The ideological dispensation of the Indian socialists was clearly spelt out in a statement made in 1964 during the formation of the Samyukta Socialist Party. In that statement the Party pledged "to achieve, by democratic and peaceful means, a socialist society, free from social, political and economic exploitation of man by man and nation by nation." It also pledged to "organize, guide and lead peaceful revolutionary class struggles, mass movements and civil disobedience; promote constructive efforts and use parliamentary methods to secure political power in order to eliminate all forms of injustice and feudal capitalist exploitation."

Originally an Undivided Movement

We must understand that from the very beginning, for about hundred years, the socialist movement was an integrated movement. Socialists and communists were together in it. Though Marx called himself a communist, when he convened the First Socialist International in 1864, the parties which constituted the Socialist International were Social Democratic and Labour Parties. From Russia, the party which participated in it was the Russian Social Democratic and Labour Party. This nomenclature of parties was kept intact when Friedrich Engels, after the death of Marx in 1883, convened the Second Socialist International in 1889 also. The position remained unchanged until the Russian Revolution of 1917. After the Russian Revolution, Lenin divided the socialist movement and splited off the communists from the socialists and established Communist parties all over Europe. Besides, in 1919 he established the Comintern or the Communist International and attached these parties with the Communist Party of the Soviet Union, and used them as instruments to promote the Soviet Union's foreign policy objectives. After the Second World War, Stalin renewed the exercise and established Cominform in 1947. As a result, the Communist parties across the world viewed the Soviet communist system as a model for them to emulate.

However, as the Soviet socialist state inevitably moved towards a totalitarian system, the non-Communist socialists began to give special emphasis to the democratic character of the socialist state which they had envisaged. From 1930s, they prefixed the term 'democratic' to the word 'socialism'. In some countries the term 'social democracy' is used as a synonym for 'democratic socialism'.

Socialist International

In 1951, the democratic socialist parties held a Convention at Frankfurt, in Germany, and established the Socialist International, with its headquarters in London. All democratic socialist parties across the world are attached to the Socialist International either as full members or as consultative parties or as observers. The Socialist International helps these parties to promote the basic values of democratic socialism, mutual assistance, and solidarity activities across the world. Today, the Socialist International has linkage with a total of 146 socialist/social democratic parties from all over the world – 102 full member parties, 44 consultative and observer parties. In addition, the Socialist International has three fraternal organizations – Socialist International Women, International Union of Socialist Youth, and Socialist Education International/International Falcon Movement.

Among the cardinal principles adopted by the Socialist International are: (1) It is possible and essential to have social and economic transformation through democratic means; (2) The socialists do not equate nationalization with socialism; (3) They do not believe in total nationalization of the means of production; (4) In the management of industrial enterprises, there should be greater participation for workers; (5) A democratic set up should be established after winning power; (6) There should be equal distribution of welfare between countries and social groups; (7) There should be equitable distribution of wealth and incomes in society; and so on.

Thus it may be found that the vision Social Democracy has presented is to effect an all-embracing development of the society, and not just in areas of politics or economics alone. Their aim is the creation of a positive state which would be responsive to the aspirations of people for liberty, equality and justice. As Asoka Mehta, a doyen of Indian socialism said: "In a depressed and oppressed world, socialism has to be the voice of conscience, it has to touch human thought with a vision of tomorrow and the faith needed to realize it."

Therefore, the philosophical foundation of social democracy is the quintessence of the ideas contained in the thinking of various socialist thinkers and philosophers who shared a common concern, a common approach and common programmes, and of the principles the socialist organizations have enunciated from time to time. Though some of these ideas are two hundred years old, they still remain valid for building social democracies in the 21st century.

II

Its Impact on People's Quality of Life

In this lecture, I would like to focus on the basic principles of social democracy, and also on what social democracy would mean in the day-to-day life of ordinary people. First, let me explain the basic principles of social democracy, in which its programmes are anchored.

Principles of Social Democracy

Social democracy has five basic principles. They are freedom, equality, justice, democracy and solidarity. Freedom, in the social democratic parlance, has a wider connotation. It implies opposition to all kinds of dictatorships, whether it is dictatorship of the proletariat or dictatorship of individuals. The concept also implies freedom from want, freedom from ignorance and exploitation, personal freedoms, political and civil rights of people guaranteed by an independent judiciary, and so on. All these freedoms are essential for a person to lead the life of a worthy citizen. The basic parametres that govern the enjoyment of freedom in a social democracy is that one can enjoy freedom to an extent that it does not curtail the similar freedom of another fellow human being.

Similar is the meaning of equality. It implies equal value of all human beings. It means that all men and women should have equal rights, equal responsibilities and equal opportunities to develop in freedom and equality. They should have equal opportunities to the well being, security and participation in the decision making. Equality does not mean uniformity, nor does it mean the levelling out. But, it does mean denunciation of a society based on class, caste and privilege. Equality is also a precondition for full development of a person's personality. Indeed, freedom and equality are complementary since freedom is the first step towards equality.

The third basic principle of social democracy is justice. Justice implies equal rights and equal opportunities. It includes distributive justice, which means that jointly achieved social product should be evenly shared, and that it should bring about a social equilibrium among various groups in society. Justice also implies establishment of welfare state systems to build caring societies. It has been widely recognized that a full employment policy holds the key to the upkeep of a successful welfare state. Therefore, employment generation is a key element of imparting justice in society. Social democracies pursue distributive justice through progressive taxation and through welfare state provisions.

Another basic principle of social democracy is democracy. It implies democratic functioning at all levels of organization in society. Universal adult franchise is *sine qua non* to it. Democracy must not be confined merely to periodic elections. It should take the form of a participatory system. Social democrats believe that a new social democratic society can be achieved by extending democracy into ever increasing areas of human activities. Also they believe that democratic procedure should be followed at all levels of decision making.

And, finally, the principle of solidarity. Essentially, solidarity means collective responsibility of individuals for one another and for the community. Social democracy envisages the construction of a new society based on solidarity among the people where they respect each other's rights, where they do not exploit each other, and where they promote common welfare. In the ultimate analysis, the kernel of social democracy is solidarity.

Conceptually, solidarity springs from a feeling of togetherness, backed by a mentality of sharing, without heartburn, a part of one's own earning and services with fellow humans. It also implies joint effort for the wellbeing of all. Initially, the concept evolved among the socialists in forms of working class solidarity, wage solidarity and trade union solidarity worldwide. In the hands of the working class, it has been a strong weapon against exploitation and oppression. But, over the years, its scope has been widened to encompass not only the whole society – national and international – but also the present and future generations. It constantly reminds us that the present generation has a responsibility for future generations.

Certainly, in a society based on solidarity, mutual assistance among the people becomes a permanent feature, which would engender a new form of social relationship, and a new form of organization based on cooperation and mutual concern and mutual sharing. As in the case of automatic extension of mutual concern and support among the family members, generally without much heartburn, solidarity can be fruitfully promoted among the people, whether in a locality, province, country or worldwide, for attaining highest level of wellbeing for the people, through an ever widening application of solidarity among the people at appropriate levels.

I may underline that all these fundamental principles of social democracy are equally important. A joint realization of all these principles, through a string of appropriate programmes, will inevitably result in the establishment of a social democratic society.

Worth of an Ideology

It is my conviction that the best way to measure the worth of an ideology is to test its social relevance by using a yardstick of how much is its potential to enhance the quality of life of ordinary people in society, and how much is its potentiality to generate a positive vision among the people for the elevation of the whole population. Social democracy should also be subjected to such critical tests.

Impact of Social Democracy

Therefore, in order to explain the impact of social democracy on the quality of life of ordinary people, it is imperative that

I draw from the experiences of countries which have imbibed social democracy as a way of life, and which have attuned their policies and programmes to the principles and ideals of social democracy. The countries which I have in mind in this context are four social democratic states of the Scandinavian region — Sweden, Denmark, Norway and Finland, in northern Europe — which have built up new social democratic societies under the leadership of the Social Democratic parties of these countries. Moreover, these are the social democratic countries which I had the opportunity to visit several times during the last 20 years to study the social democratic system they have developed during the last 70 years.

Pertinently, it is important to remember that Scandinavia is a region where social democrats have opted to follow the path of ballot box and reform to establish socialist societies peacefully when, in the neighbouring Russia, Lenin and Stalin had chosen the path of violent revolution to establish a socialist society there. Developments during the last 18 years have shown that the violent means which Lenin and Stalin had adopted could not build an enduring socialist society. While the Soviet communism collapsed, the Scandinavian social democracies, established through the ballot box and reform, remain strong and enduring. Another aspect which we have to keep in mind is that Scandinavia is a region where social democratic parties have dominated the political scene as ruling parties for a long time since 1930s. And, this is also the region where social democracy flowered first, and established successful egalitarian societies through systematic and benign state intervention.

It may also be remembered that historically Scandinavia is known as the homeland of the legendary Vikings who were nightmares of mighty powers like Russia, Germany, France, England, and so on, through their frequent forays for plundering them between the 8th and the 11th centuries. But, today that Scandinavia presents the picture of the most civilized and the most peaceful region of the world. People there now hesitate even to use an offensive language.

Indeed, until social democratic parties got established in the last quarter of the 19th century, and until social democracy gained ascendancy in these countries, they were all relatively poor and backward countries. But, the change in them is so spectacular that today they are among the most prosperous egalitarian social democracies of the world. Though they have achieved a per capita income approximate to that of the United States, the new societies they have built up in Scandinavia are far superior to the one the Unites States could build up. Not only that these countries have prospered, but the fruits of their prosperity have been almost evenly distributed among the people.

Construction of Social Democracy

Let us examine the measures the social democrats have taken to build these social democracies. A few years ago, Dr. A.P.J. Abdul Kalam had underlined the need for countries to develop a national vision. He said: "Any organization, society or even a nation without a vision is like a ship cruising on the high seas without any aim or direction. It is clarity of national vision which constantly drives people towards the goal". He said further that it is not enough to have a vision, but we should strive to make the people of the whole nation to share that vision and work together for its realization. Social democratic parties of the Scandinavian countries have succeeded in developing such national and regional visions for the construction of egalitarian societies in the region 75 years ago, and made the whole people of the region to share that vision and made them to join hands to realize it. As a result, political education and reforms went hand in hand in the process of restructuring of the Scandinavian societies.

Full Employment Policy

The bedrock of this new restructuring on egalitarian lines was laid on a full employment policy the social democrats of Scandinavia have pursued, with a keenness to put every able bodied person in society to productive work. Indeed, they have recognized the centrality of gainful employment in a person's welfare. For a person, gainful employment means a recognition of his worth. Certainly, a person would prefer a job to earn his livelihood, than joining the queue for unemployment doles. However, in Scandinavia the full employment policy of social democrats has ensured growth and prosperity, and promoted equality in society. Their governments had generated innumerable productive jobs, through public investments and appropriate social policies. They provided social security for everybody through measures like right to work, right to education and a decent place to live. They instituted uniform pensions for the aged, sick, unemployed, victims of accidents, and so on. In order to reduce the income disparity among the wage-earners, they pursued a policy of solidarity wages. They followed a policy of judicious state intervention for common good without upsetting free individual enterprise. In brief, they gave emphasis on full employment, an all-embracing welfare state system and a mixed economy.

Construction of Welfare State System

But, what has effected a dramatic change not only in the standard of living, but also in the quality of life of ordinary people of Scandinavia is the spectacular success social democrats have achieved in the construction of a cradle-to-the-grave welfare state systems in all Nordic states. The aim was to build new egalitarian communities around the concept of "people's home" and establish a new social environment which frees people from all kinds of dependencies, and, at the same time, enable them to cooperate with one another as free and equal people.

When we talk about welfare state, what do we understand of it? Welfare state system connotes substantial government responsibility for the provisions of social security, health care, medical care, education, housing, social services, unemployment provisions, family allowances, pensions, and so on for the people. And these provisions would be financed substantially from the funds generated through taxation. However, establishment of a welfare state would constitute the recognition of the social rights of everyone to enjoy a fare share of the fruits of growth in society, and would be a catalyst to develop a mentality of sharing the earnings from one's own labour in a spirit of solidarity. No doubt, it is a higher form of social engineering.

In Scandinavia, a systematic construction of welfare state was initiated in Sweden in 1930s by the Swedish Social Democratic Party. It was facilitated by the fact that the Social Democratic Party was in power in Sweden continuously for 44 years, from 1932 onwards. Sweden has conceived the welfare state as a system to promote equality and distributive justice in society, to increase state's responsibility for the people's wellbeing, and to free the poor people from the institutionalized humiliation inflicted on them by the Poor Law Administrators.

The Swedes call their system as 'cradle-to-the-grave' welfare state system. But, literally to describe their system that way is an understatement because the state's welfare benefits to a person starts when the child is in the womb of the mother. The mother at that time gets a special allowance to get extra-nutrition for feeding the child in the womb. From then onwards, the state's responsibility for the child's wellbeing continues all through its life. Every child gets a child allowance and free education. After education, the state is responsible for the provision of a gainful employment for the person, failing which it has to provide unemployment allowance for him/her. When a person retires, he/she gets adequate pension to maintain the quality of life enjoyed prior to retirement, in addition to free medical care. And, when the person dies, his/her funeral expenditure is also met by the state. That is how the cradle-to-the-grave welfare state system operates in Sweden. More or less similar is the system in other Scandinavian countries as well. Therefore, the correct depiction of this welfare state system is not 'from cradle-to-the-grave' but 'from the womb-to-the-tomb'. What is notable in it is that the welfare state in Scandinavia is attuned to ensure acceptable standard of living for everyone universally, irrespective of one's socio-economic background.

Steeply Progressive Taxation

From the very beginning, the social democrats of Scandinavia have anchored their welfare state system in a full employment policy, which could sustain the system without any problem. The resource mobilization for the purpose is the responsibility of the state by using its power of taxation. This is generally done through the application of a steeply progressive taxation system, which not only makes everybody a contributor and a beneficiary of the welfare state system, but also helps to promote equality in society by reducing the gap between the take-home pays of employees. In Sweden, for example, through the application of solidarity wage structuring, and through the application of steeply progressive taxation system, the take-home pay ratio of the lowest paid and the highest paid individual employee could be brought down to 1 : 4. But, when family was taken as a unit of measurement in this regard, then the income ratio of the lowest paid and the highest paid family came down further to 1 : 2. This was revealed in an evaluation made in 1985. In fact, no other system, including the totalitarian communist system, anywhere, could achieve such a high level of income equality in society, by consciously attuning the state's fiscal policies in that direction. It has made a great difference in the quality of life of the people everywhere, and also in the perception of people about each other. It has enhanced people's respect for one another. It has also blurred the class distinctions in Scandinavia. There is no domestic servant in Scandinavia.

People are happy to pay high taxes for the upkeep of the welfare state system since the system takes care of the interests, not only of the present generation, but also of the incoming generations. Therefore, in these social democracies, there is hardly any anxiety among the parents regarding the future wellbeing and security of their children, as the welfare state system guarantees a secure life for everybody – the young, the old, and the yet to be born. All these have been achieved through a democratic process, and without sacrificing people's freedom and liberty.

Under the system, everyone gets equal educational opportunities. The entire population is insured against illness. The system protects all employees from work related accidents. They are entitled to compensation for industrial injury. All wage-earners are granted five weeks paid annual holidays. All mothers receive maternity grants. Under a family law, either the father or the mother is entitled to 7 months leave from work, with full pay, after the birth of a child. All housewives are entitled to go for annual vacation anywhere in their country at the cost of the government.

Pension Schemes

There is a highly developed pension scheme. Under an old age pension scheme, all old people are entitled to a pension. Similarly, all disabled people, after the age of 16, are entitled to a pension. If that pensioner is a fully disabled person, he/she would get a full disability pension which is equal to the old age pension. If parents themselves nurse their disabled children, they are entitled to child care allowances.

In Sweden, medical care is free, except a nominal prescription fee. Under the sickness benefit insurance system, those who suffer income loss due to illness, injury or disability, are entitled to compensation. Sickness benefit is 90 per cent of the person's salary prior to his illness, injury or disability. The cost of health insurance is shared between the state, employers, and the self-employed people.

Social democracy has taken the democratization process to the enterprises level through the institutionalization of a co-determination system in the industrial establishments. It meant that, the employer and the employees' representative would sit together across the table, as equals, and together examine the company's accounts and performance and take decisions pertaining to the activities of the company. In addition, they give overwhelming importance to negotiations as a methodology to settle contentious issues. And, they go on negotiating until they find amicable solutions. As a result, though trade unions are very strong in all these countries, and are strongly linked to social democratic parties, they refrain from strike action, and negotiate hard, sometimes very prolonged, to settle their disputes that way. Generally, they do not upset the production schedule of their enterprises. Significantly, the work ethics among the workers remain very high in Scandinavia.

Cooperative Movement

Social democracy in Scandinavia has developed a well developed consumer cooperative movement. Although the cooperative movement absorbs only about 4 per cent of the labour force, it is a widespread movement encompassing about 50 per cent of the total population. Today cooperatives are a well entrenched sector of the Scandinavian economy and society. They practice economic democracy, as has been seen in the examples of consumer cooperatives where the dividends are distributed annually on the basis of the purchases a member has made, and not on the basis of shares a shareholder holds in that cooperative society.

Scandinavian social democracies have paid special attention to people's housing need. This was done through the establishment of state owned housing banks and through the promotion of cooperative house building schemes. The motto followed in this context was that: "No one should make a profit of somebody's housing need". As a result, by 1970 housing shortage in Scandinavia was solved.

Promotion of Equality and Distributive Justice

Though the initial objective of welfare state was alleviation of poverty, the Scandinavian welfare states have gone far beyond that agenda and inculcated in it larger programmes like reduction of inequality and promotion of distributive justice and human solidarity, besides programmes like social insurance and social services to the needy people. The agenda of distributive justice was pursued both vertically and horizontally – vertically from rich to the poor through a steeply progressive income-tax system, and horizontally through the establishment of a cradle-to-the-grave welfare state system for the entire population. Since matters touching vital interests of the people, like education, health, employment, social insurance, etc. are taken care of by the welfare state system, the popular support for it remains strong everywhere in Scandinavia.

The Scandinavian economies had experienced some strain in the early 1990s, following recession and budget deficits. It had certain impact on the social policies of the Nordic countries. As a result, governments had resorted to effect marginal reductions in social benefit entitlements. Barring these and similar marginal changes, the economic crisis of early 1990s could hardly make any dent on the fundamental features of the Scandinavian welfare state system. In the words of Dr Nimmi Kurian: "Cutbacks in benefit levels which have taken place in the Swedish welfare state in no way represent a paradigm shift away from the universal, egalitarian system."

The Scandinavian welfare state model has exercised, and will continue to exercise, enormous influence on societal reconstruction across the world. Many developing countries have drawn inspiration from it and tried to emulate it in their own limited ways. In this connection, I would like to point out that the Scandinavian welfare state model was no mean a factor which had influenced the Soviet leader Mikhail Gorbachev to introduce *perestroika* and *glasnost* in the erstwhile Soviet Union, which also triggered a systemic change in the Soviet Union and eastern Europe. The importance Gorbachev had attached to the success of the Scandinavian social democracies could be seen from the fact that he had chosen to send top Soviet economists to Sweden and Finland to study how the system worked there. Indeed, his desire was to pattern the Soviet system after the Scandinavian social democracies.

In the final analysis, Scandinavian social democracies have proved that the system they have advanced is good economics, good politics and good sociology. It is a splendid example of how public spending on welfare creates general conditions for economic growth, and how preventive policies reduce potential social problems and influence the development of a healthy, stress-free society. It has brought a remarkable change in the psyche and ethos of the Scandinavian countries.

Social democracy in Scandinavia has shown that it is possible to achieve equality and distributive justice in a peaceful and civilized way through parliamentary institutions. It has also shown the virtues of following the principle of universalism, instead of following a targeted and selective approach to benefits, so that, like in the construction of welfare state, everybody is a partner in the programme both as contributors and as beneficiaries. That has ensured wide public support for the programme. In Scandinavia, extensive social rights of people have been recognized. These social rights are non-discriminatory and universal. All people are entitled to social benefits as a matter of social right. The wealth of the community is used for the benefit of the whole population, and not of a section or of a few sections of it. It is being pursued under the broad framework of human solidarity – a very dynamic concept which can change the face of the whole world during the 21st century.

A Strong State

Social democracies of Scandinavia would not have been able to impart this range of benefits to people, to spectacularly enhance their quality of life, if the democratic state, through the central government and municipalities, has not assumed a pivotal role in the system. Indeed, social democracy apportions a central role for a strong democratic state as a regulator and also as a provider. Its judicious and benign intervention in the country's economy and social life is considered logical and necessary to promote the ideals of social democracy. Therefore, social democracy would not support any measure which would weaken the state and which would undermine the financial strength or resource base of the state and cripple its capacity to intervene in favour of the needy in society. This runs counter to the scheme of the conservatives and their philosophers who want that the state should retreat from the domain of public welfare and should function only as a law and order machinery. They want that the public welfare services, beneficial to the poor, should be left to the market forces. Obviously, it is a recipe for the destruction of the poorer sections of society. Instead of eliminating poverty, this conservative recipe, now expressed through the agenda of globalization, liberalization and privatization, will eliminate the poor from the face of the earth.

However, the appeal of social democracy is not in doubt because it deals with the day-to-day life of ordinary people. To be equal and free is a basic urge of all human beings. So long as inequality and squalor remains in the world, the appeal of social democracy will remain powerful among the people. What social democracy means for ordinary people in terms of enhancement of their quality of life has been amply proved by the Scandinavian experience.

III

Social Democracy and India: Problems and Prospects

Social democracy made its inroads in India 70 years ago, during India's freedom struggle, when leaders like Jayaprakash Narayan, Acharya Narendra Dev and others launched the socialist movement in India by founding the Congress Socialist Party in 1934 within the Indian National Congress. Records show that throughout the freedom struggle the Congress Socialist Party had functioned as a radical constituent of the Indian National Congress. In the freedom struggle, the valiant acts of young congress socialists against the British were spectacular. Their bold underground activities during the 'Quit India' movement made young socialist leaders like Jayaprakash Narayan, Ram Manohar Lohia and so on, heroes of the time. Jayaprakash Narayan's daring escape from the Hazaribagh Jail, the underground radio station other young socialists like Ram Manohar Lohia, Aruna Asaf Ali, Usha Mehta and so on, operated during the 'Quit India' movement roused the spirit and morale of the freedom fighters. As a result, from the 'Quit India' movement, the Congress Socialist Party became the symbol of radicalism and youth aspirations to establish a new socialist society in India. After India's freedom, the Congress Socialist Party had severed its link with the Indian National Congress in 1948 and founded the Indian Socialist Party.

I have already explained, in my first lecture, the ideological dispensation of the Indian socialists and its special features, which I do not want to repeat here. Therefore, I would draw your attention straight away to the Indian Constitution which contains the framework and provisions which have the potential to take India towards an egalitarian society based on principles of social democracy. The 'Preamble' of the Indian Constitution declares: "We, the people of India as having solemnly resolved to constitute

India a sovereign, socialist, secular democratic republic and to secure to all its citizens ... equality of status and of opportunity." Similarly, in the Directive Principles, it has stipulated the direction of state's governance: to "securing the right to work, to education and to public assistance in cases of unemployment, old age, sickness and disablement and in other cases of undeserved want"; to ensure equal rights for men and women "to an adequate means of livelihood"; to "minimize the inequalities in income ... status, facilities and opportunities" among the people; to provide "free and compulsory education for all children till fourteen"; and to raise the standard of living of the people and the improvement of public health. If these provisions of our constitution have been pursued seriously and sincerely, by now India would have covered a long way to become a social democracy. However, in order to make these provisions a reality, it is imperative to have a political party in power, which is dedicated to bring major reforms in that direction. Therefore, the basic question is: Do we have such a national political party today in the Indian political scene which is passionately wedded to the principles and ideals of social democracy? The answer is 'no'; but we can create one if we apply our minds positively and creatively. How can we do it is a question which we would deal with a little later. However, the lack of political will among those who wielded power in India after independence was mainly responsible for not taking the country in the direction stipulated in our Constitution. Therefore, the progress in this regard remained slow and sluggish. Economic growth in the country was not accompanied by distributive justice, nor by greater equality. As a result, a substantial number of people (26%) in India still remains below the poverty line. Those who wielded power in the country all these years have paid only lip-service to these programmes as a matter of political expediency. Their lack-lustre approach to some of these programmes did not produce the desired effects.

Socialists' 14-Point Programme

It is pertinent to recall that when the Congress government, led by Jawaharlal Nehru, failed to secure a majority of the votes polled in the first General Elections of 1952, in order to widen the popular support base of his government to more than 50 percent of the total votes polled, Nehru invited the socialists, who got more than 12 percent of the votes polled, to join his government. That gave an opportunity for the socialists to test the Congress regarding its seriousness to implement the socialist programmes in a time bound manner. Therefore, Jayaprakash Narayan and other socialists informed Nehru that they would consider his invitation to join the government provided Nehru agreed to implement certain priority socialist programmes in a time-bound manner. The 14-point programme which the socialists presented to Nehru at that time included: land reforms and re-distribution of surplus land to the landless poor; nationalization of banks, insurance companies and mining industries; administrative reforms to promote decentralization; state assistance to agriculture; co-determination in industries; promotion of cooperatives and public sector undertakings; development of state trading; scaling down of higher salaries in government to promote income equality; and so on. But, Nehru cleverly replied that while he had no disagreement with the programmes presented by the socialists, he could not give any time frame for their implementation. As a result, the socialists had declined Nehru's invitation to join his government.

But, Nehru and the Congress Party decided to take the wind out of the sail of the Socialist Party, by appropriating some of these programmes under a vaguely constructed term, "socialistic pattern of society", as the goal of the Congress. The Avadi Congress of the Indian National Congress in 1955 had adopted the establishment of a "socialistic pattern of society" as the Party's goal. The vagueness of that construct was apt to confuse the electorate. Through that exercise the Congress could retain power in India continuously for 30 years, of course, with the rich man's money and the poor man's votes. Though Nehru allowed land reform legislations, he chose to retain the right to property on the list of Fundamental Rights in the Constitution, which had effectively blocked the implementation of various land reform legislations through judicial decisions. It was only in 1977 that the Janata Party government, headed by Morarji Desai, had removed the right to property from the list of Fundamental Rights and made it an ordinary legal right.

Indeed, the Congress projection of a 'Socialistic Pattern of Society' was an exercise in hypocrisy. This was not surprising because as a party the Congress Party was not built nor equipped to implement any socialist programme, nor the party had any understanding of the socialist ideology. Indeed, under its patronage, the Indian capitalism had grown in leaps and bounds. Tata, Mafatlal, Martin Burn and so on, had grown in a big way during the prime ministership of Jawaharlal Nehru. Of course, public undertakings also made a beginning during this period, but they were generally administered in a manner which promoted unprofessionalism in them. Public Sector Undertakings were generally managed by civil servants who were temporarily drafted from the government for short durations, and who had no abiding interest in them or in their success. Many Public Sector Undertakings were also kept headless for long durations.

Sanjay Gandhi's ambition to become a rich industrialist — a big small-car manufacturer – touched the heart of his mother, Indira Gandhi, which made her to change her Government's attitude to the public sector. It may be noted that during Nehru's time, in 1956, the Government of India took a policy decision that if ever India would go for production of small cars, it would be only in the public sector. But when Sanjay Gandhi wanted to own a small-car factory, in order to fulfil the son's ambition, Indira Gandhi decided to change that policy overnight, in late 1960s, and gave her son the license, under her own seal and signature, to start the Maruti car factory in the private sector. The Parliament was informed that when Sanjay Gandhi was given the license for the production of 50,000 cars annually, he had a bank balance of Rs. 748.

The point is that under the veneer of the "socialistic pattern of society" there forged a strong nexus between the Congress Party and the big business houses and industrialists in the country on a *quid pro quo* basis. While the Congress governments helped the big business and industrial houses to grow in leaps and bounds, by integrating their interests in government policies, they reciprocated it by making huge financial contributions to the election funds of the Congress. The pattern was set during the prime ministership of Jawaharlal Nehru itself. Indeed, one of the Birlas, in the early 1960s, had disclosed that during the freedom struggle Jawaharlal Nehru himself was carrying Birla's blank cheques. Whether this had considerably influenced government's policy to promote big business houses, after independence, is another matter. However, as part of their reciprocal relationship, it has been revealed that in 1961 Tata gave Rs. 15.5 lakhs to the Congress election funds, where as Birla, Martin Burn, and Khatau Makanji gave Rs. 7.7 lakhs, Rs. 10.7 lakhs, and Rs. 9 lakhs respectively, to the Congress election funds. As a result, public policies of the Congress Government remained attuned to promote the business interests of the big industrial houses. It helped all these industrial houses to grow rapidly. At the same time, over the years the Congress policies have moved decisively against the socialist oriented reforms, notwithstanding the addition of the word 'socialist' in the preamble of the Constitution as a matter of expediency during the emergency.

Splits Among Socialists

Congress alone is not to blame for the failure to build a social democratic society in India after independence. Part of the blame should go to the socialist leaders as well, whose strong egos and the resultant bickerings had deprived the Socialist Party the necessary cohesion and team spirit to become a viable alternative to the Congress. Personality clashes, based on covert expression of egos, made their inroads into the functioning of the Socialist Party organization, causing fissions and fusions. This became more pronounced from 1954, when the first Praja Socialist Party government, under the Chief Ministership of Pattom Thanu Pillai, assumed power in the Travancore-Cochin state (now Kerala) in the midst of a Tamil language agitation to bifurcate the Trivandrum District and merge the present Kanyakumari District with Tamil Nadu. When the Tamil language agitators turned violent and started to demolish a vital bridge across the Kuzhithura River, which was the life line of communication between Trivandrum and Kanyakumari at that time, the police opened fire to stop the destruction of the bridge. A few agitators died in the police firing. On hearing the news, Dr. Ram Manohar Lohia, without consulting other leaders of the PSP, demanded Pattom Tahnu Pillai's resignation from the Chief Ministership. But Pattom Thanu Pillai did not resign, and justified the police firing. It culminated in the first disastrous split in the Praja Socialist Party. Dr. Ram Manohar Lohia left the PSP with his followers and established the Indian Socialist Party as an additional socialist party. Though police firing was the ostensible cause for the split, the real cause for the split was the clash of personal egos inside the party. Since then socialist movement in India had undergone some more fissions and fusions. Dr. Sonal Shah, daughter of Bombay's veteran socialist leader and humanist, Dr. G.G. Parikh, has written a Ph.D thesis on this phenomenon in the Indian socialist movement, with graphic details. She has published it later as a book under the title, *Indian Socialists: Search for Identity*. However, this recurring feature in the socialist movement had undermined the Socialist Party's potential to become an alternative to the

Congress at the centre. If the top leadership had kept the party/movement interest above their personal angularities, and if they had shown certain degree of accommodative spirit and respect for democratic process in the decision making, the party would have emerged as the natural alternative to the Congress in the country.

However, I would like to underline that it was the first Praja Socialist Party government of Travancore-Cochin State, led by Pattom Thanu Pillai, that pioneered the innovative land reforms Bill in India way back in 1954. It was the first government in the country to take over public utilities, like public transport for example, from the domain of the private sector. It was that government which had introduced, for the first time in India, free school education upto the 8th Standard, again in 1954. Indeed, the PSP government's land reforms bill, presented by then Revenue Minister P.S. Nataraja Pillai, provided the model for future land reforms bills in the country. That bill put a ceiling on maximum land holding upto a level which yielded an annual income of Rs. 3600 for a land holder. It was a revolutionary step when we take into account the year in which such a radical measure was launched in the country. But, ironically, for taking that radical step, the Congress and the Communists joined hands against that Socialist government and ousted that minority government before it could place the Select Committee Report of that land reforms bill before the Legislative Assembly. The innovation made in subsequent land reforms bills in the country was that instead of land ceiling fixed in terms of annual income from it, the land ceiling in the new bills was fixed in terms of the area of individual land holding.

Socialists Merge in Janata Party

Socialist Party was an active participant in the Movement led by Jayaprakash Narayan against corruption in 1973-75. Rattled by the JP Movement, and in order to protect her seat of power, Indira Gandhi declared Emergency in June 1975 and put all opposition leaders in Jail for 19 months. Besides the Socialist Party, the JP Movement was joined by Congress(O), Bharatiya Kranti Dal (BKD), Jan Sangh, and the Congress for Democracy (CFD). The JP Movement saw the realignment of political forces in India.

The socialist movement in India suffered grievously in 1977 when the Socialist Party merged with four other parties —Jan Sangh, Congress(O), BKD and CFD – to constitute the Janata Party. That decision was taken in haste, without making any hard assessment of its long-term implications. The socialist leaders had quickly agreed to it at that time because Jayaprakash Narayan, in order to achieve the unity of opposition parties against Indira Gandhi's dictatorship, insisted upon such a merger as a pre-condition for his active campaigning in the 1977 Parliament elections to defeat Indira Gandhi and her Congress Party. I was present at that meeting of the Socialist Party which decided to merge to constitute the Janata Party. But, in retrospect, it was not a wise decision. Subsequent developments in the Janata Party and the Janata Dal had clearly revealed the gravity of that mistake. Socialists never anticipated that the decision would grievously harm the interests of the poor and the downtrodden in India.

All said and done, despite internal problems manifest from 1954 onwards, and the spectacle of fissions and fusions, the Socialist Party was the principal national voice to protect the interests of the poor and the deprived people in the country. Indeed, it was the Socialist Party that had articulated the problems and aspirations of the ordinary people of the country. It had a record of examining every governmental decision against the interests of the poor. Though they were in opposition, the socialists had forced a reluctant Congress government to introduce certain public welfare measures beneficial to the deprived sections of society. It was that voice of the poor that got stifled, in 1977, when the Socialist Party merged into the Janata Party. Many distinguished international socialists, like Willy Brandt, were visibly unhappy that India, the largest democracy in the world which geopolitically occupies a central position in Asia, did not have a Socialist Party to promote the ideals of social democracy.

Socialists in India remained in disarray after the formation of the Janata Party. Although outstanding socialists like Madhu Dandavate and George Fernandes were in the Janata Party Government headed by Morarji Desai and presented great performance as Railway Minister and Industries Minister respectively, at the Janata Party deliberations, the term 'socialism' was heard less and less. For some senior leaders of the Janata Party, like Choudhuri Charan Singh for example, the word 'socialism' appeared an anathema. Keeping in view the sensitivities of such leaders, many socialists had refrained, as far as possible, from using the term 'socialism' at the Janata Party deliberations in the presence of such leaders. So, in practice, socialism and its core values like equality and solidarity were gradually ebbed out of the core agenda of the Janata Party. The disorientation was so fast that by 1981 the Janata Party President, Chandrasekhar, came out with a public statement that there was no difference between the Janata Party and the Congress Party.

That new situation forced some of us, including Mr. Pradip Bose, Samarendra Kundu, Subrata Mukherji, K.K. Panda, T.K. Oommen and numerous others, to take the initiative to establish the Indian Centre for Democratic Socialism to articulate the social democratic perception on important issues facing India and the world.

It may be noted that of all political parties which merged to constitute the Janata Party, Socialist Party was the only one which had a clear ideological base. Therefore, it was also the biggest loser in the merger process since the effective running of the Janata Party was done predominantly by non-socialists. The hope of some socialists that they would inculcate democratic socialism as the Janata Party's basic ideology was belied, as the Janata Party was getting progressively deideologised.

Janata Party's Disintegration

Janata Party's disintegration began with a group of MPs, led by Choudhuri Charan Singh, defected from it and pulled down the Janata Party government led by Morarji Desai in 1979. Soon, the BKD elements left the Janata Party and formed the Bharatiya Lok Dal. Subsequently, the Jan Sangh component went out of it and formed the BJP. Most of the Congress(O) elements became more or less inactive. Many socialists had either left the Janata Party or chose to remain in wilderness as the party, bereft of any ideology, lost its moorings, direction and sense of purpose. Yet many other socialists stayed on in it simply because they did not want to be seen as defectors. Although Lok Dal rejoined the Janata Party again and got the name of Janata Party changed to Janata Dal, it soon left it again after leaving the burden of the 'Dal' on the lap of the old Janata Party leaders.

Mandalization of Politics

Mandalization of politics saw Janata Dal drifting further away from any ideological dispensation. Indeed, Mandalization had a negative impact as it brought back the caste factor to the centre of Indian politics. Instead of unifying people by promoting ideas and attitudes away from caste and communal considerations, Mandalization had spread disaffection and divisiveness in our society, even in political parties, on caste lines. As caste based divisiveness got sharpening, the religion based divisiveness also followed suit, with more and more people found displaying, in their body, symbols indicating their religion. It had inflicted a serious blow to solidarity among the people, cutting across caste and communal divisions. Cumulatively, Janata Dal's sense of purpose became hazy, and it continued to drift in a direction which was incomprehensible in political or ideological terms. Its presence in the Parliament also became negligible. In the circumstances, in 1998, Vishwanath Pratap Singh came out with his verdict that the Janata Dal had no future. However, the message was loud and clear that the Janata Dal has ceased to be the rallying point for the social democrats in the country.

New Socialist Splinters

Disillusioned with Janata Dal's lack of direction, many socialists have left that party and launched their own small parties. But people do not see these splinters, though led by socialists, as serious alternatives to the Congress or the BJP. They are viewed as local or state parties and not as national alternatives. Many other socialists have opted to channel their energies by engaging themselves in small isolated battles or by taking up single issue campaigns, or just chose to remain in wilderness.

The Costs of Socialist Party's Absence

Ever since the Socialist Party was established in 1948 the Party's emphasis was on socio-economic reforms favourable to the weaker and marginalized sections of Indian society. As mentioned earlier, Socialist leaders like Jayaprakash Narayan, Acharya Narendra Dev, Asoka Mehta, Ram Manohar Lohia, S.M. Joshi, Madhu Limaye, Prem Bhasin, Madhu Dandavate, George Fernandes, Samar Guha and so on, had pursued this path steadfast since then and forced a reluctant Congress government to implement certain welfare measures beneficial to the poor. Therefore, the absence of the Socialist Party from the Indian political scene during the last three decades has been disastrous for the poorer sections of our society. The proportion of public funds spent for their welfare has been found constantly diminishing. Indeed, during the last 25 years we have witnessed the scaling down of the state's responsibility for the welfare of the poor people.

People's health care, education and other essential public services have been put on a commercial track. And they are increasingly left at the mercy of the private profiteers. Even government hospitals have been found forcing the poor people to buy essential costly medicines from the market for their poor in-patients. As a result, good quality essential services, like health care, have become the preserves of the rich and the privileged who have the money to buy them from the open market. Poor people have the option to slowly get perished. This is not a management question; it is very much an ideological question, which needs to be resolved within the parameters of an egalitarian society.

During the last 25 years, the rich has steadily siphoned off power, wealth, comforts, and facilities. The government policies have been attuned to cater the affluence of the richer sections of our society, with no consideration as to how far they would be beneficial to the poorest in the far end of the country. Indeed, today we see the spectacle of the ruling elite going out of the way to favour the rich, to facilitate their getting higher and higher margins of profits. The phenomenal growth of the Reliance Industries during the last 20 years is a case in point which indicates how the government policies have impacted on, and in whose favour. It may be noted that in 1963-64, Reliance did not figure at all in the list of notable Indian industrial houses, which had assets worth a minimum of Rs. 100 crores. But in 1988, its assets had grown to Rs. 2,022 crores. But, by 2005, its assets have further grown to Rs. 100,000 crores. The point is that concentration of wealth and power has been promoted in India in a big way during the last 25 years.

At the other end of the spectrum is the spectacle of small farmers who, unable to repay their small agricultural loans, are pushed to the wall, forcing them to commit suicides in several states in India. Debt-based suicides are on the increase everywhere. The profit-loss considerations in government's public welfare policies are so dominant that the problems of the poor remain in the periphery in the midst of a growing commercial culture in administration, which is carefully guided and nurtured by former IMF/World Bank employees who, on their return, have occupied key positions in the Government of India during the last 20 years. They are still there in top positions to continue to tune India's social, economic and financial policies to the wishes of the IMF and the World Bank. A debt-trapped consumerist culture, assiduously promoted by state policies, is systematically promoting a climate of social unrest in India.

Similarly, the government's pricing policies of essential commodities, like medicine for example, do not take into account the purchasing power of an ordinary Indian villager. Many advanced facilities in the health sector are just beyond the pale of the poor people, as, in the largely privatized health care system, they just cannot afford to buy them in the private market when they need them in emergencies. The result is that through government policies, the advanced medical care in India has been made the preserve of the rich people only. This situation must change. Medical care must be a fundamental social right of all people. I believe that only social democracy can do it by building up a welfare state system in India. However, such important issues affecting the poor people seldom get addressed properly in the absence of a strong Indian social democratic party.

The absence of the social democratic party has some other consequences too. During the last 3 decades there is hardly any meaningful education on the fundamentals of social democracy either through socialist study circles or through socialist training camps. Last time a socialist study circle met in Jawaharlal Nehru University was in 1975, before Indira Gandhi declared the Emergency. The position is not different in other parts of the country as well. What does this mean? It means that it is difficult to spot a young man or woman, below the age of 40 or 45, who is well-versed in the socio-political and economic significance of social democratic approach or its importance for our future. It also means that we have to start socialist education, in a political sense, from the scratch once again.

Another consequence is that when the Congress Party declined, it was not the Socialist Party but non-socialist parties and regional parties, built on narrowed visions, which have filled the political space. That situation also has not given any solace to the poor people in the country.

Value of Ideology

It has become a fashion now-a-days to say that the age of ideology is over. That is a fallacy. To be meaningful, politics in India has to be anchored in a long-range vision and in a commitment to organize a welfare state in India on egalitarian lines, in the coming years. That vision can come only from a deep commitment to the ideology of social democracy.

Certainly, in politics ideology plays a key role in the development of the vision. Without it, a person can run the state's affairs in a routine manner, with the mind set of a technocrat or of a managing director – for example, the way Rajiv Gandhi led India after 1984 or the way Dr. Manmohan Singh is leading the country now. How important it is for the political leadership to have a national vision based on an ideology and how disastrous it could be without it was once emphasized by Dr. Bruno Kreisky, former Chancellor of Austria, in 1985 at a meeting of the Indian Centre for Democratic Socialism in New Delhi, which he addressed minutes after his meeting with Rajiv Gandhi, the new young Prime Minister. Dr. Kreisky told us that during his conversation with Rajiv Gandhi, he asked Rajiv whether he had ever studied an ideology, to which Rajiv replied 'no'. After narrating the incident to us, Dr. Kreisky wondered how this young man, without a vision based on an ideology, was going to lead a vast country like India? Indeed, without having a vision Rajiv Gandhi too led India, to drift and degeneration. Form, without content, was his style and approach. A steep fall in public standards was the result. The Bofors scandal epitomized it.

Without an ideology and a vision, politics in India has become parasitic and it has degenerated into some kind of a leach-rearing activity around the seats of power in the government and parties. What India needs today is a new generation of leaders steeped in integrity and in social democratic ideology. Their main task should be to make the whole nation share the social democratic vision of constructing a welfare state in India for the welfare of the whole people, and redirect the country's political agenda to promote the wellbeing of the poorer sections of our society.

India's Critical Problems

The critical problems of India today are still poverty and squalor, inequality, unemployment, and the absence of a welfare state, and the social security it provides for the people. All these are ideological questions. Tinkering with these problems cannot do any good to the people. For the votaries of globalization, liberalization and privatization, like Dr. Manmohan Singh, P. Chidambaram and Montek Singh Ahluwalia, who are the teamsters of the present Central Government, backed by the Left parties like the CPI(M) for phoney concessions, the framework for the provision of employment for the unemployed youth in the country is 100 days casual labourers' job in a year, that too further limited to only one member of a family of unemployed people. It is making a mockery of the provision of employment for the unemployed people in the country. Young people need secure, productive jobs, with adequate income round the year. That is not the mind set that leads India today. That needs the mind set of a social democrat guiding the national policies. There should be no mistake that today we are being led by the present rulers to a state of social unrest which would manifest, in due course, in the form of growing criminalization of our society, which no amount of police force can control. This needs to be stopped. India needs policies which would meet the basic needs of all people in the country through governmental action and not through the free market. Therefore, equality, full employment, distributive justice and solidarity should be the watchwords of Indian reconstruction. Political playfield in India needs to be freed from the vote banks based on caste and religion. Only socialists can do that meaningfully by providing the people with a higher agenda and a higher vision based on the fundamental principles of social democracy.

India Needs a Social Democratic Party

For all these reasons, it is imperative to re-establish the Indian Socialist/Social Democratic Party as a truly all India party immediately in a manner in which it becomes a rallying point for all socialists in the country. The right approach for it should be the one which would bring about complete fusion of all socialist splinters, and others who believe in social democracy, irrespective of their present locations in the country's political spectrum. Keeping in view the vastness of the country, effective functioning would require enormous organizational networking and grass root vibrancy. This would mean that the new launchers will have to harness every ounce of support to build up this social democratic instrumentality nationwide. The framework of this new venture should be inclusion, not exclusion, of every socialist in the country. We must remember that division among them in the past was a key factor which had helped the non-socialists to dominate the Indian political scene, detrimental to the interests of the poorer and the deprived sections of our society. However, the new party, whether it is called Socialist Party or Social Democratic Party, should be launched at a well prepared national convention of all socialists, who remain scattered at present in various socialist splinters.

It is also desirable to simultaneously explore the possibility of associating ideologically like minded parties, like today's Communist Parties, Revolutionary Socialist Party and the Forward Bloc, which have their pockets of influence in Kerala and West Bengal, with the new venture.

Communists Have Changed

The mainstream communists in India, under the impact of India's democratic and pluralistic system started reforming themselves since 1950s. Although the Indian communist parties call themselves communists, they are really social democrats. They believe in pluralism and democracy and they, like other parties in India, use the ballot box to come to power and to leave power. They use parliamentary method of reform to usher in socio-economic changes in society. For them 'dictatorship of the proletariat' and 'democratic centralism' are dead letters, with no practical relevance to their conduct. During the last 20 years the Communists have changed a lot. Considerable bourgeoization has taken place at their leadership level. Many of them have realized that, as echoed in the deliberations of the recently held Kerala State Conference of the Communist Party of India (Marxist).

However, it may be noted that after the collapse of the Soviet Communism, some communist parties have adopted the name 'Party of Democratic Socialism' to indicate their changed character. It is high time that the Indian communist parties should recognize their transformation as social democrats and forge genuine unity, and not tactical unity, with other social democrats in the country to provide a credible alternative to the Congress and the BJP at the national level. Their present role as backers of the anti-poor policies of the Indian votaries of globalization, liberalization and privatization policies – Dr. Manmohan Singh, Montek Singh Ahluwalia and P. Chidambaram – under the palliative of some phoney concessions here and there, is an exercise in self-deception, which they cannot sustain for long without serious loss of their credibility.

We got independence to stop the drain of our resources to other countries, through establishments like the East India Company, and use them for the wellbeing of our own people. After all colonialism is primarily about the capture of markets and resources. But many of our leaders are systematically surrendering the country's hard won freedom, by inviting multi-national companies to the country to exploit us, to destroy our indigenous industries, and destroy the job opportunities of our people. It is not one East India Company, but innumerable ones which are operating in the country today on our leaders' invitation.

However, today, ideologically and programmewise, the Communists (Right and Left), RSP and the Forward Bloc are closer to social democrats. Their coming together at the national level will be more purposeful and more effective in changing Indian policies in favour of the deprived sections of our society. Together, they can build a welfare state in India, which is the best way to help the poor people in the country. In the 19th century the term social democracy meant both the communist and socialist streams. It was an appropriate flexible formation. The communist debate over democracy and dictatorship, and revolution and reform are obsolete in today's context as communists themselves are opponents of all kinds of dictatorships and accepted democracy and reform as the methodology of change. This fact should be recognized by both the Indian Communists and the Indian Socialists. Therefore, politically, there is enough justification for the Communists to become part of the mainstream Indian Social Democratic Party when that party comes into being.

Social democracy is the higher form of democracy. It recognizes not only political rights, but social, economic and cultural rights as well. We have to steadily and systematically remove the cause of inequality in India. It is imperative that every person in India is provided with the necessities of life. Our young people need secure jobs, through a full-employment policy, and not insecure jobs, that too after bribing the parasites of our society. In India social rights, anchored in a welfare state, is still a far cry. But we have to achieve it. It is my conviction that only the Indian Social

Democratic Party can make these aspirations a reality. Its re-establishment and launching of a massive ideological education on social democracy to enable the youth in the country to develop a social democratic vision, and prepare them to work sincerely for the establishment of a welfare state in India, will be the beginning of a new epoch in Indian politics, economy and society.

2

European Union and the Emerging Global System

Problems and Prospects

The Perspective

The end of Cold War and the disintegration of the Soviet Union in the early 1990s have placed the international system in a flux that the bipolar system that dominated the post-war period had instantly given way to a unipolar system commandered by the remaining super power – the United States. In the changed global power balance, which tilted heavily in favour of the United States, Washington quickly got into the track of unilateralism and assumed the role of a world policeman in tackling major international questions. But in the right perspective, and in realistic terms, this unipolarity and unilateralism of the United States are neither sustainable nor enduring. History unmistakably testifies that reality. Seminal works, ranging from Edward Gibbon's *The Decline and Fall of the Roman Empire* to Paul Kennedy's *Rise and Fall of Great Powers*, convey that message most eloquently. They tell us the story of how states/nations regularly rose to dizzy heights, remained there at the top for sometime, long or short, and then descended and gave way to new powers or faded out into the oblivion.[1] This is an unending process, which so far no power, however strong and skilful, could stop. In the present epoch we have seen how Britain, in whose empire the Sun never set, and France established great empires and became dominant powers of the world and then gradually receded from the frontline of power. During the last nine decades we have seen the rise and fall of the Soviet Union. And, there is no valid reason to believe that this time-tested process in the international system would be stopped by the present lone super power, or by anyone else, more than their ability to stop the ticking away of the time itself. Obviously, it is just beyond the pale of all 'powers'. However, what seems distinct in the near future is that a more balanced multipolar international system is bound to replace the present unipolar system. The rumblings of that change could be heard from other parts of the world – from Europe and Asia. Yet, there are analysts who believe that the present US dominated unipolar system would remain stay put for a long time to come, a perception that can be as valid as what the communists used to trumpet about the eternal life of the Soviet Union.

Therefore, from a realistic angle, what is envisaged is that during the next twenty or twenty-five years the global system would turn truly multipolar, upstaged by five effective power centres – the United States, European Union, Russia, China and India – which would be closely interacting with one another in a constructive manner to maintain peace and equilibrium in the world. It seems that for the United States, the year 2003 may prove the beginning of its descent from the peak of its dominance and to come to terms with other emerging power centres. Indeed, there is also an ongoing paradigm change in Eurasia which needs to be recognized – the consolidation of an ageing Europe, matched by the rise of China and India and a re-emerging Russia. This unfolding phenomenon is likely to change the present unipolar system fast into a multipolar one.[2] Since the focus of this paper is on European Union and its likely position in the emerging multipolar global system, it will be out of place to focus here on the metamorphoses that are taking place in other emerging power centres. However, it is appropriate to examine certain pertinent questions. What is the scope and potential of the

European Union for playing a significant role in the newly emerging global system? What are its strong points and weaknesses in this regard? What should the EU do to harness its full potential and play an effective role in the global system commensurate its aggregate strength? This paper tries to give answers to these questions.

EU Remains an Enigma

To most observers European Union is an enigma, with hardly any parallel in the world. It presents the picture of a unique hybrid, blending the federal and non-federal features, a hybrid that synthesises certain features of a state and an international organization. From the small beginning of creating a common supranational structure of six war-ravaged continental countries – France, Germany, Italy, and the Benelux countries – to control the production and use of their coal and steel in the early 1950s, the European Coal and Steel Community (ECSC) structure has graduated into a European Common Market, European Economic Community, European Community and, finally, into a European Union. Of course, between the rhetoric and the reality, the Community's rechristening moved faster than what it actually was at the given time, constantly egging on the Member States to live upto the common name given to their togetherness. It was called a 'Common Market' when it was not. It was called an 'Economic Community' when it was far from it. It is now called a European Union when it is not really a Union. Therefore, the terminologies used for characterizing the Community was just goals unrelated to the existing reality at the given time, 'sometimes allowing our rhetoric to run ahead of what we achieve – we have, by and large, managed to do it', to quote Chris Patten.[3] Therefore, there existed a gap between the image and the reality of the European Community all the time. And, it constantly evolved and grew under such misnomers deftly crafted by the Brussels bureaucracy which was in its driving seat. That approach is still in vogue.

Europe's woes in the past had germinated largely from a state of mind, of its political leaderships, dominated by the instincts of self-preservation and self-advancement through bloody wars and conquests – a Hobbesean state of nature in international relations where might was right. In a prevalent distrustful and suspicion based relationship, scheming and organizing against one another was considered a legitimate approach of all the players in the field in the conduct of their international relations. That was a feature which the European states had also preserved all through their history — from the time of the city states to the modern times of nation states. That basic approach had kept them firmly on the track of perpetual wars and conflicts against one another. Neither Renaissance nor Reformation could bring any change in it. As a result, Europe got repeatedly organized and reorganized for wars and conflicts – and certainly not for peace. Cumulatively, the continent became a vortex of internecine quarrels and endless bloody and destructive wars. As Robert Kagan observed, for better part of three centuries, European Catholics and Protestants preferred to kill each other than tolerate. During the past two centuries there was little mutual tolerance between the French and the Germans.[4] The two World Wars which Europe had hosted during the first half of the twentieth century were culminations of the basic approach the European states had followed all through their existence – intelligence backing up the instinct. The net result was that at the end of the day all warrior nations – both victors and the vanquished – got exhausted beyond redemption. The ashes of war and the untold pain and misery of the people were all what they could achieve in the end. It took centuries for the Europeans to realise the folly of the way they were managing their affairs and relations. The question that faced them starkly was: Is there any other way Europe can manage its affairs which can produce enduring positive results? Can

Europe be insulated from its age-old internecine quarrels and conflicts, and, more importantly, from turning it again into an arena of another World War and the destruction and suffering that it would entail? The positive answer came from a French bureaucrat, Jean Monnet, who gave intense thought to these fundamental questions. His answer was to shift the conduct of relations between European States from a national approach to a community approach and blunt the edges of aggressive nationalism hither to pursued by them which led to, and sustained, wars and conflicts. The road map which Jean Monnet prepared for Europe was the creation of a community based supranational structures to which nation states would voluntarily transfer parts of their sovereignty on functional basis. His solution based on common law and common institutions, while keeping the inter-governmental method also side-by-side, was found viable to begin with.

The driving force that propelled European integration in the post-war period has been viewed differently by different experts. Sociologists like Martin Kohli and Mojca Novak, are of the view that the European integration was initially driven by concerns of European countries for employment and welfare of their population.[5] According to them: 'In its early stages after the Second World War, Western European political integration was driven by the attempts of nation states to create the conditions for economic growth and social cohesion through a stable framework for European trade and cooperation.... These were the roots of the ... partial sacrifice of sovereignty that integration implied. The nation states were not following a death drive by giving themselves up into a new super-structure; they were on the contrary trying to rescue themselves by agreeing to just the loss of sovereignty necessary for their survival.'[6] They explain that in the context of the economic, social and physical ruins of Europe during the Second World War, achieving economic growth and social pacification appeared possible only through renewed social contract. 'The new social contract took the form of a social model based on full employment for male bread winners and strong social protection for those at risk of being excluded; in other words, the form of what came later to be known as the European model of the "work society". But to implement such a model was not possible for the weak nation states alone; it seemed feasible why in an institutionally secure framework of exchange and cooperation (including Germany which economically was still no *quantité negligeable*). This is the story that led six of the countries of continental Western Europe on the path towards economic and political integration which through several – partly successful, partly abortive – institutional steps resulted in the Treaty of Rome.'[7]

But, experts on international relations and security matters give higher emphasis on the security dimension of European integration. They view it as a measure drawn to contain potential threats from Germany and the Soviet Union. Indeed, it has been emphasized that in the establishment of a supranational ECSC the French objectives were to anchor Germany in Western Europe, gain access to coal in Rhur and make war between France and Germany impossible by enjoining them in a partnership venture.[8] Indeed, the French vision went far beyond the immediate horizon. The French foreign minister and statesman, Robert Schuman, prophesied, way back in 1953: 'We must build Europe in the interest not only of free countries but also in order to be able to integrate the countries of eastern Europe, once they ask us to accept them as members'.[9]

However, France and Germany, two leading continental states whose traditional antagonisms had ignited many wars in Europe in the past, were quick to grasp the potential of the new idea of Jean Monnet and came forward to build new structures of co-operation and to pool their destinies together around them. Indeed, their reconciliation and decision to live in peace and grow together has formed the bedrock of the EU edifice we find today. Therefore, the construction of the

European Union was moved by a lofty vision, sprung from the ashes of the Second World War, to build an enduring family of European states anchored in community spirit, peace, friendship and harmony. It was launched to promote a new approach based on trust and confidence, and to move away from their habitual distrust and suspicion-based relationship, with its concomitant of arming against one another. It was aimed to achieve prosperity by pooling their destinies together under a new European architecture. However, the immediate concerns that clinched the issue were the search of France, in 1950s, for stable security through the containment of Germany by integrating it in a broad supranational framework, complemented by Germany's aspirations to gain equal status and a respectable place in the comity of nations. So in concrete terms, the birth of this functional type Community was made possible partly by the French desire not to return Germany full control over the Rhur and partly by the German manoeuvre to escape the humiliations the victors had imposed on her.

Though the initial objective behind the construction of a United Europe was political, and to blunt the edges of nationalism of the nation states, a wholesale merger of nation states – whether into a federation or a confederation – was sheer impractical at that time. Therefore, to begin with, Jean Monnet preferred to choose certain sectors of common interest and build supranational institutions for those sectors in Europe on functional lines. The basic idea was to increase the number of such supranational institutions so that a point would be reached when unification of nation states in Europe into a political union would become more easier. Began with the establishment of a supranational structure, the European Coal and Steel Community, in 1951, the process quickly moved upward to integrate their markets and international trade, by establishing a European Common Market in 1957, which could cement a new relationship firmly among the Member States. That constituted the bedrock of a new peace structure for Europe.

It may be noted that, in tune with the changing character and role of the new evolving European architecture, the objective of the Community had also kept on changing. As a result, while the 'Preamble' of the ECSC treaty, signed in 1951, stated that the direction of the new venture was 'to create... the basis for a broader and deeper community among peoples long divided by bloody conflicts', the Treaty of Rome of 1957, which established the European Common Market, had underlined its determination 'to lay the foundations of an ever closer union among the peoples of Europe'. This formulation remained unchanged in the Maastricht Treaty also.[10] The new draft EU Constitution, published in 2003, has underlined the determination of the peoples of Europe to get 'united ever more closely, to forge a common destiny'.[11]

The French Perception

Being a key actor involved in the construction of European Union the perception of France about the whole project assumes special significance. Pertinent are the views expressed by two French statesmen – Robert Schuman and Charles De Gaulle. In his book *Pour L'Europe*, published in 1963 in Paris, Robert Schuman, the enunciator of the Schuman Doctrine which gave birth to the ECSC in 1951, explained: 'Instead of persisting in the old nationalism, in a grudging, distrustful independence, we are linking the interests, decisions, and destinies of this new community of states, which heretofore have been rivals. This new policy rests on solidarity and increasing trust.' (p. 45). The other French view which has to be kept in mind, and which continues to influence the French thinking on European integration during the last three decades, is the view held by Charles De Gaulle, Former President of France. The cardinal features of De Gaulle's perception are that nation is a fundamental political reality and that Europe is not a nation, but a collection of nations. Therefore, forging a European nation is contrary to the nature of things, and that the continent can have a confederal set up, an association of nations, obviously under the French leadership. He was against supranational European institutions for two reasons: (1) fear of German hegemony; and (2) he was opposed to granting of power to the stateless and faceless technocrats in Brussels. He favoured intergovernmentalism than supranationalism and supported a political Europe sans supranationality, which implied that nations will remain with all the authority vested in them. But, there could be certain extra-national specialised organs which could do the groundwork for taking decisions by the nations through mutual cooperation. He rejected all military ties between Europe and the United States and wanted that the French defence and French deterrence should remain truly national and strategically free. For him a European federation was a 'totally unrealistic plan'. Instead the plan should be of an 'organized cooperation of States' which is in tune with what the European nations really are. He opposed supranational arrangements for Europe since they would submerge France as a nationless entity. While he favoured close consultation among the six founding members of the European Community he was emphatic that Europe should not remain tied to the Atlantic system in contravention with a genuine European Europe.[12] Although the French made certain compromises here and there after De Gaulle left the Presidency, the spirit and content of De Gaulle's ideas remained a core element in the French approach towards European Union, which has become more manifest in the growth of intergovernmentalism pursued at the level of European Council.

European integration has been harnessed through constant upgradation of the project's stated objectives. Although the project was launched with a single agenda of containment of the potential power of Germany, this was quickly achieved greatly with the conscious cooperation of

Germany itself. Enveloped by an economic agenda for the future construction of Europe, the process was pursued through a combination of patient negotiations, diplomacy, constructive political engagements and cooperation, besides launching a plethora of confidence building measures. In the process they shifted their policies away from traditional concepts of balance of power and deterrence doctrine. These fundamental changes have helped to condition the European psyche gradually in favour of the rejection of reliance on military might for security and for the construction of a new Europe, wedded to the ideals of a community life for the entire region. They rejected power politics and use of force as instruments to preserve peace in Europe. It has led to a new perception of not looking at military power as the core of national security in Europe. Instead, the rule of law and multilateral governance have been made the bases of national security. This new system has defied all existing definitions of the systems of governance, 'a novel form of polity without historical precedent,' to quote Magnus Ryner.[13]

It is significant that European integration in the post-war period has taken place concurrently with a diminishing emphasis on military capabilities and reductions in defence budgets. Indeed, in international relations Europe's new strategy relies to a great extent on diplomacy and use of its 'soft-power'. It appears that regionally and globally, the European Union tends to reject power politics. Barring Britain and France, no other EU Member State seems to entertain any ambition to play a global power role. Therefore, the general ethos growing in EU today is not supportive of EU playing a global military power role nor for seeing itself as a big military power. Rather, it would like to be seen as a soft power. Indeed, it has considerably devalued the role of military power as an instrument in international relations. It also means that there is little political will in EU to acquire more military might and project itself as a global military power.

For four decades since its inception, the main preoccupation of the European community was to transform the European Common Market into a single European market. Indeed, since 1958 the Community's efforts have been to lower the trade barriers between them to facilitate the progressive establishment of a broad, synchronized, economic system for the Community. Yet, all along, they functioned effectively as 12 markets inside the Common Market, with many internal non-tariff barriers attached to them, mainly to protect the domestic products of Member States. As a result, it had necessitated the enactment of the Single European Act, in 1986, to dismantle all internal barriers and establish a single integrated market of the European Economic Community, which was achieved only in 1993. As a result, all goods produced in the Community, on EC stipulated standard, could be marketed freely anywhere in the Community. It enabled free movement of capital across borders, either by shifting their production units to advantageous locations or by effecting mergers or take over of companies from different Member States and establish trans-national European companies. It had removed all barriers of economic activities in the Community and stopped Member States from practicing discrimination in favour of their own products, enterprises or citizens. Competition within the Community was made completely free from restrictions. Therefore, from the very inception in 1958 upto 1993 the main focus of attention of the Council of Ministers and the EC Commission was the pursuance of the economic aspects of the single market. The effort was to attune the single market to strengthen the position of European trade and industry internally and externally. It enabled big companies to apply economies of scale in production thereby to maximize their profit, and to promote joint research and development programme.

The Maastricht Treaty of 1992 had taken the deepening process in the European Union further by programming the Economic and Monetary Union, launching of a single currency, establishment of a Common Foreign and Security

Policy, and creation of a European Central Bank and a European Investment Bank. The Amsterdam Treaty and the Nice Treaty have made further inputs into these programmes. Thus by 1993, EU was able to create a single European market, with a free trade area and a customs union. The launching of Euro in 1999 and distribution of Euro notes and coins in 2002, has made the Union a global player in the currency field also. Therefore, in economic and trade terms, the EU functions like a super power. Indeed, during the last one decade the Union's visibility in the global economic scene has increased spectacularly.

It may be noted that as the character and scope of the European Community has changed, its nuances also have kept on changing, expanding its ambience from a mere common market to a European Union. Simultaneously, the geographical frontiers of the Community have also kept on expanding. From the original six countries of Central Europe — France, Germany, Italy and the Benelux countries – it expanded to other parts of Europe, bringing in countries like Britain, Sweden, Spain, Portugal, Denmark, Greece, Ireland, Austria and Finland and became an organization of 15 European countries. In 2004, 10 more countries from eastern and southern Europe – Poland, Hungary, Czech Republic, Slovak Republic, Slovenia, Estonia, Latvia, Lithuania, Malta and Cyprus – are slated to join the European Union. This would take the Union membership to 25, with a combined population of about 450 million.

It has been widely recognized that in the post-war period, the EU has provided an effective answer to the age-old rivalries in Europe and promoted cooperation and economic development in the region by voluntarily transferring part of the Member States' sovereignty to a supranational structure, although this approach has not made much significant headway in the non-economic sectors of state policies. As Chris Patten, EU Commissioner for External Relations, said recently: '...sharing sovereignty between 25 countries is hell of an enterprise. And I think some of us know the difficulties of reaching an agreement with one other country. So when you are talking about 25, it is like playing chess on a multitude of different levels'.[14] In the non-economic areas the approach is basically inter-governmental decision-making process. Because of the presence of this dual nature of decision-making, the European Union displays partially the characteristics of a state and partially those of an international organization. This hybrid nature of the Union makes it hazardous to explain or predict the general behaviour pattern of the European Union. Perhaps, this may be a reason for the glaring gap between the EU's economic and political influence in the world.

A spectacular result of the European Union process is that the venture has achieved and consolidated the much needed reconciliation between France and Germany whose antagonisms had ignited many wars in the past. Their coming together for common good was wrapped up with stable common institutions, as a result of which construction and consolidation in the EU integration process went hand in hand, leaving little room for setbacks. Multilateralism was made its basic framework in dealing with intra-Community matters and international questions. Joint or coordinated approach, pooling of resources, lowering of intra-Community barriers, and so on were its other features. All these features have made EU a unique experiment in regional integration and in transforming the Community into a force for stability and growth, and a rallying point for the European countries.

Institutionalization

A notable feature of European integration in the post-war period has been a simultaneous process of the Community's institutionalization which has synchronized both construction and consolidation of the new European architecture and minimization of possible setbacks. For administering the supranational structure, the system has created a machinery composed of a Council, a Commission, a Parliament and a Court of Justice, and their competencies have been clearly defined (modified subsequently) by the six founding members when they established the Community. The structure also gave the Union some attributes of a state. Subsequently, a new institution, the European Council, composed of Heads of State and Government of Member States, was added to the superstructure in 1974 as an intergovernmental machinery, which began to meet regularly, at least once in six months, for taking major decisions pertaining to the Community. The Maastricht Treaty of 1992 had formally recognized these meetings of the European Council and made the President of the European Commission also a participant in it, but without the voting right. It gave inter-governmentalism a strong position in the EU decision-making process. However, the EU's basic institutional structure, rules and regulations were initially framed keeping in view a small number of prospective Member States. It remained still viable, with some modifications, when the Community membership got increased from six to nine, and then to fifteen. But that initial mould would be found wanting when the Community membership would be swelling to twenty-five in 2004 or thirty in a few years from now. That has made a major institutional reform imperative.

European States' five-decades long musings with the Community building experiment have entailed substantial change in their perceptions, attitudes, direction and framework. It helped them to break with the past, and enhance their mutual cooperation and flexibility to an extent that they are able to pool their energies and resources for their collective well-being and for peace in the region. It has provided an answer to the prolonged insecurity in Europe. Building a common market and promoting common policies are part of that answer. The European Union, thus evolved during the last half a century, therefore, presents a good example of a truism that intelligent human intervention can change considerably the course of history. However, the resultant Union has become a novel entity built upon a semi-supranational structure. All these years, it has tried to permeate a community spirit, though limited, across Europe which today constitutes the bedrock of Europe's peace, prosperity and stability. Looking back to what Europe was 60 years ago, this is undoubtedly a tremendous feat. It has created a region of limited solidarity.

Though constructed with great care and perseverance, this novel construction still remains quite fragile and presents a metamorphosis where convergence and divergence manifest all the time in quick succession. The high level of market and currency integration has not substantially obliterated the strong cultural boundaries within Europe. So is the identity of peoples inside Europe. They remain staunchly, and proudly, British, German, French, Italian, Spanish, and so on, laced with a veneer of Europeanness wrapping them, as they were ever before since the establishment of the Roman Empire. However, while appreciating what has been done during the last 50 years, it must also be recognized that, except in the economic sector, the structure of European Union is still not sturdy enough to make any strident advances in playing an effective political role in the international system. Of course, the biggest task of establishing a European political and social community is being attempted now. But that construction seems to be beset also with problems the present EU enlargement will be carrying with it.

EU'S EFFECTIVENESS

Strong Points

European Union's effectiveness as an autonomous actor in the emerging global system will depend greatly upon the degree of integration it is able to achieve in various important facets of its activities. Pertinently, the EU has achieved a high degree of integration in the economic sphere, which has created a tremendous potential for the Union's unified autonomous action. As a result, the Union is well set to follow an autonomous policy on economic matters which is manifest particularly in trade and competition policies. It has been quite effective in the deliberations of the WTO and also in the framing of the rules governing the intellectual property rights. Similarly, the Union has gained considerable ground to play an influential, effective and autonomous role in the global currency market, and in the international financial institutions, especially after the launching of the Euro notes and coins as the common currency of the Union, except in three Members States – UK, Denmark and Sweden. With 25 countries in its fold, the EU today is obviously an important actor in the world economy and world trade. This has been recognized by other major global economic players as well.

Problem Areas

Common Foreign and Security Policy (CFSP)

But, if one looks at other facets of EU activities, the picture that emerges is different. There the level of integration remains quite shallow and weak. This is quite explicit in areas like Common Foreign and Security Policy. In fact EU is not able to assert itself in these areas partly because national agendas of Member States are still being pursued in them, although at times they are being tempered marginally by a desire to remain together.[15]

Although there have been initiatives for strengthening the theoretical foundations of an EU foreign policy, by adding a chapter on it in the Maastricht Treaty, there are many areas in which the policies pursued are divergent, where interests and linkages are quite diverse. Britain's worldwide interests and special ties with the United States and the Common wealth, France's special interests in the Francophonie, Spain's and Italy's special interests in Latin America, Germany's special interests in Central Europe, and so on are ground realities which can not be brushed aside so easily for the sake of forging a Common Foreign and Security Policy for the EU. Though EU has put a consultative process and a convergence machinery in place, they do not mean much in this regard. In the circumstances, in effect, the Member States virtually follow their own national policies. If we get a little deeper into it, it is just beyond anybody's imagination how the Union can resolve a question like who should represent the EU in the UN Security Council, if ever EU wants to present itself as a single entity in foreign and security matters. Today, as permanent members of the UN Security Council, Britain and France separate their functions as EU Member States and as UN Security Council members and take independent positions in UN and act separately. And, under the current dispensation, they are unlikely to agree for a single European Union seat in the UN Security Council and give up their two permanent seats in it in favour of a permanent EU seat there, a line which a Member State like Germany espouses. If that ever happens, the battle royal will be on the question of who should occupy that seat. Italy does not want Germany to occupy it, as it wants that seat for itself. The point is that it is unrealistic to gloss over these ground realities of sharp disagreements based on certain degree of hidden suspicion and secret jealousies about status of the Member States. Therefore, when it comes to international organizations like the United Nations, International Labour Organization, and so on, the perspectives that are being presented by the EU Member States remain basically national – the British, French, German and so on. And they sharply disagree when it comes to the question of reforming international organizations like the United Nations. The EU framework hardly exists on such matters.

Clearly, there is no coherent debate among EU member states about what EU foreign policy should be about or how, as a collectivity, they should see the rest of the world. Obviously, they do not see the rest of the world from a single perspective. Despite the existence of various mechanisms and committees in Brussels, and the display of cooperation among the European embassies in third countries, at the micro-level, national debates on foreign policy question in each Member State are very different and are based on very different perspectives. It makes it very difficult for Prime Ministers or for senior officials of all EU Member States to reach a common view on any major issue because each one has his/her national problems and they have been found pulling off in different directions on major issues. Therefore, progress towards forging a Common/Single Foreign and Security Policy for the European Union is hampered by the fact that the international objectives and ambitions of Member States vastly vary and do not converge. Pertinently, it must to be recognized that the European Union is a collection of small and medium sized countries, many of them do not tend to look beyond their neighbourhood or their region. Many of them have never entertained the idea of a global foreign policy nor were they found taking positions or keen interest on issues pertaining to distant parts of the world. Indeed, most of them have not shown any intention to go beyond making certain symbolic gestures. Even a country like Italy, for example, generally pursues that kind of an approach in its responses to important foreign policy questions.

If we examine this question keeping in view the depth of involvement of EU Member States in world politics, Britain and France are the most active ones, which also have the will and capacity to project their power independently beyond their borders. At the same time, it must also be admitted that many other Member States simply do not have that will or capacity to project their power or influence beyond their borders in any significant way. But the Member States which do show some interest beyond their borders are confined largely to their neighbourhood – like Spain and

Italy in the Mediterranean and Latin America, Scandinavian countries in the Baltic, and so on. Since the external interests of Member States in other regions vary vastly from country to country, like Spanish territorial interest in Morocco which obviously is not the same for Finland or Sweden, for example, it is incorrect to surmise that a neat process of historical convergence of perspectives is taking place in the EU on CFSP. Therefore, that possibility remains quite distant. But, what is in vogue is that, by slowly promoting a habit of working together, Europeans are trying to harness a lack-lustre process of convergence in the field of foreign policy on the basis of their shared values, if not of shared interests—commercial, territorial or political. Therefore, it remains a difficult task for the Union to cobble up the divergent foreign and security policies of Member States together and bring them under a single unified structure, especially in areas where multilateralism and coordination remain the evolving norms. From that angle EU has to go very far to realize the CFSP.

It may be recalled that integration of foreign and security policies of Member States was not a priority for the Community when the European Common Market was launched in 1957. In fact, the moves for a concerted approach among the Member States on foreign and security policy issues was initiated only in 1970 when they established European Political Cooperation (EPC) as an intergovernmental forum outside the framework of the European Community structures. Although the EPC's initiatives had helped to open up a new process of Euro-Arab dialogue in 1970s and early 1980s, the degree of coordination the EPC process could achieve among the Community Member States on foreign and security policy questions remained marginal. The degree of consultation and cooperation was also negligible. The situation improved under the Single European Act of 1986 which incorporated a provision in it (Art.30, Title III), theoretically committing the Member States, 'to coordinate their positions more closely on the political and economic aspects of security', and established an EPC Secretariat to assist the process. But the Maastricht Treaty of 1992, (Title V, Article 'J') gave the Common Foreign and Security Policy (CFSP) a prominent position in it, and made it the Union's second pillar (European Community, the first pillar). Article B of the Maastricht Treaty said that the objective of the EU is 'to assist its identity on the international scene, in particular through the implementation of a common foreign policy, including the progressive framing of a common defence policy, which might lead to a common defence'.[16] Article 'J' of the Treaty has defined the specific objectives of the CFSP, which include: (1) to safeguard the common values, fundamental interests and independence of the Union; (2) to strengthen the security of the Union and its Member States; (3) to maintain peace and to strengthen international security; (4) to promote international cooperation; and (5) to develop and strengthen democracy and rule of law and respect for human rights and fundamental freedoms.[17] Despite these provisions in the Maastricht Treaty, there exists a lot of confusion regarding the content of the CFSP. No one is clear how far CFSP is distinct from the general European line on critical issues of foreign policy. Since a distinction has been made between 'common' and 'single', the CFSP's ambience remains quite misty. However, since the Maastricht Treaty there has been incremental advancements in the CFSP process as efforts, though generally unsuccessful in situations like the Kosovo Crisis in 1999, were made to take agreed positions towards various international crises which had taken place since then. But, in real terms, the CFSP made very little progress for a number of years, barring making efforts to cobble up common positions or to make high sounding declaratory statements on some peripheral issues and distant problems, and getting Javier Solana, former NATO Secretary General, appointed in 1999 under the Amsterdam Treaty, as the Union's High Representative responsible for the CFSP.

Rudiments of a European Force Construction

But, a new beginning in the European Union's force construction was made at the Anglo-French bilateral summit, at St. Malo in November 1998, when the two countries decided to have 'an autonomous capacity for action based on credible military forces with the means to use them and the readiness to do so'. This Anglo-French initiative was later supported by other EU Member States at the European Council meeting, held in Helsinki, in December 1999 which launched the European Security and Defence Policy (ESDP). As a follow up, the EU summit, at Laeken, in December 2001, decided to raise a Rapid Reaction Force (RRF) comprised of 60,000 troops, drawn from national armies of Member States, for carrying out 'humanitarian and rescue tasks, peace-keeping tasks and tasks of combat forces in crisis management including peace-keeping'. To provide pertinent advice to the concerned ministers and the European Council, three advisory bodies were also established: (1) A Security and Political Committee composed of high-level representatives; (2) A Military Committee composed of Chiefs of Staff of Member States; and (3) a Military Staff composed of about 100 officers. The Rapid Reaction Force was provided, in 2002, with an annual budget of € 25 million.

Apart from the 60,000 troop component, the RRF would be equipped with a 15 squadron airforce and 15 Warships, besides a contingent of about 200 airbus jets which could be used as military transport for air lifting. These steps EU has taken in recent years have been viewed as initiatives to strengthen the military arm of the European Union and an increasing readiness of it to gradually reduce Europe's dependence on NATO for the security cover. It has been widely speculated that the RRF may constitute the nucleus of a potential European Army. However, the RRF has already taken over, from NATO, the peace-keeping responsibility in

Macedonia from March 2003. But, on the whole, CFSP's progress so far remains marginal, although on certain issues pertaining to the Middle East, Russia, Ukraine, Mediterranean, Balkans and eastern Europe, the EU Member States could work out certain common strategies.

However, of all the EU reforms set in motion, the most difficult one to achieve seems be to put in place a Common Foreign and Security Policy. Under the burgee of CFSP what the Union has now is independent foreign policies of 15 or 25 countries which differ from one another in their perspectives and objectives. Clearly, big Member States like Britain, France and Germany have different international interests to protect. To serve these divergent interests under a Single/Common policy will not be easy or realistic, compared to organizing their trade together. Therefore, the Union's aspiration to have an effective foreign and security policy is beset with enormous difficulties. It is unimaginable, at the moment, that foreign policies of all EU Member States could be fused together to create a clear and coherent foreign policy for the Union. It also involves the forgoing of a very important competence of the Member States. As the EU Member States hold diverse views on foreign and security policy issues, which the national governments freely express at critical times, giving up of that national autonomy of Member States in favour of an integrated EU foreign and security policy is not on cards. Therefore, the pace of CFSP is bound to be very slow, and its evolution may take a long time.[17] Whether the introduction of QMV in this sector would be acceptable to large states like Britain and France is doubtful. The institutional structure which the EU has put in place to promote CFSP is also mired in confusion as there are two anchorages to it – a Commissioner for External Relations, Chris Patten, who has the resources but no mandate, and a High Representative, Javier Solana, who has the mandate but no resources. So there is no sensible decision-making process in the foreign policy field. The European

Convention has now come up with a solution to bridge this hiatus by merging these two positions. But, this will still not produce the situation where EU will speak with one voice on foreign and security policy matters. Another pertinent question is whether all Member States – old and new – want EU to play a political or military role outside the European region? The US would like the Europeans to do that. But a number of EU Member States would not agree for it. The extent to which the EU could agree so far is to undertake the peace keeping responsibility – the least controversial – in Macedonia, the first European Security and Defence Policy (ESDP) operation. In the opinion of Peter Wilson of the British Foreign office:

> I don't think you can see in short-term any EU common foreign policy developing in exclusion of national interests. EU foreign policy unanchored in national realities will have big problems. Underpinning that policy would be ESDP. Even now policies are still debated at national levels. Trade, aid, sanctions, etc. are all mechanisms outside the CFSP which can be used to strengthen the CFSP. All these mechanisms can be communitized. I think our understanding of foreign policy interests is also changing – terrorism, weapons of mass destruction and energy security are top foreign policy interests today. So it is not CFSP anymore – it never was. It needs greater coherence and sophistication.... We simply do not believe in the Commission and the Community method to conduct our foreign policy. I don't think it is happening and I don't think it should happen. It is going to be a little more sophisticated than the classic internationalist model of 1960s. The Union we have now is much more complicated. It is hard for anybody outside to understand. It is hard even for anybody inside to understand. Coherence is now the biggest problem in EU.[19]

Similar sense of pessimism was sounded by some other strategic experts also. For example, Dana Allin of the IISS, London, was emphatic: 'I don't think that during this century Europe will have a single foreign policy in the sense that US has a single foreign policy. A single foreign policy needs a single unified state. That does not happen in EU. There can be greater coordinated foreign policy which may look like a single foreign policy, but it won't be a single foreign policy'. He said that, 'a coordinated foreign policy in EU can rest on a lowest common denominator. The question is how far you can raise that lowest common denominator.'[20]

Building a separate military structure for Europe is likely to face problems. During the last 3 years, except in Britain and France, there is a general slow down in the defence budgets of most other EU Member States. It raises the question whether the EU Rapid Response Force will have the needed capability to conduct separate military operation. The other factor is the changing attitudes of a large number of EU Member States towards military solutions which Robert Kagan has focused. These European States repose more faith in non-military solutions to problems because of the success they had achieved in creating the European Union by renouncing the use of military force. Although there are Member States in EU who still believe in use of force if necessary, as a general proposition, there is general resistance in EU against use of force. Most of them prefer use of soft power, by using economic clout, to solve contentious international issues, and not hard power.

Whatever the interpretations of CFSP and its perceived direction, the articulation of foreign policy in European Union remains essentially a matter of national governments. Inter-govermentalism is the core feature of it, and the lowest common denominator remains its benchmark. Indeed, there is an in-built incapacity in EU to be effective in foreign and security policy since the Member States are too divided, vertically and horizontally, to act effectively and are having different priorities. It is important to underline that all Member States of EU are not equally concerned about foreign policy issues, nor do they entertain similar aspirations in playing roles in the international arena. The differences are quite conspicuous in the attitudes of countries like Britain and France on the one hand, and of countries like Germany, Italy, Spain, Greece, Denmark and Ireland, who are very reluctant to play any larger international role; some of them do not want to go beyond making grand gestures and impressive suggestions, with nothing meaningful behind to back up. The EU enlargement is likely to heighten this incapacity. Therefore, making the EU to speak in single voice or to convey a single message from EU during major international crises remains very difficult.

A notable feature of EU's CFSP is that it accepts the existence of 15 or 25 foreign ministers pursuing their own independent foreign policies. Therefore, what is envisaged under CFSP is to ensure a high degree of consultation and cooperation to reach a common position on various international issues. Therefore, CFSP is not envisaged to become a single foreign and security policy, which is also not possible unless the EU becomes a single European State, which no one wants it to be at present. The Member States are still not ready to toss their national interests for a hazy 'European' interest. Therefore, the construction of a common foreign policy by cobbling up agreed positions on some peripheral issues can hardly be taken seriously, and the effectiveness of such a policy will always remain doubtful.

In a statement made in December 2002 Romano Prodi, President of the European Commission, said in Brussels that 'We cannot afford to remain an economic giant and a political dwarf. We must wield more authority in international affairs.... That calls for a more robust common foreign and security policy.'[21] Chris Patten, European Commissioner for External Relations, has cited three developments which have led EU to pay more attention to CFSP in 1990s: (1) As EU matured as an economic entity, there was realisation that it was lagging behind in the sphere of foreign policy; (2) the collapse of the Berlin Wall and the haplessness EU had experienced during the crisis in Balkans; and (3) Europe's changing relationship with US, especially after Washington has displayed a tendency to pursue unilateralism disregarding others.[22] According to him, the CFSP remains weak 'because it is an area in which the Member States are rightly jealous of their national prerogatives. There are distinct limits on how far they want to go in pooling their capacity, and on how much they want to spend. But in recent years they have begun to fashion a Common Foreign and Security policy which can be more than just declaratory. They have recognized that this needs to integrate three strands: national policies, Community Policies, and CFSP itself (the so-called second pillar). European Foreign Policy must combine all three, and it will become stronger as that 'combination' becomes seamless.'[23] He said: '...people don't die for interest rates. But they are prepared to die for crucial issues of foreign and security policy issues that go right to the heart of national sovereignty'.[24]

The general opinion among specialists in Europe is that the EU integration process is yet to reach a level from which it can function as an autonomous actor on foreign and security matters. And, therefore, the nation state would continue to play an independent autonomous role in the strategic, foreign and security policy fields. According to Antonio Missiroli, there are real difficulties for the EU for having a 'single' security policy than for having a 'common' security policy. A Member State like Britain is more closer to US than to any other EU state.[25] In the opinion of a French expert, the problem is that in foreign policy and defence, the EU Member States are not in the same wavelength. They do not share a common perception on the question of use of force. And generally they do not want to spend more on defence. A contributory factor to EU's ineffectiveness in foreign and security policy, according to him, is the vagueness with which the EU project has been pursued. He says:

> First of all they had a very strange idea that they have to start with economics. Therefore, there was no need to declare their aims beyond saying "an ever closer union" in the Treaty of Rome which is a very vague objective. But if you look at it today and ask Europeans what they aim now, it is equally vague, something like a state but not a state. State will remain, but EU will be an international entity, and so on. So where are we? You cannot still define what you are. The result is that you do not devote sufficient energy to try and define its aims in international terms.... If we want to be taken seriously in international scale, we need to define the means whereby we can define our policies and get them implemented. What we need is a continuum, starting with definition of policy when a problem occurs, including all the means as far as the implementation by using the force. That is what foreign policy is. It starts with the definition of the problem and it ends with the implementation of the decisions, including the means of using force as the last resort. We are very far from that because in a sense behind the slogan there is a great ambiguity .... Clearly, Europe is not going to be a significant power in the complete sense of the term, unless international situation changes, US decides to leave Europe or a clash takes place on a sensitive issue.[26]

It is widely recognized that on foreign and security policies, EU is not in a position to speak with one voice nor one person can speak for the entire EU. Big countries speak for themselves. In the opinion of a German official: 'The drawback is that Europe has structures which have not yet fully adapted to play a major political role. Ten years have passed after CFSP was adopted in the Maastricht Treaty. The progress is very slow. Lowest common denominator has become the benchmark of the CFSP. So one should not be overoptimistic that Europe is becoming one of the poles in a multi-polar world'.[27] But, on certain issues like Kyoto Protocol and International Criminal Court of Justice, there is unanimity in EU.

Distrust in Brussels Bureaucracy

A key European Union institution which has come under constant scanning and attack and has generated much criticism and suspicion in the public mind, over the secrecy and insensitivity that envelope its functioning, is the 20-member European Commission, the steel frame of the Union, assisted by about 20,000 faceless bureaucrats, which administers the Union and its € 90 billion annual budget. On many occasions its activities have been mired in controversies, as it was seen as the main source of 'petty and irritating' regulations for which, generally, the Union is criticized. At the popular level, the unelected Commission is seen as a remote secretive bureaucratic institution which, through its imposition of all kinds of directives and regulations from Brussels, posed a threat to their traditional ways. As a result, since its inception in 1957, the European Community has acquired the image of a bureaucracy-driven project from above. And the European Commission has been solely responsible for the Community's trade policies, development assistance and framing of EU regulations, and thus functioning as the fulcrum of the EU system. Indeed, the centrality of the Commission is a strong feature of the EU set up. The Commission's key position in the system was made explicit, in a speech at the European Parliament, by Romano Prodi, President of the European Commission. He said:

> The Commission is the melting pot into which the various national interests and tensions are poured, and from which emerge proposals that seek to reconcile these often conflicting interests. In this way it provides not only a synthesis and analysis of the problems at issue but also a starting point for negotiations in which, once national differences have been aired the common European interests can be identified. This executive, that combines independence with a sensitivity to the balance of powers and interests in all the Member States (both large and small) is the *sine qua non* for the effective pooling of sovereignty in the Community.[28]

But, recent developments gave rise to an apprehension in the Commission that its predominant role in the system was getting eroded as the inter-governmental system, represented by the European Council, has increased its role in the system. The Commission was unhappy over the growing strength of the inter-governmental system and launched an attack on it. The Commission President, Romano Prodi, has stated that the inter-governmental model would be unsuitable for the European Union because 'it can lead to only two possible outcomes, both of them undesirable – either it will turn the Community into an international talking shop, incapable of producing a real pooling of sovereignty around the common interest or it will deceive people constantly by creating new bodies which are exempt from any form of democratic scrutiny – a real government of bureaucrats. Giving new powers to some sort of Committee of Ministers, served by an unaccountable secretariat, would not represent any sort of progress either for democracy or for effective decision-making'. According to him: 'Enhancing the inter-governmental model at the expense not only of the Commission but also, ultimately, of the Council would therefore undermine the democratic nature of the whole

European structure and would be a seriously retrograde step.'[29] He said:

> If development of the Union is pursued while weakening the political role of the Commission, if our capacity for executive action is eroded, if the extension of the inter-governmental model corrupts the judicial and institutional mechanisms of the Community, if the democratic legitimacy of the system, guaranteed by this House, is undermined, if all this is allowed to happen, then the achievements of the single market, the common policies, the solidarity mechanisms, and the strength Europe exercises by speaking with a single voice in international negotiations, will all be at risk.[30]

But, Paul Taylor holds the view that the Commission's position is not as exalting as it has been projected. According to him, the Commission is a unique international organization. Its right to initiate is provided in the Treaty of Rome. But the Council, which takes the decisions, controls the policy. The Council has representatives of States that makes law. It is also acting as the guardian of law. The European Parliament, though it is not a true legislature, has gradually increased its negative powers – it has strengthened its right to be consulted and has strengthened its powers over the EU budget. The EU budget works out something like 2.3 percent of the GNP, which is pretty small in size compared to the national budgets. Therefore, according to him, the Commission does not have an overbearing power.[31]

Shallow Europeanness

A factor that militates against crystallization of EU's potential strength is the continued dominance of national loyalty and national feeling embedded in the psyche of the people which keeps the national identities in Europe (sans its aggressiveness) still very strong. The Europeaness EU has inculcated has not yet acquired much depth in the people's psyche, although one may find more younger people, not in any significant size, in the original six Member States stressing their European identity. Even within the original six, the number of such 'Europeans' seems comparatively more in Italy than in other states. However, the general trend appears to be to gradually develop a framework of multiple identities in which the national identity would remain the core and the European identity would take its place in the periphery. In the words of an Italian academic: 'Our identities are multi-layered. At present our European identity is not as strong as our national identity. But European identity is growing among the new generation.'[30] However, the number of people who might say that they are primarily Europeans remains insignificant. For example, in a Member State like Britain it is very hard to find this category of people. What it indicates is that on the whole the national identities in Europe are unlikely to get submerged by the European identity in the foreseeable future. It is quite obvious that the Member States still vigorously pursue their national objectives within the European Union, although in the process they do go through a series of compromises with other EU members. As a result, a point has reached today that nationalism cannot be pursued rabidly or aggressively by any EU country. That gets tempered constantly with the general interests of other EU States as well. This change apart, there is no indication that national identities in Europe will disappear. What is expected is a flexible framework in which national and European identities can amicably coexist in which national identities will continue to occupy a pride of place. As Dick Gupwell said: 'A French man can regard himself as French and European and not French or European.'[33]

Several European scholars think that national objectives are still being pursued in EU and will r emain strong although compared to 1950s they are less vigourous.[34] According to Gianni Bonvicini, pursuit of national interests always existed in the European Union. They will continue to remain as guiding forces. Therefore, in future there will be more complex picture of national interests. At the same time EU has succeeded in introducing certain moderation in the pursuit of national interests through procedure mechanisms like majority voting, QMV, EU Commission's independent role as the guardian of the treaty, and so on.[35]

So every Member State is engaged in constantly fighting for its own national interest in the EU. According to Axel Queval, 'this is going to continue even if we have the United States of Europe. So, Germans, British, French, Italians, Spaniards, and so on will battle for their cornors in EU. That is absolutely normal.'[36] At the same time, it must also be noted that not every Member State in EU has national ambitions. For example, Member States like Britain and France still clearly have national ambitions to remain as global powers. They are permanent members of the UN Security Council, and do possess the wherewithal to project their power outside Europe, alone or in coalition. But, if we turn to other EU Member States, the picture becomes more complex – should Germany behave like a power or it should refrain from joining a foreign policy course which would entail military operations, like in the middle east for example. Italians pursue a foreign policy which, observers think, does not have much substance.[37] Julie Smith observes: 'Italy was originally one of the pro-integration countries. But, under Berlusconi that attitude is changing. It does not mean that it will pull out. But it is very different. We see that also in The Netherlands – a good European country. But anything that affects its national interests it resists'.[38]

A notable new trend in Europe today, a spillover effect of the EU process, is a more accommodative attitude on the part of Member States towards the re-emerging local and regional identities, which is manifest in the British attitude towards the creation of the Welsh Assembly and the Scottish Parliament, in the Spanish attitude towards the Basques, in the French attitude towards Brittany, and so on. In the past, regional movements for autonomy was seen as a threat to national integrity and unity. But in EU such fears are less today. Indeed, today to aspire for greater regional autonomy within the EU system is considered legitimate in a multi-layer identity framework for EU citizens.

However, despite many changes at various levels and intensities, it is unlikely that national identities in Europe will be overwhelmed by the European identity. Yet, the European identity can clothe the national identities, as it has always been a feature of European nations, but this time it is with a little more political sanctions than ever before. National identities will still remain central since they are keyed into geography, history, public opinion and character of societies. Therefore, they will remain even in a United States of Europe, if ever it comes into existence. It may be recalled that European Community was established in a framework of diversity. That is where primarily the European Union still is. When asked whether nation states in EU would eventually wither away, Christopher Hill made a thoughtful observation. He said:

> I think the nation states are not going to wither away. I don't think the European Union is going to disappear either. It is an important historical achievement. EU will continue to coexist with nation states. The smaller states may be willing to be absorbed within it and see their identity lost in a political sense. But, short of a major war and crisis, I don't see a single United States of Europe is being created in the model of India or United States federal system. It is impossible to measure the circumstances in which it can come about because it would mean that each individual country like Britain and France and Germany will have to opt

> for suicide, the destruction of themselves as independent actors irrevocably. There has been some discussion about it in France. A French writer said: "Wait a minute. What are you doing? Des est libre France?" France will never say yes to it. Britain will say : 'never' 'never'. There will always be an England.[39]

Another factor that inhibits the shaping up of EU as an autonomous centre of decision making on political matters is the absence of hard boundaries around the European Union. In a territorial sense there is the Schengen system. But, in a political sense, the boundary is breached by US-UK special relationship, the NATO and so on. 'There is no solid shell which holds Europe together. Therefore, any given decision it takes is based on a kind of penetrating system from away by some outside actors – especially the US. In the Copenhagen EU summit in December 2002, the US supported Turkey's membership in the EU. The Europeans made it clear to US to mind its business. But US manages so subtly to influence the EU agenda and decisions.'[40]

UK's Reluctant Partnership

EU's effectiveness in the global arena will depend upon how united and strong a voice it can build up for itself to respond to international developments. If the concert it represents has to be sturdy and effective, there should be unity of purpose among the Member States. From that point of view, EU is still not an accomplished architercture. When major Member States assemble, they sit together with different objectives and agendas in mind. They do not show much enthusiasm to take supranational arrangements in the Community beyond trade and currency matters. An important Member State like Britain has been cautious in its approach to the European Union for various reasons. Its special relationship with the United States inhibits Britain from thinking and acting as an ardent member of the European Union, especially on matters pertaining to foreign and security policy. Therefore, it shows reluctance to make a clear choice between US and EU on political issues. As Thomas Meyer said, there is need to bring Britain back 'to the integrated action and concert building' and arrive at 'a clear understanding of what the role of Europe should be and how it should be developed.'[41]

Britain's semi-insular position in Europe is based on its sense of sovereignty, on its sense as a major global power. This sense has been fortified by its special relationship with the United States, which the latter reciprocates liberally at critical times.[42] Therefore, when it comes to international issues, Britain generally takes a pro-American position. Besides, the British voters also seem to be more cautious about an integrated political Europe. Julie Smith explains: 'There is a genuine economic difference between Britain and Europe. UK-EU economies do not appear converging. So synchronization becomes difficult. There is a huge amount of historical legacy in the British psyche that we have to go alone instead of following Europeans in international politics'.[43] According to Peter Wilson, Britain's close relationship with the United States would 'mean that sometimes we have to see things differently from what our EU partners see. We think that our good relationship with US is good for all and not just for us. Every EU member has its own perception about the world and its position in the world. EU is relatively a large number of countries. The EU as such does not have a particular view about its relationship with the US, and also in part, due to the similar kind of mindset, about the occasional need to intervene in international situation in order to enforce decisions of international and multi-lateral institutions'.[44] There are experts who think that if Britain joined euro, the new currency would have been stronger than what it is today. At the same time, they also feel that if it joined the recession that gripped other parts of the European Union also would have instantly affected the British economy. Similarly, it would have deprived Britain the right to decide interest rate independently. 'It is our desire to control our fiscal policy and to control our interest rates that we want to remain national than international in decision-making on our fiscal policies. So Britain's refusal to join euro is much more than the differences between the functioning of European Central Bank and the British Banking system. So staying away from euro was beneficial to Britain.'[45] The British position in euro would not change in the near future, according to Christopher Hill. A lot of people don't want to join euro because the British economy is doing well while most of the continental economies, including Germany's, are not. 'It would be crazy if Britain joins a system in which interest rates are higher, where Britain will not be free to spend more money to public services programmes.'[46] He apprehends that, if Britain does join euro and if it works well, the next pressure would be for a European Economic Council to act as a government. As a result there would be a kind of an implicit European government at that point, which will raise the question whether European Union has to become a state or not, whether it has to be a super power. 'I would say Europe of nation states – diversity. I don't want Europe to become a super power like US and spend a lot of money on military force.'[47] What Britain follows in EU today is a cost-benefit approach. It is more careful and acts on the basis of what is best for Britain.[48]

There is plenty of evidence to show that Britain has been a reluctant partner in EU. It has always been reluctant to get deeper into the integration process and even to get into a customs union. Every forward movement Britain made in the EU integration process beyond the frame of a free trade area was made with great reluctance. It has opposed federalism, refused to join euro, criticized the CAP and got annual financial refund from the EU. This reluctance is not simply by accident, but because of Britain's history. For Britain, the continent for centuries has been a source of sorrow. Though that is past, the fact remains that many in Britain do not trust the continental countries sufficiently to share power with them. As Paul Taylor says, basically they remain Euroskeptic.[49] They trust the British people, the House of Commons, and Westminster not Brussels. That is why they are extremely reluctant to transfer power from Westminster to Brussels, with all its consequences for the performance of the EU architecture. But some continental scholars see in Britain's reluctance a refusal to see itself as a European country. According to Ernst Reichel, 'the British accent on sovereignty, power projection, its world role and so on are manifestations of the British failure to come to terms with the fact that UK is a European country.'[50]

The Problems of CAP

European Community's Common Agricultural Policy (CAP) has fermented considerable rancour in the European Union in the past. It is also an example of how Member States have pursued national interests steadfastly in the European Union. It may be noted that the bedrock of European integration was laid on the Franco-German reconciliation which was cemented by the German promise to support the CAP, which was clearly beneficial to the French agriculture, as a *quid pro quo* for the benefits Germany would receive from the industrial expansion in a European Common Market. Therefore, no German Chancellor after Konrad Adenauer could obtain the consent of his French counterpart to modify the CAP. For the French, the matter was non-negotiable. As a result, every effort of German Chancellors, after 1965, to change the CAP was met with failure for purely political reasons. In France, to be fair, if any President or Prime Minister or Farm Minister ventured to contemplate any change in the CAP, he invariably met with aggressive rebellion from the French countryside. Therefore, CAP was considered a core national interest for France. It may be recalled that in order to protect it from attacks, in 1965-66, the French had resorted to an 'empty chair' policy in the Community, until it was resolved to the French satisfaction by the 'Luxembourg Compromise' in 1966. These developments have shown that a change in CAP is not in the hands of anyone else, but solely in the hands of France.[51]

There is no doubt that CAP is an important aspect of the European Union. But its problems are: (1) it takes away a chunk of EU budget; and (2) it provides product subsidy to farmers. At one stage, it took about 70 percent of the Community budget. But now it has fallen to 50 percent, still a big chunk, which is creating problems inside and outside the Union. No doubt, so long as EU spends this much amount for CAP, it will limit EU spending on other sectors. For the French it is a vital issue. To some extent Italy and Spain also want it to continue as they also have sizeable farm sectors. The CAP reforms introduced after the Berlin Summit of 1999 have changed the CAP from a price guarantee system to an income guarantee system. The new Member States, slated to join the Union in 2004, also have strong farm sectors. If their farmers are not treated equally at par with farmers of older Member States, there can be problems. Whether these farmers could be treated discriminately for long, or whether the EU budget can sustain a non-discriminatory CAP are open questions. Therefore, the CAP can cause strain in intra-EU relations. As a policy which is in place for the last 45 years, it is difficult to discontinue it. Moreover, it is an important element in EU's internal and external relationship, affecting agricultural imports and exports. The discriminatory deal EU had recently with Poland and other new members – a cap of 25 percent as subsidy and not more – does not seem to be an enduring one, and will have to give way to a uniform system. It is neither feasible nor desirable to keep a completely different or discriminatory system forever within the European Union itself for the new members without serious political fallouts.

However, now new pressures are mounting from US, Canada, Australia, and the WTO to change the CAP. In the circumstances, France ultimately will have to give in. But, a fundamental question is whether France would give in without substantially undermining the continued French adherence to European integration? In other words: Is there a way of opening Europe for international agricultural trade without destroying the French countryside? These are big questions. In the opinion of Weizacker:

> The French are not going to be in a position to defend the present system of sharp export subsidies. They are extremely expensive for the European tax payers. And they are very destructive to the third world. Although they have defended this non-sense in the past, this does not mean that they will go on subsidizing their own farmers for non-exportable agricultural products. You have to find a basis for self-nourishment of the countryside of the Continent, which should not be destroyed and which should not make itself hostage to Australians, Canadians or Americans. Switzerland after the Second World War had a popular vote for an amendment to the Constitution which made the existence of small-scale farms in the country as part of the Constitution. So the Swiss government is not permitted to negotiate about opening their market to anybody which can destroy their farmers. In Europe, we don't have that constitutional barrier. So EU is not going to dismantle CAP, but modify it in a way that it is no longer truly destructive to developing countries.[52]

I have heard angry reactions in Germany against the CAP. An official in the German Foreign Ministry said that in economic terms 'it is a non-sense'. In political terms it deprives resources for other purposes, like regional development. Some others called it 'irrational', 'anti-third world' and 'causes huge waste of resources'.[53] Yet some others focused on financial constraints of EU and pressures from WTO which would compel EU to reform the CAP and cut down the CAP expenditure.[54] Of course, there is justification for Germans to feel that way. CAP costs Germany 20 to 25 per cent of tax-payers' money which goes to the EU budget, against which the flow back to Germany from the EU budget is about 10 percent. So Germany is a net payer to EU. Therefore, it has an interest in cutting down the EU's agricultural spending. Notably, Germany, unlike Britain, does not get any rebate from EU. That apart, the CAP reform would require French acquiescence. So a solution will have to be found with the consent of France. Enlargement will necessitate it since the EU will not have enough money to sustain the present policy in the enlarged Union. However, the general opinion in EU today is in favour of reforming the CAP in the light of trade talks in WTO since the old CAP is no longer sustainable. The CAP will continue, but it will have to be shifted away from subsidies for production to subsidies for income. So a reformed CAP may decouple subsidies from production so that it does not disturb the market.[55]

How does the French view this changing CAP scenario? The French radiate more confidence about the international competitiveness of their agriculture today than ever before. And they are not opposed to CAP reforms. According to Axel Queval, CAP has already been revised quite a lot. Fixed prices have diminished. Reforms were also carried out within the framework of WTO. And they would continue. He said: 'French soil is very fertile and it can produce grains – corn, maize, barley, oats and so on – at a price which is competitive in the world market because we have a good climate and a fertile soil. A lot of other European countries cannot do it. Neither Britain nor the Scandinavians can produce for a world market. But France can do it and compete at the world market.' He holds the view that there is no justification for the rich farmers getting assistance from the CAP. 'Only poor and small farmers should be helped from the CAP. In CAP the subsidy should diminish. There is now a dual system envisaged for the east European countries because we can't afford to pay to the east European farmers what the French, German or British farmers are now getting. The issue of CAP reforms will reappear all the time until it is reformed.'[56] Another French scholar, Guillaume Parmentier, said: 'If one country whose agriculture can survive without price subsidy in the world market it is France. There is no doubt about that. So it is in our interests to get out of the system. Politically, we are a democracy. Therefore, CAP and support for farmers is also a political issue. Support prices benefit large parts of the farming sector.' CAP will be reformed. But it will not give up support to farmers, but reorient the support base to their social needs, he says.[57]

Clearly, the CAP cannot continue in the present form after enlargement if we take into account the state of agriculture of the newly admitted Member States. The Polish agriculture in 2004 is where the European Community agriculture was at the time when European Common Market was launched. Therefore, the CAP reform is inevitable. According to one analyst, Antonio Missiroli, CAP will change by 2010 or 2012, and even French would accept it. 'What is being done today is to postpone that moment of truth. All EU decisions are subject to the WTO. So WTO will not accept decisions which are not compatible with WTO regulations and agreements. So there will be pressures also from WTO for changing the CAP. In the short-term, of 3 or 4 years, the CAP is unlikely to change drastically. But in the medium term, for various reasons – due to external and internal pressures – the CAP will change. France also will face that moment of truth.'[58] In the opinion of Paul Taylor: 'The French argument that protectionism is useful keeping in view the massive international farming organizations which try to get control of farms, is bound up with genetic modification to control the seed that is going to be put as part of the politics of CAP. The agro-business is a big threat. The Europeans are having anti-GM policy. And Americans don't like that. So CAP has a positive side of protecting the European farmer from the onslaught of GM farm products and against international farm organizations. CAP will continue, but in an amended form.'[59] An EU official, James Gilbert said: 'There will be some form of CAP, whether it receives the same expenditure in the budget, I can't say. But certainly it cannot continue in the present form. If it is extended to all new Member States it will bankrupt us. Something has to give. Change of CAP will be forced upon the EU. But eventually the system has to be harmonized to apply to everybody.'[60]

The Impact of Enlargement

The European Union is in for a major enlargement, from the present 15 to 25 Member States, in 2004, which can have a major impact on its political unity, cohesion and effectiveness as an actor in the emerging global system.[61] While the impact of enlargement cannot be assessed in advance, since it can also be affected by strategies pursued after enlargement, certain forebodings are there for anyone to see. In economic terms, quantitatively, it would add more European economies to the European Union, which can strengthen the economic clout of the European Union and expand the Euro zone, although the new Member States are relatively backward, and will take a long time and would involve considerable cost from EU for levelling them up economically. But considering the political advantages, and long-term economic advantages, of having countries like Poland, Hungary, Czech Republic, Slovak Republic and so on in EU, it is worth for the EU to spend for the transition towards their levelling up, some have argued. But, overwhelmingly, there is skepticism among a cross-section of experts in EU about the likely overall impact of enlargement on the European Union. The general opinion is that the enlargement will weaken the coherence in the European Union. An Italian Professor said that the enlargement will be 'dangerous' to the European Union.[62] A French expert said that it would make the construction of CFSP more difficult. A British expert thought that the enlargement would make EU decision-making more difficult, as reaching agreement among 25 countries would be difficult.[63] It can dilute the process of integration, and weaken EU's ability to perform as a common actor. 'The core element of EU is the common market – a free trade area – and a customs union. The customs union will survive unless the economic conditions change dramatically, like in 1930s, and economic nationalism taking over. The CAP may go down. The CFSP too may go down. Thus the EU will be left with the common market and the customs union, technical cooperation; and may be human rights provision. What it might be, if we start with 25 or 27 countries, and if there is no enforcement mechanism? European common law without European police force to enforce it? So, we don't have a common judicial space. There are too many legal systems. So it is difficult to move towards common standards.'[64] Another British academic also holds similar views. He says that though enlargement is an important factor in EU, the problem will be about getting agreements among 25 or 30 states. 'There is talk about extension of QMV in the area of foreign policy. I am not convinced that that actually will prove to be the way of achieving effective coordination because as we know big states can be unhappy about such voting. So every attempt will be made to seek consensus. That takes time. Also one is talking about a group of as many as 10 countries which have no experience in European foreign policy, which would take a lot of time for learning of about 15 and even about 6. It will take time to learn all this. How they will be affected by the new addition of Member States, one does not know. One tends to know that they are on the pessimistic side because there are possibilities that a group of West European states will emerge again ahead of others .... EU is now striving for coordination. But the mechanism of coordination is not very strong.' He said, 'I am very much concerned that enlargement is very damaging for EU's achievements.'[65] However, what comes out of these expressions is that enlargement will make the EU decision-making more difficult. This is particularly so in the field of CFSP. Of course, to have a coherent CFSP for the enlarged EU is logical to make it effective. But that prospect is going to be more difficult. A lot of Europeans think that enlargement is not a good idea. According to Axel Queval, 'If every single country has a right to veto, imagine Latvia, which has a common border with Russia, will veto any EU policy that will offend Russia. So an island with a million population will have a right to veto the whole EU policy. Also on defence, some countries – neutrals – can veto moves. Some may oppose common taxation policy. Another problem is the unwillingness of many countries to spend for defence. You need a strong defence so that it works as a deterrent. But unfortunately, barring Britain and France, all other EU countries want to spend less for defence.'[66] In the words of Dana Allin: 'The original concept of Europe was a fairly a small place. It was an ideology, mainly of Christian Democrats in the border regions around Alps – Benelux, France, Germany and Italy. It was about the people of the border regions of Alps. In that sense, Britain has been a non-European in the coordinated club on foreign policy.'[67] Therefore, enlargement is likely to apply brake on CFSP, because of the sheer size of the enlarged EU.

EU has meetings where everybody has to speak. It makes a big difference in having 15 heads of state and 25 heads of state. Each has to speak at the meeting in their languages because there is national pride attached to language, which is a big issue in EU. How important it is for a delegate to speak only in his national language at formal meetings of EU has been explained by Dana Allin. He explains: 'I heard stories about it, the experience of a UK friend a number of years ago, a story about how he went to attend a meeting in Brussels. Everybody flew to Brussels and the Spanish translator was sacked. They could not find another Spanish translator. Probably, the Spanish representative could have spoken in English, as a practical solution. But, as a matter of national pride he would not speak in any other language. The meeting was cancelled. This is an example.'[68]

There is an apprehension that enlargement's widening process will apply brakes on the deepening process and will eventually transform the EU into a *de facto* free trade area, by reducing all other existing features, barring the customs union and the Euro, to frills attached to it. Of course that was Britain's initial layout for the Community when it conducted negotiations in 1957-59 in the OEEC to establish linkages with the European Common Market by establishing a European Free Trade Area.[69] That was also what Margaret Thatcher desired when she said that the European Community should widen as much as possible because then EU would become a free trade zone. Whether the present enlargement will eventually lead the Union towards that destination is matter one has to wait and see since this enlargement is pregnent with many practical log-jams for the Union in the coming years.

There are different perceptions about the present enlargement. Some view it as furtherance of the British wish for widening and not deepening. Others content that widening does not mean that it cannot also deepen. Since the European Union framework is a constant experiment, one cannot at present be certain about which view will prevail ultimately. There is also a perception that the present enlargement will strengthen the pro-American voice in European Union as some of the Balkan states and Poland have closer ties with the United States, and that the new members would not support any CFSP move which would undermine NATO relationship. But others disagree with this perception. In their view, this may be true in the short-run since some of the conservative parties in eastern Europe would probably be pro-Americans because they were anti-Russians. But this is not possible in the long-run because the long-term interests of these Europeans would be different.[70]

However, in economic terms, the key beneficiary of EU enlargement in 2004 is Germany as it brings in all the areas charted under the *Lebensraum* doctrine peacefully under the European Union, which could bring to Germany all the benefits expected of from the *Lebensraum* doctrine. As an Indian Diplomat remarked, through the EU Germany has achieved what it could not achieve through the world wars. No doubt, the main long-term benefit of enlargement will go to Germany. In political and cultural terms, all these countries are very close to Germany for historic reasons. 'I think it will strengthen Germany in the European Union. So Germany will be stronger. But, I don't think that enlargement will strengthen the possibility of political unity of Europe.'[71]

The German Question

As mentioned earlier, building a community structure and culture for Europe was aimed partly to contain a potentially powerful Germany. Perhaps, this was the prime motive behind the French initiative in this direction. But, Germans have shown understanding of this French concern and remained cautious about its own empowerment with traditional attributes of power. As a result, instead of building itself up as a hard military power, Germans chose the path of becoming a soft power, an economic power, in Europe, a path which Japan chose in Asia in the post-war period. In that vein, even when France became a nuclear power, Germans refused to match that French power, and decided to stay as a non-nuclear power. Their emphasis was more on the strengthening of the diplomatic and pacifist content in Germany's foreign and security policy. That shift in approach has made a positive change in the nature and ethos of Germany. Yet, when the Berlin Wall collapsed in 1989, it stirred up a lot of suspicion in France about the potential of reunified Germany. But, after 14 years now, the situation is quite different and more relaxed. According to a French academic, Germany, a big country, often shows diffidence and gives out the signal that it does not want to be an international power, and shows reluctance to participate in military operations in combat positions. Indeed, it is extra-cautious in the exercise of power. But, 'at times it looked like a bully. During the early recognition of Croatia and Slovenia it looked like that. But the fear of German garishness is a matter of the past. Germans keep the views of France in mind when they take decisions. It is a complex question. It is not based on French fear or German overbearing. Germany is seen in France sometimes not as a decisive actor.'[72] In the words of a British academic:

> France and Germany have their disagreements and moments of tension. But they always come together again. They are aware that European Union's future depends on their togetherness. Relationship between Mitterand and Kohl was close. Schroeder and Chirac have their disagreements, but still they have a strong sense of togetherness. They know that EU's success depends upon them. Together they remain the centre of Europe. Britain feels that it is left out, or at least does not constitute the centre of Europe. Britain gets worried when French and Germans visibly get closer together. There was a speedy phase of integration from 1984 upto the Maastricht Treaty when Britain was actually being led along by its nose. As far as Germany and France are concerned there is nothing to worry about it at the moment. France is actually a

> successful country in many ways. Germany is bigger, but has its own problems. Higher level of unemployment, continuing difficulties regarding integration between West and East Germany and so on. Yet I am optimistic about Franco-German relations. Germans have put their investment in political integration in Europe precisely because they realize that French are sensitive to German unilateralism in Europe. Germans recognize that and act accordingly. They are anxious to prove that they are good citizens of the European Union.[73]

Yet, though not one of dominance, Germany will continue to play a significant role in Europe because of its geo-political position and its strong connections in the continent. But, some experts see the prospective German position in Europe differently. In their perception, Germany is a problem, not by its active dominance but by its passive dominance. Though there is no German dominance in any active sense, it is there in a passive sense which could make things difficult without German support. They site the observation of Joachka Fischer the other day about Germany's playing a 'small role'. 'Even if it tries to play a "small role", it is so large that it is as good as doing it.'[74] In the words of Lord Wallace:

> Germany is the central country in Europe. Everything Europe does unavoidably revolve around Germany. The French elite thinks that they need to carry on playing a leading role in Europe. They want to carry Germans along with them accepting that they have a secondary role. What is going on now is an attempt to revive that relationship. The problem is that they disagree in a large number of issues. The current set of Franco-German declarations we have, do narrowly disguise their substantial difference. During the negotiations of the Nice Treaty, the French were

> refusing to accept that Germans could have more MEPs. Then Germany and France worked together to remain the key core.... The strong point of German foreign policy has always been that Germany is too big than its partners. So it is in Germany's interests to have a more deeply integrated Europe, where as the French, like the British, wanted to have strong national governments so that they can retain their national autonomy. That is the underlying contradiction in the French position.[75]

The problem for Germany today is economic. Recession is making an adverse impact on the country. It has stimulated rightwing nationalism in Germany, which was manifested in the attacks on Turks in the country. Therefore, it is wrestling with domestic problems, particularly with a sluggish economy. When Germany was reunified in 1990 Chancellor Helmut Kohl promised the German reunification without tears. But that was not to be. The pain of reunification has been felt deeply in east Germany. Reunification has brought down the growth rate and heightened unemployment. That has put Germany under serious economic problems. Germany accounts for 25 percent GDP in the European Union. But, the enlargement has positioned Germany at the centre of EU logistically, geo-politically, financially and industrially. Although politically the new Member States may now be closer to United States, economically they will be more dependent on Germany. Half of Eastern economies of EU will still deal with Germans. Fearing a German take over, Poland and Slovenia have decided not to sell land to foreigners (effectively Germans) for ten years. Despite such hostile expressions, all these countries are dependent economically on Germany. For a decade now, Germany has low growth, which has constrained Germany from acting as a dominant power in EU. The current growth rate in Germany is 0.5 per cent and the country is faced with recession.

It is incorrect to suggest that the change of German attitude to military power in the post-war period, and the ongoing difficulties the German economy is faced with after the German reunification, have totally removed the lurking mistrust of Germany, which makes its appearance on rare occasions. It surfaced at the time of the collapse of the Berlin Wall in November 1989 when older generation in France and elsewhere in the continent tried to stop German reunification because they were 'frightened' by the prospects of a reunified Germany.[76] According to Prof. Jean-Paul Chagnollaud: 'Older generation (in France) mistrusts Germany. They tried to stop reunification because they were frightened by the prospects of a unified Germany. Mitterand in 1989 tried to stop the unification. Many French specialists believed that there will be two German states. They did not believe that there will be only one unified German state. This was in 1989. They did not want reunification.'[77] Although the French no more sleeps with one eye open for fear of Germany as a result of the military superiority the French enjoys as a nuclear weapon state, it is still premature to say that the French mistrust of Germany is totally dead and is not in the back of the minds of the States in the neighbourhood of Germany. In the words of a French academic: 'French suspicion of Germany is not "completely" buried. But I think there is a new generation which is no more suspicious of Germany. We expect no problem from Germany. Our concerns now are how to build a new Europe. How to deal with Turkey and so on, and not Germany. I think Germany will play its own role. And it will serve its national interests. We are too many in Europe. We don't have a single political perspective. That is my concern.'[78]

Germany's rise as the epicentre of Europe's economic and technology power in early 1990s has caused some anxiety among Germany's immediate neighbours.[79] German unilateralism in according recognition to Croatia and Slovania had added to this anxiety. With the realization of an age-old political objective of *Lebensraum* peacefully through an EU process, Germany has got the economic space it aspired under that doctrine peacefully without resorting to wars and conquests. The enlargement would bring a large number of new countries around Germany, making Germany's geo-political position literally as the heart of Europe. How Germany is going to deal with them will be interesting to watch. The German psyche is basically accommodative upto a point. But, then it can become coldly assertive and stubborn. The post-war German leadership has shown sensitivity to this perception about them outside. Prosperity and security can change the psyche of a nation sometimes for good and sometimes for bad.[80] So German responses during critical situations will continue to draw interest not only in EU but elsewhere too.

But currently, Germany is faced with deep seated problems. There is little sign of solving them. Problems and difficulties have increased after the country became bigger following reunification. But, according to Axel Queval, Germans don't realize that they have economic problems. The French economy performed better in recent years than the German economy. 'During the last 7 years the French growth rate is bigger than the German growth rate. French inflation is lower than German inflation. French budgetary deficit is smaller than German budgetary deficit. The French trade balance is more positive than the German trade balance. Now France has a surplus trade balance. The French current account balance is bigger than the German current account balance because France has a large surplus from the invisibles whereas Germany has a deficit from its invisibles. So today the French economy is faring better than the German economy. The biggest problem is that the Germans have become complacent. They don't work hard as they used to be. They are not organized as they used to be.'[81]

DRIVE FOR COHESION IN EU

Crafting of A New Constitution

The European Convention

Since 1957, the European Community functioned mainly with the basic structures and instrumentalities provided in the Treaty of Rome, with certain modifications made in subsequent years to meet the demands of changing times. The structures the Community had adopted in 1957 were meant for a small number of Member States. That was adequate for the then six Member States which were pursuing a limited agenda of establishing a Common Market among themselves. But as the Community got enlarged, and transcended its scope beyond the economic sector to encompass other areas, the instrumentalities and procedures stipulated earlier were found wanting to meet the requirements of the changed situation. Therefore, it became imperative to attune these structures to the needs of the time. In addition, besides the Treaty of Rome, the Community was loaded with many other treaties, like the Single European Act, the Maastricht Treaty, the Amsterdam Treaty and the Nice Treaty, and also with many other legal instruments composed of rules, regulations, procedures and so on, the nebulousness of which has baffled people who tried to understand how the EU functioned. Therefore, there was a need to end the nebulousness of the EU instrumentalities and to codify them into a comprehensive document which can be understood by the ordinary people. The European Convention on the Future of Europe was constituted in 2001 to do that exercise and make suitable recommendations. The discussion and deliberations that followed had taken the direction of the convention towards the drafting of a new Constitution for the European Union. Among the broad objectives of the Constitution making were : (1) to make a consolidated text of various treaties and agreements; (2) to do a popularizing exercise and give people a comprehensive document which they can keep and refer; (3) to get EU integration further advanced and overhaul the institutional arrangements; (4) to define the competencies of various institutions and structures and of States and the Union; and (5) to achieve greater clarity, cohesion and compactness in the functioning of the EU. The Convention was headed by the former French President, Valery Giscard d' Estaing.[82]

Expectations From the European Convention

Prior to the drafting of the EU Constitution, the European Convention had generated a lot of hopes and expectations. Many leading Europeans have made their expectations explicit. In a significant speech at the European Parliament, on 4 April 2001, German President Johannes Rau made explicit his expectations from the Convention. He said: 'What concerns people in Europe is how the not very transparent integration process is organized and how little influence they seem to have on it. Many citizens are rightly asking: who is actually driving the locomotive of the European integration train... and what is our destination? These are not academic questions. They are questions which are being asked in all European countries by the sovereign, that is to say by the people.'[83] He said that the objective of the Constitution making should be: '. . . preserving what has been achieved so far, preventing what is not wanted and remaining open to new ideas – that is the basic idea behind a Constitution for a federation of nation states.'[84] He said: 'No one wants to do away with the nation states and their sovereignty. On the contrary, we will need them and their distinctness for a good while yet, as guardians of diversity in Europe.' He was emphatic that 'Europe is not moving towards a centralized state, nor should it.... The basic political principle is the federation,' a federation in which 'every member state makes its own sovereign decisions on its Constitution and system of government.' He said, the EU Constitution should be a 'grammar book of freedom' and particularly here in Europe, 'a grammar book of solidarity.' It should determine 'who is responsible for what'.[85] He said that 'the European Constitution should prescribe that Europe will not become a centralized super state but, rather, we are building a federation of nation states.'[86] Rau desired that the EU Constitution should have 3 parts : (1) A Charter of Fundamental Rights; (2) A part that divided the competencies between the Member States and the European Union, which would determine the relationship between the Member States and the federation – with two essential features interwoven into it : (a) the principle of subsidiarity should be integrated into it as a guiding principle; and (b) the residuary powers should remain with the Member States; and (3) it should lay down Europe's future institutional framework. He was emphatic that in the new Constitution as well, the European Commission's present right to initiate legislations should remain intact.[87]

More ideas were also set afloat by other European leaders as well. In an attempt to give a boost to the idea of a federal Europe, German Foreign Minister, Joschka Fischer, said that the EU should have an elected President with executive powers, a federal Parliament with power to legislate, and a written Constitution. But, the French President, Jacques Chirac, following the footsteps of De Gaulle, wanted the EU Member States to move on and build a new European family based on nation states, which could mean even a confederation. At the same time, Tony Blair, the British Prime Minister, has chosen to uphold the nation state against a federal union. Other European leaders like Helmut Schmidt and Jacques Delors wanted basic constitutional reform for building the European Union, but were not explicit about its details.

A Public Controversy

It may be noted that while the European Convention's deliberations were in progress, there erupted a public controversy over the divergent perceptions held between the European Convention and the European Commission. While the Convention favoured a more federal decentralized set up for the Union, the Commission wanted a more centralized structure, with entrenched powers for the Commission itself. It may be noted that at present on economic policies, the Commission sends its recommendations to the Council of Ministers for framing broad economic policy guidelines, the contents of which the Council can easily amend. But, now the Commission wanted that this right to make 'recommendations' should be upgraded to make 'proposals' which would mean that any amendment to these 'proposals' would require the agreement of the Commission. The tenor of the Commission argument is that an enlarged EU would require a stronger centralized power centre, like the Commission, as the guardian of EU interests. There are experts who share this perception of the Commission.

The Commission's perception on these matters were presented to the European Convention by its President, Romano Prodi, on 5 December 2002. He proposed radical changes in the EU institutions and EU decision-making process. His proposals included a higher role for the EU Parliament in the legislative and budgetary matters, scrapping of unanimity rule in the decision making of the Council of Ministers and its replacement with a majority rule of Member States representing a majority of the EU population, more powers for the European Commission, and so on.[88] Prodi said: 'We need to simplify the way in which Europe's institutions work and make them more effective. The *status quo* is not an option, even less so in view of enlargement. National leaders should act on their commitment to make Europe a superpower: speaking with one voice is essential to defend Europe's social model in a globalized world and to promote our values.'[89] He said that 'all the institutions here represented have in fact the duty to call themselves into question', including the EC Commission.[90] He wanted that a Charter of Fundamental

Rights should form the basis of the EU Constitution. 'Peace, freedom and solidarity' should be the motto of the Union. There should be more democracy in EU. The Commission President should be elected by the European Parliament, with two-thirds majority, and then be confirmed by the European Council. Other members should be designated by the European Council in agreement with the Commission President. The whole Commission should be approved by the European Parliament, and should be accountable to it and to the European Council. All legislative powers of the Union should be divided between the Council of Ministers and the European Parliament. 'An EU legislation should be proposed exclusively by the Commission for adoption by the Council and the European Parliament acting by co-decision. And no Member State should have a veto.'[91] He said that keeping in view the prospect of a Union of 25 members, majority voting should be the rule. But in sensitive cases the decisions should be based on enhanced majorities—'twofold majority of the member states and of the population of the Union.' He held that the economic policies must remain a national responsibility. At the same time the EU Commission should be given the power 'to monitor both compliance by the Member States of the Broad Economic Policy Guidelines and budgetary discipline.' The decisions of the Council 'should be based on Commission proposals, and not just "recommendations".'[92] On external relations, he said that Europe has to play a role in the world. 'It has its own values to defend and a social model to promote. To do this, it needs to be strong and speak with a single voice.' To ensure that he proposed the appointment of a Secretary of the European Union to represent the Union and implement common measures. He should also be a Vice President of the EU Commission. He should be appointed by agreement between the European Council and the Commission President and should be personally accountable to them and to the European Parliament.[93]

For quite some time, the Union's decision-making process and its opaqueness have been under public criticism. The secrecy that shrouds the decision making process in Brussels has led to criticisms like concentration of too much power in Brussels bureaucracy, democratic deficit, and so on. Of course, the EU has a double executive – the Council and the Commission. While the Council is composed of representatives from the Member States, the Commission, though appointed not elected, is generally composed of leading politicians drawn from Member States, who, after appointment, do not accept or seek advice from Member States. And they are seen as the guardians of the Treaty and the Union. Of course, there are checks and balances in the exercise of their executive authority. The right to initiate legislation is vested in them. And they have exclusive control over the execution of decisions, which in practical terms, gives them enormous power. Since the Commission acts as a collegeate body, expressions of confidence and no-confidence are on the whole Commission, and not on individual Commissioner.

However, in the context of the public criticism regarding the overbearing role of the Commission, there was apprehension in the Commission circles that the Member States would make use the opportunity of drafting the new EU Constitution to 'claw back' as much national executive authority as possible from the Commission and place it with the Council. That was obviously the context in which the President of the Commission, Romano Prodi, made a presentation before the European Convention on 5 December 2002, demanding a stronger position for the Commission in the Constitution. In the debate that followed many in Europe had underlined the need to keep a strong Commission as the hub of EU administration, keeping in view the impending enlargement. At the same time, some have argued that the Commission is not as powerful as it has been perceived. A German Foreign Office official, for example, has pointed out that there is a lot of institutional checks and balances in the working of the European Commission.. Although the Commission has the right to initiate, while doing so it has to be careful not to initiate a proposal which would be unacceptable to the Council of Ministers.[94] However, what happens now is that the EU does legislate on a whole range of areas in which national governments have been legislating in the past. Since sovereignty on certain areas have been transferred to the Union, EU takes decisions on behalf of Member States based on political circumstances. This, probably, makes the Member States more cautious about further transfer of sovereignty to Brussels which would limit the competence of the Member States in EU. Therefore, there should be a dividing line which should protect the Member States from intrusion of the Commission and the Council.[95] According to Detlef Weigel, the Commission was right in what it has suggested. But it does not have democratic legitimacy. One can ask whether it was tactically wise to overstress the role of the Commission before the Convention. 'The Commission is trying to integrate. The public is not confident about what the Commission does. So they think that there is something wrong in what the Commission does.'[96]

While Germany and smaller states had favoured the proposals Romano Prodi made before the Convention, Britain, France and Spain favoured the strengthening of intergovernmental cooperation method and are set against further strengthening of Brussels.

A Draft EU Constitution

The Convention on the Future of Europe has prepared a Draft Constitution for the European Union and submitted it to the European Council in June 2003, which was to be considered by the EU Inter-Governmental Conference proposed to be held in May 2004.[97] When the Convention began its work on the Constitution making, hopes were raised that it would give clarity to many ambiguities in the European Union, including what the Union is and what its direction would be. Although its direction has been spelt out as one towards building 'a common future' for the people of Europe by coordinating the policies of the Member States, the Draft Constitution has left the question of what the European Union is, or what it would be in political terms, unanswered.[98]

The Draft Constitution has defined the Union's objectives as promotion of peace and well being of its peoples and of sustainable development of Europe based on balanced economic growth, a social market economy and aiming at full employment and social progress. 'It shall combat social exclusion and discrimination, and shall promote social justice and protection, equality between women and men, solidarity between generations and protection of children's rights'. Globally, the Union 'shall contribute to peace, security, the sustainable development of the earth, solidarity and mutual respect among peoples, eradication of poverty, and protection of human rights and in particular children's rights, as well as to strict observance and development of international law, including respect for the principles of the United Nations Charter'. It guarantees free movement of persons, goods, services and capital and prohibits 'any discrimination on grounds of nationality'. It would 'respect the national identities of Member States, inherent in their fundamental structures, political and constitutional, inclusive of regional and local government.'[99]

Fundamental Rights

The Draft Constitution contains an elaborate Charter of Fundamental Rights. It has listed 50 rights in all, which include right to life, right to the integrity of the person, right to freedom of thought, conscience and religion, freedom of expression and information, freedom of assembly and association, right to engage in work, right to education, freedom to choose an occupation, right to property, right to asylum, right to equality, workers' right to solidarity (collective bargaining and so on), right to social security and social assistance, health care, citizen's rights, right to good administration, and right to justice. It prohibits death penalty or execution in the Union, eugenic practices, reproductive cloning of human beings, torture, slavery, forced labour and trafficking in human beings, and provides for protection against unjustified dismissal, right to vote and to contest for European Parliament and municipal elections (nationals only can contest for national parliaments), and so on.[100]

EU–A Legal Personality

The Draft Constitution is aimed to give the Union a legal personality and has made provisions for dual citizenship – national citizenship and the Union citizenship – for the people. As per the Draft, 'the Union's competences are governed by the principle of conferral', under which 'the use of Union competences is governed by the principles of subsidiarity and proportionality'. The Union's right to actions are limited to 'the competences conferred upon it by the Member States in the Constitution.' The residual competences would remain with the Member States. The ambience of the principle of subsidiarity is that 'in areas which do not fall within its exclusive competence the Union shall act only if and insofar as the objectives of the intended action cannot be achieved by the Member States either at central level or at regional and local level, but can rather, by reason of the scale or effects of the proposed action, be better achieved at Union level.' On the conferred competences to the Union, the Union law 'shall have primacy over the law of the Member States.'[101] In certain areas the Union shall have exclusive competence, like 'to establish competition rules necessary for the functioning of the internal market', and in areas like the monetary policy for the Euro area, Common Commercial Policy, Customs Union, and conservation of marine biological resources under the Common Fisheries Policy. Areas of shared competence include internal market, agriculture and fisheries excluding the conservation of marine biological resources, transport, energy, social policy, environment, consumer protection, and common safety concerns in public health matters. At the same time there is a provision to the effect that the 'Union shall adopt measures to ensure coordination of the economic policies of the Member States'. There would be specific provisions for the Euro area.[102]

Position of the Commission

The Draft Constitution provides for ensuring 'closer coordination of economic policies and sustained convergence of the economic performances of the Member States' and 'the Council of Ministers, on the basis of reports submitted by the Commission, shall monitor economic developments in each of the Member States in the Union....' It empowers the Commission 'to monitor the development of budgetary situation and of the stock of government debt in the Member States.... In particular, it shall examine compliance with budgetary discipline....' It says: 'If the Commission considers that an excessive deficit in a Member State exists or may occur, it shall address an opinion to the Member State concerned'. Then the Council of Ministers, on a proposal from the Commission, would send its recommendations to the Member State, confidentially, to bring an end to the deficit within a given period.[103]

No doubt, such provisions can have their adverse potential implications for the tax systems of various EU Member States which can cause the erosion of advanced welfare state systems like the ones in Scandinavia, which depend on high taxation. In addition, such provisions would give enormous leverage to the Commission and the Council to do quiet arm twisting of the Member States, particularly of the smaller ones, in the Euro area. In the name of budget discipline and sound financial management, they can use this as a lever to control and hamstrung national budgets.

European System of Central Banks

However, under the Draft Constitution, the main role of the European System of Central Banks, composed of the European Central Bank (ECB) and the National Central banks (NCBs), is to maintain price stability and to define and implement the Union's monetary policy. At the same time the ECB alone has the 'exclusive right to authorise the issue of Euro bank notes in the Union', which may be issued by the ECB and the NCBs. But as far as the Euro coins are concerned they may be issued by the NCBs with the approval of the ECB regarding the volume of the coins to be issued. But the technical specifications of such coins are laid down by the Council of Ministers in consultation with the European Parliament and the ECB. The President of the ECB would participate in meetings of the Council of Ministers when it discusses matters pertaining to European System of Central Banks.[104]

CFSP

The Draft Constitution gives details of the Union's competence in the field of Common Foreign and Security Policy. In this respect, the Union's competence would cover 'all areas of foreign policy and all questions relating to the Union's security, including the progressive framing of a common defence policy', and it says that the 'Member States shall actively and unreservedly support the Union's common foreign and security policy in a spirit of loyalty and mutual solidarity and shall comply with the acts adopted by the Union in this area'.[105] It states that the Members 'shall refrain from any action which is contrary to the interests of the Union or likely to impair its effectiveness as a cohesive force in international relations'.[106] The policy would be 'based on the development of mutual political solidarity among Member States, the identification of questions of general interest and the achievement of an ever-increasing degree of convergence of Member States' actions'. The European Council would identify the Union's strategic interests and decide the objectives of the CFSP, and the Council of Ministers would frame the policy based on the guidelines provided by the European Council. These decisions would be taken unanimously by them and would be implemented by the Union Minister for Foreign Affairs and Member States by using resources of both the Union and the States. On CFSP matters, the EU shall be represented by the Union Minister for Foreign Affairs. It stipulates that prior to any international action Member States would consult each other at the European Council and Council of Ministers levels, and would show mutual solidarity. On the main aspects and basic choices of the CFSP, the European Parliament also would be consulted. However, it is important to note that the European Commission plays hardly any role in the CFSP, except in the sense that the Union Minister for Foreign Affairs would be the Vice President of the European Commission and that the President of the Commission would be a non-voting member of the European Council.[107]

In addition, the Common Security and Defence Policy (CSDP) has been made an integral part of the CFSP. Under the CSDP, the Union can have an operational capacity drawn from the civil and military assets of the Member States, and the policy would include the progressive framing of a common defence policy for the Union, which, if the European Council so decides unanimously, can lead to common defence. The Member States are obliged to make civilian and military capabilities available to the Union for implementing the CSDP. However, it has been made explicit that the Member States' CSDP obligations would not prejudice their NATO obligations. All CSDP decisions would be taken unanimously on a proposal either from a Member State or from the Union Minister for Foreign Affairs. In the execution of CSDP, the participating EU Member States would work in close cooperation with NATO.[108] An interesting provision in the CFSP section is the stipulation that 'Member States which are also members of the United Nations Security Council shall concert and keep the other Member States and the Union Minister for Foreign Affairs fully informed.' Similarly, it says that at the UN Security Council meeting on a matter in which the Union has taken a position, those Member States which sit on the Security Council, 'shall request that the Union Minister for Foreign Affairs be asked to present the Union's position'. Such wishful thinkings are there in abundance in this Draft Constitution.

The Draft Constitution provides for 'enhanced cooperation' among a group of Member States of the Union—at least one-third of the membership – if it gets established that 'the objectives of such cooperation cannot be attained within a reasonable period by the Union as a whole'.[109] As this opens up the possibility of smaller formations within the larger EU formation, this provision contains mixed potential for the Union. It can give rise to groupism and centrifugal tendencies in EU sooner or later.

Institutional Structure Remains Unchanged

The European Union's institutional structure remains by and large unchanged in the Draft Constitution – European Parliament, European Council, Council of Ministers, European Commission and the Court of Justice. The legislative functions are shared between the Parliament and the Council of Ministers. Apart from its traditional legislative and budgetary roles, the European Parliament now has a new role of electing the President of the European Commission. In addition, it gives the European Parliament the right to propose amendments to the budget and send it back to the Council and the Commission.[110] The European Council defines EU's political directions and priorities. The new Draft Constitution has created a new position of the Union Minister for Foreign Affairs after merging the two earlier positions – European Commissioner for External Affairs and the High Representative. He will be appointed by the European Council with the agreement of the President of the European Commission. Another innovation in the Draft Constitution is that the President of the European Council would be elected by the Council by a qualified majority for a term of two-and-half years, and his term is renewable once. He will not have the voting right in the European Council. This will end the six-monthly rotation of the EU Presidency. Similarly, in the Draft Constitution although the European Commission's earlier key role has been kept more or less intact, in a comparative sense its position has been made less pivotal by raising the domain of inter-governmentalism under the European Council, on areas like the CFSP. The Commission's right to initiate proposals has been kept intact. But the innovation that has been introduced in the Commission is the reduction in the number of the Commissioners from the present 20 to 15, and the creation of a new category of non-voting Commissioners, to be appointed by the Commission President (from 2009). These non-voting Commissioners would be chosen by the Commission President from all other Member States which could not get representation in the regular Commission.[111] This innovation has been made keeping in view the imminent enlargement of EU from 15 to 25 members. Similarly, it stipulates that any addition of new members required unanimity in the Council of Ministers. This would make EU membership for Turkey more difficult.

Social Policy

The Draft Constitution makes promotion of employment opportunities as a factor in the formulation and implementation of the Union's policies and activities.[112] Under its social policy, the Union would support measures to improve the working environment, working conditions, social security and social protection of workers, protection of workers who have lost their jobs, co-determination, gender equality in the labour market, combating of social exclusion, and so on. It says that the European laws adopted in this context 'shall not affect the right of Member States to define the fundamental principles of their social security systems and must not significantly affect the financial equilibrium thereof'; and 'shall not prevent any Member State from maintaining or introducing more stringent protective measures compatible with the Constitution.'[113] This provision gives certain degree of safeguard for Welfare State Systems in the Scandinavian countries, though they could still be attacked stealthily by using certain other provisions of the Constitution.

Under the Draft Constitution, the Parliament seats allotted to the Member States vary from 5 (Malta) to 99 (Germany). The weighting of votes of Member States in the European Council and Council of Ministers also vary from 3 (Malta) to 29 (to all big countries), which makes structural inequality among Member States a permanent feature of the democratic functioning of the European Union.

The Draft Constitution defined what constitutes a qualified majority. It provides for a Commission administered European Social Fund for vocational training and retraining of workers to improve their employment prospects, and also for a European Regional Development Fund to reduce the regional disparities in the Union. The Constitution recognises 21 languages, of 25 would be Member States of the enlarged EU, as official languages of the Union. The new Constitution, when approved would repeal the earlier treaties which have established the European Community and the European Union.

There is no doubt that the new Constitution, if and when gets approved, would give the European Union a legal personality and would provide the Union with a document which would give greater clarity regarding the rights and responsibilities in the European Union, and a comprehensive instrument to understand what the EU is all about. It would also give greater clarity regarding the division of powers between the Union and the Member States. It has merged and reorganized the provisions of existing treaties and has provided clarity and simplification of the Union's instruments and procedures by codifying them from a vast array of an estimated 80,000 pages of rules and regulations. Besides, many innovations have been introduced at the institutional level to contain potential problems of EU ostensibly after its enlargement from 15 to 25 Members States. But a conspicuous void in the Draft Constitution is its failure to clarify what the European Union is, and how the world should characterize it – a Europe of nations, a federation, a confederation, an international organization with semi-federal features? However, it may be noted that, as an entity, the European Community has all along been a gigantic exercise in ambiguity and that it flourished under that ambiguity. That ambiguity still persists under this new Constitution also. Many *de facto* federal features have been infused in it without clearly stating what a political entity the European Union really is. It remains a hybrid structure of supranationalism and inter-governmentalism which defies all known political models. Since it is more than an economic association and less than a state there has always been an existential crisis present in the EU. The grey features of this hybrid entity are still considerable even under the new Draft Constitution. National perceptions, and national interest identities, and national interest approaches remain entrenched elements in the Union's overarching veneer of Europeanness that clothes it. Yet, basically, EU remains an evolving structure embodying a process of dialogue and multilateralism towards the promotion of solidarity and pooling of destinies as solutions to numerous vexed problems of the Member States. Since the EU construction is still an ongoing process, it is still hazardous to forecast what kind of a hybrid it would eventually become and what would be its final shape. However, even now the Union's common market image remains the strongest. Therefore, broadly speaking, it is still moving to an unknown destination.

Draft Constitution Disapproved

The failure of the European summit of Prime Ministers, Presidents and Chancellors of the present and future EU Member States, held in December 2003 in Brussels, to approve the new EU Constitution drafted by the Convention on the Future of Europe, and the debates took place around it has unmasked the complexities involved in the firming up of a genuine European Union. The last straw that broke the camel's back was the ruckus over the distribution of power among the Member States in the decision making – the failure of Germany to honour its commitment at the Nice Treaty of 2000 and the insistence of Spain and Poland to honour them. It may be noted that in the wee hours of 11 December 2000, in order to break a major deadlock during the negotiations at the Nice Summit, Germany had accepted a voting system under which the Member States were given certain fixed weightage for their individual votes at the Council of Ministers meeting. The system incorporated in the Nice Treaty was not based on any uniform formula – like proportional to the size of the population, and so on. It was based on a political decision. Under the system, Germany, France and Britain were given 29 weighted votes each, and Italy, Spain and Poland were given 27 weighted votes each. Others were also given certain specific number of weighted votes each. The Nice Treaty, which incorporated these provisions, was ratified by all countries, including Germany. But, at the Brussels summit in December 2003 Germany wanted to go back from this commitment and wanted to cut down the weighted votes of Spain and Poland, by bringing in a new formula based on the strength of their populations, which would undermine their potential to block EU legislations. At the same time, the new formula can also establish Germany's pre-eminent position in EU as the Member State with the largest population (82 million) – ahead of Britain and France. That was the substantial issue on which the approval of the draft EU Constitution at the Brussels summit got derailed. The other pertinent aspect which needs to be noted is the whittling down of EU's effectiveness in matters like CFSP, Defence and Taxation by taking them out from the domain of majority voting and placing them under the principle of unanimity, which would have its impact on the integration process of all these vital sectors. Indeed, inter-governmentalism would remain strong in all these sectors. A more disturbing development during the summit debates in December 2003 was the resurfacing of the talks, even by some Heads of Government, about the possibilities of creating a two-speed or even a 3-speed Europe – with the original Six Member States moving ahead separately at top speed, whereas others would be left behind to follow the integration process at lower speeds, which again would raise question marks on the longevity of this European integration process based on equity of participating Member States. Of course, notably, of the original six, Italy and Luxembourg had rejected the idea of a two-speed Europe.[114] But, this move has the potential to quietly set a reverse process in motion or create a new mindset which, even if would not undo in the near future what has been achieved so far, can prevent any further progress in the European integration process. The debate at the summit has also brought out clearly how the big Member States want to maneouvre the preservation of their leadership roles in the Union after keeping the smaller Member States as partners without influence.

Europe–US Relations in a Flux

The exigencies of 1940s and 1950s had forced Europe to accept a subservient relationship with the United States, which got established through the Marshall Plan and the North Atlantic Treaty Organization, and reinforced by the perceived potential threat from the Soviet Union and the Warsaw Pact. As US and Europe joined hands in the Cold War, their relationship, in many ways, became the key to world politics because the flash point of Cold War during the first two decades was Central Europe. That, and the perceived Soviet threat to Western Europe, together provided a sound basis for the United States and Europe to craft a shared security strategy. The Marshall Plan helped the fast recovery of the war-damaged European economies and putting them back on the rails, which was proved beneficial also to the American economy itself.

The economic and political relationships thus forged between Europe and the United States when Europe was in distress have undergone a tremendous change during the last half-a-century, following changes in Europe and in its external environment and in the attitudinal changes they have brought about on both sides of the Atlantic. As Europe gradually moved up in the path of integration and became a stronger economic entity, and reached approximate parity with the United States in the economic and trade fields, its old dependent relationship with Washington has given way to a more mature and balanced relationship between the US and the European Community. Competition, cooperation and divergence became a simultaneous feature of the new relationship.

Trade Competition

In the economic sphere, particularly in the sphere of world trade, EU and US became truly competitors, and their trade conflicts became more pronounced during the last 3 decades. These trade conflicts became more structured when the United States fortified itself with NAFTA on its side. As their trade disputes could not be resolved bilaterally, they had to take recourse to the WTO grievance redressal mechanism for settlement. But, even WTO is unable to find satisfactory solutions to their disputes over agricultural trade issues like exports of genetically modified food items and so on. Though both sides subscribe to free trade, they have erected trade barriers as part of their protectionist measures, and trade wars between them have become a regular feature. Now, with the enlargement, the European Union's economic clout *vis-a-vis* the United States is expected to grow further as the enlarged EU would be a larger market than the United States. It can also be a bigger investor. Moreover, in trade terms, the enlarged EU would be a dominant partner in the neigbourhood, in the middle east, Africa, Russia, Belarus, and so on. Therefore, economically, the EU's power is on the increase. It tries to build alliances to counter the economic weight of the United States. Therefore, on trade matters, United States and Europe match each other and are functioning today as equal autonomous entities. According to Malcolm Subhan, the United States no longer dominates the EU's economic thinking and that the transatlantic economic ties are getting weakening. In his opinion, as trade with East Asia has become more important for EU than with US, the importance of US market for EU is also diminishing. The European investment has also started diversifying.[115]

Currency Competition

The launching of Euro as a common currency for EU has further strengthened EU's position *vis-a-vis* the United States in the global financial market. As a trade organization with a common market and a common currency, European Union has further strengthened its economic position as a soft power. Euro can help improvement of EU's economic performance as well, and play an important role in the global financial market. No doubt, the Euro will be the leading currency for a geographically larger part of the world than the dollar. That will include Russia, parts of Africa and increasingly even parts of Asia. It has been reported that the Reserve Bank of China has accumulated and has a steadily growing amount of its foreign exchange reserves in Euro. With the enlargement, ten more countries are expected to adopt Euro as their currency. This will also expand the Euro area. As David P. Calleo said, being the currency of a large economic area, there is no doubt that Euro has become an alternative currency for dollar. International financial market cannot ignore the existence of Euro.[116]

Introduction of Euro is a big step in Europe's integration process. Since the Europeans have not yet put Euro into direct competition with dollar, there is no direct 'war' yet between these two hard currencies. But their competition is inevitable since they constitute the biggest currencies in the global currency market. Today, a lot of third world countries are tied to the dollar. But, as they become aware that they can drive the Euro against the dollar, they may increasingly align their currencies with Euro. This may be the case with countries like Russia, China, India, countries in the middle east, and so on.[117] It may be noted that the Iraqi President, Saddam Hussain, was one of the earliest OPEC leader in the middle east to accept payment in Euro, instead of dollar, for his petroleum products, which seems to have alarmed Washington. It seems that it was to nip in the bud such a dangerous initiative in the middle east, which could have had dangerous implications for the future of the dollar, that Washington had decided to eliminate Saddam Hussain from Iraq on the basis of fictitious accusations. In that sense, the American war on Iraq in 2003 was the inaugural of the war between dollar and Euro.

However, so long as US dollar remained the only major international currency, US enjoyed tremendous power. But by launching the Euro, EU is quietly challenging that US power with a credible alternative to the US dollar. Since the Euro covers a huge geographical area governed by the European Central Bank, it will also adversely affect foreign direct investments in US. US is known to have a long-standing external deficit, a viable solution to it will become extremely difficult after Euro gets established as a credible currency alternative. Therefore, Euro can cost US dearly in the coming decades.

Therefore, in two important areas of economic activity – trade and currency – Europe and United States are already in a collision course.

Bridging Technology Gap

Although economically Europe is comparable to US, technologically the United States has maintained a big lead over the European Union. This was mainly because till 1980s technology development and the R&D related to it were done by individual EU Member States. Serious joint approach in this regard was launched only in late 1980s and early 1990s. But the gap between the EU and US in the technology field remained quite wide. In order to bridge this technology gap and enhance the Union's competitiveness in this field, the EU has launched, at the Lisbon Summit in 2000, a major technology innovation programme in order to take the European technology to a leading position by 2010. According to Vinzenzo Nazo, an active participant in the EU's Technology Innovation Programme, there are six strategic programmes of science and technology that the European Commission had decided to start in December 2003. It is an important indication of the Union's new strategy for science and technology. The EU Member States would be spending a lot of money for these programmes and the technology projects under these programmes have also solicited international cooperation.[118] One such EU project, Galileo

Satellite Navigation Programme, has invited India to participate in it. In a reference to it, the Indian Prime Minister, Atal Behari Vajpayee, said in New Delhi in November 2003, at the India-EU Summit, that India would be interested in participating in the project as an equal partner and not as a mere customer. He said: 'In this multi-billion Euro project, exploring new frontiers of technology, India's expertise in cost-effective space technologies can bring both technical value and price competitiveness.'[119]

Similar invitation has been extended to China as well. However, the objectives of EU's technology innovation programmes are many, in which R&D is one aspect. But the most important objective of these programmes is to push strongly for a European technology, and one finds a general political support to this larger objective, which is quite promising. But, there are two difficulties, according to Nazo. 'In Europe we are still experiencing nationalism, and some difficulty for governance, to push for improving the rate of integration. But as a bottom up strategy, scientists, researchers, professors, and people in industry who are working for research, are more and more attracted by the idea of cooperating as Europeans. That is just one aspect, but an important aspect.'[120] For the implementation of these programmes, it has been stipulated that each of these EU sponsored programmes on science and technology must be joined by at least 3 EU Member States, a policy that was followed by EU since 1980s. Programmes like Eureka are still on. In addition, there is promotion of an impressive number of scientific networking for special kind of programmes – like applied physics, genetics, and so on – which involves a large number of networks. The expectation is that if these efforts succeed, EU would be able to reduce its technology gap with the United States. Of course, the EU Commission would select the projects for financial support, check and monitor the programmes and their results. 'That is the only way to raise EU's technology level and its competition level.

The contribution of scientists from Poland, Norway, Czech Republic, and so on will improve this capability.'[121] Nazo sees Europe as a potentially powerful alternative to the United States. 'If you look at the positions in the areas of energy and environment, Johannesberg and Kyoto events, I can see even now that Europe has a tendency to be different from the position of the United States. Of course, not all European countries have the same position.'[122] The quintessence of all these technology innovation initiatives is to make EU the strongest knowledge-based economy by 2010.

Of course, all these EU moves need not be viewed as deliberate anti-American measures. Rather they are measures aimed to consolidate the growth of EU as an autonomous entity which will have the spillover effect of EU finding itself placed in competition with the United States.

Unilateralism in a Unipolar World

At the political level, the notable change in the American attitude towards the management of international system, since the collapse of the Soviet Union, has led to a growing disenchantment between the European Union and the United States. It appears that, the EU-US relations are moving towards a tense phase as differences in values and attitudes in a number of areas are growing between the Union and the United States. The collapse of the Soviet Union has left the United States as the sole super power in the world. It has resulted in the development of a new mindset in the United States which has emboldened it to slight its traditional European allies in the formulation of its global policies, making it increasingly difficult to work closely together. Some Americans have started thinking that the Americans can do things on their own without Europeans. Indeed, increasingly, the United States has got into a unilateralist mode in setting its agenda on world politics and developed the psyche of a hegemon of the world, assuming that it had the right to order things around as it pleased. US has assumed that it has the right to intervene to ensure democracy and stability in other parts of the world. But, Europeans do not agree with such interventionist policy of the United States. During the last 13 years the world has witnessed a unipolar syndrome, with the United States as the sole super power setting the global agenda. Europeans were peeved at this unilateralism which US has displayed in recent years, but remained more or less forlorn spectators. In the words of Ernst Ulrich Von Weizacker: 'US unilateralism does annoy most European leaders. I do not see at present a determination on the part of European leaders to really confront this unilateralism. They will continue to express their annoyance with what Washington does and it is quite possible that after President Bush, there will be a new American leader who may think differently.'[123] According to him unipolarity is a fact of life today. "I don't see at present any power of the world that has the capacity to reverse that trend and, probably, able to stop it. United States, I seem to see, is still increasing arrogance and self-centredness, having little interest in anything that happens outside America, and in particular, contempt for the Europeans and hatred against much of what is called the third world, the kind of enchantment with China, contempt for Japan and Latin America and an unparallel build up of military power and the clear intention to maintain that position as the only military power of significance left."[124]

According to an Italian academic, Gianni Bonvicini, the future of international relations will largely be settled by the nature of relationship that would be established between the United States and the European Union, the core concerns of which today are the US hegemonic role and the European Union's moves for autonomous role. 'It means that the relationship between US and the EU will depend upon the way EU succeeds to emerge as an international player. EU has a potential to do that. There is a need for EU to move more autonomously from US'. According to him: 'If the present US emphasis to play a hegemonic role continues, the future will be of conflicts between US and the emerging powers. If we offer a more structured multipolar world to US, we and US will be managing international relations in a regulated international set up that will be a solution for a complete alternative – by creating a European entity capable of managing its own international interests.'[125] As an American scholar said, the US vision of a unipolar world would set the United States in a collision course with many other emerging powers. The political elite in Washington is trying to give shape to the idea of the United States as a world ruler dominating a unipolar world. This unipolar vision of US is ill at ease with the vision of a strong united Europe. And that US vision is bound to clash with Europe due to geo-political ambitions.[126] However, Europe is unlikely to accept the US hegemonic approach for long. As Malcolm Subhan said, 'A unipolar world, even with a democratic hegemon, is not a good idea. Unipolar world is a world of military hegemony. Global war on terrorism is a façade under which this unipolarism is perpetuated. We need a multipolar world.'[127] Europe aspires to have a more equitable relationship with the United States, and not the way Tony Blair maintains Britain's relationship with Washington, which critics call 'poodle like'. Blair thinks that Atlantic alliance is crucial for Britain. Therefore, he does what Americans want him to do unmindful of consequences. That irritates many continental Europeans. However, if Europe wants to establish an equitable relationship with the United States on foreign and security policies, Europeans will have to act together, as they now do on trade and economic matters. But, today, on foreign and security policy matters Europe is in a subordinate position to the United States. But if Europeans can act together on these matters, during the next 20 or 25 years EU can become much more an equal partner to the United States, because by then EU would have become less and less dependent on the United States and would have acquired a new personality of its own. In the opinion of Dick Gupwell: 'A lot depends on policies of the US administration. If the US policy does not substantially diverge from the general policies of EU then there is no reason for the Atlantic alliance to get weakened. Under Bush Presidency, there are very many more strains placed on the transatlantic relationship than under Clinton. Clinton was much more appreciated in Europe than Bush.'[128] According to him, if US begins to behave in an irrational manner, Europeans may have to re-think about the future of the Atlantic alliance. 'There are a lot of Europeans, not all, who would like Europe to be autonomous from US. But, I don't see the weakening of the Atlantic alliance. That does not mean that Europeans would do what Americans are going to say.'[129]

Hollowness in US Economy

A larger question in this context is: Is there an overestimation of American strength and superiority? It seems to be so. According to David P. Calleo, the US economy is not as sturdy as it appears to be. There is considerable hollowness in it. No doubt, the United States today is the world's richest economy. At the same time, it is also the world's biggest borrower from savings. Its external deficit also remains high, which raises question marks in the horizon on the long-term sustainability of such an economy. What sustains its apparent prowess today is the big flow of external capital, based largely on the deftly crafted image building of the US economy as a strong economy, boom economy, and so on, which also enables the US to sustain a high rate of employment and a low level of inflation. According to Calleo, such booms contain potential crashes. Federal deficit is a serious problem for the US economy, which remains concealed under the mirage of a boom economy.[130]

According to Immanuel Wallerstein, US is on the decline. Many events like Vietnam, Balkans, September 11, the Middle East and so on have exposed the limits of American supremacy. The question, according to him, is whether US will learn to fade quietly, or the US hawks, by their foolhardy decisions, would transform a gradual decline of America into a rapid and dangerous fall? According to him, if the rise of US power began with the world recession of 1873, the fading of US as a global power began 3 decades ago in the 1970s. 'The economic, political and military factors that contributed to US hegemony are the same factors that will inexorably produce the coming US decline.' He says:

> The United States' success as a hegemonic power in the post-war period created the conditions of the nation's hegemonic demise. This process is captured in four symbols: the war in Vietnam, the revolutions of 1968, the fall of the Berlin Wall in 1989 and the terrorist attacks of September 2001. Each symbol built upon the prior one, culminating in the situation in which the United States currently finds itself – a lone superpower that lacks true power, a world leader nobody follows and few respect, and a nation drifting dangerously amidst a global chaos it cannot control.[131]

Hawks in US want their country to assert its position in the world by launching military attacks here and there. This strategy can only contribute to a rapid decline of the United States. It will transform 'a gradual descent into a much more rapid and turbulent fall. Specifically, hawk approaches will fail for military, economic and ideological reasons.'[132] Although US is projected as the robust economy, in reality it is also the most indebted country in the world, with a domestic and international debt burden of about $ 3.4 trillion or a per capita debt of $ 12,000.

Differing Attitudes

However, as unipolarity and unilateralism define the US attitude and keep itself ever ready in a fighting mode, its expectation of cooperation from the European Union is unlikely to materialize mainly because of the different path the Union has chosen for itself – promotion of peace and prosperity by refraining from waging war against each other and make the future secure for everybody. In the ultimate analysis, European Union is a peace project. Under its influence, the Europeans have developed a new attitude to power and to the use of military power to settle international disputes. Indeed, it is difficult to politically organize these EU Member States sensibly in terms of power because many of them believe that power is dangerous and, therefore, they refrain from looking for more power. Instead of clamouring for more power, they are looking for more welfare, in the traditional sense of the term of welfare state. They aim at united economic well-being and not at becoming a power centre in the traditional sense of the term because they, particularly Germany, for example, see that historically the use of traditional power proved disastrous. It was disastrous for other small EU Member States too. In fact, barring Britain and France, EU Member States are basically not in favour of the Union becoming a power in the traditional sense. Embedded in it is the reluctance of Europe to increase its military expenditure to catch up with the Americans militarily. This runs counter to the American perception. After September 11, America looks at the traditional instruments of power as being the most significant. But in Europe it is the opposite. They tend to rely more on the effectiveness of the use of soft-power to achieve enduring results. The general EU opposition to US war on Iraq in 2003 was, to a great extent, conditioned not only by the lack of credible justification for it but also by the EU approach that war is not a solution to problems when other means are still open. Although from among the EU Member States America could enlist support from the governments of Britain, Spain, Italy and Portugal for its war on Iraq, public opinion in all these countries were overwhelmingly against that support. Notably, Romano Prodi, President of the European Commission, said recently: 'A big, majority of European public opinion was against the war [on Iraq] which did not have the backing of the United Nations. What is important is that six months after the end of the war there was a poll inside the EU which demonstrated that the opinion had not changed. European people are still against war and what is even more interesting is that there is no difference between public opinion in countries that participated in the war and those who were against it.'[133] Similarly, one cannot ignore the basic difference in the attitudes and approaches of both societies. As Paul Taylor explains, the habit in continental Europe is social democracy, exemplified in well developed welfare state systems. In other words, it is a home of social democracy and welfare state. But, that is being viewed with suspicion by the right wing American political leadership. Continental Europeans have a favourable view about social democracy, welfarism, multilateralism and attitude towards business. This is different from the neo-liberalist economic agenda steered by the United States. Similarly, there is increasing resentment in Europe, even in UK, against America's application of extra-territoriality over others' legal systems. So there is a potential for increase of tensions.[134]

There are fundamental attitudinal differences now between the European Union and the United States. In many ways, US has become interventionist and antienvironmentalist. The US aspiration to be the policeman of the world has been pursued through enhanced interventionist approaches to impose its values or will on others, an approach the EU does not share. Presumably, the US will pursue it until a new concert develops against that US attitude and approach across the globe. But, at the moment such a concert has not got shaped. But, if the United States does not change its perception and approach, the crystallization of such a concert would become inevitable, leading to a clear decoupling between Europe and the United States, with Britain positioning somewhere in-between. But much will depend up on the US approach to world politics in the coming years.

If US persists with the present approach, a concert composed of EU, Russia and China is a distinct possibility. But, a British Foreign Office source has expressed more optimism in this context:

> I don't believe that the more developed EU is, more challenging it will be *vis-a-vis* the United States. During the next 20-30 years there will be increasing coherence on the EU side and more cooperative relationship with US. The lines of communications will be more clear and positive between United States and European Union. But at the moment there are minor frictions between them on a few issues – on trade front and on Iraq. On Iraq some countries of EU want to demonstrate independence from US line. But it is not necessary that as coherence in EU grows friction with US also should grow. The EU is a young method of cooperation among old European nations and the feeling of casting of Europe as bigger and overbearing power, I don't think it is there in our own psyche in the same way.[135]

But another leading British specialist on EU affairs has said that some decoupling and recoupling are inevitable in EU-US relationship.

> Certainly, there have been a number of regular clashes, especially in economic areas, over the last 30 years. But these have been compartmentalized away from politics. So it is quite interesting to see how neither side wants to link the economic side with the political side. Here they have a basic interest. Both sides would like to have a good relationship basically. US wants Europe to be basically united, but not too united. More united, it could be weak as well. Divide and rule all the time. On the International Criminal

> Court issue, there was a deadlock – Europeans like it and US dislikes it. So what the Americans do is to make bilateral agreements with every individual European country that if an American officer gets arrested he will not be sent to the Hague, but to US. Italy and Greece have already signed it. That is a classic divide and rule policy US has already implemented.[136]

In the Iraq crisis, European Union was not actually an actor involved. It was the individual Member States which were involved in it. In Iraq, Europeans and Americans disagreed a great deal about the course of actions to be adopted against Iraq. In any case Europeans did not want a war against Iraq. They favoured only sanctions against Baghdad. The deep disagreement between EU and US on Iraq has considerably weakened the American influence in Europe, as major European countries like Germany and France were forced to take public positions against the US attack on Iraq. After the war in Iraq, America is seen in Europe in an unfavourable light. According to a French academic:

> US is very dangerous because it considers itself as the balancer of the world. I am very skeptical about the capacity of the US to think broadly. It thinks only in terms of its own national interests. Europe could do something against it but it tries to propose other ways.... US policy today is dangerous. It does not respect national borders, nor international law. It has no respect for principles. European Union is a peace process. But US is asking Europe's support for its war. US supported CTBT. But it did not ratify it. Now it says that it would use nuclear weapons.[137]

European Union's readiness to play a more active role where US has failed to produce positive results is reflected in what Romano Prodi, President of the European Commission, said on 2 April 2002. He said that since US has failed totally in finding a solution to the middle east problem it is time that the US should step aside to enable others to try for its solution.[138] Indeed, while US gives one sided support to Israel Europeans are much closer to Muslims and their countries and know more about the situation there. Although EU is a major aid donor in the middle east, when US is involved in the process, it is difficult for Europe to play a meaningful role there.

Many experts think that the EU-US relations are on the track of growing disharmony, which has been amplified in their approaches towards issues like International Criminal Court, Arab-Israeli conflict, the Iraqi question, the Kyoto Protocol, Bio-weapons Convention, steel imports, agricultural imports, and so on. Europeans appear getting exasperated over the US unilateralism and Washington's refusal to accept any constraint on America's freedom of action and its readiness to bypass international organizations and international law. Therefore, on fundamental issues EU and US are drifting apart. Europe does not obviously share the US 'grand strategy' for the emerging world.[139]

What kind of scenario is envisaged in the US-EU relations in future? In the words of Christopher Hill:

> The already huge disparity between US power and that of the next most significant international actors will become so great as to risk unbalancing the whole system. Indeed, it would call the very notion of an international system... into question. The stakes would be raised for every international crisis, for all those unwilling simply to acquiesce in US policy, and the risks of conflict significantly increased.... If this analysis is correct, it is not the adversaries of the United States who will face the great challenges but Washington's allies, notably the Europeans .... The

> contradictions in the Atlantic Alliance ... will emerge more clearly. If the Europeans are forced to fall in with a less emollient style of American leadership, resentments will grow. If they manage to make a *saut qualitatife* in their own collective capabilities, a sharper rivalry between the two major Western powers becomes inevitable.... There is a danger of a broad front opening up both in US commitments and in US European disagreement over the next few years from which retreat will prove impossible.[140]

In this context, a German academic writes: 'The neo-conservative theory that currently governs official thinking in Washington identifies Europe as the principal future rival and potential challenger of the United States. And Germany, whatever its current difficulties, is the most powerful economy in the European Union, and will remain a leader of Europe no matter what happens. This is the first time that a German government has taken a stand against Washington and refused to back down. The Chancellor who does this must not, in the current Washington view, be allowed to get away with it. What Schroeder has done is all the more dangerous to Washington because he reflects popular opinion across Europe.'[141]

In a widely discussed article in Europe and United States, Robert Kagan has explained more vividly why time has come for Europe and the United States for parting their ways and stop pretending that they 'share a common view of the world, or even that they occupy the same world' since they diverge in their perspectives on the 'all important question of power.' As Europe is turning away from power 'into a self-contained world of laws and rules and transnational negotiations and cooperation', America continues to exercise power 'in the anarchic Hobbesian world where international laws and rules are unreliable and where true security...still depend on the possession and use of military might. That is why on major strategic and international questions...they agree on little and understand one another less and less.' He contends further: 'When it comes to setting national priorities, determining threats, defining challenges, and refashioning and implementing foreign and defence policies, the United States and Europe have parted ways.'[142] So there exists a dichotomy in the mindsets of Americans and Europeans. While Americans look for application of unilateral coercive methods to find solutions to international problems, Europeans look for diplomatic solutions. The truth, according to Kagan, is that 'the United States and Europe are fundamentally different today.'[143] In Europe, only Britain shares, to a considerable extent, the American perspective. Therefore, the differences in the transatlantic relationship are more fundamental than what has been recognized so far. Basically, it is a power problem born out of the American readiness to use its military power to solve international problems, and the European aversion to it.[144] According to him, European tolerance and preference for less confrontationist approach is born out of its psychology of weakness as a power, and its incapacity to respond to threats. He asks: 'If Europe's strategic culture today places less value on power and military strength and more value on such soft-power tools as economics and trade, isn't it partly because Europe is militarily weak and economically strong?'[145]

By integrating internal and external marketing and by introducing Euro as the common currency of 12 Member States (of 22 Member States in 2004), European Union has established itself as a powerful actor in the global economic system and has asserted its autonomous position in trade and currency sectors. With the attainment of an edge over the United States in terms of GDP and share of world trade, the European Union is beginning to take on the United States in both these sectors. In terms of GDP the EU stands at $ 8,361 billions against the US GDP of $ 8,179 billion. Similarly, the EU share of world trade is 20 percent against the US share of 18 percent.[146] But, the battle royal between EU and US in the currency front has just began, with its inaugural shot through the recent US war on Iraq. This battle for the supremacy of their respective currencies is going to be more ruthless in the coming decades than their trade wars. Both of them have a clear perception that whichever hard currency, euro or dollar, that is used in the energy trade, the main commodity of exchange of our times, would dominate the global economy in the coming decades. For historical circumstances, during the last 4 decades, US dollar enjoyed a monopoly in oil trade which had a multiplier effect on the US economy. It afforded the United States to run huge fiscal deficits year after year by printing more dollars to absorb the deficit because all other countries had accepted US dollar as the main currency of their energy trade. But that dollar monopoly cannot be preserved since euro has become the currency of 22 states of Europe whose energy trade is bound to be in euros. As many other countries will also accumulate euro reserves, they will also be partially switching their energy trade to euro. Therefore, US is bound to battle bitterly to preserve the dollar monopoly and EU is bound to do everything possible to break this monopoly and establish euro as the dominant global currency. But, that battle will be fought between EU and US from an even keel because both these currencies today are backed by two comparable economies, and is going to be a long drawn affair. While Japan remains a competitor in trade and currency, other growing economics are far behind in this respect. It will take some more time before they also become effective trade competitors in the world market, and much longer before they become competitors in the currency market.

EU and the Emerging Power Centres

It is axiomatic that the present unipolar world would create new poles in the global system sooner or later. The new poles thus envisaged to emerge during the next two or three decades are Russia, China and India, besides, of course, the European Union, and the United States, the ring master of the present unipolar world. It is also axiomatic that if the United States continues to anchor its policies in unipolarity and unilateralism, soon it will find itself in collision course with the rest of the world, which can eventually lead to a steady decline of the US power, reminiscent of the way the Soviet power had drained off and declined between 1960s and 1990s.

However, as the EU is likely to grow in power and stature and become increasingly an autonomous centre of activity in the coming years, provided it can achieve more cohesion politically as well, it would be forging a closer relationship, both economically and politically, with these newly emerging power centres. Therefore, a pertinent question that needs to be addressed to is the kind of attention EU has paid to these emerging power centres in its scheme of things for future.

Russia

The Soviet Union's enemy image was a political factor that was used partially to promote European integration during the cold war period. But that anchorage got dissolved with the end of the cold war and the dissolution of the Soviet Union, which was facilitated also by the European Union. Perhaps if the EU and the G-7 countries had responded more positively to Mikhail Gorbachev's request for fiscal support, it could have helped a more orderly change in the Soviet Union than its collapse. However, the politico-economic changes in the successor state, Russia, enabled the European Union to look at Russia from a different angle – of a potential partner – and build a cooperative relationship with Moscow. The new relationship between EU and Russia in the post-Soviet era has been built up around several bilateral agreements and instrumentalities generated during the last

10 years. Most important among them is the Partnership and Cooperation Agreement concluded between them in 1994, which came into effect in 1997, which has provided a broad institutional framework and details of the common objectives they should pursue. They encompass trade and economic cooperation; cooperation in science and technology, energy development, environment, and so on; cooperation to prevent illegal activities; and political dialogue on international issues of common concern. At the same time, the Union has also formulated a common strategy for Russia with certain specific objectives to promote a convergence process between the two entities in areas like democracy, rule of law, economy, security and stability in Europe. In pursuance of these objectives, several agreements have been signed between the Union and Russia, encompassing sectors like steel and textiles, science and technology, nuclear safety, energy, environmental protection and so on. It was also made quite obvious that the EU would like to have a politically and economically stable Russia as its immediate neighbour. To promote these objectives in a systematic manner, new bilateral consultative structures have also been put in place, which included 6-monthly summit meetings among the EU Presidency and Presidents of the EU Commission and of the Russian Federation; annual ministerial level meetings (Cooperation Council); and senior official level meetings (Cooperation Committees) which can meet more frequently at any time whenever necessary. Consultation on CFSP matters has to take place at the monthly meetings between EU's Political and Security Committee and the Russian Ambassador to EU in Brussels. Added to this is the Northern Dimension partnership between EU and Russia on areas like environment, nuclear safety, energy development, and so on.

Over the years, the European Union has developed a strong trade connection with Russia. Indeed, EU is Russia's largest trading partner, accounting for more than 70 per cent of Russia's foreign trade. Russian exports to EU include strategic exports like oil and natural gas, and steel and textiles. After the enlargement this trade figure is expected to go upto 80 percent. Similarly Russia is EU's sixth largest trading partner accounting for 6.5 percent of its external trade. The EU exports to Russia are mainly industrial products. And in their bilateral trade, the trade balance is heavily favourable to Russia. In 2002, against € 47.5 billion worth imports from Russia, EU's exports to Russia was worth € 30.4 billion, which gave Russia a surplus of € 17.1 billion in its trade with EU. [147]

Russia was not happy with the way NATO was expanded, in March 2004, upto the borders of Russia, and has recently warned NATO against expansion.[148] The hidden grievances connected to it can be problematic in the long-run. The EU enlargement in 2004 has made Russia a country having common borders with the European Union, besides the Russian enclave, Kaliningrad, getting located inside the geographical boundary of the European Union. However, apparently Russia seems to have adjusted itself with these new realities in a positive spirit, indicating that it looks forward to a relationship of constructive cooperation with the EU Member States. The NATO-Russia Council can facilitate such cooperation. Although Russia is down, it is naive to imagine that it is out. Under Putin, Russia is in the process of a serious economic and strategic reorganization and readjustment. Its global disengagement will expedite the resurrection of a more sturdy Russia as a major actor in world politics and in European politics during the next two decades. Of course, at the moment Russia is in a great deal of confusion — socially, politically and economically. And nobody expects Russia to stage a come back as a great power in a short-run and become again an equal to the United States in military or economic terms. But, it will not be surprising that, given the current pace of development, in about two decades Russia gets to act together and bounce back to the frontline because that country has a very talented people, active economy, strong technological base and rich natural resources like oil and natural gas. 'If its domestic situation gets stabilized, Russia would once again rise as a major power.'[149] During the last three years Russia's average economic growth is 6.4 percent and it is now pursuing an ambitious target of doubling Russia's GDP by 2010.[150] However, despite its declined position, psychologically Russia is viewed in Europe as a big power, and the EU is set to follow a good neighbourly policy with it. It would entail the EU to keep a distinct relationship towards Russia. The prevalent attitude in EU towards Russia has been explained by an EU official in Brussels. He said: 'We would like to lock Russia in with EU in cooperative ventures, which we possibly can. Russians are not backward people. The process of change in the system, one diametrically opposite to the system they had, is taking place. They need a lot of sympathy. We try to be as helpful as possible. The nature of relationship we have with Russia is totally new. When the Soviet Union collapsed, big investors from Europe and America went to Russia to invest. Many of them have backed off now. I am sure that there will be a second wave of investment in Russia from EU and US.'[151]

However, today the EU Member States do not see Russia as a military threat or as an economic threat. As a result, EU and Russia are now developing a more relaxed relationship. Indeed, Europe is less cautious about Russia now. On its part, Russia is developing a close relationship with the European Union. The Russian President, Vladimir Putin, has established a good rapport with the French President Jacques Chirac and the German Chancellor Gerhard Schroeder. And, he is also trying to strengthen bilateral relationship with various other EU Member States, and also with the European Union in a broader framework. However, the NATO expansion may make certain impact on Russia in the long-run. In the words of Dana Allin, a strategic expert of International Institute of Strategic Studies, London, 'I don't think expansion of NATO was a good idea. But right now the President of Russia doesn't seem to have any great difficulty with it. In the long-run, if NATO becomes a strong and serious military institution, then Russia will feel left out. To some extent the Treaty will be viewed as one against Russia and will feel beleaguered. It is not so much a threat to Russia as it is a dividing line that it emphasizes.'[152]

China

The two other major emerging power centres are in Asia – China and India – which, according to James Gilbert, EU has decided to make its 'principal partners in Asia' keeping in view their enormous potential and increasing importance in terms of trade and investment.[153] Of the two, EU has paid more attention to China during the last one decade.

Although European Community's trade interaction with China dates back late 1970s, following the EC-China Trade and Cooperation Agreement in 1978, and a similar agreement in 1985, a more broad-based EU-China interaction began in 1994. As a result, a dialogue process was carried forward at various levels, including at the Foreign Ministers' level, on a regular basis. From 1998, they hold EU-China annual summits at Heads of Government level; the sixth such summit was held in Beijing in October 2003. This structured dialogue process has made their cooperation multi-faceted and transcended trade and investment matters to encompass areas like education, science and technology, environment management, village governance, forest management, enterprise reforms, and so on. In addition, many bilateral agreements, including a Science and Technology Agreement, and a Maritime Transport Agreement, have also been signed between EU and China. China is a participant in the Galileo Satellite Navigation Programme, and in about 40 other EU sponsored projects, worth about € 260 million, aimed to promote mutual cooperation. The special attention EU gave to China during the last one decade has taken their trade and investment ties to a high level that the EU-China annual trade today stands at € 115 billion (2002), with a trade advantage of € 47 billion for China. This phenomenal growth of trade ties between EU and China seems to have inspired the European Trade Commissioner, Pascal Lamy, to sing in Beijing, on 13 June 2003: 'As EU-China ties continue to deepen, as our interdependence grows and grows, as our political relationship blossoms, the EU and China are becoming ever closer partners.' However, China is EU's most important trade partner after the United States and Japan. For China too, EU is the largest export market after the United States and Japan. But, the many restrictions that China still maintains against EU's market access has been cited as one of the reasons for EU's huge trade deficit with China. EU hopes that China's accession to the WTO would remove many of these trade obstacles in China. Notably, the EU seems to have assumed a self-appointed role of monitoring the Chinese compliance of WTO stipulations, which has the potential to cause tensions in EU-China relations in the coming years. However, during the last ten years, China was a major destination of EU investments. Of late, the EU companies have invested in China to the tune of about $ 4 billion annually. As a result, the EU FDI in China today stands at about $ 34 billion. In the flurry of such trade and investment promotion, the Tiananmen Square massacre of 1989, China's poor Human Rights record, and so on have been conveniently swept off to the backburner, and have been raked up rarely for the sake of record.

All these developments show that the EU has taken its relationship with China seriously and has structured it carefully to carry forward in future. Since the European Union is basically a market driven enterprise, for it China's huge potential market is a great attraction. So China has become a trade and investment destination of EU Member States. It seems that as a trading partner, China has made a good impression in the EU circles. They find it easy to invest in China because there is much less bureaucracy and better infrastructure in the Middle Kingdom. They think that as long as political situation in China remains stable, it would remain an attraction for the Europeans. They also realize that China is also a potential trade competitor worldwide. 'The question is: how long China will remain a stable country? China is economically prosperous and successful, but politically without sail.'[154] European businessmen are attracted to China as a promising economic power which is in a better and stronger position in Asia. It has improved its technological capabilities and has created special economic zones in the country to attract business cooperation from Europe and elsewhere. According to William Wallace: 'EU-China relationship will depend upon how the Chinese economy develops. A number of European companies have invested in China. There is a huge surge of Chinese students in Europe. That is actively building relationship between China and Europe. Links are growing economically, but not politically or in terms of foreign policy. Europeans are increasingly going there, but more tourists from Europe go to India.'[155]

In China, the European Union seems to have a long-term programme of building business relationship. As part of it, the European Commission has set up in China a successful International European Business School, in Shanghai, to impart training to future Chinese businessmen and to give them management tools to help them to deal with the global economy. Indeed, it is seen as a significant EU project in China. However, most Europeans see China as a trade partner with a huge market, but not as a partner in political or security terms. Whether it can be an EU partner in these areas also, one is not sure at this point of time. However, there is a willingness, a determination in EU, to establish a close linkage with China, although the rather difficult Chinese language still remains a great wall against any kind of large-scale natural exchanges at the people-to-people level. But the EU's potential to act in concert with China in the international fora in times of need is very much there.

But, so far, the tangible relationship EU has developed with China is economic – trade and investment areas, with little political content. While for EU the economic networking with Beijing is relatively easy, political networking with China will not be that easy. But the American pursuit for hegemony can make it relatively easier. According to Rosita Dellios and Heather Field: 'While it appears probable that China and EU will each increase its global power without reference to the other, it is also possible that they might do so jointly in specified areas of common interest. This is likely to occur through institutional and networking means. A China-EU concert for now does not suggest the development of special relationship, as both have their regions of influence and EU's natural "cooperators" are the US and Russia.'[156]

India

Where does India stand in the emerging global system at the dawn of the new millennium? What importance European Union accords to India in its global vision for future? During the last 50 years India has made strident advances in many critical sectors to enable it to take its rightful position as a front rank power. Apart from its strategic geopolitical location in Asia, rich resource base, and its position as the home of a billion people, India is fastly acquiring the position of a great responsible global power. Being a nation steeped in intellectual tradition, India has already been acknowledged as a super power in the field of information technology. In areas like space technology, super computer technology, missile technology, satellite technology and so on, India has the capability to match any other power in the world. Today, it is in a position to produce world class hardware, including electronic hardware. Many international automobile companies depend on Indian firms for components. India is one of the six satellite launching nations. It is also one of the three countries which have produced super computers – the others being United States and Japan. India's *Param* super computer can match the US *Cray* supercomputer. India's pharmaceutical and infotech industries are much feared ones in the world. In the new situation, India has stopped seeking aid from other countries. Instead, today India is an aid giver to 10 or 11 countries. Recently, India has loaned $ 300 million to the IMF.[157]

India has a long-standing relationship with the European Community. Indeed, India was the first Asian country to recognize the European Common Market and establish diplomatic relations with it in early 1960s. Since then the relationship between India and the Community remained stable, and has been promoted through Trade/Economic and Commercial Cooperation Agreements and Joint Commissions. It was further expanded through the 1994 India-EU Cooperation Agreement. In all these agreements the emphasis was on economic and commercial relations, although the 1994 agreement has provided room for political cooperation in the form of annual meetings at Foreign Ministers' level. By the turn of the new millennium, India and European Union decided to hold annual summit meetings, and a beginning in this direction was made when the first Indo-EU summit was held, in June 2000, at Lisbon and issued a Joint Declaration which said that 'EU and India shall build a new strategic partnership founded on shared values and aspirations, characterized by enhanced and multi-faceted cooperation.' The Declaration stressed their commitment 'to promote socio-economic development and prosperity, as well as international peace, stability and security.'[158] Similar impressive declarations have been reeled out after every Indo-EU summit meeting held since then. The last Indo-EU summit was held in New Delhi in 2003 which was attended only by the Indian Prime Minister and the President of the EU Commission. The Prime Minister representing the EU Presidency was conspicuous by his absence at the summit. But in brass tacks, the emphasis remained mainly on the promotion of trade and investment, and little beyond. Political relationship has been kept at the margins, and that is likely to remain so until the Union's CFSP takes proper shape and the EU begins to play a more cohesive political role in world affairs, which can bring India and EU closer under the framework of a more meaningful political partnership.

India has a stable trade link with the European Union. EU is India's largest external market, and it accounts for about 25 percent of India's foreign trade. But, for the European Union, India accounts only for less than one percent of its foreign trade, a critical factor that defines EU's attitude towards India. In 2002, India's exports to EU was worth € 12.96 billion where as its imports from EU was worth € 12.83 billion, with a marginal trade balance of € 0.13 billion in favour of India.[159] However, their trade relationship could not achieve its full potential because it was dogged by many persistent problems. India's major exports like textiles, clothing and agricultural produce, which together constitutes about 41 percent of Indian exports to EU, are faced with severe protectionist measures from the EU Member States which has made it difficult for the Indian exports to enter and compete in the EU market with equity. Non-tariff barriers like product standard, health standard, and so on have also been used to effectively keep Indian exports, like food stuffs for example, out from the EU market. For about 25 years now India has been asking the European Community for the removal of an irrational and unfair quota and sub-quota system the Community had imposed against Indian exports like textiles and clothing. But, all along, the EU had played truant with that Indian demand without addressing that problem squarely, and delayed a decision as long as possible. Now, it has made a commitment to remove it by the end of 2005. But, the enlargement is likely to deprive India whatever benefit this much belated step of the Union would be bringing in for its exports to the Union. European Union's success in forcing India, through WTO intervention in 1997, to remove quantitative restrictions, which would hit millions of small and medium-scale domestic producers and their livelihood, has not gone well with the Indian public opinion, and has been widely criticised in India. This push, unmindful of its consequences to India's domestic industries and domestic products, has suddenly brought back in India the past memories of Europe's imperialist ventures in the 18th and 19th centuries.

Similarly, India has not been a preferred destination for EU's foreign direct investments. Although India's total FDI approval from EU Member States between 1990 and 2002, came to about $ 13.94 billion, the actual EU FDI flow to India, mainly from 5 EU states – Britain, France, Germany, Belgium and the Netherlands – during the period was a meagre $ 3 billion.

In India, a strong impression has been orchestrated that India matters a lot in the EU circles, in Brussels and elsewhere. New Delhi has been led to imagine that it is being accorded considerable importance in the European Union. But the picture one gets from Brussels and other EU capitals is quite different. When looked at from the ground realities in Brussels, India remains peripheral in the EU agenda. When asked about India's rating in the priorities of the European Union, a perceptible European expert said: 'There are straws in the wind. That is all.'[160] Another expert said: 'I can't say at policy level India is a priority for EU. Economically, India is potentially an important market. There are prospects for joint ventures. British Airways are using Indian telephone system. In the IT sector India and EU can cooperate.'[161] A Paris based Italian researcher, Antonio Missiroli has pointed out the absence of a coherent EU policy towards India. He said: 'On the one hand Europe wants to attract Indian skilled workers. On the other, there is a lack of strategic view as to what kind of relationship EU should have with India. EU recognizes that India is a potentially huge market. So it would like trade cooperation with India and selective immigration from it.'[162] An Italian Professor, Vinzenzo Nazo, was brutally frank. He said candidly: 'India is not a priority for EU programmes at the moment. At the moment China is more attractive for EU. But potentialities of India are very large.'[163] There are European experts who think that India's importance in EU's scheme of things has been grossly exaggerated. The fact is that 'India is not very important for EU in terms of external policy. Relationship between India and EU is good and healthy for a long time. It is such a smooth relationship that the EU States and the European Commission do not give too much significance to India. I think the EU has not given much heed to India, as the Community had given a lot more attention and time to its relations with China because China is economically much more important than India, and politically a problem than India.'[164] Some other experts have tried to explain away why India does not receive the attention it deserved from the European Union. According to Julie Smith, since the European Union is concerned with countries with whom it can do business, the key countries in EU's priority are Russia and Japan. 'I have not heard much about EU-India relationship. It would make sense if EU develops relationship with India as an emerging centre of power.'[165] EU's domestic preoccupation has also been cited as a reason for the Union's lack of attention to countries like India.

> When you are creating a new system and new institutions you look at yourselves, which is not a good thing, but that is the reality. Therefore, India is important in one way as an economic power in the making. Everyone accepts that. India is also complicated, a complex partner to work with. It is democratic and has complex environment with very different influences on decisions and so on. So it is not easy to work with such a partner, which is known partner as well. So I think it will take time to precisely

> understand its culture. Once we start we will have more and more formal dialogue. One of the problems we have in the India-EU relations, to be frank, is that any entrepreneur in Europe has assessment chart. China is an enormous market. It is easy to negotiate with China. It has a thriving private sector, with very few rigmarolls. China is very good in beating the drums, makes it impressive by saying that they are the coming power, their economy is growing at the rate of this speed and so on. But the Indians are not doing enough. India is an immense market, an open society, developed in high-tech sectors. These elements are not very well known.[166]

Similarly, it has also been pointed out that since the European governments are so preoccupied now with their own region that it is hard to find time and energy to think about the world outside the region.

> If you look at foreign policy priorities of EU, they are Russia, South Eastern Europe – the Balkans, Turkey and the Mediterranean – Israel-Palestine, Algeria, Morocco and Tunisia. Those are all immensely difficult and preoccupying problems. Then if you add the problems of West Africa, it is not surprising that we don't have much time. That is why European countries don't spend much time on India. But, there are growing economic links between Britain and India. But, I don't see why we need stronger political partnership between India and EU. Important issues of India's foreign policy are different from important issues of European foreign policy. European governments underplay their relationship with India and give more importance to China.[167]

Other reasons are also cited in this context. 'In trade

negotiations, India is a tough partner. That does not help with the development of technology transfer, cooperation and investment in high tech. India is reluctant to get involved in the international system in the technology field'.[168] Some have characterized India self-centered, interested in itself or in its neighbouring countries like Pakistan, Bangladesh, Sri Lanka and Afghanistan, and the Gulf. 'The Indian newspaper coverage are mostly about these regions in their international affairs section. Small items on US, Russia and Britain. Nothing on France, Germany, Africa, and so on. That is self-centered India. It has one billion people. The potential impact it can have on the world scene is enormous – in consumer industry, import and export, production, and so on.'[169]

But many European scholars have underlined the growing importance of India and the need for the EU to establish stronger relationship with New Delhi. In the words of Thomas Risse: 'India is very important. It is one of the major power centres in Asia and also the biggest democracy. EU is a Union of democratic states. Therefore, its relationship with India is very important. India is a nuclear power. So in security terms, it is pretty significant. I presume that the more EU increases its role as a global player in foreign policy, the more it will develop its relationship with India. EU will try to cooperate with India in a whole range of global governance issues.'[170] They also underline the top position India occupies in the IT sector and the global role it may be playing in future as a big power of Asia.[171] However, on the whole, there is a general recognition in Europe about the potential roles of India and China as major global players. 'India and China are two important players in the world. They are nuclear powers. So we have to be in touch with them. They are large markets and ancient cultures.'[172]

In many respects, India fits in to be a natural partner of EU intellectually, politically and institutionally. There are considerable similarities between the two entities. Though the current relationship between them does not commensurate these plus points, that could be developed in due course if there is a will. The British, the French, the Dutch, and the Portuguese have traditional links with India. Germany and other EU Member States also have established strong bilateral relations in recent decades. Apart from the fact that India is a vast market of a billion people, there is more scope for the Europeans to go to India. 'India's middle class is probably as big as Japan, if not more. English is the language in which most Europeans can communicate. India has a stable political structure. It is an open country, with a free press and independent judiciary. It is a huge potential market, which is an economic attraction. India is a great cultural attraction because it has an extremely rich culture. Therefore, intellectually and culturally, it is much easier for Europeans to interact with Indians than with the Chinese and the Japanese.'[173] A German scholar who has a long association with India has observed: 'There is not much discussion in EU about India's emergence as a major power centre. It is possible for India to become a major power centre because, in terms of size and its relevance, it can be a very crucial actor, particularly in the region. India should play a regional role and would be able to play a global role as well.'[174] A strong India, no doubt, is important in a multipolar world.

India is a country of growing importance in world politics, economy and technology. Many indices are pointers to this unfolding Indian potential. There is a general appreciation in Europe that a strong India would be an important actor in a multipolar world. But, there is no adequate appreciation of this fact in Brussels. While a lot of attention is paid in EU to China in fostering closer relationship with that country, India has not yet been accorded due importance in Brussels, despite the hyped public relations exercise of the recently established Indo-EU annual summits. But, according to a former German Vice Chancellor, Ernst Ulrich von Weizacker, 'Europe and India has so much in common that there is going to be splendid relations between the two.'[175] The French Ambassador to India, Dominique Girard, has said recently: 'If Europe succeeds in implementing a common foreign and security policy, it may drastically change for the better the relation with the other players in a multi-polar world, beginning with India.'[176]

However, clearly, the European Union has established a reasonably sound and stable relationship with all the emerging power centres of the world. Therefore, if and when the EU decides to play an active role in a mutlipolar world, it would have the necessary linkages to establish a concert of emerging major powers to act internationally together to promote justice, peace and stability in the world.

Problems and Prospects

Taking into account all aspects of the situation in which the European Union finds itself today, what are the problems and prospects of its playing an effective role in the emerging multipolar global system? Certainly, the degree of its effectiveness will very much depend upon the common will and the extent of cohesiveness the EU can achieve in different facets of its activities.

Lack of Cohesion

European Union's main focus is economy and markets. Naturally, therefore, of all its facets, the level of integration and cohesion in EU is highest in the trade sector. Achieving cohesion in this sector was also comparatively easy because the commonality of interests among the Member States for doing so was explicitly high, and the equity level in the sharing of benefits accruing from it was also high. The resultant effectiveness of EU was clearly manifest in all multilateral trade negotiations in the world in recent decades.

To a considerable extent this is true also in the international currency sector following the launching of Euro as the common currency of 12 EU Member States – to be of 22 Member States from 2004 – though its impact is being felt very slowly as Euro is only beginning to take on the US dollar as an alternative hard currency of the world. Indeed, the Europeans have not yet put Euro in direct competition with US dollar. But, it is inevitable that Euro and dollar will be competing soon in the market because they are the biggest currencies in the global financial market.

Therefore, by achieving a substantial level of economic and market integration through the establishment of a free trade area, customs union and a common currency, and the resultant prosperity the Community has achieved during the last half-a-century, the EU has beefed up its profile as an effective 'soft power' which can exert considerable diplomatic influence on other countries. Indeed, a vast majority of EU Member States would, therefore, prefer diplomacy and persuasion, wherever possible, to settle international problems. They rely increasingly on the use of 'soft power' and have developed a new concept of their own – how to get the activities of different States and different peoples coordinated and get them to work closely together. This is an approach different from the use of military power – a more long-lasting approach, which can produce durable results. The success which the concerted move of the Foreign Ministers of Britain, France and Germany has achieved, on 21 October 2003, in making Iran to agree for the IAEA inspection in that country is an example where the joint application of EU's 'soft power' has succeeded in achieving satisfactory results.[177]

But the picture is different if we lifts our sights a little up, to other facets of EU activities where the level of integration and cohesion have not yet reached high. In most other facets of EU activities, the Union's effectiveness is shackled by the lack of cohesion and other internal problems which deprive the necessary unity of purpose in those facets.

Institutional Deficiency

To a considerable extent, the EU's problems in playing an effective role in the global arena emanate from the deficiencies in the Union's institutional arrangement itself. It may be noted that originally the European Community's decision-making apparatus was conceived keeping in view a small number of six Member States in it. Six ministers or six officials could meet together and discuss any matter at length. But today there are 15 Member States in it, which will soon be 25. In practical terms, even if a minister or an official takes only 5 minutes in a meeting to present his country's perception on a particular matter, it will still take a minimum of 125 minutes to complete the first round of discussion. So, it will not be easy even to manage the meetings of 25 representatives, especially if everyone insists on speaking in his own national language as well. It can only stifle meaningful discussion on any subject, however important it may be. Therefore, in the changed context, the present EU decision-making structure seems to be thoroughly inadequate to meet the requirement of an enlarged EU. The other aspect is the problems pertaining to the decision making process. Along with the structural deficiency, ingrained in its decision-making process is the right to national veto on many important matters which can apply effective brakes in the process. The Council of Ministers generally takes decisions by consensus. As a result, if any Member State has reserve, voting on that issue will be put off until all reserves are removed. But that method could work, with 6, 9, and even 15 Member States in EU. Whether this method can still work with 25 Member States around the table is a big question. So the old system is in for serious log-jam after the enlargement. The question is, will big States in EU wait for a tiny Member State's agreement on every move? The option for the big States then would be either to increasingly use the QMV to placate the small Member States, or a number of them get together, in concert, and act outside the EU system. According to Gupwell, it is likely that the QMV will be used increasingly to placate the small Member States.[178] Yet, during the discussion on the Draft EU Constitution at the Brussels Summit in December 2003, subjects like CFSP, Defence and Taxation have been kept under the principle of unanimity at the Council meetings, which also raises question marks on the future progress of integration on these important sectors.

A Stiff-necked Commission

The centrality and the overbearing attitude of the European Commission are factors which inhibit national governments from transferring more powers to Brussels. Indeed, if possible, some Member States would like to 'claw back' powers from the Brussels bureaucracy by infusing higher dosage of inter-governmentalism in the decision making process and by slowly dissipating the supranational vision and content of the European Union.[179] It is true that the European Union process has been carried forward by the relentless pursuit of the huge, Brussels based, bureaucratic machinery led by the European Commission, which also plays the role of the guardian of the Treaty. Since the Commission is not democratically elected, though manned generally by leading political personalities drawn from the Member States, the Commission has been under prolonged criticism of democratic deficit in it. Some supporters of the Commission contest this point by arguing that this criticism of the Commission is misplaced since the Commission is controlled by the Council of Ministers, the political wing of the EU executive. They argue that since the Commission takes decisions through a long cooperation process with the Council of Ministers, they do constantly influence each other. To buttress the point further, they stretch the argument that since the Ministers in the Council are controlled by their national Parliaments, it is incorrect to say that there is democratic deficit in the functioning of the Commission. Another argument advanced in favour of a strong Commission is that, if you have to keep the Europe of 25 Member States together, it is imperative to keep the central structure in Brussels strong. Since a conglomeration like the EU would be prone to the pushes and pulls of centrifugal and centripetal forces, it should have a strong centralized institutional structure which can withstand such pressures.[180] These arguments apart, the fact remains that there is a lot of resentment and irritation among the public, even in governmental circles, about the Commission's attempt to effect harmonization through 'regulations' and 'directives' and 'executive decisions' from Brussels, which results in considerable intervention in their daily lives, and also about the lack of transparency in what is going on at the Commission level in Brussels. However, during the last 10 years the Commission's powers have been curbed quietly through the Maastricht and Amsterdam treaties. As a result, in today's EU set up, considerable real power now rests with the Council of Ministers and its Secretariat in Brussels. But, as a process, Brusselsization and resistance to it from Member States are constant features of the EU evolution.

Moreover, the beehive in Brussels does not radiate the impression that the EU is preparing itself to become a major actor in world politics. What is going on in Brussels is horse trading on a regular basis. That is one of the reasons why the EU institutions are not the first choice of promising politicians in Europe. Important national politicians, looking for a future, are seldom attracted to the European Parliament or to a position in Brussels. They opt for Brussels when they get ejected from their national political arena. Indeed, a national MP commands more prestige than an MEP. When the European Parliament itself has very little power, what an MEP does there is not much noticed. However, so long as strong national parliaments are there in every Member State, the European Parliament is not expected to acquire more power and prestige. If the European Parliament is going to have 800 MPs, nothing effective can work at that level; its public image will continue to remain that of a glorified talking shop.

Blurred EU Vision

When the European Community was launched in 1950s, it had a clear vision. But, that vision got blurred over the years. As a result, today the EU does not seem to be guided by any vision – like a ship cruising in the ocean blown off by the wind and guided by exigencies. There is a good deal of confusion in EU as to which direction the Union should move on. Concepts, like federalism, nationality, etc, for e.g., are adopted and interpreted by Member States according to their convenience. They mean different things to different people. Some favour a quasi-federal approach and others favour an inter-governmental approach. But the EU has adopted a mixture of both, which helped to bring many European countries together under the European Community umbrella. Yet, there exists an overall skepticism, which has prevented, and which still prevents, Europe from becoming a cohesive, integrated great power. This skepticism is stronger in countries like Britain, Ireland, Sweden and Denmark. Norwegians have repeatedly rejected the proposal to join the Community. Perhaps, this is because these countries never belonged to the Roman System (Britain was part of the Roman Empire, but the English were not. English settled in England after the collapse of the Roman Empire). While the Germans, French, Italians and the Berelux countries think that they are Europeans, the British do not think that way. For them Britain is a sovereign country, which has given up some of its sovereignty reluctantly to the European Union.[181] So as a nation the British are not enthusiastic about the European Union. A few minutes talk with any British would reveal it. So, though many countries have joined the Euro, Britain stayed away from it, because the British people are against it. Tony Blair is in favour of Britain joining Euro, and promised a referendum on the question, which he does not expect to win. According to a German socialist, Ernst Ulrich von Weizacker:

> Of the two visions of Europe – a federalist or a centralist solution – a centralist solution could be a bit risky because too many anxieties are still around among the people. For example, Hungarians who are now joining EU may lose their enthusiasm for EU once elements of cold capitalism destroy much of what they were trained or educated to see as their propriety or their rights, their aspirations in their later years and so on. Then they would not blame capitalism but EU. They would put all their anger and anxiety against Brussels and not against Budapest. So, perhaps, the federalist solution is a little more stable with regard to potential outcry of social nature during the next 30 or 50 years. In the end there is going to be a fairly centralist kind of embodiment for Europe. There will be a lot of diversity in Europe.[182]

Diverse Cultural Fortresses

In a recent book, an American writer has characterized the European Union as 'big, bloated, and undemocratic and is snuffing out the charming diversity of European life.'[183] It is an evaluation which can stir up mixed reactions regarding the degree of its validity in today's Europe. While 'European' symbolisms, like use of European flag, European number plates in cars, European Union driving license, separate (preferential) Customs Channel in EU Airports for passport holders of EU States, and so on, are galore in the European metropolises, whether they have really touched the cultural domains of Member States and made any significant impact on them needs a deeper study and analysis. But, on the face of it, it seems no. In a speech in the European Parliament on 4 April 2001 President of Germany, Johannes Rau, cautioned the Europeans that the 'diversity of our cultural wealth must not become the victim of uniformization.'[184]

Traditionally, Europe has been a multicultural entity, with a weak pluralistic base.[185] They are successful confessional societies, fortified by their developed national languages. How to integrate them into a single politico-economic entity with a *lingua franca* is a big challenge before EU. Recently, a German academic, Volker Bornchier, was quite emphatic about what the new European Union would be. He said: 'It has become clear ... that there will not be a United States of Europe in the foreseeable future since that would be implying a melting pot of nations.... The European state project rests for the time being on the acknowledgement of its constituent nations, which have developed in the course of history. What the Union contributes to this is an increasingly European identity – not as a replacement for, but as an addition to, national, regional and local bonds. Such an overarching European identity has existed for long in Europe's history, albeit to varying degrees and restricted to elites.'[186] Therefore, the current search to invent a common European identity is unlikely to fructify and also looks considerably artificial since the boundaries of new Europe is still not clear, politically, culturally and geographically as, even today, antagonisms and commonalities coexist in Europe in large measure, manifested in their multiple, overlaping and even conflicting identities. The debates in Europe surrounding Turkey's membership in EU exemplifies this phenomenon most spectacularly.

CFSP Problems

The EU seems to aspire to harness its great power position

also through the CFSP. That calls for defence cooperation among the EU Member States. But here again perceptions vary. For Britain, NATO is a key ally, and a military alliance with US is paramount for London. But, the French are more skeptical about the United States. France and many other Europeans would like to develop an exclusive European defence set up. A European defence force would demand EU budgeting. It would mean that all members should finance it equitably through the European Union, even though all forces will remain under the national control. They pose many psychological and practical problems in a group of countries like in EU whose attitudes towards military spending and power projection vastly vary. Many small EU States do not entertain any big international ambitions. Indeed, in a general sense, there is apathy in EU to play a global political role. In the sector of foreign policy, only big EU countries like Britain and France are interested. And, they act individually and independently without coordination, and they are effective. So, the European Union's coming together under CFSP, excluding these big powers, means little. According to a European analyst based in Brussels, despite the EU move to raise a force of 60,000 personnel in uniform, it is unlikely that during the next 25 years EU would have a credible military force.[187] Moreover, except on specific issues, many EU States are not in favour of a general experiment in CFSP. It must also be recognized that despite having a Chapter on CFSP in the Maastricht Treaty, EU does not have a common foreign policy. What the EU has is only national foreign policies of the Member States who are very often unable to take any common position on important issues. So, there is inadequacy in the institutional structure which has been built to back up the CFSP. The Member States do not show sufficient enthusiasm to transfer sovereignty on foreign policy decisions from the national capitals to Brussels.

The European Union states, taken together, have a strong military potential. Together they spend annually about

$ 140 billion for defence. They together have 1.8 million troops, compared to 1.3 million troops of the United States. Similarly, they have a highly advanced military-industrial complex, aero-space industry, high-tech capabilities, satellite and missile launching systems, nuclear arsenals, nuclear submarines, aircraft carriers, and so on.[188] If organized intelligently and coherently, and if the Union has the will to do so, it can quickly organize its own security outside the US/NATO umbrella. But, the major impediments to it are the British, Danish and the Dutch attitudes and the imminent entry of a good number of pro-American States from eastern Europe into the Union. Otherwise, the potential of EU to emerge as an effective autonomous power centre, even in traditional terms, is very much there all the time. But, the problem is the lack of will to effectively integrate this combined strength into an independent collective entity, which can easily upstage the global security scene.

Despite having a big paraphernalia in terms of elaborate structures and diplomatic establishments, EU's effectiveness in the non-economic field is comparatively less remarkable. EU Member States today altogether have 45,000 diplomats across the world, compared to America's 10,000. But since these 45,000 EU diplomats are not connected, this big number does not bring commensurable effectiveness. As a result, the 10,000 US diplomats prove more effective than their larger number of EU counterparts. It is also due to the fact that some countries, like Britain for example, do not want EU to play any political role. They are interested mainly in its large market. 'So the great question today is that do you want a political unit? Or do you want only a big market. I feel that there is a strong trend in favour of the market. I am sure that Americans will be glad that Europe develops only as a market and not as a political unit.'[189]

There are pessimistic voices in Europe regarding EU's emergence as a cohesive actor in world affairs. They base their pessimism in EPC's 30-year record, and the problems the CFSP is faced with during the last 12 years. They argue that before 1973, when the European Community was composed of only six members, it was possible to become a strong cohesive unit. But, it was not possible even at that time because contradictions were already there. A French academic said it candidly: 'I am pessimistic about the EU role because we are not a single political unit. If we could not do it with 6, 9 and 15, how is it possible with 25? So we are losing a big chance of becoming one of the big centres of power in the world. EU would be a big single market and not a political centre. We cannot play an active role without some military strength. There is some progress in it. We have only some 20,000 soldiers which would be used in crisis.' He says: 'Originally the EC goal was not to build a political unit. We wanted our nations. We still have them.'[190]

The non-performance of the Barcelona process was cited as another example of EU's ineffectiveness. Nine years have passed after the Conference in Barcelona, in Spain, was held in 1995, to sign an agreement between Europe and the Mediterranean countries to create a large zone of peace and stability. The agreement has also been ratified. Although eight years have passed since then, this process is faced with difficulties because this project was supposed to create an area of peace. But EU did not try to impose peace in the region, and it seems that it is unable to do it. Europe does not exist in that sense, says J.P. Chagnollaud. 'Even today we are not able to think as Europeans. French play the European game. So is Germany. Italians play the American game. So is the British. When an important issue comes up, EU countries take national positions. We have a European vision. But we have national visions which dominates our thinking. As far as foreign policy is concerned, European Union does not exist.'[191]

Similarly, on the question of use of force, there is no single opinion in the European Union. A good number of EU

Member States are basically reluctant to use force to settle issues in international relations. They favour solutions through negotiations, discussions and diplomacy. A careful look into the attitudes of various EU Member States will show that not all of them want to play active roles globally. Only Britain and France have that clear intention to play a big extra-regional role. However, it is mainly the former imperial powers which show some degree of interest in developments outside Europe, but generally confined to their former colonies. Others like the Irish, Austrians, Danes, Finns and many new Member States are not interested in playing any global role, partly because they will also have to spend for playing that role – for weapons, for organizing military operations, and so on. Germans do not want to play any role in the world stage because in the past it was proved catastrophic for Germany. And, they don't want to increase their defence spending. After the collapse of the Soviet Union, Germans are not motivated to spend more money on defence. For many years they took umbrage on constitutional provisions in the Basic Law to support their position not to send German troops outside the NATO area. But, even after the decision of Germany's Constitutional Court, in 1994, in favour of German servicemen's participation in peace-keeping operations outside the NATO area, Germany's reluctance to send troops for out of NATO area operations still continues although German troops are there in Bosnia and Macedonia at present as part of peace keeping forces. So, basically the vast majority of EU Member States do not want the Union to play a global role. So, inevitably, the compromise between countries which want to play a global role and which don't want to play such a role, is that the EU plays only a weaker role. So, in the midst of such divergences in basic approaches, the crafting of a meaningful CFSP will be very difficult. Britain's close ties with the United States is also another big problem for crafting the CFSP. In the words of Detlef Weigel:

> During the last century, as powerful States, European countries were fighting for something, right or wrong. That time is over. Now we are in a globalized world. Alliances are built around subject matters. So we may be fighting together for Kyoto Protocol. We might disagree on other issues. We might have an alliance with China on another subject. I don't see any stable coalition on a permanent basis between one State and another or between one group of States and another group of States. But the grouping will be on subject matters. I think the times are over when we have to do a power play – with a coalition of all countries working in all fields together. In the globalized world we have to move beyond the power centres, to coalitions of the willing around subjects, to networking.[192]

However, the indecisiveness inherent in such an outlook will have a weakening effect on EU's influence in international relations. As a result, whenever the United States becomes assertive, Europe has a record of pulling apart and part of it has been found going along with the American wish, right or wrong. Continuation of that approach can only undermine the EU's potential to play any meaningful role in a multipolar world.[193]

Clearly, many EU Member States do not believe that the Union should become a global power. Their aspiration is to turn EU into some sort of a welfare state entity. But, the British would like EU to become mainly a free trade zone, through a limited integration process. They have a concept of power whereby Britain would like to act not with all members of the Union, but with some of them. The French would like integration, but they would hesitate when it comes to the giving up of its permanent seat in the UN Security Council or the handing over of more power to Brussels. But, for most other Member States, the aim is not to create power, but to create something which would make EU more cohesive. While a German would read the history of the use of power as disaster, for the French and the British, it is the opposite. So, when there exists such deep-seated differences, it is still difficult for the EU countries to have a common vision of the European Union. That is why the Franco-German cooperation still continues to be the centre-piece of the European architecture since their disagreement can spell disaster for the European Union. But, perceptions differ. For Britain, the Anglo-American special relationship is indispensable, which does not square well with the concept of EU growing as an autonomous centre of activity. The Dutch see the coalition of large countries of Europe as dangerous. Therefore, for them the continued US presence in Europe is far more desirable and reassuring. Of course, these perceptions are changing, but very slowly. Therefore, the EU gives out mixed signals all the time.

Of course, EU today is effectively a soft power, an economic power. In trade it can exercise enormous power. But, its military role is nascent. And even the military role it is ready to play – the peace keeping role in Macedonia and Bosnia – is on the softer side of the military operation – humanitarian tasks. Perhaps this is the maximum what the EU Member States could agree. To get support for anything further from the EU is not easy. Indeed, EU is not inclined to spend any big amount of money for military, or for a military build up. Therefore, EU will participate in peace keeping operations, and nothing more than that. The Union is inclined to remain largely as an economic power, with the diplomatic weight of a soft power.

Is EU a Transcient Phenomenon?

During the last half-a-century, European statesmen have been trying to firm up a united Europe through the twin process of deepening and widening. But, this twin process does not go hand in hand. Although widening has been achieved to a great extent, the deepening process continues to face problems which keep the EU structure comparatively fragile and shaky. It refuses to get firmed up in a political sense because the Member States are not willing to stake their entire future in it, nor to irrevocably close their other options forever. In the circumstances, a fundamental question that comes up is: Is it because in the back of their mind they do entertain doubts about EU's longevity, and that, given the historical processes of Europe in view, the European Union is not the end structure for Europe, but only a transcient one? According to Martin Kohli: 'The two experiences of the sudden break down of the Soviet Union and Eastern bloc have brought home the point that such integrations are contingent on certain conditions. They need to have sufficient degree of openness to say that they are simply structures of obligation forced from above. So they have to take account of the extent to which populations and people's psyches or mentalities are really to go along, and to what extent it is possible to create common institutions that allow for participation of all parts.'[194] However, while the institutionalization of the European structures, and the relentless pursuit of the powerful bureaucratic machinery in Brussels to constantly strengthen the European Union, the Member States' reluctance to transfer more powers to the Union show that, apparently, they are yet to see in the European Union more than a transcient European structure. Of course, experts differ in their assessment of the future of EU in this regard. While some of them pin their faith in the strong institutional structure of the Union, which, of course, is stronger than any intergovernmental organization, and in the establishment of the ECB and the launching of the Euro, which would presumably make it difficult for the Member States to move out of EU at will, there are many others who give the EU experiment another 50 years to go on.[195] According to an expert: 'Sometimes we take the EU association for granted, particularly when we look at it from a global developmental perspective. European Union will stay if it becomes more successful with demonstrative benefits for the Member States, and for the people it serves. If it stops doing that, I don't think EU has any inevitability or the right or duty to survive regardless.'[196] What it means is that there is a flexible geometry involved in all these experiments. Many countries which were once firmly attached to the Soviet Union had quickly moved away from it for economic reasons. 'If the economic situation in Europe goes bad, really bad, then we will be returning to the pre-1914 or post-1918 situation. During the next 25 years there will be ups and downs, but I think the European ideal will continue to shape Europe.'[197]

Potential Problems from Enlargement

However, there are others who believe that the EU enlargement of 2004 will make the Union an 'ever looser' organization and would impede its progress as a cohesive entity. It may stimulate fissiparous tendencies in the European Union. 'The internal difficulties may grow in the Union of 25. It can stir certain degree of disintegration. There is also a discussion about the idea of a Europe of flexible geographies – for e.g., some parts of Europe enter into a looser integration than others. So, there is a possibility that Europe will take a direction of development which is not foreseen now. With the new questions posed by the eastern enlargement, disintegration is an open question. There is no guarantee. But, does anything which is created out of politics lasts forever? Such a guarantee is not there. The danger is also present.'[198] Besides, the enlargement also casts doubts over the smooth functioning of EU in future.

National Mould and National Visions

It is premature to say that nationalism and the urge of nations for dominance are dead and gone in Europe. The veneer of Europeanness on an essentially Common Market mechanism has not yet succeeded to bring the Member States out of their strong national moulds and national visions. Indeed, a mature analysis will show that the EU structures are not deep rooted, compared to the deep-rooted civilizational pasts of countries which constitute the European Union. Dismantling single market and single currency and going back looks difficult for many reasons. But things can change. 'The real test will be the enlargement. One solution could be to establish a multi-layer, multi-speed system where old Member States move ahead with further integration process and the newer ones are helped to catch up.'[199] However, there are enough indications that nation states, national visions and national ambitions are not going to wither away in Europe under the impact of the European Union. It is possible that European Union will continue to coexist with nation states. According to a French academic:

> Disentanglement of Member States from the Union is not impossible because the Member States are very strong. But it is unlikely that the whole thing will be reversed. What we could end up with will be a system where all these economic integration will survive but with no political backing which will make economic integration far less effective because we would keep what we have without making any further progress. European construction is like a bicycle. It functions when it runs. When it does not, it falls. And, therefore, that is a bit of a problem for us. After the next enlargement we are going to have a problem. We have to digest these ten countries. It will be very difficult to stomach them. But it is not going to be as difficult as integrating Britain. The question is whether we will be able to move forward again after that. I can't answer that question.[200]

In the words of a German expert: 'It is possible that with

the enlargement we don't manage to adjust European structures the way to make the EU workable. The political dynamism which kept the integration process so far may stop to exist after the enlargement. There is no example of any international organization getting dissolved. So will be the European Union. What can happen is that when major actors of the organization get withdrawn, things change and the organization dies without dissolution. I don't see a situation where EU gets dissolved. Common currency is a stabilising factor.'[201]

Clearly, the European Union will not be able to play any meaningful autonomous role so long as it gives the impression that it sychronizes its basic approach with the United States. It has to show its independence more unambiguously to judge international issues on merits, as have been shown by some EU Member States during the US invasion of Iraq in 2003. Of course, head on clashes between US and EU are on cards on a number of issues like the genetically modified organisms, development of welfare policy, Kyoto Protocol, application extra-territoriality, International Criminal Court of Justice, and so on. The differences between the United States and some important EU Member States, which came in the open during the Iraq war, indicated that a powerful section in EU is prepared to follow a path independent of the United States. At the same time, it has also revealed that there is another section in EU which would continue to follow the US footsteps, right or wrong, in world affairs. This divergence in the approaches of powerful EU conglomerations, casts doubts on EU's ability to take clear cut positions on any serious issue involving the United States. Enlargement seems to have enhanced the US influence in the European Union.

This inner weakness of EU apart, EU is a power centre in its own right. It has made Europe a continent of peace and prosperity. Indeed, today, Europe does not need US protection as it can take charge of its own security and has sufficient resources of its own to meet it. But, what is conspicuous in Europe is the lack of will to unite, the half-heartedness in taking positions, a tendency to remain a prisoner of indecision when critical issues come up in the world – make bombastic statements and declarations using fine phrases, but with little follow up action, a kind of pussy-footing in world politics. This must change. EU has to join other emerging power centres like Russia, China and India and become a front-line actor in world politics, which can change the global power equations drastically during the next 2 or 3 decades. For that there should be cohesion in the crust of the EU, which is conspicuous by its absence at the moment.

Whatever the shortcomings of the European Union, for Europe EU today is a factor of stability and prosperity. It has freed the European nations from their traditional suspicion-based confrontationist approach towards one another and has created a new European structure in which powerful nations of Europe can cooperate without fear of one another, and prosper together in a more transparent environment. Certainly, a community approach among countries has enhanced cohesion in Europe in an impressive manner. It has built up an ethos of conflict prevention and has provided a conflict prevention model by building bridges across nations through structured dialogues and enhanced transparency. As a result, internally, EU's peace dividend is impressive during the last half-a-century. Through a Community approach the Member States have conserved their energy and resources for people's development and prosperity and spent very little for military ventures. The fact that they have stopped planning against each other itself is a great achievement.

Europe has No Enemy

At the same time, we have to admit that the political environment in Europe today is not conducive for further deepening of the integration process. Of course, the surest and easiest way to build a common identity and direction in foreign and security policy is to locate a common enemy – real or phoney – without which building up cohesion and unity of purpose in world politics is said to be difficult. The post-war Europe's unity was fostered, to a great extent, by projecting the Soviet Union, and the communist system it represented, as the common enemy of the West, for about 3 decades. But today it is of no avail. Europe enjoys the luxury of not having an enemy, which becomes a disincentive to further build a common identity and cohesion. As the potential threat from the Soviet Union has vanished, attempts to invent new phoney threats, in the form of fantasies like the 'Clash of Civilizations', have not clicked to catch the imagination of the European psyche. Therefore, without identifying the 'other' against whom Europe can define its common interest, it is not easy to agree on what fundamental question Europe must necessarily remain united. But, there are scholars who hold the view that disappearance of the Soviet Union has not weakened the resolve of EU members for further integration. In support, Thomas Risse cites developments in 1990s, like the development of CFSP, introduction of Euro, the move to craft a new EU Constitution and so on.[202] A French scholar, Guillaume Parmentier, also shares this view. He also underlines that today Europe is not faced with serious security problems. 'Russians do not pose any threat to Europe in the foreseeable future. You may have some dictator emerging somewhere, but that can be taken care of. The Balkans are much quieter. The example of Milosovich [in Jail] is not going to encourage anyone to follow his path. That helps. It is going to be more difficult because Europeans are not going to concentrate on issues of security.'[203] He says: 'When we created NATO in 1949, the Prague coup had just happened. So there was an immediate comprehensible reason to do so. Today Europe has to create a European defence and security identity policy in a vacuum.

It is not easy to do that, to get the means to do that, to get over the obstacle that the national governments are going to create against that. It is not easy when there is no obligation. Therefore, if the situation does not change, it is going to take a very long time for Europe to develop all instruments of power.'[204]

Europe of Nation States to Stay

There is wide recognition across Europe that nation states still remain as strong entities in the European Union and pursue their own agenda and that that process will continue as a legitimate activity. Under the subsidiarity principle, national Parliaments remain strong and more prestigious. In the words of Parmentier:

> Europe is not a federal system. Even in a federal system, states pursue their interests. In Europe, at the moment they are not completely subservient. It will take longer before something like that takes place. There is certain amount of hesitation to relinquish all national instruments of power for European aspiration, especially on the part of larger nations because there are times when the overall European interests will not overwhelm the national interests. It will be much more difficult for us to make a federation than for the US. In US it was easy because they all use the same language and cultural background. But, for Europe it is different. Look at what we have succeeded in doing since the Second World War, in mere 60 years. We have achieved quite a bit. I think, in short term, there will be a lot of competition between the national element and the European element. I do not believe that we are going to abolish national policies, unless we face a sudden threat. I don't see that is coming about.[205]

EU: Unlikely Global Military Power

For various reasons, EU is unlikely to be a global military power because it is not a nation state but a collection of nation states. It is a structure in which nation states remain the primary source of political power and political will. Therefore, EU can grow to the extent the Member States permit. While doing so, every Member State pursues its national interests. If pooling is beneficial to national interests, they agree to it. Otherwise they staunchly oppose. Unity of markets and currencies was found beneficial to Member States. So they agreed for a united approach in those sectors. But, studiously, foreign policy, security policy, social welfare policy, and so on are kept away from the domain of the centralized bureaucracy in Brussels.

There is great potential for the European Union to play a major role in the non-economic facets of the global system as well. But many factors are pitted against the realization of that potential. Their aggregate hard power does not get added up. Britain and France are nuclear weapon states and their arsenal is next only to those of US and USSR. But they remain independent national programmes. They are permanent members of the UN Security Council and function there as independent states not only from one another, but also from other EU Member States, although EU has set up consultative machineries for greater coordination. Their navies have aircraft carriers and ballistic nuclear submarines. The EU Member States' national armies are under independent national commands. The European battle units, or the 'Rapid Reaction Force', are assemblies of small numbers of service personnel drawn temporarily from national defence forces of EU Member States and are 'European' only notionally. These are symbolisms of a reluctant organization, which can hardly be seen as effective ones. However, the EU plan to establish a new autonomous European army of 60,000 men drawn from Member States, supported by an air contingent of 15 squadron air force and a naval contingent of 15 warships, besides a fleet of 200 military transport planes for strategic airlifts, and so on are indicative of the readiness of the EU to assume greater role in the maintenance of international peace and security. How this grandiose plan would get implemented – its budgeting and so on – one has to wait and see. If pursued seriously, it can become the nucleus of a potential European defence force. The million dollar question is, whether all EU Member States are on the same wavelength on this matter? It is a fact that in the non-economic sectors, there is not enough cohesion in the attitudes of the EU Member States. Their global visions, global interests, and their expectations from EU membership vary widely. In fact, many Member States look at EU only for economic benefits accruing from free trade in EU. Many of them do not want EU to play a global role at all, and do not want to spend any money for that purpose. Barring Britain and France, other Member States hardly have the will or capacity to play that role. The CFSP is a grandiose plan. But, it does not perform the way it was expected. On foreign policy questions it is not EU, but Britain, France, Germany, Italy, Netherlands, and so on which are speaking. On paper there is CFSP. But in practice EU has no meaningful voice in dealing with major global questions. Its failure to make progress has been shrouded by a thin veil of a clever twist of the connotation of the word 'Common' that 'Common' is not 'Single'. Every failure to get agreement on CFSP questions has taken umbrage on this interpretation that 'common' is not 'single'. Inter-govermentalism in CFSP and twist in the interpretation of the word 'common' that it does not mean 'single' make this EU agenda a programme meant largely on paper. The Iraq War of 2003 has exposed the hollowness of CFSP beyond doubt. EU Member States adopted their own independent lines throughout the Iraqi crisis.

However, there are clear indications that in geo-political terms the EU and US are moving at different wavelengths.

During the last one decade the Union has become a more autonomous centre of power than ever before in the post-war period. That trend is likely to continue unabated for various geo-political reasons. Clearly, America's unipolar vision of world's future does not square well with the vision of a strong and cohesive Europe. The US attempts to dominate are bound to generate a lot of resentment in EU against it. If that leads to the creation of economic and political systems which could generate counter influence, it can weaken the US legitimacy politically in international affairs. But that will take some time. After all, Americans will have to realize that their power in the past has been built upon their ability to create coalitions around them. That power was based on the way the US has been traditionally seen as a benign benevolent country, not as an arrogant power scheming for dominance. However, more than clash of interests, for political reasons and for reasons of differing view points, such major changes can take place in the transatlantic relationship. There can be more vociferous differences over the fundamental question of use of hard military power in international relations. Europeans are not enthusiastic about it. According to Thomas Meyer, since US is following a hegemonic policy with Europe, Europe is likely to counter it. It means that in Europe US is producing its own countervailing force. In the next few years it will become more clear that Europe plays its own role *vis-à-vis* United States.[206] The aggressive pursuit of unilateralism and unipolarity by the United States is likely to cause increasing estrangement in the transatlantic relationship.

For the European Union to play an effective role in world politics, it has to assert its autonomy from the United States and remove the ambiguity in its position as an appendage of the United States. The question is: Is EU ready for it? A critical factor in EU's future role in the emerging global system is how it will refashion its relationship with the United States in several areas of world politics, strategy, economy and technology. While a decoupling with US seems to be the need of the hour, a clean break with Washington is not envisaged in the immediate future, although more acrimony in their relationship in every area of their activity is on cards. Moreover, signals of a slow decoupling in several sectors of transatlantic relationship are being given out by the unilateralism pursued by the United States, particularly more virulently after George W. Bush became the US President. Though US enjoys a commanding lead in the technology sector, the EU has taken measures to reduce its gap with the United States through joint efforts. In the aerospace industry, a raging competition is on between Europe and the United States. There exists stark differences between US and EU on the question of handling the Arab-Israeli conflict. As mentioned earlier, in a statement made on 2 April 2002, Romano Prodi, President of the EC Commission, openly suggested that the US should 'step aside' as the primary peace-maker in West Asia and give way to 'a broad alliance of countries' to mediate a durable peace agreement between Israel and the Palestinians. These are straws in the wind of an increasing EU readiness for a slow parting of the ways with US, and, at the same time, getting itself slowly organized to restore its autonomous position and assert its independence in its responses to international questions. It seems that the old paradigm of Europeans to remain content with their position as an economic power, while leadership role in other important areas, like political and security matters, should be left to Washington is in the melting pot and has become a less attractive framework for the Europeans. It is true that during the post-cold war period US has relentlessly pursued a superiority policy and established its dominance as an economic, political, military, and technological power. But, without getting overawed by that scenario, the EU is also re-organizing itself in all these sectors, without appearing confrontationist. It is true that today's EU's military position does not match its economic strength. If that matching takes place, it is unlikely that EU will acquiesce into unreasonable demands of US in many areas of international politics. The spectacle we saw during the Iraq war of 2003 between France and Germany and US and UK was the birth pangs of EU's parting of ways with US. At the same time, US still maintains a capacity to keep the EU house divided. Yet, more Member States are showing readiness to assume greater autonomous role in the world. But the problems of the realization of that wish are also considerable.

The notable impediments in achieving EU's objective of playing an effective role in the global system are partly internal. EU is likely to remain engaged, for quite sometime, in its domestic problems. The enlarged EU will be an area of tremendous inequality, in people's quality of life and income levels. The per capita GDP of the EU of 15 States is $ 23,000, which is 4 times higher than the per capita GDP of Poland. The per capita GDP of some other new Member States are much lower. Levelling them up and bring them on a par with other EU members will be a great task for the prosperous parts of the EU. When West Germany tried to do that in East Germany, the West German economy suddenly got into difficulty, from which it has still not recovered even after 14 years. Therefore, the task of elevating the 10 new Members to a reasonable level in terms of per capita income and quality of life, and tackling their unemployment problems will engage EU in a big way. Even synchronizing national standards, without venturing to totally eliminating national differences, will be a stupendous task. There are promising traits in EU. But their realization requires a more deeper integration process and unity of purpose among the Member States in the non-economic areas of their activities. That needed strong cohesion which is conspicuous by its absence in EU. That can deprive EU the full realization of its potential as an effective autonomous global actor in the emerging global system.

Enlargement seems to put the EU in a multi-speed track, some will move ahead and others will be left behind to tread at a lower speed. The spectacle that was witnessed at the failed inter-governmental conference in December 2003, which considered the new Draft EU Constitution, gave an impression that the big three – Britain, France and Germany — seem to give shape to a triumvirate to give leadership to the enlarged EU in future when the multi-speed EU becomes a reality. The rumbles of that could be heard when the big three met separately in February 2004, in Berlin, along with their ministers responsible for health, social welfare, industry, trade and labour. Already, resentments, among the medium and small EU Member States against this new top formation, have been publicly expressed by some of their leaders. They see in this tripartite summit an attempt of the 'big three' to dominate the smaller EU Member States and promote their national interests.[207] The way the 'big three' leaders had posed for photograph at the end of the summit, with the French President Jacques Chirac on the right, British Prime Minister Tony Blair on the left and German Chancellor Gerhard Schroeder at the centre, was symbolic to the way leadership of Europe is going to unfold in the coming years.

During the last ten years EU has been trying to project its political image by acquiring certain features of a state, and complement its economic weight with its political weight. Yet EU's political profile continues to remain low. It is not surprising that a mindset steeped in profit and loss, market, and promotion of consumerism and interests of the business elite of Europe, the EU is not able to attune itself to the social, political or foreign policy aspects of international life. That is the malady the European Union is faced with. Politically, Member States like Britain and France have higher political profiles than EU's political profile and these countries are cautious against miring themselves into the EU quagmire which, they apprehend, would pull them also back into inaction on international questions.

If EU wants to show that it is not one of the exploitative structures of the 21st century, it has to moderate its rabid shopkeeper approach and raise its sights up and show more benign features of social concerns, internally and externally, through genuine transfer of resources from the North to the South on the lines Willy Brandt had envisaged in the Brandt Commission Report. Sophisticated protectionist measures in the EU market against products from developing countries do not bestow that benign image for EU. A dwindling development assistance is not the answer. As Thomas Meyer said: 'Good relations of even-footing between EU and other countries are not enough. The EU should attune its policies towards faster distribution of resources and wealth. It should strive for a world order where all human beings have a basic feeling of living, are able to lead a secure life.'[208]

A polarization between the haves and the have-nots will be dangerous. Globalization and technological advancements enrich people, but not everyone and everywhere. Development sans equity is a framework for the preservation of an exploitative structure. External aid is not the right solution. EU is boastful that it is the source of 55 percent of all international official development assistance and about 66 percent of it are grant aid. But how meagre it is becomes clear when the amount spend on it is compared with the annual resource flow from the developing world to the developed world. EU's association agreements with poor countries have not brought prosperity to them. EU can become more attractive if it enlarges its Community approach seriously to the social sector and transform the EU into a welfare state zone, a zone of human solidarity – a Nordic model applied Europe wide.

European Union is the latest Concert experiment in Europe. Europe had experimented it, though not in this scale and dimension, in the past as well, after the Napoleonic wars through the Congress of Vienna of 1815 when a European Concert redrew the map of Europe to guarantee peace and stability in the Continent. But, the Europeanness embedded in that concert did not kill the national spirit and ambitions of its participants, which, in due course, flowered and expressed themselves in the most virulent form. It may also be noted that at every turn in the history of Europe, there has always been an element of surprise in making radical shifts. And, there is no logic in believing that that element of surprise in European politics has now ended with the establishment of EU, if one keeps in view the varied basic psyche of European peoples hailing from various nationalities. Of course, during the last 50 years EU has helped a major transformation in the relationship between European States. But the level of unity they have achieved so far remains mainly in the economic field. That is not enough to make EU an effective centre of power in the emerging multipolar world. For that they have to achieve more cohesion among the Member States by acquiring firm features of a state, and present themselves as a genuinely united power centre *vis-à-vis* other power centres of the world.

REFERENCES

1. B. Vivekanandan, *In Retrospect: Reflections on Select Issues in World Politics*, 1975-2000 (New Delhi, Lancer's Books, 2001), p. 30
2. The trajectory of the current pace of India's resurgence as a great power is focused in three articles published by Dr. Arun Shourie in the *Indian Express* (New Delhi), 15-17 August 2003.
3. See Chris Patten's interview in *The Hindu* (Madras), 24 November 2003.
4. Robert Kagan, 'Power and Weakness', *Policy Review* (Washington DC), No. 113, Autumn 2002, p. 7.
5. Martin Kohli and Mojca Novak, eds, *Will Europe Work?: Integration Employment and Social Order* (London & New York, Routledge, 2001), Chapter 'Introduction: Will Europe Work?', p. 1.
6. *Ibid.*, p. 5
7. *Ibid.*
8. Brigitte Vassort–Rousset, 'France and European Integration', a paper presented at a seminar in New Delhi in May 2003.

9. Quoted in Malcolm Subhan, 'EU Enlargement', *Eurasia Bulletin: European Institute for Asian Studies* (Brussels), Vol. 6, No.10, October 2002, p.1. 50 years later EU has reached that point to take them in.
10. EC Council and EC Commission, *Treaty on European Union* (Brussels, EC, 1992), Title I, Article A, p. 7.
11. The European Convention, *Draft Treaty Establishing a Constitution for Europe* (Brussels, European Convention Secretariat, 2003), Preamble p. 3.
12. Charles De Gaulle, *Memoirs of Hope* (London, Weidenfeld and Nicolson, 1971), pp. 171-2.
13. J. Magnus Ryner, 'European Integration', in Mary Hawkesworth and Maurice Kogan, eds, *Encyclopaedia of Government and Politics* (London, Routledge, 2004), p. 1150.
14. *The Hindu* (Madras), 29 November 2003.
15. See Susan Mathai, *National Interests and Community Building: A Study of European Community*, Ph.D Thesis, Jawaharlal Nehru University, New Delhi, 2002
16. EC Council and EC Commission, *Treaty on European Union*, n.10, p. 8.
17. *Ibid.*, pp. 123-24
18. James Gilbert, Principal Administrator, European Commission, in an interview with the author on 2 January 2003, in Brussels.
19. Dr. Peter Wilson, Head, Strategy Policy Team, British Foreign Office, in an interview with the author on 30 January 2003, in London.
20. Dr. Dana Allin, Senior Fellow for Transatlantic Affairs, International Institute of Strategic Studies, London, in an interview with the author on 23 January 2003, in London.
21. Romano Prodi, 'Europe in Transition: Hopes and Fears', speech at the Fifth Europa Forum, in Brussels, on 3 December 2002, p. 3.
22. Chris Patten, 'A European Foreign Policy : Ambition and Reality', speech at the IFRI, Paris, 15 June 2000, in Antonio Missiroli, ed., *Coherence for European Security Policy: Debates – Cases – Assessments* (Paris, ISS-WEU, 2001), pp. 42-3.
23. *Ibid.*, p. 49.
24. See Chris Patten's interview in the *The Hindu* (Madras), 29 November 2003.
25. Dr. Antonio Missiroli, Research Fellow, Institute for Security Studies, Western European Union, Paris, in an interview with the author on 8 January 2003 in Paris.
26. Dr. Guillaume Parmentier, Director of French Centre for United States (CFE), IFRI, Paris, in an interview with the author on 7 January 2003, in Paris.
27. Dr. Detlef Weigel, Deputy Head of Policy Planning Staff, German Ministry of Foreign Affairs, in an interview with the author on 17 December 2002, in Berlin.

28. See Romano Prodi's speech in Antonio Missiroli, ed., *Coherence for European Security Policy: Debates – Cases – Assessments* (Paris, ISS-WEU, 2001), p. 66.
29. *Ibid.*, p. 67.
30. *Ibid.*, p. 69.
31. Prof. Paul Taylor, Director, European Institute, London School of Economics (LSE), in an interview with the author on 22 January 2003, in London.
32. Prof. Fulco Lanchester, President, Department of Political Studies, University of Rome, in an interview with the author on 10 December 2002 in Rome.
33. Dick Gupwell, Secretary General, European Institute for Asian Studies, Brussels, in an interview with the author on 2 January 2003 in Brussels.
34. Prof. Vinzenzo Nazo, Department of Mechanical and Aeronautical Engineering, University of Rome, in an interview with the author on 11 December 2002, in Rome.
35. Prof. Gianni Bonvicini, Director, Institute of International Affairs, Rome, in an interview with the author on 11 December 2002, in Rome.
36. Axel Queval, Head, International Department, Jean Jaurés Foundation, Paris, in an interview with the author on 6 January 2003, in Paris.
37. Prof. William Wallace, London School of Economics, in an interview with the author on 24 January 2003 in London.
38. Dr. Julie Smith, Royal Institute of International Affairs (RIIA), in an interview with the author on 28 January 2003, in London.
39. Prof. Christopher Hill, LSE, in an interview with the author on 28 January.2003, in London.
40. *Ibid.*
41. Prof. Thomas Meyer, Professor of Political Science, Dortmund University, Germany, in an interview with the author on 20 November 2002, in New Delhi.
42. Dr. Nimmi Kurian, *The High Noon: Anglo-American Special Relationship Under Thatcher and Reagan* (New Delhi, Lancer's Books, 2001).
43. Dr. Julie Smith, RIIA, London, in an interview with the author on 28 January, 2003, in London.
44. Dr. Peter Wilson, n. 19, in an interview with the author on 30 January 2003, in London.
45. Dr. Julie Smith, n. 38, in an interview with the author on 28 January 2003, in London.
46. Prof. Christopher Hill, n. 39, in an interview with the author on 28 January 2003 in London.
47. *Ibid.*
48. Dr. Karen E. Smith, International Relations Department, London School of Economics, in an interview with the author on 22 January 2003, in London.
49. Prof. Paul Taylor, n. 31, in an interview with the author on 22 January 2003 in London.

50. Ernst Reichel, German Foreign Office, in an interview with the author on 18 December 2002, in Berlin
51. Dr. Ernst Ulrich Von Weizacker, SPD MP and Former Vice Chancellor, and currently Chairman of Environment Committee, Bundestag, Germany, in an interview with the author on 19 December 2002, in Berlin.
52. *Ibid.*
53. Prof. Thomas Risse, Free University, Berlin, in an interview with the author on 16 December 2002, in Berlin. '
54. Dr. Detlef Weigel, n. 27, in an interview with the author on 17 December 2002, in Berlin.
55. Dr. Christoph Jessen, Botschafter, German Foreign Office, in an interview with the author on 17 December 2002, in Berlin.
56. Axel Queval, n. 36, in an interview with the author on 6 January 2003, in Paris.
57. Dr. Guillaume Parmentier, n. 26, in an interview with the author on 7 January 2003, in Paris.
58. Dr. Antonio Missiroli, n. 25, in an interview with the author on 8 January 2003, in Paris. According to William Wallace, 'in ten years from now CAP will be something different'. Prof. William Wallace, n. 37, in an interview with the author on 24 January 2003, in London.
59. Prof. Paul Taylor, n. 31, in an interview with the author on 22 January 2003, in London.
60. James Gilbert, n. 18, in an interview with the author on 2 January 2003, in Brussels.
61. Belgium Ambassador to India, Guy Trouveroy, has characterized the latest enlargement as 'mutation' of the European Union which will make EU 'look completely different from the Union we know today.' See his speech, 'The Future of the European Union' in New Delhi on 6 September 2001.
62. Prof. Fulco Lanchester, n. 32, in an interview with the author on 10 December 2002, in Rome.
63. Dr. Guillaume Parmentier, n. 26, in an interview with the author on 7 January 2003, in Paris.
64. Prof. Christopher Hill, n. 39, in an interview with the author on 21 January 2003, in London.
65. Prof. Paul Taylor, n. 31, in an interview with the author on 22 January 2003, in London.
66. Axel Queval, n. 36, in an interview with the author on 6 January 2003, in Paris.
67. Dr. Dana Allin, n. 20, in an interview with the author on 23 January 2003, in London.
68. *Ibid.*

69. For details, See Chapter VII, 'Movement for a European Union' in B. Vivekanandan, *The Shrinking Circle: The Commonwealth in British Foreign Policy*, 1945-1974 (Bombay, Somaiya, 1983), pp. 240-74.
70. Axel Queval, n. 36, in an interview with the author on 6 January 2003 in Paris, n. 66.
71. Prof Jean-Paul Chagnollaud, President, Cergy-Pontois University, France, in an interview with the author on 9 January 2003, in Cergy, France.
72. Dr. Guillaume Parmentier's interview with the author on 7 January 2003, in Paris, n. 26.
73. Prof. Paul Taylor, n. 31, in an interview with the author on 22 January 2003, in London.
74. Prof. William Wallace, n. 37, in an interview with the author on 24 January 2003, in London.
75. *Ibid.*
76. See Chapter on 'German Reunification: A Decade After', in B. Vivekanandan, *In Retrospect: Reflections on Select Issues in World Politics*, 1975-2000 (New Delhi, Lancer's Books, 2001), pp. 160-77.
77. Prof Jean Paul Chagnollaud, n. 71, in an interview with the author on 9 January 2003, in Cergy, France.
78. Ibid.
79. B. Vivekanandan, 'German Re-unification', n. 76.
80. Malcolm Subhan, Vice Chairman, European Institute for Asian Studies, Brussels, in an interview with the author on 31 December 2002, in Brussels.
81. Axel Queval, n. 36, in an interview with the author on 6 January 2003, in Paris.
82. Jean-Luc Dehaene and Giuliano Amato were Vice Chairmen of the Convention. See Delegation of European Commission in India, *EU-India Update* (New Delhi), Vol. 2, No. 2, Nov.-Dec. 2003, p. 3.
83. *See* the speech of Johannes Rau, German President, at the European Parliament on 4 April 2001. *The Future of European Union Debate, http://europa.eu.int/futurum/documents/speech/sp040401_eu.htm*, p. 2.
84. *Ibid.*, p. 3
85. *Ibid.*
86. *Ibid.*, p. 2
87. *Ibid.*, p. 3
88. E.C. Commission, Commission Press Room, 'Commission Proposes a Radical Simplification of How the European Union Works,' Brussels, 5 December 2002, p. 1
89. *Ibid.*
90. See the text of Romano Prodi's speech at the European Convention on 5 December 2002, in *http://europa.eu.int/rapid/start/cgi/guesten.ksh?p_action..../617/o/rapid&ig=EN&display*.

91. *Ibid.*, p. 3.
92. *Ibid.*
93. *Ibid.*, p. 4
94. Dr. Ernst Reichel, n. 50, in an interview with the author on 18 December 2002, in Berlin.
95. Ibid.
96. Dr. Detlef Weigel, n. 27, in an interview with the author on 17 December 2002, in Berlin.
97. Keeping in view the impending enlargement of the European Union from 15 to 25 members, the European Convention on the Future of Europe was established by the European Council meeting at Laeken (Belgium) in December 2001 for preparing a Constitution for EU in order to give it a legal personality, to demarcate competences between the Union and Member States, to merge various European Union treaties, to simplify the Union's instruments of action and decision-making process, and so on.
98. See the *Draft Treaty Establishing a Constitution for Europe* (Brussels, European Convention Secretariat, 2003), Part I, Article 1.
99. *Ibid.*, Articles 3 and 4.
100. *Ibid.*, Part II.
101. *Ibid.*, Part I, Articles 9 and 10.
102. *Ibid.*, Articles 12-14. Such provisions can have their adverse potential implications for the tax systems of various EU countries, which can cause erosion of advanced welfare state systems which depends on high taxation, like the Nordic States.
103. *Ibid.*, Part III, Articles 71 and 76. Such provisions would give enormous leverage to the Commission and the Council to do quiet arm twisting of the Member States, particularly of the small ones, in the Euro area. In the name of budget discipline and sound financial management they can use this as a lever to control and hamstrung national budgets.
104. *Ibid.*, Part III, Articles 77, 78, 84 and 85. It may be noted that the ECB's Governing Council is composed of the 6-member Executive Board of ECB and the Governors of the NCBs.
105. *Ibid.*, Part I, Article 15.
106. *Ibid.*, Article III-195.
107. *Ibid.*, Part I, Article 39.
108. *Ibid.*, Part I, Article 40
109. *Ibid.*, Articles 42 and 43.
110. *Ibid.*, Article III-310.
111. *Ibid.*, Part I, Articles 18-27.
112. *Ibid.*, Part II, Article III-99.
113. *Ibid.*, Article III-104.

114. See *Newsweek* (New York), 22 December 2003, *The Hindu* (Madras), 19 & 20 December 2003; and *International Herald Tribune* (Paris), 16 December 2003.
115. Malcolm Subhan, n. 80, in an interview with the author on 31 December 2002, in Brussels.
116. David P. Calleo, Director, European Studies, John Hopkins University Washington DC., in a speech at RIIA, Chatham House, London, on 20 January 2003.
117. Axel Queval, n. 36, in an interview with the author on 6 January 2003, in Paris.
118. Prof. Vinzenzo Nazo, n. 34, in an interview with the author on 11 December 2002, in Rome.
119. *The Hindu* (New Delhi), 30 November 2003.
120. Prof. Vincenzo Nazo, n. 34.
121. *Ibid.*
122. *Ibid.*
123. Ernst Ulrich Von Weizacker, n. 51, in an interview with the author on 19 December 2002, in Berlin.
124. *Ibid.*
125. Prof. Gianni Bonvicini, n. 35, in an interview with the author on 11 December 2002, in Rome.
126. Prof. David P. Calleo, Director of European studies, John Hopkins University, Washington D.C., in a talk at RIIA, London, on 20 January 2003, in London.
127. Malcolm Subhan, n. 80, in an interview with the author on 31 December 2002, in Brussels.
128. Dick Gupwell, n. 33, in an interview with the author on 2 January 2003, in Brussels.
129. Ibid.
130. Prof. David P. Calleo, Director of European Studies, John Hopkins University, Washington D.C., in a talk at RIIA, London, on 20 January 2003, in London.
131. Immanuel Wallerstein, 'The Eagle has Crashlanded', *Foreign Policy* (New York), July-August 2002, p. 63.
132. *Ibid.*, p. 66.
133. *The Hindu* (New Delhi), 1 December 2003.
134. Prof. Paul Taylor, n. 31, in an interview with the author on 22 January 2003, in London.
135. Dr. Peter Wilson, n. 19, in an interview with the author on 30 January 2003, in London.
136. Prof. Christopher Hill, n. 39, in an interview with the author on 28 January 2003, in London.
137. Prof. Jean-Paul Chagnollaud, n. 71, in an interview with the author on 9 January 2003 in Cergy, France.

138. *The Hindu*, 3 April 2002.
139. Steven Everts, 'Mission Impossible? Managing the Growing Divide Between Europe and the US', *International Spectator* (Rome), Vol. 37 No.3 July-Sept.2002, p. 32.
140. Prof. Christopher Hill, '11 September 2001: Perspectives from International Relations', *International Relations* (London), Vol.16, No.2, pp. 260-61.
141. William Pfaff, 'Crushing German Dissent: Why the US Fears Europe', *International Herald Tribune* (Paris), 1 February 2003.
142. Robert Kagan, 'Power and Weakness', *Policy Review* (Washington DC), No.113, Autumn 2002, p. 1.
143. *Ibid.*, p. 2.
144. *Ibid.*, p. 7.
145. *Ibid.*, p. 9.
146. Alan S. Milward, 'Historical Teleologies', in Mary Farrel, et.al., eds, *European Integration in the 21st Century: Unity in Diversity* (London, Sage, 2002), p. 121.
147. Eurostat, Comext *http://trade-info.cec.eu.int/doclib/docs/2003/august/tradoc_113540.pdf*
148. *The Hindu*, 26 March 2004.
149. Prof. Christopher Hill, n. 39, in an interview with the author on 28 January 2003, in London.
150. Vladimir Radyuhin, 'Rebuilding Russia's Global Role', *The Hindu*, 26 July 2003. Also see Vladimir Radyuhin, 'Putin Looks to Turn the Economy Around', *The Hindu*, 21 March 2004.
151. James Gilbert, n. 18, in an interview with the author on 2 January 2003, in Brussels.
152. Dr. Dana Allin, n. 20, in an interview with the author on 23 January 2003, in London.
153. James Gilbert, n. 18, in an interview with the author on 2 January 2003, in Brussels.
154. Dr. Ernst Reichel, n. 50, in an interview with the author on 18 December 2002, in Berlin.
155. Prof. William Wallace, n. 37, in an interview with the author on 24 January 2003, in London.
156. Rosita Dellios and Heather Field, 'China and the European Union: Potential Beneficiaries of Bush's Global Coalition', *Australian Journal of International Affairs* (Deakin, Australia), Vol.56 (2002) No.1, p. 96.
157. The current pace of India's resurgence has been analysed in 3 articles published by Dr. Arun Shourie in the *Indian Express* (New Delhi), 15-17 August 2003.
158. For text of the Joint Declaration, see Delegation of European Commission in India, *European Union News* (New Delhi), May-June 2000, p. 6.
159. *Indian Express* (New Delhi), 29 November 2003.

160. Prof. Paul Taylor, n. 31, in an interview with the author on 22 January 2003, in London.
161. Prof. Christopher Hill, n. 39, in an interview with the author on 28 January 2003, in London.
162. Dr. Antonio Missiroli, n. 25, in an interview with the author on 8 January 2003, in Paris.
163. Prof. Vinzenzo Nazo, n. 34, in an interview with the author on 11 December 2002, in Rome.
164. Dick Gupwell, n. 33, in an interview with the author on 2 January 2003, in Brussels.
165. Dr. Julie Smith, n. 38, in an interview with the author on 28 January 2003, in London.
166. Dr. Guillaume Parmentier, n. 26, in an interview with the author on 7 January 2003, in Paris.
167. Prof. William Wallace, n. 37, in an interview with the author on 24 January 2003, in London.
168. James Gilbert, n. 18, in an interview with the author on 2 January 2003 in Brussels.
169. Axel Queval, n. 36, in an interview with the author on 6 January 2003, in Paris.
170. Prof. Thomas Risse, n. 53, in an interview with the author on 16 December 2002, in Berlin.
171. Author's interviews with Mr. James Gilbert, n. 18, on 2 January 2003 in Brussels, with Dr Ernst Reichel, n. 50, on 18 December 2002, in Berlin, and with Dr. Detlef Weigel, n. 27, on 17 December 2002, in Berlin
172. Dr. Christoph Jessen, n. 55, in an interview with the author on 17 December 2002, in Berlin.
173. Dick Gupwell, n. 33, in an interview on 2 January 2003, in Brussels.
174. Thomas Meyer, n. 41, in an interview with the author on 20 November 2002, in New Delhi.
175. Dr. Ernst Ulrich von Weizacker, n. 51, in an interview with the author on 19 December 2002, in Berlin.
176. Dominique Girard, Ambassador of France to India, in an address 'European Union in World Politics', in New Delhi on 22 May 2003.
177. *The Hindu*, 22 October 2003.
178. Dick Gupwell, n. 33, in an interview with the author on 2 January 2003, in Brussels.
179. Malcolm Subhan, n. 80, in an interview with the author on 31 December 2002, in Brussels.
180. Dr. Christoph Jessen, n. 55, in an interview with the author on 17 December 2002, in Berlin.
181. Dick Gupwell, n. 33, in an interview with the author on 2 January 2003, in Brussels.
182. Ernst von Weizacker, n. 51, in an interview with the author on December 2002, in Berlin.

183. Fareed Zakaria, *The Future of Freedom : Illiberal Democracy at Home and Abroad* (New Delhi, Viking, 2003), p. 243.
184. See Johannes Rau, 'Plea for a European Convention', *The Future of European Union Debate, http://europa.eu.int/futurum/document/speech/sp040401_eu.htm*, p. 1.
185. Prof. Imtiaz Ahmed, Jawaharlal Nehru University, New Delhi, at a seminar on 'Multiculturalism in India and Europe', at JNU, New Delhi, on 6 November 2003.
186. See Volker Bornchier, 'European Processes and the state of the European Union', in Alison Woodward and Martin Kohli, eds., *Inclusions and Excluions in European Societies* (London & New York, Routledge, 2001), p.199.
187. Dick Gupwell, n. 33, in an interview with the author on 2 January 2003, in Brussels.
188. Martin Walker, 'Europe's Existential Crisis', *Wilson Quarterly* (Washington D.C), Winter 2001.
189. Prof. Chagnollaud, n. 71, in an interview with the author on 9 January 2003 in Cergy-Pentios University, in Cergy, France.
190. *Ibid.*
191. *Ibid.*
192. Dr. Detlef Weigel, n. 27, in an interview with the author on 17 December 2002, in Berlin.
193. Dr. Antonio Missiroli, n. 25, in an interview with the author on 8 January 2003, in Paris.
194. Prof. Martin Kohli, Department of Social Policy, Free University, Berlin, in an interview with the author on 20 December 2002, in Berlin.
195. Prof. Jean-Paul Chagnollaud, Mr. James Gilbert, Dr. Ernst Reichel, Claudio Franzius, Axel Queval and Thomas Risse give at least another half a century for this experiment to go on without much problem.
196. A European government official, not to be named, in an interview with the author during his visit to Europe in December 2002-February 2003.
197. Malcolm Subhan, n. 80, in an interview with the author on 31 December 2002, in Brussels.
198. Thomas Meyer, n. 41, in an interview with the author on 20 November 2002, in New Delhi.
199. Dr. Antonio Missiroli, n. 25, in an interview with the author on 8 January 2003, in Paris.
200. Dr. Guillaume Parmentier, n. 26, in an interview with the author on 7 January 2003, in Paris.
201. Dr. Ernst Reichel, n. 50, in an interview with the author on 18 December 2002, in Berlin.
202. Prof. Thomas Risse, Centre for Transatlantic Foreign and Security Policy, Free University, Berlin, in an interview with the author on 16 December 2002, in Berlin.

203. Dr. Guillaume Parmentier, n. 26, in an interview with the author on 7 January 2003, in Paris.
204. *Ibid*.
205. *Ibid*.
206. Thomas Meyer, n. 41, in an interview with the author on 20 November 2002, in New Delhi.
207. *The Hindu* (Madras), 19 February 2004.
208. Prof. Thomas Meyer, n. 41, in an interview with the author on 20 November 2002 in New Delhi.

3

Austria Viewed from India

I

Viewed from India, Austria gives the image of a picturesque country that has attracted the world's attention in the post-war period through its sensible propositions to find solutions to pressing international problems. Being a nation with a glorious past, long traditions and rich in culture, art and architecture, in the vicissitudes of the last thousand years of European history, Austria had its share of Europe's delights and sorrows. Its geographical location in Europe exposed Austria to repeated occupations, which were followed by struggles for restoration of independence. Its geopolitical position as a land-locked country, sharing common borders with seven countries – Germany, Czech Republic, Slovakia, Hungary, Slovenia, Italy and Switzerland — and its position as an important junction of traffic in Central Europe, have endowed Austria with a certain degree of sustained influence in Europe's thinking and outlook.

Despite the short-lived success Adolf Hitler had accomplished in erasing Austria from the map of Europe through the inglorious *Anschluss*, this seven-year interruption between 1938 and 1945 could not rupture Austria's link with its glorious past and rich heritage. From the *Anschluss*, Austria rose once again like a Phoenix and re-established itself as a vibrant nation, enjoying a high reputation in the international arena.

What are the significant traits Austria had shown during the last one thousand years that are still relevant to be taken note of? Despite the pulls and pushes of history and short interruptions, during the last thousand years, Austria has been a stable state in Central Europe, smoothly adjusting itself to changing times and situations. The fact that for about nine and-a-half centuries starting from the 10th century Austria was ruled only by two dynasties – the Babenbergs and the Habsburgs – is a pointer to this trait. Austria's dominant position in Central Europe began to plummet following the rise of Prussia under Otto von Bismarck who, after defeating Austria in the battle of Sadowa (Königgrätz) in 1866, got Austria expelled from the German Confederation. Although Austria tried to limit the damage caused by the onslaught of Bismarck by forging a confederation between Austria and Hungary and by establishing a dual monarchy in 1867, which continued to ensure Austria's self-sufficiency, the Austro-Hungarian empire collapsed under the pulls of national aspirations within the empire, which had reached their crescendo during the First World War, and under the weight of the unrest caused by the hardships and shortages of essential commodities to the civilian population during the course of the war. Under their impact, the empire gave way to the birth of a few nations like Austria, Hungary, Czechoslovakia, Yugoslavia, and so on. The Danubean landmass thus got splintered in such a way that Austria's self-sufficiency was totally destroyed and its dependency on its neighbours irreversibly heightened. The empire was disintegrated in a manner in which the new small Austria and its 7.5 million people were placed under chronic economic difficulties and shortages of essential articles. That became a perennial problem for Austria. And these new constraints had a recurring limiting impact on Austria's domestic and foreign policies. Away from confrontation, Austria relied more on diplomacy, negotiation, and compromise to obtain enduring results.

For centuries Austria remained a bulwark against the westward expansion of the Ottoman empire and the eastward expansion of Germany, which had made Austria geo-politically vulnerable to conflicts and rivalries. The active diplomacy such vulnerability demanded, the cross-cultural currents – of Germans, Magyars and Slavs – which had passed through Austria and which had made Austria the meeting point of three major European civilizations – Roman, German, and Slavic –, the travails and tribulations Austria had suffered following Hitler's occupation of the country, the struggle it carried on in the post-war period to end occupation and to regain its sovereignty by harnessing international support enabled Austria to develop a unique personality in Central Europe. If, in the dawn of the 20th century, the Austro-Hungarian empire functioned as an effective buffer between Russia and Germany and prevented any direct conflict between them in the heart of Europe, in the post-war period, at least for a decade, Austria functioned as a strategic outpost of both the East and the West, a factor which encouraged the big powers to prolong their stay in Austria in order to gain an advantage. Therefore, cumulatively, Austria had developed an international mind which had dissuaded it from pursuing a narrow nationalist approach to world politics, and had shown a natural inclination to view problems and their solutions from an international perspective. This basic psyche of Austria expressed itself through Austria's active participation in world politics in the post-war period as well. Moreover, ever since the Austro-Hungarian empire disintegrated, Austria, as the most important and high profile country among the Danubean states, had maintained a hope and a vision of building up a community of Danubean states. Though not much progress has been made in this direction so far, peace and security of this region remains a major concern of Austria.

Seen from the outside, the political mind of Austria is basically anti-authoritarian. The people of Austria have shown this trait repeatedly. When Chancellor Engelbert Dollfuss suspended the Austrian Parliament and established his dictatorship in the country in 1933, to follow the footsteps of fascism in Italy, there was stiff resistance to it from the people under the leadership of the Social Democrats and they organized, though unsuccessfully, a revolt against the Dollfuss regime. Not dissimilar was the revulsion people had shown when Hitler invaded Austria in 1938, contrived its *Anschluss* with Germany and brought Austria under his dictatorship. The Western democracies chose to remain mute spectators to the demise of Austria. Only a few countries like Mexico, the Soviet Union, Chile and China protested against the German annexation of Austria. In a letter to Joseph A. Avenol, the League of Nations Secretary-General, the Mexican envoy to the League of Nations, Isidoro Fabela, wrote on 19 March 1938: "The political demise of Austria ... constitutes a grave violation of the Covenant of the League of Nations and the sacrosanct principles of international law. Austria's existence as a sovereign nation was terminated by an act of violence. This intervention is a gross breach of our Covenant. ... The Government of Mexico ... protests in the strongest terms against the external aggression to which Austria has fallen victim." However, the establishment of a dictatorship in Austria forced many eminent political leaders to flee the country and to take refuge abroad and live in exile under the benign care of an international solidarity approach of the host countries. The experience of foreign occupation, statelessness, forced refugee status, sustenance on the goodwill generated by the international solidarity of the Labour Movement, made deep imprints on the political mind of Austria that had a lot of bearing on Austria's international policies in the post-war period. It enabled Austria to show a better understanding of the problems of the Third World and to pursue more humane policies.

Viewed from New Delhi, Austria's image is intertwined with a galaxy of great personalities the country has produced over the years. In the background are the notable political personalities like Prince Metternich, King Joseph I, Otto Bauer, Victor Adler and Bruno Kreisky. Others include many Nobel Laureates (16 during the 20th century, including the Austrian writer Bertha von Suttner, the author of the famous book *Lay DownYour Arms* which inspired Alfred Nobel to institute the Nobel Peace Prize) in the fields of Medicine, Economics, Physics, Chemistry, Peace and so on, Alfred Fried, the progenitor of the idea of peaceful European integration (who was also a Nobel Laureate), Sigmund Freud, and the famous composers like Joseph Haydn, Wolfgang Amadeus Mozart and Ludwig van Beethoven – the trio famous for the "Vienna Classics".

Similarly striking in the profile of Austria is the aura of the city of Vienna, famed for its architectural splendour, studded with marvellous structures like the Opera House, Burg Theatre, Volks Theatre, Academic Theatre, Belvedere Palace, and so on. The city also bears the footprints or Europe's political, social and cultural history which, being a scene of pitched battles between the Germans and the Allied Forces in the last phase of the Second World War, also contains plenty of war scars. The city is also famous for music, jazz and orchestra. For centuries, Vienna has played host to many historic international conferences. After the Napoleonic wars, during the course of which Napoleon twice occupied Vienna, the Congress of Vienna of 1814-15 redrew the map of Europe and made the balance of power as a basis for the maintenance of international peace and security. That conference tradition of the city of Vienna has been preserved in the post-war period as well. In 1961, Vienna hosted a meeting between the US President John F. Kennedy and the CPSU General Secretary Nikita S. Khrushchev. Similarly, in June 1979, Vienna hosted the signing ceremony of the SALT II agreement by the US President Jimmy Carter and the Soviet President Leonid Brezhnev. It was also the venue of the CSCE Review Conferences and of negotiations on Conventional Forces in Europe and also of the Conferences on Confidence and Security Building Measures. Moreover, today the Vienna International Centre is a permanent seat of the United Nations, housing organizations like the International Atomic Energy Agency and the UN Industrial Development

Organisation. The OSCE General Secretariat is also located in Vienna.

Similarly striking is Austria's position as one of the most advanced welfare states in Europe. Its social security schemes are, in a general sense, comparable with similar schemes introduced in Sweden. Austria also enjoys the distinction of the first country in Europe, after Russia, to establish Works Councils. Similarly, it was one of the earliest to formulate a social policy by law. In 1919, it passed an Act that stipulated paid holidays for workers. Moreover, as early as 1920, the Parliament enacted legislation establishing statutory associations (Chambers of Labour) for blue and white collar employees and introducing employment insurance. In the wake of the Bolshevik revolution, the Austrian Social Democrats wanted the "Austrian revolution" to be peaceful. The SPÖ leader, Victor Adler, stated confidently: "We shall show the world how a revolution is started and implemented in the smoothest, most classic and simplest manner." That was accomplished in the most impressive manner through the establishment of a highly advanced welfare state system in Austria.

II

The first ray of hope for the restoration of Austria's independence appeared on the horizon on 1 November 1943 when the Moscow Declaration on Austria was published. The declaration, jointly agreed by the Foreign Ministers of the Allied Powers – Anthony Eden, Cordell Hull and Vyacheslav Molotov – on 30 October 1943 and published two days later, said that Britain, the United States and the Soviet Union had "agreed that Austria, the first free country to fall a victim to Hitlerite aggression, shall be liberated from German domination". They said that the annexation of Austria by Germany was null and void. "They declare that they wish to see re-established a free and independent

Austria, and thereby open the way for Austrian people themselves ... to find that political and economic security which is the only basis for lasting peace." While the Allied Powers made an unequivocal commitment to establish "a free and independent Austria", they added a rider in the Declaration which said: "Austria was reminded, however, that she has a responsibility which she cannot evade for participation in the war on the side of Hitlerite Germany, and that in the final settlement account will inevitably be taken of her own contribution to her liberation."[1] This rider assumed great significance when the war was over and when the Allied Powers and Austria began their negotiations for the conclusion of the Austrian State Treaty. In the run-up negotiations to the State Treaty, Austria was forced, unjustifiably, to share the responsibility for Hitler's ambitions and atrocities and share the "collective guilt", which obviously was not Austria's creation.

After the fall of Hitlerite Germany in 1945, Austria had to struggle for ten years to regain the national sovereignty it had lost in 1938, despite the declaration of Austria's independence and the re-establishment of a 'Democratic Republic of Austria' on 27 April 1945 by the Provisional National Government headed by Karl Renner, at the end of War in Europe.[2] This was largely due to the fact that although the allied forces had liberated Austria from the German occupation 1945, it put Austria instantly into the vortex of cold war power politics. As the liberation of Austria was achieved jointly by the Western and the Soviet forces, they refused to vacate Austria after the liberation and remained as occupation forces, making Austria a laboratory for their cold war experiments. Owing to its significant geographical location and the final positioning of the Western and the Soviet occupation forces, the fault line of the cold war passed not only through the heart of Germany but through the heart of Austria as well. The fact that the Soviet Union had instantly recognized the new national coalition government formed by Karl Renner caused suspicion in the minds of other allied occupation powers whether Austria would function as a Soviet outpost in Central Europe and establish communism in Austria. Therefore, in the post-war period Austria became the first testing ground of big power politics. The ideas that had been thrown up and the diplomatic moves and counter moves that entailed during the prolonged negotiations for the State Treaty had a direct bearing on the big power's future plans for Europe. Therefore, Austria's decade-long relentless struggle to regain its sovereignty has received world-wide attention including in the newly independent India.

A controversial issue that cropped up during the negotiations for the State Treaty was the extent of responsibility Austria should be apportioned for the damages caused by Hitler's war machine and the amount of compensation it should be made to pay in the form of war reparations. While the Soviet Foreign Minister V. M. Molotov was keen that Austria should not go unpunished for the damages it, as part of Hitler's war machine, had caused to the Soviet Union, the Americans and the British did not agree to such a proposition. As a result, though Joseph Stalin temporarily relented on the question of war reparations from Austria, he stuck to his claim for Germany's external assets in the Soviet occupation zone in Austria and brought under its ambit assets which really belonged to Austria. In this context, Austria's argument that it had no responsibility for the damages since it was annexed by Germany before the war, was not accepted by the Soviets. In the end, Austria was not given any exemption from the war reparation claims of the Soviet Union. Unmindful of Austrian resistance, the Soviet Union, under the facade of Germany's extended assets, seized Austria's Zistersdorfer oil fields and other industrial establishments and shifted their plants and machinery to the Soviet Union. Indeed, the sharp disagreements that surfaced between the Soviet Union and Britain and the United States over the Soviet insistence on the shifting of Austrian plants and machinery had marked the beginning of the end of the big power cooperation and signalled the onset of the cold war. However, in the process, a settlement on Austria was delayed to the extent that it made Chancellor Karl Renner observe that the State Treaty was delayed because 'the powers are negotiating over Austria, but they are dealing with Europe.'[3] Therefore, although agreements have been reached on major issues, for three years between 1949 and 1951, the big powers, in order to prolong their occupation, refused to engage in serious negotiations on Austria to end their occupation. Under those circumstances, in order to end the impasse, Brazil, Mexico, Lebanon and The Netherlands took the initiative and sponsored a resolution in the UN General Assembly and forced the Assembly in November 1952 to discuss the issue of the end of occupation and restoration of the sovereignty of Austria. Following this, the General Assembly passed a resolution in favour of starting negotiations to find a fruitful solution.

India's role as an interlocutor between Austria and the Soviet Union came during this phase of negotiations that followed the UN resolution. In 1953, the Austrian Foreign Minister, Karl Gruber, met the Indian Prime Minister, Jawaharlal Nehru, at the famous Swiss tourist spot, Bürgenstock, and requested that he uses his good offices to quickly get the Soviet Union to the conference table to negotiate Austria's State Treaty. Gruber asked Nehru to find out from the Soviet Union whether Moscow would accept a neutral Austria.[4] As a follow up to this request, K. P. S. Menon, India's Ambassador to the Soviet Union, discussed the matter with the Soviet Foreign Minister V. M. Molotov in Moscow. During the discussion, Molotov indicated that if Austria chose to stay away from military pacts and would not provide foreign military bases in Austria, it would not be difficult to find a solution to the problem of Austria. Thus, Moscow made it explicit that neutrality would be the policy the Soviet Union would like to see Austria following.[5]

Obviously, Moscow wanted to keep Austria away from the West and wanted it to remain neutral between the east and the west. Austria accepted the line indicated by Molotov to K. P. S. Menon. Chancellor Julius Raab did not take much time, thereafter, to formally adopt neutrality for Austria so that the State Treaty could be concluded expeditiously and the country's sovereignty could be restored quickly. In the words of Bruno Kreisky: 'In 1953 Foreign Minister Gruber had what I consider to have been a most original idea, that of using Nehru, whose friendly attitude towards Austria was well-known, as a mediator in the State Treaty negotiations: he was to sound out the Russian attitude to Austria's adoption of neutrality.'[6]

Obviously, Austria turned to India for help and assistance as an interlocutor between the Soviet Union and itself for two reasons. Firstly, India had the reputation of a credible non-aligned country which, after independence, chose to follow an independent foreign and security policy by staying away from bloc politics. Indeed, India's non-aligned approach was an attractive proposition for Austria as well. Secondly, India by then had established a cordial relationship with the Soviet Union and Moscow had begun to appreciate India's non-aligned position as a contribution towards promotion of peace, reconciliation and international understanding. However, undoubtedly, India's friendly intervention with the Soviet Union in favour of Austria had helped the early resumption of serious negotiations for Austria's State Treaty.

It may be noted that though Moscow was agreeable to Austria's neutrality, it continued to couple the settlement of the Austrian problem with the simultaneous settlement of the German problem, a proposition which Austria vehemently opposed.

The four powers took up Austria's State Treaty for discussion on 12 February 1954, in which the Austrian Foreign Minister Leopold Figl made a fervent appeal to the big four to give Austria the State Treaty and contribute to a genuine relaxation of tensions in international relations and to the preservation of security in Europe.[7] But Molotov was still arguing that the troop withdrawal from Austria should be linked to the conclusion of a peace treaty with Germany. Austria was upset over this continued Soviet attempt to delay the State Treaty. With the support of the United States, Austria rejected the Soviet demand.[8] However, in the final round of bilateral talks with the Soviet Union in April 1955, prior to the conclusion of the State Treaty, Austria made it clear that it would follow a policy of military neutrality after it attained independence. And, for its part, the Soviet Union had agreed to withdraw its troops from Austria soon after the State Treaty came into effect.[9] The *modus operandi* finally agreed upon was that the four powers would restore Austria's sovereignty first, and, afterwards, Austria would declare neutrality subsequently on its own. Indeed, Austria insisted that its neutrality should be a self-proclaimed policy of the Austrian government. And it was accepted. The Austrian State Treaty was signed on 15 May 1955.[10] Significantly, the treaty did not mention Austria's neutrality. Following the conclusion of the State Treaty, the Austrian government voluntarily declared Austria's 'perpetual neutrality' and pledged not to enter into any military alliance nor allow the establishment of any foreign military base on its territory.[11]

From the angle of the peace process in Europe, the Austrian State Treaty marked the beginning of detente in East-West relations, provided a framework for conflict resolution and improved the prospects of East-West accord on many outstanding issues through multilateral negotiations. It also raised the hope that the vexed German problem could also be resolved peacefully in the same manner through negotiations. However, on the role India had played during the negotiations for the Austrian State Treaty, a former Austrian Ambassador to India, Wolfgang Schallenberg, observed:

> It was India, which gave us important diplomatic assistance in the earlier stages of the negotiations for a State Treaty. In 1953, the Austrian Foreign Minister Gruber met Prime Minister Nehru in Switzerland and requested him to find out in Moscow whether an offer of Austria's neutrality would be useful in the context of the current negotiations on Austria's future. This request was addressed to India because of the good relations it had with Austria and with the Soviet Union, because of its non-alignment and because of the high international reputation of Jawaharlal Nehru himself. Nehru acceded to our request and upon his instructions the Indian Ambassador to Moscow, K. P. S. Menon, discussed the case of Austria with the Soviet Foreign Minister Molotov, pointing out that India felt an Austrian undertaking not to allow foreign military bases or to conclude any military alliance could form a basis for the Soviet Union agreeing to an Austrian State Treaty. To this Molotov was said to have replied that a solemn declaration of Austrian neutrality, though of undoubted value, would not be sufficient for a withdrawal of the Soviet troops. The Indian initiative was, therefore, not crowned with success, but we shall always remember with gratitude the assistance India gave us in our struggle for independence. [12]

III

In the developing countries, Austria enjoys a high reputation which no other developed country of Europe enjoys. There are solid reasons for it. Apart from the natural affinity generated by Austria's active neutrality policy and the non-alignment pursued by most of the developing countries, Austria's relentless espousal of the causes of the developing countries since 1960s has earned it a special place in the hearts of the developing countries. Austria's initiative to support Third World causes began to unfold soon after the conclusion of the Austrian State Treaty in 1955, and after it had completed its annual war reparation payments, worth $ 45 billion, to the Soviet Union over six years from 1955. Bruno Kreisky, in his various capacities – first as the State Secretary in the Ministry of Foreign Affairs then as the Foreign Minister, and finally as the Federal Chancellor – became the torch bearer of Austria's policy towards the developing countries. The preliminary ground for a major Austrian initiative in this regard was prepared by Bruno Kreisky, then State Secretary, when he told the Congress of the Austrian Socialist Party (SPÖ) on 14 May 1958: 'We are opposing the exploitation of peoples by other peoples. But today this is no longer enough. ... We have to assist the peoples fighting for their independence to develop their economies, to increase their standard of living.'[13]

Austria did not formulate any clear policy towards the problems of the developing countries until it took the initiative in 1962 to establish the Vienna Institute for Development to focus on the problems of development in the Third World. The impetus for it came in December 1961 when the United Nations designated the 1960s as the First Development Decade. Soon after, Austria took the initiative to organize an International Conference of eminent personalities, drawn from both developed and developing countries, to deliberate on the question of economic cooperation and partnership between the developed and developing countries. This conference, which was held in July 1962 in Salzburg and Vienna, came out with an important document entitled the 'Vienna Declaration of Cooperation for the Furthering of Economic Development.' The preamble of this Declaration stated that the continuance 'of the conditions of poverty, misery, disease and degradation for two-thirds of the human race' was 'the most urgent problem of our times.' The Declaration observed: 'While the income of this fortunate third of humanity continues to increase, the underdeveloped world continues to stagnate, thus widening rapidly the already large gap that exists between the poor nations.' It added:

> We regard the continuance of this state of affairs as immoral. The kind of inequality that exists between nations would never be permitted within the frontiers of a modern progressive nation-state; for the human conscience no longer tolerates the provision of luxuries for a few when the many are deprived of necessities. ... There are enough resources in the world today ... to wipe off poverty from the face of the earth. We believe that it is the inescapable obligation of the whole of humanity, whether rich or poor, to cooperate in this task. [14]

Stating that the world has become 'too small for fellow feeling between man and man to stop at political frontiers', the Declaration said that the developed countries had an obligation to extend support to the developing countries for their development by providing them with the needed resources. They should be helped in selling their products 'by removing the barriers that are now placed in their way in the markets of the developed countries'. It also pleaded for providing capital assistance to the developing countries 'so that non-commercial capital transfers reach the minimum level of the one per cent of the total combined national income of the developed countries'.[15]

The establishment of the Vienna Institute for Development as a 'public relations institute on development issues which could inform the world about the real problems' was the immediate follow up of this international conference.[16] Since its establishment, the Vienna Institute for Development has done commendable work in focusing the problems of development of the developing countries, besides adding to the image of Austria as a country which has made genuine efforts to concretize a concerted global strategy to promote the development of the developing countries.

International solidarity was the general framework under which Austria tried to harness international support for the development of the Third World. The model around which the Austrian effort revolved was the Marshall Plan, launched in 1948 by the United States to rebuild war-ravaged Europe, and the *modus operandi* it had followed. It is significant that the basic idea that gave birth to the Marshall Plan had also sprouted from the fertile mind of an Austrian Social Democratic leader, Otto Bauer, who, in order to meet the Great Depression in Europe, made a proposal in 1931 to adopt an international public loan system. Pointing at the vast unutilized resources lying idle in countries like the United States, France and some other European countries, Bauer suggested:

> Vast capital is not being utilized to advantage in the United States of America, in France and in the neutral European countries and, while it is not being used, the national economy of Central Europe is desperately in need of such capital. Undoubtedly, one of the most effective methods of controlling the world crisis and unemployment would be to redirect this capital into production, thereby reviving the latter. [17]

Although the idea embedded in this suggestion was not taken up immediately by the then captains of the global economy, the idea became attractive following the devastation Europe suffered due to the Second World War, and it gave birth to the Marshall Plan — a pioneering international solidarity programme the people of the United States offered to the people of Europe. Of course, the Marshall Plan was a great success as an act of international solidarity, and it was implemented without offending the susceptibilities of the recipient countries. Bruno Kreisky, both as Austria's Foreign Minister and later as the Federal Chancellor, made laudatory references to the success of the Marshall Plan, and pleaded for a similar approach to bring about the development of the developing countries. As early as 1958, when he was still State Secretary, Kreisky said: 'We have experienced a grandiose act of international solidarity in the form of the Marshall Plan, and I want to state that we will soon have to be prepared for an even bigger act of grandiose intemational solidarity.' [18]

Soon after the Vienna Declaration, Austria's Foreign Minister, Bruno Kreisky, spoke on 17 September 1962 in the United States at the Economic Club of Detroit on the subject: 'What are the Possibilities for Worldwide Economic Cooperation?' He urged the developed countries to foresee the potential opportunities cooperation between the developed and the developing countries would generate for everybody. He said: 'We would be confronted with a boundless development in world trade if we found the philosopher's stone which could give Asians and Africans a higher purchasing power. ... Only if we succeed in raising the standard of living for a billion people, who suffer bitterly from the consequences of underconsumption to a level which would make them modest consumers – if we succeed through our partnership to transfer a part of our buying power to them, will there be created new, nearly inexhaustible possibilities and markets.'[19] He said that this could not be done merely through grants. 'This can only be done by helping these countries to build up their infrastructure to rationalize their agriculture, and to construct new, adequate industries there.'[20] He said further: 'I believe that we ought to be clear about one thing: all this is only possible when we are ready to invest in those parts of the world where rentability has to be measured with other standards than we use in our developed economy. But this is primarily a political, not an economic question.'[21] He observed: 'The most important question is whether the political leaders of the rich countries will succeed in convincing their peoples that they must dedicate a larger part of their national income to conquer hunger and disease in Asia and Africa.'[22] Acknowledging that Americans had pioneered the international solidarity programme through the Marshall Plan, he told his American audience: 'By your assistance you have initiated the first steps toward a new idea: The economic integration of Europe. Now since we are more prosperous we understand that we, too, have to participate in this task.'[23]

Underlining the significance of the Marshall Plan, he said in 1978: 'When the European economy lay in ruins after the Second World War, when we were standing practically on the edge of an economic abyss, the people of the United States decided to undertake a great, I would almost say a gigantic programme of assistance to the shattered economies of Europe. At that time vast resources were made available to us. ...'[24] In 1965, in a speech at Dallas, he said that the industrialized countries should come up with a realistic global programme of action 'which could mean to the developing countries as much as the Marshall Plan meant to European States.'[25] In 1968, when he was out of office, Kreisky wrote that there was need to 'establish cooperation with the Third World and bring about the measure if international solidarity which is needed if the hunger in the world is to be abated.'[26] He reminded the developed countries that if Europe was set on its feet economically by the Marshall Plan, it was incumbent on the developed countries of Europe to 'make up their minds to carry out a similar programme for the Third World countries'.[27] The basic policy the Austrian government had adopted on the question of development assistance for the Third World was explicit in two policy declarations the Federal Chancellor made in 1971 and 1979. In a policy statement, made in 1971, the government declared:

> Since this phenomenon [development assistance] will probably be applicable to most European industrialized nations alike, it might be worth-while to consider preparation of a concept as an initiative of the government of Austria which, based on experiences of the Marshall Plan, makes available to developing countries so-called drawing rights within the framework of an overall European plan – initially within the framework of OECD – which would permit developing countries to cover their requirements of essential commodities, notably capital goods, in those countries which take part in such a Plan. The obligation to extend know-how would, of course, be part of it.
>
> We believe that in times of extreme prosperity little room exists for such considerations. However, in periods, in which idle capacities exist, such considerations gain substantial economic importance. Thus, development assistance might very well be economically motivated as one among the anti-recessional policy instruments.[28]

In a similar policy declaration made in Parliament on 19 June 1979, the Federal Chancellor stated:

> Austria considers development assistance policy an instrument of international cooperation. In this she is guided by the principles of partnership and solidarity, whose objectives consist in lessening existing dependencies without creating new ones, in reducing differences in social and economic levels and in promoting self-determination of developing countries and of their people. Austria will continue to work for a comprehensive international programme, which would assist the developing countries in the rapid development of their infrastructure.[29]

The core idea of Kreisky's New Marshall Plan was the use of counterpart funds generated by the sale of goods and services from the developed countries, and also from the petroleum exporting countries, for the economic development of the recipient developing countries. On the New Marshall Plan, an Indian newspaper wrote:

> ... by broaching the 'Kreisky Plan', moderate and neutral Austria has at least acknowledged the need for a suitable mechanism for funding Third World development. The Austrian Chancellor has expressed his country's willingness to inaugurate a pilot scheme under his plan in association with other advanced and OPEC countries. As a statement of intentions, the 'Kreisky Plan' is unexceptionable and it strives valiantly to lift the issue of Third World industrialization above the current North-South polemics. But one cannot visualise any takers for it at this stage. Will the OPEC, for instance, agree to the creation of counterpart development funds in oil-importing developing countries by the sale of oil?[30]

Clearly, Austria's emphasis was on concerted global action. Its concern for the development of the developing countries was voiced on 31 July 1975 when 35 Heads of Government assembled in Helsinki at a summit meeting of the Conference on Security and Cooperation in Europe to sign the Helsinki Final Act. After noting how inadequate the quantum of development assistance the developed rich countries had extended to the Third World was, the Austrian Chancellor urged the leaders of the developed world:

> Here the industrialized states must be prepared to make far greater efforts, must make it their goal to set up infrastructures in the developing countries to preserve the people of those countries from starvation

> and misery. ... I am convinced that we could all fulfil these commitments if they were part of a great continental concerted operation. Only thus shall we be able economically to strengthen the developing countries and raise them to the level where it will be possible for them to enter into a real partnership with the industrialized world.[31]

Why did Austria choose to articulate its thought on Third World development under the framework of a new 'Marshall Plan for the Third World.'? Bruno Kreisky, the main architect of this idea, gave the following four reasons:

> It was firstly because I hoped to arouse the interest of the United States by suggesting that it was time to set our sights on a variant of the Marshall Plan; secondly because I thought that within the framework of a global idea it might be possible to achieve a far greater degree of European commitment; thirdly because it seemed to me that some of the arrangements for repayment used for the Marshall Plan would work equally well in the case of the developing countries; and fourthly because I believe that bilateral development aid, as practised in exemplary fashion by the Scandinavian countries, Holland and Belgium, is indispensable, but that many projects are beyond the means of individual countries. I would also like to mention in this context that I have for many years actively opposed the West's lending policy, because for a number of reasons I consider it inappropriate and not always morally defensible.[32]

Austria gave highest importance to the building up of infrastructures in the developing countries. It believed that the most essential prerequisite for the development of the developing countries was to equip them with infrastructures.

Therefore, a primary objective of the development assistance should be to help the developing countries to build infrastructures. As a measure to deal with economic crises, Austria favoured 'large-scale international action in which the industrialized world – being immensely rich – is prepared to help to build the infrastructures of the Third World on a continental scale in a planned way in order to give employment to the people of these countries, to create opportunities to develop their resources, by assisting them to increase their agricultural output through enlarging irrigation facilities, by developing their transport systems, by enabling them to use their energy reserves'.[33] It held the view that 'global economic and political cooperation is only possible if the industrialized states are able, through large-scale joint actions, to assist in building up the infrastructure in the broadest sense of the word, ranging from building of a sub-continental railway system to the development of telecommunication. ... If the economies of the Third World nations are to be placed on a sound footing and if industrialization is to be promoted, the prime requisite is the development of the infrastructure'.[34] At the UNIDO Conference in New Delhi in 1980, the Austrian Chancellor said: 'The economically developed countries have a duty to render the countries of the Third World decisive assistance in developing their infrastructure, because that is the only way in which they will be enabled to achieve their own economic goals and exploit their wealth to the full. Also, that is the only way in which they will be increasingly able to gain equality as partners of the industrialized nations.'[35] He reasoned his proposition by arguing 'that the modernization of an economy is less risky and has more lasting results when it is accomplished on the basis of a well developed infrastructure. A sound infrastructure has to reduce the costs of industrial production: its establishment and operation provide better service to broader groups of the population and less considerable impetus to the economy'.[36] He added:

... the development of a modern infrastructure also creates employment, income and prosperity for a large number of people. The international community should therefore devote itself more than ever before to these great tasks and make a special effort to promote establishment of infrastructural facilities in the developing countries.'[37]

Austria gave special attention to the nitty-gritty of raising adequate funds for the development of infrastructure in the developing countries. In this context, it found the terms and conditions, and the methodology followed by the Marshall Plan satisfactory and viable as it was offered to the recipients without imposing any political conditions, and that the 'counterpart funds generated by payments in the national currency of the recipient state for goods and services supplied would accumulate and would then be available to that state for other economic purposes ... as a result of the re-circulation of funds that went on year after year, the original aid was perpetuated and fed back into the economy again.':[38] The Chancellor said:

> We fully appreciate the fact that infrastructural development on a large scale in developing countries calls for the expenditure of vast sums of money, and it will be no easy task to raise these funds. Even if we endeavour to use existing financial institutions to the widest possible extent, the establishment of a special mechanism for cooperation cannot be ruled out altogether. This idea might perhaps be put into effect more readily if the funds could be raised through joint action by the industrialized and the oil exporting countries, naturally referring to all industrialized countries.[39]

That was the thoroughness with which Austria drew up the blueprint for the development of the developing countries. Pertinently, Austria also referred to the movements of capital between Europe and North America, which had led to the accumulation of 'considerable amounts of US dollars outside the United States.' Austria favoured the use of 'part of this "overhang" of US dollars for low-cost development financing' and make available to the developing countries in the form of loans 'at interest rates attractive for the developing countries.'[40]

But, subsequently the Chancellor expressed dissatisfaction over the piecemeal approach based on bilateral aid. He told the UN General Assembly in 1979: 'I feel that something is lacking in this (North-South) dialogue; namely, a "grand design" based upon strong feeling of responsibility and international solidarity, from which everything else would follow.'[41] He said, for Austria, the North-South cooperation 'concerns us in Europe as much as it does those who come from other continents'.[42] He said: 'Should a large scale multinational action of the North come about, Austria will certainly shoulder the part which will be due to her on the basis of her national product and her economic strength.'[43]

Austria tried to drive at home the point that the development of the developing countries would be in the long-term interests of the developed countries as well. In this context, Austria pointed out that the developed countries would find development assistance for the developing countries attractive and economically motivated as it could be one of their 'anti-recessional policy instruments'.[44] In other words, a large-scale economic solidarity programme with the developing countries would be in the interest of the developed countries as well since it would enable them to preserve domestic employment, along with growth and prosperity. Austria believed that in the ultimate analysis, although the development of the developing countries might appear to be a dominant economic issue, it primarily is a political task.[45]

Austria's constant drive to promote development cooperation between the developed and the developing countries gave no mean inspiration for the launching of a movement in the West in favour of an institutionalized North-South dialogue towards the establishment of a New International Economic Order and for providing the necessary philosophical foundation for it. One may find that the broad line that was generally followed by the Brandt Commission on North-South Cooperation was largely the one that was espoused by Austria and its Chancellor Bruno Kreisky. Therefore, Austria not only took keen interest in the deliberations of the Brandt Commission on North-South Cooperation, it also took keen interest in the follow up measures and worked hard to convene the North-South summit at Cancun (in Mexico) in 1981.

The proposal for the North-South summit was made by the Brandt Commission Report.[46] Subsequently, the Commission Chairman, Willy Brandt, asked the Austrian Chancellor Bruno Kreisky to organize the summit. Along with Lopez Portillo, President of Mexico, as co-chairman, Bruno Kreisky took measures to organize the summit – an International Meeting on Cooperation and Development – at Cancun in 1981. The preparations for the summit were made in Austria, and two preparatory meetings were also held in Vienna – one in November 1980 and the other in March 1981 – both under the chairmanship of the Austrian Chancellor. At the insistence of President Lopez Portillo and Chancellor Kreisky, Austria's Foreign Minister Willibald Pahr invited Foreign Ministers of four developed countries - Germany, France, Canada and Sweden - and six developing countries - Nigeria, Algeria, Mexico, Tanzania, India and Yugoslavia - to Vienna 'to consider the possibility of convening an International Meeting on Cooperation and Development at the level of Heads of State/Government'.[47] The Press Release issued on 8 November 1980, after the first meeting of the Foreign Ministers, said:

> ... problems of cooperation and development need to be given urgent attention at the highest political

> level. The proposed meeting would, therefore, be political in character, informal in its proceedings, comprehensive in its scope and adequately prepared. The meeting would not be a negotiating forum, rather it would be oriented towards an exchange of views leading, *inter alia,* to a greater understanding and a deeper appreciation of interdependence among nations, its relevance, importance, and implications.[48]

The second meeting of Foreign Ministers, held in Vienna on 13 March 1981, decided to hold the summit at Cancun (Mexico) on 22-23 October 1981 and finalized the list of the Heads of State/Government to be invited to it. The countries thus invited to the summit were: Algeria, Austria, Bangladesh, Guyana, India, Ivory Coast, Japan, Mexico, Nigeria, Philippines, Saudi Arabia, Sweden, Tanzania, United Kingdom, United States of America, Venezuela and Yugoslavia. Further, they decided 'to convey to the Soviet Union their wish for the participation of its Head of State/ Government at the summit.'[49]

The summit meeting was held at Cancun (Mexico) on 22-23 October 1981. It was obvious that Austria and its Chancellor Bruno Kreisky's main objective at the summit was to get the summit's endorsement for their pet idea of a New Marshall Plan for the Third World. But, unfortunately, due to illness, Chancellor Kreisky could not attend, or chair, the summit. In his place, Pierre Trudeau, Canada's Prime Minister, presided over the summit. Kreisky's absence proved costly for the summit, and it made a lot of difference in its outcome. No doubt, if Kreisky had presided over the summit, its outcome would have been markedly different. However, that happened to be the first and last North-South summit. Although, at the policy level, Austria's interest in the development of the developing countries remained intact during the Chancellorship of Fred Sinowatz, its priority in the government's agenda receded during the Chancellorship of Franz Vranitzky. After 1986, Austria's foreign policy converged increasingly towards the neighbouring states and to the European Community, particularly towards the issue of Austria's membership in the European Community. The issue of the development of the Third Word received less and less attention. During this period there was no appreciable improvement in Austria's ODA level. Despite this shift in Austria's priorities, Austria's image as a friend of the Third World remained undiminished.

Another Third World problem to which Austria paid attention was the debt crisis of the developing countries. On this issue, Austria held the view that the poor developing countries should be relieved of their international debt burden and be given a real chance to develop. Fred Sinowatz, who succeeded Bruno Kreisky as the Chancellor of Austria in 1983 and who was still following the policies pursued by his predecessor towards the Third World, said that behind the debt crisis 'we find a terrible and most bitter form of dependence where a state is no longer the master of its own economic development, and its people can no longer benefit as they should from the fruits of their labour.'[50] His successor Franz Vranitzky held similar views.[51] However, though out of office, Bruno Kreisky continued to express Austria's concern for the debt problem of the poor countries. In 1984, he warned the Europeans over the reluctance of the rich countries to write off their loans to the poor countries. He said: 'Let's be quite frank about it: the industrial countries – this is my view – will have to write off a good deal of that money. Through their unrest and continuous conflicts, the thousands of millions of starving people will very soon create a situation in which our Western world will be in danger. According to this view, a system of economic cooperation has to be built up in good time, and very efficient sacrifices have to be made by the Western industrial states. We are on the point of becoming the victims of our own false conceptions.'[52] In an interview with the author Bruno Kreisky underlined that the rich countries could afford it: 'We are rich enough', he said.[53]

In addition to these expressions of solidarity with the developing countries on the issue of their development, Austria simultaneously took the initiative to expand its diplomatic ties with the developing countries. Indeed, during the Chancellorship of Bruno Kreisky between 1970 and 1983, Austria opened twelve new embassies in Asia, Africa and Latin America and stepped up interactions with the developing countries of these regions.

IV

In the post-war period Austria had a lively interaction with one of the most important countries of the Third World – India. Indeed, in any Austrian analysis pertaining to development issues, like the need to build up infrastructure, etc. India figured prominently as a reference point. This was particularly true during what is known as the Kreisky era. India's non-aligned position had considerably facilitated this interaction between Austria and India and became quite useful during the negotiations for the Austrian State Treaty. As mentioned earlier, in its endeavour to conclude the State Treaty early, Austria made use of India's good offices in 1953 as a friendly interlocutor to ascertain the likely response of the Soviet Union if Austria opted for a policy of neutrality. The encouraging response which India got from the Soviet Union was conveyed to Austria promptly and became an important input, at a critical time, in Austria's foreign policy formulation. In a pointed reference to the Indian contribution in this regard, the Austrian Chancellor Bruno Kreisky said, during his visit to India in 1980 when Austria was celebrating the 25th anniversary of its independence, that he 'should like to recall once again Jawaharlal Nehru, whose government's willingness to assist us in 1953 during the international negotiations for the conclusion of an Austrian State Treaty is still very much in our mind. India was among the first who recognized our neutrality'.[54] In an interview he said: 'Now ... in a retrospective way I have the impression that Nehru made a tremendous contribution for us in being ready to accept his role as a mediator because in doing so he confronted the Soviets for the first time with our idea of neutrality.'[55] After the conclusion of the Austrian State Treaty in 1955 and the restoration of Austria's sovereignty, barring an aberration during the period of internal Emergency in India between 1975 and 1977, the relationship between Austria and India remained close, friendly and respectful. As Kreisky said: 'On the political level India's significant role in non-alignment and Austria's permanent neutrality offered ... many points of contact for a closer working together in the international field. ...'[56]

For about three-and-a-half decades, a live wire of Austria's close relationship with India was the former Austrian Chancellor Bruno Kreisky. And he had assiduously nurtured this relationship by interlocking both the official and personal relationships he had maintained with the Indian political leaders. Being a Social Democrat who supported freedom of colonies, Kreisky watched with interest India's freedom struggle, which 'excited' him a great deal. Moreover, over the years he had developed a bond of 'admiration and respectful friendship' for Jawaharlal Nehru.[57] To quote Kreisky:

> Nehru had become one of my mentors at a very early stage. ... The living symbol of the liberation of India was Mahatma Gandhi; the way in which he conducted his campaign, non-violently, quietly, apparently passively, was no doubt far more in tune with the attitude of mind of the Indian people than was Nehru's *realpolitik*. Nevertheless, for good or for ill, it was Nehru who played the major role in the creation

> of the State of India. He was certainly the figure whom from the start I found most fascinating.[58]

He wrote further: 'The anti-colonial movement produced some strange effects. At times it even led the subject people to cooperate with enemies of the colonial power. The Indian Subhas Chandra Bose, for instance, for a long time supported Hitler's war policy ....'[59] Besides, Kreisky had a first hand knowledge about the resurgent India, on the one hand, and the widespread drudgery still persisting in the country on the other. He visited the famous Bhakra Nangal Hydro-Electric project – an artery of industrial development and agricultural growth in North India – in 1963. At the same time he had a direct exposure to the appalling living conditions in the slum dwellings of Bombay. In the company of his Indian Socialist friend, Nath Pai, MP, who was in Vienna for many years as the Secretary-General of the IUSY and who was married to an Austrian woman, Christl, Bruno Kreisky ventured a night-walk through the streets of Bombay. In his memoirs, Kreisky recorded his impressions of this walk: 'I was deeply shocked by our nocturnal walk through Bombay: some Indian police men walked ahead of us with long batons, making the people who were sleeping on the ground at least leave us space to pass. The terrible poverty of the masses in that city and the silence in the squares did not fail to have an effect on our discussion.'[60] The point is that there was a good deal of understanding in Austria's political circles about the socio-econornic and political developments in India.

India's views received due respect in Austrian political circles. When the United Nations in 1961 declared the 1960s as the First Development Decade, Austria took the initiative in 1962 to establish the Vienna Institute for Development to focus on the problems of development of the Third World and make Vienna a centre of activities in support of the development of the developing countries. And ultimately, the aims, objectives and the character of the Vienna Institute for Development were considerably attuned to the lines which India had suggested. According to Bruno Kreisky:

> During my visit to India in 1963 Nehru had advised me not to direct the efforts of the Vienna Institute towards concrete development projects but to create a kind of public relations institute on development issues which could inform the world about the real problems. This would not then impose a responsibility on Austria to give development aid herself. That should be done by other states which were very much richer than Austria. It would be better not to set up a purely Austrian institute but one which many nations were involved. ... Nevertheless he supported the proposal to call the institute the Vienna Institute.[61]

A close look at the working of the Vienna Institute will reveal how close its activities are with the suggestions Nehru made to then Foreign Minister Bruno Kreisky. The special position Austria enjoyed in New Delhi was discernible in an instance, which Kreisky fondly remembered, in which Prime Minister Jawaharlal Nehru, in an unusual gesture to demonstrate India's close relationship with Austria and much to the surprise of all the diplomats in New Delhi, attended a dinner hosted at the Austrian Embassy in New Delhi on 7 November 1963, in honour of Kreisky. On the event Kreisky wrote: 'In his speech in which he displayed a profound knowledge of Austro-Marxism, Nehru paid tribute to me in a way which I found deeply moving; he obviously knew that I was under heavy attack from the People's Party at the time and so made a special point of emphasising his cordial relationship with me.'[62] The point, however, is that apart from the official and formal relationship, which is true of India's relationship with most other European countries, except Britain, the relationship between Austria and India had the underpinning of close personal ties between the political personalities of both countries. One may find the maintenance of that close personal friendship, along with official ties throughout the period when Bruno Kreisky was in office, whether as the State Secretary, or as the Foreign Minister, or as the Federal Chancellor, which lend the relationship between the two countries a specialness which is rare in India's relationship with other countries of Europe. As a result their requests received sympathetic consideration in each other's capital. For instance, when Austria contested for a seat in the UN Security Council in 1970, the Austrian Chancellor sought India's support. He prefaced his letter to the Indian Prime Minister by saying: 'Encouraged by the friendly spirit which distinguishes relations between the two countries', and ended it by saying: 'I do so in the fraternal spirit of our common political aims', and in view of 'the great prestige which she [India] enjoys in the Third World'. He wrote further: 'As a neutral country, Austria cannot for obvious reasons count on the support of certain countries belonging to the great alliances of either the West or the East. The success of Austria's application is therefore intimately linked with the support given by the countries of the Third World.'[63] In response, the Indian Prime Minister wrote:

> I need hardly assure you of the regard and esteem in which we hold you personally and the value we attach to the warm and friendly relationship with Austria. The various considerations you have urged in support of Austria's candidature for the Security Council have led us to decide to give our support to it. ... I have no doubt that Austria's participation in the deliberations of the Security Council will be conducive to the cause of peace in the world.[64]

Ten years later, in September 1980, the Indian Prime Minister Indira Gandhi, in a letter to Chancellor Kreisky, sought Austria's support for T. N. Kaul's candidature for UNESCO's Executive Board .[65] Austria readily agreed. In reply, the Austrian Chancellor wrote: 'I have pleasure in informing you that the Austrian delegation to the General Conference of UNESCO had been instructed to support the candidature of Mr. Kaul.'[66] Austria was one of those countries in the West that had shown great understanding of the tremendous problems the Bangladesh crisis had created for India. Pertinently, the crisis erupted when the leaders of West Pakistan, such as President Yahya Khan and Zulfikar Ali Bhutto, who was also a leading contestant for prime ministership, refused to hand over power to the majority leader, Sheikh Mujibur Rahman, from East Pakistan, whose party, the Awami League, won an absolute majority in National Assembly of the undivided Pakistan. Instead of inviting Sheikh Mujibur Rahman to form the government, the West Pakistani power elite imposed military rule and unleashed repression and committed genocide in East Pakistan. This had resulted in the influx of 10 million refugees from East Pakistan to the neighbouring Indian state and caused severe strain on the Indian economy. In view of this mounting problem, the Indian Prime Minister Indira Gandhi sent a personal emissary, Moinul Huque Choudhury, to Vienna with a personal letter to Chancellor Bruno Kreisky to appraise him of the problems India was facing due to Pakistan's action in East Pakistan. In her letter the Indian Prime Minister wrote: 'The two problems – Pakistan's war on the people of East Bengal and its impact on us in the form of millions of refugees – cannot be separated.'[67] She wrote: 'In this grim situation, I feel I am entitled to seek the advice of all friendly governments on how they would wish us to deal with the problem .'[68] Underlining that 'the loyalty of a people to a State cannot be enforced at gun point,' she wrote to Kreisky:

> I believe that the Government of Austria under your wise and humane leadership, is interested in peace

> and stability of the sub-continent and its evolution along democratic lines. I have no doubt that you are giving thought to the long-term consequences of the events in East Bengal. In the meantime, it is our earnest hope that the Government of Austria will impress upon the rulers of Pakistan that they owe a duty towards their own citizens whom they have treated so callously and forced to seek refuge in a foreign country. It is also our earnest hope that the voice of Austria and the prestige it enjoys in the community of nations will be used to persuade the military rulers of Pakistan to recognize that the solution they have chosen for their problem in East Pakistan is unwise and untenable. ... If you consider sending any message to the President of Pakistan, we would appreciate your taking up this matter with him.[69]

Although, due to illness, the Austrian Chancellor could not meet the personal emissary of the Indian Prime Mnister, he had adopted a sympathetic attitude and took prompt action on the letter. In his reply Kreisky wrote to Mrs. Gandhi: 'I can assure you that the Austrian Federal Government has followed with sympathetic concern these tragic developments from their very beginning. The Federal Government, and with it the Austrian people, are deeply impressed by the size of the population movement into West Bengal, and the grave problems India has to overcome in providing shelter, food and medical care to the refugees.'[70] He said that every effort should be made to reverse the refugee inflow to India 'as soon and as smoothly as possible ... by repatriating them to their homes'. In addition, as requested by the Indian Prime Mnister, 'the Austrian Government appeals through its Ambassador to the Pakistani Government to bring about an early return to normal conditions of life in East Pakistan and show mercy to East Pakistani political leaders and other persons detained or expelled in connection with the recent events in East Pakistan'. He reminded the Indian Prime Minister that 'neutral Austria always advocates a peaceful settlement in all international conflicts' and expressed the hope that 'some compromise can be found' to solve the refugee problem acceptable to both sides'.[71] Austria was one of the few Western countries which the Indian Prime Minister Indira Gandhi subsequently visited in order to personally appraise the Chancellor about the grave situation. As no peaceful solution could be found, the Bangladesh crisis led to a bloodless war between India and Pakistan in December 1971, and the war ended with the surrender of the Pakistani army to the Indian army in Bangladesh. The crisis ended with the birth of an independent Bangladesh.

Austria's relationship with India entered a troubled phase in 1975 when Prime Minister Indira Gandhi, following a court verdict which had found her guilty of electoral malpractice and unseated her from the Parliament, declared a national emergency and brought India under her dictatorship on 25 June 1975. Simultaneously, she imprisoned, without trial, 40,000 opposition leaders and activists, including Jayaprakash Narayan, the founder of the Indian socialist movement, and Morarji Desai, the veteran Gandhian. The detainees included her own Congress Party MPs who had opposed her dictatorial ways. All fundamental rights, including the citizens' right to life, were suspended. The Parliament was reduced to a cypher. And press censorship was introduced. As a freedom loving country, which valued human rights and personal freedom, and which had suffered Hitler's dictatorship for seven years from 1938 to 1945, Austria was dismayed at the way in which the Indian democracy was derailed by Indira Gandhi to usher in her personal dictatorship. Although Austria was upset over her actions, the personal friendship between the Austrian Chancellor and the Indian Prime Minister put considerable restraint on the public reaction in Austria. Therefore, Austria initially acted only through the Socialist International.[72] But this restraint was tapered off partially when George Fernandes, Chairman of the Indian Socialist Party, was arrested and detained by the Indian government in 1976 on criminal charges. Following this, the Austrian Chancellor Bruno Kreisky, along with his West German and Swedish counterparts, Willy Brandt and Olof Palme, sent a joint telegram to Indira Gandhi, appealing to her to free Fernandes from detention. But the telegram evoked an angry, rather undiplomatic, outburst from Indira Gandhi. On 30 June 1976, she wrote to Kreisky: 'It is indeed an astonishing communication for a person of your eminence to send, and I can only surmise that you have allowed yourself to accept the version of certain individuals and groups without attempting a correct assessment of the situation.' She continued:

> I am pained that you should have felt it necessary to raise your voice at the arrest of a fugitive from justice. Perhaps you are not fully aware of his activities or the threat posed to orderly government in India. Mr. Fernandes had taken it on himself to carry out an underground campaign of subversion and disruption. He has publicly claimed responsibility for numerous clandestine acts of sabotage. Would you condone use of such methods in similar circumstances? ... If the efforts to paralyze the Government of India had been allowed to succeed, the very integrity of the country would have been in peril. ... In moments of grave internal peril ... it is not unusual for certain civil liberties to be suspended. ... You have spoken of India's reputation in the democratic world. May I point out in all earnestness that many of these democratic countries had no hesitation in extending military, economic and moral support to dictatorial and authoritarian regimes on our own sub-continent as well as in other parts of the World. ... Our people

> are as mindful about their integrity as about their liberty. Any dispassionate student of the Indian scene will tell you that the overwhelming majority of the people have welcomed our actions to improve the level of responsibility in our country.[73]

In response, in a joint letter sent to Indira Gandhi on 23 July 1976, Kreisky, Brandt and Palme clarified their position that their telegram on behalf of George Fernandes 'was by no means our intention to interfere in the internal affairs' of India. 'But we wouldn't neglect to request from you to take care that the Chairman of the Socialist Party of India, George Fernandes, well known in trade union circle, is treated as a leader of an oppositional political party and not as a vulgar criminal that – if really it should be unavoidable to charge him – he gets a fair trial and a fair treatment.' The letter had noted how 'in Europe Social Democrats like ourselves have been following for a long time the fate of India with the greatest attention and with very much sympathy', and said:

> ... it is precisely this very attentiveness which moved us to call upon you, dear Mrs. Gandhi, and your government to timely prevent a development which, in our view, would do harm to your government's reputation. So we want to underline once again that it was not contempt for your country, but friendly care for one of the most important nations of the world, which made us send our telegram.[74]

Austria was generous to those who had to flee India for safety and security during the Emergency. Among those who took refuge in Austria during this period were Leila Kabir Fernandes, wife of George Fernandes, and their small son Sushanto Fernandes. In gratitude, on the eve of Chancellor Bruno Kreisky's arrival in India on 29 January 1980 for a five day official visit, in a touching hand-written letter Leila Fernandes wrote to Kreisky on 28 January 1980:

> I can never forget the warm welcome I and my 2 ½ year old son received from you and other beautiful friends in Vienna in October 1976.
> Many things have happened, to us personally, and to our country in these past three and a half years. The wheel has turned full circle ... I know that you are in India only briefly, and also that you have a very full programme. Still, I wish to express the hope that I, and Sushanto (who has now completed 6 years) will have the opportunity to meet you to renew the friendship which you offered me when the clouds were without silver linings.[75]

Indira Gandhi's dictatorship in India continued till early 1977. And George Fernandes was not released until the General Election in India was over, in March 1977, in which not only Indira Gandhi's Congress Party, but she as well, had ignominiously lost the election, while George Fernandes, who contested from prison, won it. Nevertheless, what is conspicuous is that though, through diplomatic channels, Chancellor Bruno Kreisky, along with Willy Brandt and Olof Palme, made serious efforts to have the Emergency in India lifted, Austria had refrained from making any public criticism of Indira Gandhi or any condemnatory public statement against the Emergency in India. Not only the governmental circles but even the SPÖ circles, though critical of the Emergency, also had refrained from making any public statement condemning it. This strange paradox in Austria's reaction to India's Emergency had baffled the Indian observers. When questioned on this eerie silence, Peter Jankowitsch, International Secretary of the SPÖ and a former Foreign Minister, in an interview with the author, said: 'It is possible that the Government reaction towards Emergency might have been tempered by the friendship that existed between Bruno Kreisky and Indira Gandhi. The SPÖ, however, was critical.'[76] In another interview with the present author, Bruno Kreisky explained that the Austrian Socialist Party 'did not take a view on it. It is difficult to explain it to you'. He added: 'We [Kreisky and Brandt] tried to talk about the Emergency to Mrs. Gandhi. But we were not successful. You are not satisfied with my answer. We both tried. But we were not successful in convincing Mrs. Gandhi on it.'[77]

Following the electoral defeat of Indira Gandhi in 1977, the Emergency in India was lifted and democracy restored. Thus, the relationship between Austria and India was relieved of the temporary strain it suffered during the Emergency. Since then Austria has maintained a close and friendly relationship with India, irrespective of the change of governments. Aside from that, Austria maintained a close relationship with the new Janata Party Government, headed by Morarji Desai, in which George Fernandes was also a Cabinet Minister. Kreisky maintained a warm relationship with Jayaprakash Narayan, the founder of the Indian Socialist Movement, who led the mass movement against corruption under Indira Gandhi's regime. In a message sent to Jayaprakash Narayan, which was delivered personally by Wolfgang Schallenberg, Austrian Ambassador in New Delhi, Kreisky expressed the hope that Jayaprakash Narayan, whose contributions towards democracy and social justice had earned world-wide recognition, would be able to 'continue his dedicated work for India for many years to come and strengthen freedom and democracy in the world.'[78]

Though out of office, Indira Gandhi also maintained her interaction with the Austrian Chancellor. In 1978, former Prime Minister of Pakistan, Zulfikar Ali Bhutto, was given the death sentence by the Lahore High Court for his complicity in the murder of Nawab Mohammad Ahmad, father of an Opposition Member of Parliament, on 10 November 1974 when Bhutto was the Prime Minister. The High Court found that the murder was committed as a result to a conspiracy by Prime Minister Bhutto to get rid of an Opposition MP, Ahmed Raza Kasuri 'owing to their violent political differences.' Instead of Kasuri, his father fell victim to that conspiracy. Bhutto's appeal against the verdict was dismissed by the Supreme Court of Pakistan on 6 February 1979. In a bid to stall the execution of Zulfikar Ali Bhutto, Indira Gandhi, then out of office, approached the Austrian Chancellor Bruno Kreisky and requested him to use his 'considerable influence to arouse public opinion and to persuade the Government of Pakistan to show leniency to Mr. Zulfikar Ali Bhutto.'[79] In pursuance, the Austrian Chancellor made an appeal to the Government of Pakistan 'not to execute the death sentence to which Mr. Bhutto is convicted.' Kreisky informed Indira Gandhi: 'I have done this ... because of my longstanding personal acquaintance with Mr. Bhutto and out of my general conviction that the capital punishment should be abolished.'[80] Obviously, Kreisky never thought that Bhutto was innocent.[81] However, Bhutto's death sentence was finally carried out.

After a long gap after she ceased to be the Prime Minister, Indira Gandhi sent her first letter of political nature to the Austrian Chancellor Bruno Kreisky, in May 1979. In a four page letter, dated 29 May 1979, Indira Gandhi prefaced it with a conciliatory note, saying: 'I have long wanted to write to you, but have hesitated because in the years since we met much has happened that was misinterpreted by you and it seemed that you had definitely taken sides. Yet I cannot believe that a person of your stature, who continues to uphold the great liberal traditions of Europe, could have a closed mind and would hesitate to speak up for justice.' After explaining at length the circumstances which had forced India to fight a war with Pakistan in 1971 over the crisis in Bangladesh, she wrote: 'It is our feeling, backed by many abroad, that powerful elements in Europe and America do not approve of strong leadership in the developing countries.' Then she listed her personal woes to the Austrian Chancellor:

> There could not be many cases in history when the entire governmental and administrative machinery,

> with the vast public and private funds at their command, were being used to annihilate a single individual. For more than two years, the [Morarji] Desai Government has tried to prove some corruption or other wrong-doing against me. ... Now they are reopening the case of the [L. N. Mishra] murder [which took place in January, 1975] of my staunchest and most effective supporter, whose death greatly weakened me and my party. ... A fresh enquiry is clearly in order to implicate me. The whole thing is reminiscent of Mr. Bhutto's politically motivated trial and murder.'[82]

She complained about a campaign of character assassination against her. 'People who could possibly help me are pressurised to turn against me by threats, intimidation, and inducements', and said that there was a growing feeling that 'there is only a mockery of justice in most courts.'[83] She found it strange that 'those who are deeply concerned with human rights [indirectly referring to the Socialist International] should close their eyes to the persistent persecution that is taking place in all the countries of our sub-continent, and should be willing to accept the version of their governments without any attempt to find out the truth'.[84] She told Kreisky that 'there is no law and order' in India and that 'there is simmering discontent in the armed forces also'. In the end she wrote: 'I hope I have not bored you by this long letter. I have written at length to try to give you a glimpse of what is happening in India because of my great regard for you and the feeling that you would raise your voice for justice.'[85] To this long letter, Kreisky replied that since there was the possibility of a direct meeting between them when he would be visiting New Delhi to attend the Third UNIDO Conference at the end of January 1980, 'I do not wish to go into the details of the many points you are taking up in your letter.' He informed her that 'it was George

Fernandes, passing through Vienna recently, who convinced me that I should meet with you when coming to New Delhi for the Third UNIDO conference'.[86]

Yet, answering to some points in her letter Kreisky wrote: 'You are of course quite correct in pointing out that Europeans ... use different standards in evaluating democratic conditions in other countries. India has been observed more closely – and the declaration of the state of Emergency judged more severely – precisely because it was thought that India could have done better.' He continued: 'I do not see any valid comparison with Bhutto's case where I did intervene, as you know, although I am convinced that Bhutto was responsible for some of the grave wrongdoings he had been accused of.'[87] However, by the time Chancellor Kreisky reached New Delhi on 28 January 1980 to attend the Third UNIDO Conference, there was a change of government in India, and Indira Gandhi was back in office as the Prime Minister. As a result, many issues which Indira Gandhi had raised in her letter of 29 May 1979 became either irrelevant or redundant. However, at a dinner hosted in his honour by Indira Gandhi on 31 January 1980, Kreisky observed: 'India was one of the first nations to oppose the division of the world between the super powers and their interference in the affairs of other countries. The non-aligned movement emanating from these efforts has in the meantime become an important factor in world politics. As a permanent neutral country Austria's views coincide with those of non-aligned countries.'[88]

Austria was concerned about the Soviet intervention in Afghanistan in December 1979. For Austria, India, particularly after Indira Gandhi returned to power in January 1980, once again became a friendly interlocutor with the Soviet Union. After her discussion with the Soviet Foreign Minister, Andrei Gromyko, during his visit to New Delhi, Indira Gandhi reported to Kreisky: "We urged the rapid withdrawal of Soviet troops from Afghanistan. The Soviets strongly feel that the total stoppage of assistance to insurgents on Afghanistan by Pakistan and other countries is indispensable for such a process. We recognize that any solution must fully take into account all these elements in this complicated situation."[89]

Indira Gandhi once again sought Chancellor Kreisky's intervention in favour of the Bhutto family in Pakistan who were under house arrest and later released. In June 1980 she wrote to Kreisky that 'even though Begum Bhutto and her daughter Benazir have now been released from house arrest, they and their supporters are subjected to all kinds of indignities and humiliation. Every effort is being made to suppress the Bhutto family and their cause should not go by default. Otherwise one cannot say what their fate will be'. In the letter she also wrote about genocide of the Buddhist tribals in the Chittagong Hill Tracks of Bangladesh, persecution of Mrs. Sirimavo Bandaranaike and her family and about injustice and hardship suffered by Tamil minority in Northern parts of Sri Lanka. She asked: 'Is it possible for any international organization to look into the grievances and allegations of these parties in the various countries?'

> All these different peoples are approaching me with such desperation in their eyes and voices. What can I do? Such matters can be said to be the internal concern of the respective countries. But seeing what great interest various international organizations and governments took in Indian affairs not so long ago, the reverberations of which have not ended, I thought these developments should be brought to your notice in the hope that your voice will be raised to arouse the conscience of the world.[90]

In deference to the indication contained in Indira Gandhi's letter, Kreisky should not go unnoticed: 'and I have therefore taken the liberty to passing a copy of your letter of June 9 on to Willy Brandt.'[91]

After Bruno Kreisky relinquished the Chancellorship of Austria in 1983, he tried to develop a joint approach between Austria and India on major international issues. He was perturbed over the attempts of some big powers to weaken the United Nations and its specialised agencies, by starving them of funds and so on and wanted this trend to be reversed. He wanted India to play a key role in this regard. Bruno Kreisky and Indira Gandhi discussed the matter in June 1983 when they were travelling together on their way to Alpbach. In a letter Kreisky wrote to Indira Gandhi in June 1984, after he was selected to receive the Jawaharlal Nehru Award, he recalled their conversation in June 1983. He wrote:

> You had then mentioned the selfishness and arrogance of the rich and the powerful. You were worried because their attitude was beginning to have an adverse impact on the entire international system. You were already then concerned about the cynical attacks on the U.N. and its specialised agencies, e.g. ILO, UNESCO, FAO etc. Valid or honest criticism, in these matters, I feel, is permissible; but attacks motivated by arrogance and peeve, and threats to leave these organizations cannot be considered permissible. ... It is worth remembering also that both the Americans and the Russians strongly support the concept of zero-real-growth budgets for the U.N. and all its specialized agencies. As regards the World Bank and IMF, the Americans have prevented obstinately, either reappraisal or restructuring. Efforts like the Cancun meeting have run into the sands of inaction and indifference.
>
> What affects me most powerfully is the reminder of similar attacks against the League of Nations system that were made by then great powers in the late thirties, just before the Second World War began. This

> memory in itself must cause anxiety to all those that seek to strengthen peace. ... I feel the time has come for us to do something about this. ... There is nobody, in my view, as capable of doing something purposeful in this context, as you are. A high level international dialogue on all these matters must, therefore, be initiated under your guidance and leadership.[92]

He suggested that a small group of leaders and intellectuals should begin the dialogue. 'If I may think aloud, perhaps you could invite for a two-day conference in India. ... You could select the invitees from amongst the great internationalists and thinkers of our time. The list could include those leaders who are still in office, and those who have recently retired from active politics; political scientists; experts in international law, economists, etc..' In this connection he suggested a number of names as potential invitees to this conference.[93] Indira Gandhi agreed with Kreisky on his proposal to hold an international conference of eminent personalities for a dialogue on the issue of the strengthening of the United Nations and other pressing international problems. 'I think you will agree that we should not have a set agenda or a declaration. Would we need to commission any papers for the meeting? And do you visualise any follow-up action arising out of the deliberations of the conference?'[94] This happened to be the last letter Bruno Kreisky received from Prime Minister Indira Gandhi. Unfortunately, the move became unfruitful as, before this venture got under way, Indira Gandhi fell victim to the bullets of an assassin, her own guard, on 31 October 1984. While speaking at the Memorial Meeting for Indira Gandhi in Vienna, Kreisky said: 'Through her power of persuasion and the strength of her convictions, Indira Gandhi has tried to give a new orientation to the movement of non-aligned countries. ... Had she not been torn from life, her position in the middle of the big power blocs - regardless of likes and dislikes - would have indeed allowed her to achieve much.'[95]

Although much of the political interaction between Austria and India in the post-war period was on larger international issues, except during the period of Emergency in India, efforts were made to strengthen bilateral economic and technological cooperation. Notably, the Austrian technology (L-D process) was used for building India's Rourkela Steel Plant. Later in 1984, Austria offered technological assistance to modernize Rourkela Steel Plant. VOEST-Alpine, in a joint venture with the Government of India, set up a steel construction company, Triveni Structures, Ltd., in Allahabad. Austria provided technological assistance to a few irrigation schemes, water treatment plants and coal washeries. During his visit to India in 1980, the Austrian Chancellor Bruno Kreisky said that he would be discussing the possibilities of bilateral economic cooperation between India and Austria. He said that Austria was starting a very intensive programme of economic exchange with Asian countries .[96] He said that his country favoured collaborating with India in the industrial sector.[97] During a visit to Plasser (India) Pvt. Ltd., an Indo-Austrian venture near Faridabad (close to New Delhi), which manufactures sophisticated railway track maintenance machines and components, Kreisky described it as an outstanding collaborative venture between India and Austria, especially in marketing the products all over the world. He praised India's industrial development programmes as 'very significant'. He said: 'I am a Social Democrat. Beyond political conviction, our economic interest is to participate in the countries of the Third World'.[98] During his visit, Austria sanctioned a loan of about Rs. 8.43 crores to India for import of capital goods from Austria. The loan was given on soft terms - repayable over a period of 20 years, with a grace period of 10 years, and an annual interest at the rate of 2 percent.[99] Notably, when Kreisky and Indira Gandhi discussed, for 90 minutes, bilateral economic relations and the world situation, including the situation in Afghanistan, no aides were present.[100] However, in order to promote economic and commercial ties between the two countries, in 1983, an Indo-Austrian Joint Commission was established.

Austria took interest in the promotion of Indo-Austrian ventures and extended support to large-scale irrigation projects, particularly in the field of sprinkler irrigation, in India. When an Austrian Company (Roehren und Pumpenwerk Rudolf Bauer Ges.m.b.H.), was negotiating with the Andhra Pradesh Government in India for a large scale irrigation project, Chancellor Kreisky wrote, in 1982, to Prime Minister Indira Gandhi and conveyed the Austrian Government's full support to the Bauer Company in this venture. Kreisky wrote:

> ... this company is a well-renowned Austrian enterprise which has a long tradition of very successful cooperation with a great number of countries, particularly of the Third World. ... I am personally interested in the realization of this project because it would help to secure full employment, a goal to which my government attaches the greatest priority.[101]

Indira Gandhi replied to the Chancellor informing him that the project was being examined by the Central Government and the Government of Andhra Pradesh. She added: 'We are deeply concerned about the development of areas where water is scarce and are conscious of the need to evolve methods to get maximum benefit out of the minimum use of water. Sprinkler irrigation can be one such method. But we have to evaluate such projects for their cost-benefits and other features. Our Ministry of Irrigation will contact your authorities regarding this matter soon.'[102]

Similarly, in December 1982, Chancellor Kreisky wrote a letter to Prime Minister Indira Gandhi in support of an

Austrian bid for the supply of Howitzer guns to India. He wrote:

> Only recently, VOEST-Alpine AG together with other Austrian firms, offered to supply Howitzer guns and to assist in establishing a facility for the production of such equipment in your country. As I have been informed, tests undertaken by the Indian army of this material were positive. VOEST-Alpine AG is, as you know, one of Austria's most important and internationally experienced enterprises and I would welcome any assistance you could provide in the realization of this project.[103]

But, a final decision on the Howitzer gun deal was still pending when Indira Gandhi was assassinated on 31 October 1984. By the time a final decision on the Howitzer gun contract was due, Rajiv Gandhi succeeded Indira Gandhi as Prime Minister. Bruno Kreisky also ceased to be the Austrian Chancellor. Meanwhile, various other considerations and influences came in, which included alleged kickbacks. However, Rajiv Gandhi's government gave the Howitzer gun contract to the Swedish firm, Bofors. The controversy the Bofors deal had generated in India had cost Rajiv Gandhi his Prime Ministership, and its reverberations are still heard loudly in the Indian political scene. However, referring to the Bofors gun deal, the Austrian Foreign Minister Alois Mock during his visit to India in February 1990, said: 'This was a question of commercial competitive strength probably in some strange environment but it did not affect the relations between the two countries.'[104]

In the scientific and cultural fields too Austria and India had strengthened their relationship. A good number of Indians are now working in Austria especially in the public health sector.

It is difficult to say whether in the post-Kreisky era

Austria's relationship with India could maintain the closeness and personal touch Kreisky had given to it. Doubtful. It appears that since then it has seldom gone beyond the formal bilateral official relationship.

V

The significant contribution Austria made to promote reconciliation between Israel and the Arabs in West Asia had considerably enhanced the prestige of Austria in the Third World. Although Europe was the main theatre of Austria's activities in the post-war period, from mid-1970s it took active interest in search of a peaceful and negotiated settlement to the Arab-Israeli conflict in West Asia. Despite the wording of the UN General Assembly Resolution 181 (II) of 29 November 1947, which spoke of 'Independent Arab and Jewish States and Special International Regime for the City of Jerusalem', when Israel was created in 1948, the displaced Palestinians were left high and dry without a homeland. Moreover, since the inception of Israel, clear cut battle lines were also drawn simultaneously between the Arabs and Israel. While the Arabs vowed to destroy Israel, Israel asserted its right to exist, and the Palestinians waged a violent struggle for a homeland. These virulently acrimonious, rigid positions persisted relentlessly for a long time. More than the issue of homeland for the Palestinians, the focus was more on Israel's right to exist against the Arab countries' determination to destroy it. Under the circumstances, the Socialist International, in which Mapai (The Israeli Labour Party) was a member, from the very beginning adopted a pro-Israeli stand on the Arab-Israeli conflict. The crucial role Austria played in this context was the initiative it took to unfreeze the hitherto followed rigid position and to effect a qualitative change in the partisan attitude of the Socialist International, and to bring about a certain degree of equanimity in its approach to the Arab-Israeli conflict. The other crucial role Austria played in this connection was that by taking a sympathetic attitude to the Palestinian cause, Austria could wean away the key Palestinian militant organizations from the hitherto followed militaristviolent path and help them to increasingly put their faith in peaceful negotiations for an enduring settlement to the Palestinian question. It had also succeeded in convincing all belligerents in the region that co-existence was the only realistic way. In retrospect, certainly, this was the most decisive turning points in harnessing the peace process in West Asia. And the credit for it should go squarely to Austria and its Chancellor Bruno Kreisky who played the key role in effecting it.

The path for this sea change in the basic attitudes of the key players in the Arab-Israeli conflict in West Asia was laid by the Report of the Socialist International's fact-finding mission, headed by the Chancellor Bruno Kreisky, which was submitted to the Socialist International in October 1977. It took three years, from 1974 to 1976, for the fact-finding mission to meet the leaders of the 13 countries of the region involved in the crisis. It also enabled Chancellor Kreisky to establish fruitful personal rapport with all Arab political leaders. However, the report of the fact-finding mission, submitted by the Austrian Chancellor, was a classic document which had not only dissected with precision the Arab-Israeli problem and stated sharply the basic issues involved, but also suggested ways and means to solve it.[105]

In fact, the report was the pace-setter that also provided the necessary canvass for everyone involved in the conflict, and its solution encouraged them to turn to the negotiating table, rather than the battle field, for a settlement. Significantly, the fact-finding mission found that most Arab Governments, except Libya and Iraq, supported a peaceful solution to the Arab-Israeli conflict 'under certain circumstances.' [106] However, for its part, the fact-finding mission had prescribed certain preconditions for the restoration of peace in the Middle East. They included, among other things: (i) Israel should return to the borders of 1967; and (ii) A Palestinian state should be established. Kreisky urged: 'It is therefore the task of the Socialist International to do everything in its power to work for a peaceful solution which guarantees the acceptance of the right to live for the Israeli people and the Palestinian people.'[107]

The report gave a detailed account of the Palestinian Liberation Organization (PLO) and the different shades of opinion within its nine constituents, including Al Fatah. It also focussed on how the PLO represented politically the Palestinian aspiration for a homeland, how it enjoyed the widespread support of the overwhelming majority of the Arab governments, and how the PLO enjoyed the recognition as the legitimate representative of the Palestinian people from 105 countries.[108]

In Bruno Kreisky's perception, the centre-piece of the Arab-Israeli problem was 'the unsolved Palestinian question.'[109] Therefore, the main effort of Austria was centred on how to resolve this question. Early on Kreisky realized that for a peaceful political settlement, it was necessary to get the PLO under Yasser Arafat recognized, in the Western countries as well, as the legitimate representative of the Palestinian people and obtain support for a formula which had recognized the legitimate right of the Palestinians to have a Palestinian state. In pursuance of these objectives the Austrian Chancellor organized, in February 1978, a round table discussion in Vienna which helped to convey that Israel's intransigence toward the PLO was unsound and unjustifiable. In a further step, Kreisky officially invited the PLO leader Yasser Arafat to Vienna and accorded a warm welcome to him in July 1979 – the first European government to do so – and arranged a meeting between Willy Brandt, President of the socialist International, and Arafat. This action of the Austrian Chancellor was very significant is that it considerably enhanced the standing of both PLO and Arafat in the West as the potential chief negotiator on behalf of the

Palestinians. A few months later, in March 1980, Austria officially recognized the PLO. These moves by Austria had a tremendous impact on the PLO and the Arabs which strengthened their faith in a peaceful, negotiated settlement. However, Chancellor Kreisky pursued this steadfast line despite the violent attempts of the Abu Nidal group of Palestinians to sabotage these positive developments by orchestrating terrorist attacks in Vienna and elsewhere. It all eventually led to the mutual recognition of Israel and the PLO and to the start of reconciliation between the Arabs and the Israelis. Austria's interest in the West Asia peace process remained undiminished even after Bruno Kreisky had stepped down as the Austrian Chancellor in 1983. During his visit to Israel in June 1993, in a reference to the West Asia peace process, the Austrian Chancellor Franz Vranitzky observed: 'Now ... a solution seems to be within reach, and I wish all the parties who soon will meet for the tenth round of negotiations all the best for their quest for a lasting peace in the region.' He said :

> Austria is following the negotiations with keen interest, for peace in our world is indivisible. ... This is why it is in the interest of the whole international community to support the present negotiations with constructive and confidence-building measures. Austria is therefore actively participating in the multilateral peace process, organizing meetings and seminars, and offering its expertize in the various fields. Human contacts, interaction and the free exchange of ideas ... offer the best chance for peace and understanding. Intimidation through terrorism and repression only deepen the trenches. I therefore congratulate the Israeli government on its decision again to allow direct contacts between Israelis and the PLO.[110]

Although the final West Asia peace accord was worked out later in Oslo, the decisive role Austria had played at a crucial point to turn the direction of the Arab-Israeli conflict to the path of a peaceful negotiated settlement needs to be recognized as an outstanding contribution to the West Asia peace process. Indeed, it was the Austrian vision and perseverance which had culminated in the West Asia peace accord and the establishment of the Palestinian State under the leadership of Yasser Arafat.

VI

Therefore, for an Indian observer, post-war Austria gives the image of a nation which has upstaged most other countries of Central Europe by radiating innovative ideas and methods born largely out of the joint feeling of compassion and international solidarity. The country has also been viewed as one which has built up a humane society marked by a considerable degree of compassion in its state policies and by a unique system of social partnership which, by and large, ensures industrial peace in the country. Of course, this post-war image of Austria has been bolstered up by the great aura it has inherited from the past as a meeting point of three important European civilizations, as a country which had endured several invasions, as a home of illustrious personalities in the fields of science, culture, art, music and architecture, and as a land of good natured people who have possessed salutary qualities of patience, perseverance, humaneness and catholicity of mind, and who have refused to give up their faith in the future, even in the most adverse circumstances. Pertinent is the ringing the words of Karl Renner who, before signing the State Treaty of Saint-Germain on 10 September 1919, which accused Austria of 'war guilt' and effected major territorial losses to it and also undermined its self-sufficiency, had exhorted the Austrians on 6 September 1919: 'Let us work, work and not despair, let us believe in the future, believe in our common interest within this [truncated] state. ...' That has remained the creed of Austrians in the post-war period too. Similarly, Austria has also imbibed an approach which Bruno Kreisky had articulated for his fellow socialists: 'Socialists must constantly find themselves confronted with the fact that their ideas are ahead of their time. The day when socialists stop having ideas which are ahead of their time will be a sad one.'[111] Similarly pertinent is his observation underlining perseverance: ' ... it has never been the case in history that the struggle to achieve new and great aims has been abandoned simply because of a little resistance. On the contrary, the more opposition there is, the greater the efforts must be.'[112] Imbibing the spirit behind these words, in the post-war period, Austria radiated many innovative ideas which have made their impact on the thought process in the world. Its vast experiences in war and peace and diplomacy have made Austria more mature and balanced in its reactions to crises and in its prescriptions to resolve them. Reconciliation through patient dialogue and negotiations, however prolonged they might be, is the basic approach – peaceful methodology which Austria had demonstrated through its ten year long negotiations for the Austrian State Treaty. Austria's neutral status and the objectivity it has shown has made Austria a welcome interlocutor in the resolution of international conflicts.

Though landlocked, Austria's geographical position in Central Europe has made Vienna a capital of great significance. Not only because the city draws the attention of the world for its beauty, fame and history and has made a tremendous contribution to culture and civilization, but also because of the reform work the city municipality has undertaken has made it an example of how a welfare state system could be constructed through a social democratic reform process. Many world leaders, including Jawaharlal Nehru of India, were deeply impressed by what Vienna had achieved through the reform process. But, equally important is the strategic position of Vienna as a key observation post in Central Europe from where one can observe developments in Europe more clearly and objectively than from anywhere else in the region. It gives a different perspective, perhaps a more correct perspective, than what one could obtain from anywhere else. That was, perhaps, one of the reasons why, when many other nations were talking in terms of war, conflicts and confrontations, Austria spoke in terms of negotiations, dialogue and reconciliation – a civilized way of resolving conflicts – which has ultimately carried the day in Europe and in the Middle East, two critical areas of conflicts in the post-war period, where Austria became actively involved in their resolutions. In Europe, Austria's somewhat semi-open door policy between the East and the West and its liberal asylum laws, enabled a large number of East Germans to reach West Germany via Hungary and Austria, besides enabling a large number of Soviet Jews to reach Israel via Austria's transit point, Castle Schönau.

In the post-war period, Austria has made an outstanding contribution to promote detente in Europe, peace in the Middle East and to promote North-South cooperation. Indeed Austria was the pace-setter of detente in Europe, which was achieved through the Austrian State Treaty. The second detente and the Helsinki Final Act were the universal confirmation of the detente policy which had steadily and systematically eroded the cold war psyche and promoted East-West cooperation. Consequently, their threat perception and confrontationist attitude had also changed remarkably.

Austria's intervention in the Arab-Israeli conflict in the Middle East was one of its most outstanding contributions towards world peace in the post-war period. The intervention was timely and effective and constituted the turning point in a peaceful resolution of the Arab-Israeli conflict. The fact that Austria was the first European country that could win the trust and confidence of Arabs in their conflict with Israel at a critical time when they viewed the entire West with suspicion and cynicism was a tribute to Austria's trustworthiness and objectivity. Indeed, through a rational approach, Austria could tilt the balance in the Middle East in favour of the PLO and the Palestinian State. Without Austria's timely intervention the Arab-Israeli conflict would probably have taken a more tragic course and a devastating end. This change of track for a peaceful solution to this conflict was effected decisively by Austria and its Chancellor Bruno Kreisky. The Oslo Accord, ending the Middle East conflict, was only the logical culmination of the course Austria had chalked out in the mid-1970s.

Austria's engagement in the espousal of Third World causes, particularly to promote the economic development of the Third World, enabled Austria to win the hearts of a large number of developing countries and to enjoy great esteem among them, despite Austria's weak performance in respect of ODA (0.24% of the GNP). Its sense of justice and compassion found its expression in its persistent effort to get approval of a concerted international plan for the development of the Third World. It tried to convince the rich countries how important it was for them to help the Third World. In doing so, Austria was moved by a conviction that many problems, like recession, unemployment, economic crises, etc., in the developed world could be resolved only through international solidarity actions like a massive transfer of resources from the rich to the poor countries and the conversion of millions of poor people world-wide into potential consumers by enhancing their levels of prosperity. Poor should be helped to become richer. That was the only way, he believed, for the world to move on without crisis. In the post-war period, Austria used every conceivable opportunity to put forth all possible arguments in favour of a New Marshall Plan for the developing countries to help them to build up infrastructure and doing it as part of an international solidarity action. Bilateral aid, though important, was no substitute for such a massive international assistance plan. The idea is still valid. Austria's support for the North-South dialogue was also significant. It was also partly instrumental in the establishment of the Brandt Commission and in the convening of the Cancun summit of the developed and the developing countries. The line Austria had followed in this regard greatly enhanced its standing among the developing countries.

Among the developing countries, India received Austria's special attention. Being the first country to become independent after the War, its position as the largest stable democracy, as the leader of the non-aligned movement, its size and potential, and its responsive and responsible political leadership made India a major attraction for Austria. Equally attractive for India was Austria's basically constructive and outward looking approach on major international issues and its willingness to resolve larger international issues with a sense of commitment. Therefore, they maintained a very friendly and respectful relationship all along. Perhaps, from among the Third World countries, Austria's interaction with India was the closest and most frequent and their relationship remained free from any bilateral problems. Moreover, Austria's permanent neutrality and India's non-alignment had provided them with many meeting points in world politics in the post-war period. Indeed, during the cold war, both of them had played a bridge building role between the power blocs. Austria's current perception of India has been summed up by Alois Mock, Foreign Minister, during his visit to India in 1990. He said: 'We should do everything to increase our economic cooperation. We have by far not explored and used the huge market this dynamic economy is offering in India, with its 700 million people. There is the purchasing power of a middle class of 150 million people. The strong economic development of India has already given it an important political position world-wide and it will become more important. The area between New Delhi and Tokyo is the focal point. We should pay much more attention to the economic and political points.'[113]

Although neutrality was imposed on Austria in 1955 as a price for freedom, its active neutrality became an asset for the country to outshine most other European countries of similar, or even superior, position in the world scale of diplomacy and influence. For a small land-locked country to attain that distinction was no mean an achievement. However, Austria's image in the Third World was considerably boosted by its position as a 'permanently neutral' country in the midst of a polarised Europe. And till late 1980s, Austria had desisted from any act which had even remotely raised a question mark on that status and image. But after Franz Vranitzky succeeded Fred Sinowatz as the Austrian Chancellor in 1986, and after he became the Chairman of the SPÖ in 1988, a marked shift took place in Austria's policies and priorities. The European Community and Austria's immediate neighbourhood became the areas of concentration of Austrian diplomacy. In doing so, it seems that Chancellor Vranitzky was persuaded by a hope that Austria's membership in the European Union would act as a panacea for most of the difficulties the country was faced with. Whether that was a sound assessment or not, the future alone will tell. However, soon the question of Austria's membership in the European Community was placed at the top of the national agenda, which also instantly generated a debate on its implications for Austria's 'permanent neutrality'. When the Executive Committee of the SPÖ passed the resolution in favour of Austria's EC membership on 3 April 1989, it had made Austria's 'political neutrality' a precondition. The SPÖ resolution said categorically:

> Any negotiation of legal and political requirements arising from the permanent neutrality of our country is out of the question. ... Any application for admission as a member, therefore means to ask the EC the

> question if it is willing to guarantee Austria with contractual obligation those freedoms that enable us to perform our political function as a permanently neutral state even if the EC as such are temporarily or principally willing to take a different stand than Austria. Closely connected thereto is the question of political identity the EC is more and more wanting to attain itself. ... Permanent neutrality and the question of how to protect it are undoubtedly the central items in negotiations following an Austrian application. ... The Socialist Party is in any way unconditionally committed to this concept being the basis for its foreign and military policy and would not accept to pay with new and additional barriers against other states for a closer participation in Western Europe.[114]

It may be recalled that Bruno Kreisky once made a pertinent observation that while Austria favoured European economic integration, 'the possibilities of Austria in regard to participation in this European integration are more limited than those of non-neutral states. At every step we have to take into account how far it is compatible with our neutral policy'.[115] It seems that he did not envisage for Austria anything more than an association arrangement with the EC. However, it is not the intention of the present author to go into the details of how Austria had resolved this basic issue before it joined the European Union, particularly after the Maastricht Treaty on European Union which had clearly stated the EU convergence towards the formulation of a common foreign and security policy for the Union – though the subject matter has been kept outside the purview of the EU Commission.

From the angle of Austria's image in the Third World, the pertinent fundamental question is wether, in reality, Austria's 'permanent neutrality' could ever be reconciled with the European Union's projected common foreign and security policy, without causing damage to its own standing outside Europe. However, it appears that Austria will not be able to keep away from the stipulations which the Maastricht Treaty has made for the member countries. Under these circumstances, EU membership is likely to cage Austria's international mind within the EU straight jacket on foreign and security policy, causing considerable limitations to its freedom on the one hand and the loss of the advantage Austria had hitherto enjoyed as a neutral country with an independent approach. Therefore, Austria is likely to have less and less space in taking independent initiatives outside the European Union in favour of, for example, the developing countries. In this event, the developing countries might begin to look at Austria, as they look at other EU members. Its image as a country detached from other major political actors of the continent might also suffer in the process. How to minimize this likely fallout of its EU membership is a challenge for the Austrian leadership. The point is whether Austria will continue to be viewed by the developing countries with the same spirit of equanimity as before after its image gets completely merged with the European Union.

In the aftermath of the shifting of priorities in Austria's foreign policy in the late 1980s, due to sheer neglect and lack of initiative, considerable erosion has taken place in recent years in Austria's high profile and international influence, particularly in the developing world. Of course, the general international climate and attitude also have changed significantly. After a period of enlightened approach in the 1970s and 1980s, foreign policy, in general, has reverted to abrasiveness, business nationalism, intrigues, courtesies and routine. As a result, big agenda items like international solidarity and cooperation, feeling for the whole of humanity, etc., are found missing. However, it seems that in its new foreign policy perspective, internationalism has given way disproportionately to provincialism. As a result, Austria's visibility in the arena of international politics has become less and less. The reasons could be many. But the lack of will to play an active international role seems to be the main reason. However, this new trend can be reversed if once again international interests and provincial interests are put on an even keel, as part of a larger vision, as before, in the external policies of Austria. For the developing countries, Austria is still viewed as a reliable friend that would stand up for them in the international fora. Will Austria live up to this expectation of the developing countries in the 2Ist century? That is the key question.

REFERENCES

1. US, *Department of State Bulletin* (Washington, D.C.), 6 November 1943, p. 310.
2. Karl Renner, *Österreich von der Ersten zur Zweiten Republik* (Wien, 1953), p. 235.
3. Karl Renner, 'Austria: Key for War and Peace', *Foreign Affairs* (New York), vol. 26, 1947-48, pp. 589-603.
4. Günter Bischof and Anton Pelinka, eds., *The Kreisky Era in Austria*, Vol. 2 (New Jersey, 1994), p. 42.
5. See Ludwig Jedlicka, Die Neutralität Österreichs und der Staatsvertrag, *Österreichische Militärische Zeitschrift* (Wien), Heft 3, 1965, pp. 149-51.
6. Bruno Kreisky, *Memoirs*, Chapter 25, 'Third World', Typescript, p. 421.
7. UK, HMSO, Cmd. 9080 (London, 1954), Miscellaneous no. 5, pp. 131-3.
8. For a detailed analysis of Austria's negotiations for the State Treaty, see Janko Musulin, 'Austria Between East and West', *International Affairs* (London), Vol. XXX, pp. 431-3.
9. For the Soviet-Austrian Communique of 15 April 1955, see Soviet Embassy in UK, *Soviet News* (London), 19 May 1955.
10. US, Department of State Publication, 6437, *Austrian State Treaty* (Washington, D.C., 1957). Significantly, on 14 May 1955, on the eve of the conclusion of the Austrian State Treaty, Moscow concluded the Warsaw Pact to legitimize the continued stay of the Soviet troops in other East European countries.
11. *Bundesverfassungsgesetz* vom 26. October 1955 ueber die Neutralität Österreichs, *Bundesgesetzblatt für die Republik Öterreich*, Stück 57, 4 November 1955.
12. Wolfgang Schallenberg, *The Austrian Concept of Neutrality* (Laski Memorial Lecture, 1977), (Ahmedabad, India, 1978), pp. 7-8.
13. Arne Haselbach, *Bruno Kreisky's Drive for a Large Scale Economic Solidarity Programme with Developing Countries* (Vienna, 1981), p. 3.

14. For the text of the Vienna Declaration, see Vienna Institute for Development, *Conference for Economic Cooperation and Partnership: The Vienna Declaration on Cooperation for Development* (Vienna, 1962), pp. 11-7.
15. *Ibid.*
16. According to Bruno Kreisky, the institute's objective was devised on the advice of the Indian Prime Minister Jawaharlal Nehru. See Bruno Kreisky, *Memoirs*, n. 6, p. 422.
17. Bruno Kreisky, *A Programme for full Employment in the 1990s: Report of the Kreisky Commission on Employment Issues in Europe* (Oxford, 1989), p. xx.
18. Arne Haselbach, n. 13.
19. Austrian Foreign Minister Bruno Kreisky's Lecture, *What are the Possibilities for Worldwide Economic Cooperation*, on 17 September 1962, at the Economic Club of Detroit, USA, pp. 9-10.
20. *Ibid.*, p. 10.
21. *Ibid.*
22. *Ibid.*, p. 11.
23. *Ibid.*
24. Chancellor Bruno Kreisky's speech at the UN Interregional Symposium on 'State Petroleum Enterprises in Developing Countries', in Vienna on 7 March 1978. See *Kreisky-Reden*, Vol. II, pp. 713-15.
25. Bruno Kreisky's speech 'Foreign Policy in the Affluent Society', at the Dallas Council of World Affairs, Dallas, on 18 October 1965. See *Kreisky-Reden*, Vol. 1, pp. 655-60.
26. Bruno Kreisky, 'Austria's Place in the World', *Socialist International Information* (London), 21 December 1968, p. 280.
27. Chancellor Kreisky's speech at the UN Interregional Symposium in Vienna on 7 March 1978. See *Kreisky-Reden*, Vol. II, pp. 713-15.
28. See Chancellor Bruno Kreisky's Declaration of the Government Policy in Parliament on 5 November 1971. See 'Regierungserklärung', Nationalrat, Wien, 5 November 1971. See *Kreisky-Reden*, Vol. II, pp.158-85.
29. See Chancellor Bruno Kreisky's Declaration of the Government Policy in Parliament on 19 June 1979. See 'Regierungserkläung', Nationalrat, Wien, 19 June 1979. See *Kreisky-Reden*, Vol.II, pp. 795-820.
30. "The Kreisky Plan" (Editorial), *Hindustan Times* (New Delhi), 3 February 1980.
31. Chancellor Bruno Kreisky's speech on 31 July 1975 at the Summit Meeting of the Conference on Security and Cooperation in Europe. See *Kreisky-Reden*, Vol. II, pp. 490-93.
32. Bruno Kreisky, *Memoirs*, n. 6, pp. 425-6.
33. Chancellor Bruno Kreisky's speech at the SPÖ meeting in Vienna on 19 May 1978. See *Kreisky-Reden*, Vo1. II, pp. 730-46.

34. Chancellor Bruno Kreisky's speech at the UNIDO III in New Delhi on 31 January 1980. See Bruno Kreisky, *Massive Transfer of Resources and Development of Infrastructure* (Vienna Institute for Development, Vienna, 1980), Occasional Paper 80/1, p. 2.
35. From the "Summary" of Kreisky's speech at UN1DO III on 31 January 1980. See Arne Haselbach, n. 13, p. 23.
36. Bruno Kreisky, *Massive Transfer of Resources*, n. 34, p. 2
37. *Ibid.*, p. 3.
38. *Ibid.*, pp. 3-4.
39. *Ibid.*, p. 3. Earlier, in 1975, Kreisky put forth the idea that the developed countries and the oil exporting countries should come forward and jointly finance this large-scale international solidarity programme for the development of the developing countries. He said this while receiving Freedom Award of the International Rescue Committee, New York, on 14 April 1975. See *Kreisky-Reden*, Vol. II, pp. 460-64.
40. Austrian Foreign Minister Rudolf Kirchschläger's speech at the UN General Assembly on 5 October 1972. See UN, GAOR, session 27, plen. mtgs., mtg. 2054, 5 October 1972, p. 6.
41. Chancellor Bruno Kreiskyl's speech at the UN General Assembly, New York, on 29 October 1979. UN, GAOR, session 34, plen. mtgs., mtg. 49, 29 October 1974, p. 983.
42. *Ibid.*
43. Chancellor Bruno Kreisky's speech, "The World Economy in the Eighties", under the joint auspices of the Friedrich Ebert Stiftung and the Renner Institute, in Vienna on 16 June 1980. See *Kreisky-Reden*, Vol.II, pp. 896-902.
44. See 'Regierungserklärung", Nationalrat, Wien, 5 November 1971. See *Kreisky-Reden*, Vol. II, pp.158-85.
45. Foreign Minister Bruno Kreisky's speech at Dallas on 18 October 1965. See *Kreisky-Reden*, n. 25.
46. Brandt Commission, *North-South: A Programme for Survival: Report of the Independent Commission on International Development Issues* (Cambridge, Mass. 1980).
47. Vienna Institute for Development, *Preparations for the Mexico Summit Press Releases on the First and Second Vienna Consultation of Foreign Mmisters* (Vienna, 1981), p. 1.
48. *Ibid.*, p. 2.
49. *Ibid.*, p. 5.
50. Bruno Kreisky and H. Gauhar, *Decolonization and After: The Future of the Third World (London, 1987)*, p. 15.
51. SPÖ, '30th Federal Congress of the Socialist Party of Austria, 1987,' *Social Democratic News from Austria*(Vienna), 2/87, p. 12.
52. Bruno Kreisky, *Is There a Chance for a New and Global Detente?* (Laxenburg, Austria, 1985), p. 8. (Lecture delivered on 21 November

1984 at the International Institute to Applied Systems Analysis, Laxenburg, Austria).

53. Bruno Kreisky, former Chancellor ofAustria, in an interview with the author on 30 August 1989, in Vienna.
54. Austrian Chancellor Bruno Kreisky's reply to a toast at the dinner hosted in his honour by Prime Minister Indira Gandhi in New Delhi on 31 January 1980. See StBKA, VII, Länderboxen, Indien 2.
55. Interview with Bruno Kreisky, Chancellor of Austria, by B.R. Nanda in Vienna on 11 November 1971.,See StBKA, VII, Länderboxen, Indien 1.
56. Kreisky's reply to a toast on 31 January 1980, n. 54.
57. Bruno Kreisky, *Massive Transfer of Resources*, n. 34, p. 1.
58. Bruno Kreisky, *Memoirs*, n. 6, pp. 419-20.
59. *Ibid.*
60. *Ibid.*, p. 429.
61. *Ibid.*, p. 422.
62. *Ibid.*, p. 428.
63. Chancellor Bruno Kreisky's letter, dated 30 July 1970, to the Indian Prime Minister Indira Gandhi. See StBKA, VII, Länderboxen, Indien 1.
64. Indian Prime Minister Indira Gandhi's letter, dated 4 September 1970, to the Austrian Chancellor Bruno Kreisky. See StBKA, VII, Länderboxen, Indien 1.
65. In the letter, Indira Gandhi prefaced: 'You may perhaps be surprised to get this letter from me as I have never before written on such matters'. See StBKA, VII Länderboxen, Indien 2.
66. Ibid., T N. Kaul got elected to the UNESCO Executive Board.
67. Indian Prime Minister Indira Gandhi's letter, dated 28 May 1971, to the Austrian Chancellor Bruno Kreisky. See StBKA, VII, Länderboxen, Indien 1.
68. *Ibid.*
69. *Ibid.*
70. See Chancellor Kreisky's reply to the Indian Prime Minister.Ibid.
71. *Ibid.*
72. For the reaction of the Socialist International, see B. Vivekanandan, *International Concerns of European Social Democrats* (London & New York Macmillan Press & St. Martin's Press, 1997), pp. 127-30.
73. Prime Minister Indira Gandhi's letter, dated 30 June 1976, to the Austrian Chancellor Bruno Kreisky. See StBKA, VII, Länderboxen, Indien 1.
74. Joint letter of Willy Brandt, Bruno Kreisky and Olof. Palme, dated 23 July 1976, to 1ndira Gandhi. See StBKA, VII, Länderboxen, Indien 1.
75. Leila Kabir Fernandes' hand-written letter, dated 28 January 1980, to the Austrian Chancellor Bruno Kreisley. See StBKA, VII, Länderboxen, Indien 1.

76. Peter Jankowitsch, International Secretary of the SPÖ (former Foreign Mnister), in an interview with the author on 1 September 1989, in Vienna.
77. Bruno Kreisky, former Chancellor ofAustria, in an interview with the author on 30 August 1989, in Vienna.
78. *Indian Express* (New Delhi), 26 September 1977.
79. Indira Gandhi's letter, dated 28 December 1978, to the Austrian Chancellor Bruno Kreisky. See StBKA, VII, Länderboxen, Indien 1.
80. Austrian Chancellor Bruno Kreisky's letter, dated 15 February 1979, to Indira Gandhi. See StBKA, VII, Länderboxen, Indien 1.
81. Bruno Kreisky's letter in January 1980 to Indira Gandhi. See StBKA, VII, Länderboxen, Indien 1.
82. Indira Gandhi's letter, dated 29 May 1979, to Chancellor Bruno Kreisky. See StBKA, VII, Länderboxen, Indien 1.
83. *Ibid*.
84. *Ibid*.
85. *Ibid*.
86. Bruno Kreisky's letter, in January 1980, to Indira Gandhi. See StBKA, VII, Länderboxen, Indien 1.
87. *Ibid*.
88. Chancellor Bruno Kreisky's reply to the toast at the dinner hosted by Indira Gandhi in his honour in New Delhi on 31 January 1980. See StBKA, VII, Länderboxen, Indien 2.
89. Prime Minister Indira Gandhi's letter, dated 6 March 1980, to Chancellor Bruno Kreisky. See StBKA, VIII, Länderboxen, Indien 2.
90. Prime Mnister Indira Gandhi's letter, dated 9 June 1980, to the Austrian Chancellor Bruno Kreisky. See StBKA, VII, Länderboxen, Indien 2. Later Begum Bhutto was allowed to go abroad for medical treatment. Subsequently, Kreisky wrote to Indira Gandhi: 'I am convinced that our joint efforts contributed towards making this fortunate turn of events possible'. See Chancellor Bruno Kreisky's letter, dated 20 December 1982, to Prime Minister Indira Gandhi. *Ibid*.
91. Kreisky's reply to Indira Gandhi. See StBKA, VII, Länderboxen, Indien 2.
92. Bruno Kreisky's letter, dated 19 June 1984, to Prime Minister Indira Gandhi. See StBKA, VII, Länderboxen, Indien 2.
93. *Ibid*.
94. Prime Minister Indira Gandhi's letter, dated 10 July 1984, to Bruno Kreisky. See StBKA, VII, Länderboxen, Indien 2.
95. For the text of Bruno Kreisky's speech at the Memorial Meeting for Indira Gandhi in Vienna, see StBKA, V11, Länderboxen, Indien 2.
96. *The Statesman* (New Delhi), 30 January 1980.
97. *The Statesman*, 2 February 1980.
98. *Ibid*.

99. *Ibid.*
100. *National Herald* (New Delhi), 1 February 1980.
101. Chancellor Bruno Kreisky's letter, dated 27 October 1982, to Prime Minister Indira Gandhi. See StBKA, VII, Länderboxen, Indien 2.
102. Prime Minister Indira Gandhi's letter, dated 9 December 1982, to Chancellor Bruno Kreisky. See StBKA, VII, Länderboxen, Indien 2.
103. Chancellor Bruno Kreisky's letter, dated 20 December 1982, to Indira Gandhi. See StBKA, VII, Länderboxen, Indien 2.
104. *The Hindu* (Madras), 3 February 1990.
105. For the text of the report of the fact-finding mission headed by the Austrian Chancellor Bruno Kreisky, see *Socialist Affairs* (London), Jan-Feb. 1978, Vol. 28, no. 1, pp. 9-12.
106. Bruno Kreisky, 'Socialist International Middle East Mission (Introduction)' *Socialist Affairs*, Ibid., p. 6.
107. *Ibid.*
108. See the report of the fact-finding mission. Ibid., p. 10.
109. Bruno Kreisky, *Is There a Chance for a New and Global Detente?* (Laxenburg, Austria, 1985), p. 9.
110. Address of the Austrian Chancellor, Franz Vranitzky on the occasion of the Special Convocation of the Hebrew University of Jerusalem on 9 June 1993. See Austria, *Federal Chancellor Franz Vranitzky in Israel* (Vienna, 1993), pp. 26-7.
111. Bruno Kreisky, 'Internationalism Today', *Socialist Affairs*, no. 1, 1984, p. 37.
112. Bruno Kreisky, 'Austria's Place in the World', *Socialist International Information* (London), 21 December 1968, p. 279.
113. *The Hindu* (Madras), 3 February 1990.
114. For the SPÖ Executive Committee Resolution, see 'Resolution on a Possible Membership', SPÖ, *Social Democratic News From Austria* (Vienna), no. 1, 1989, pp. 11-12.
115. Bruno Kreisky, "Austria's Place in the World", *Socialist International Information*, 21 December 1968, p. 280.

4

Britain and the Iraq Invasion

I

In July 2004, Lord Butler's Report on the British Intelligence Report on Saddam Hussain's WMD, and Lord Hutton's inquiry report on the suicide of David Kelly, Britain's UN weapon expert, have made it absolutely clear that the British Prime Minister Tony Blair and the US President George Bush had lied to their voters to garner support for an unjustifiable invasion of Iraq. They have shown that the MI6 intelligence dossier was doctored at the Prime Minister's Office as a matter of expediency to exaggerate Saddam Hussain's possession of weapons of mass destruction and their state of readiness to fire in '45 minutes'.[1] But a year after the 'successful' invasion of Iraq, this lie is haunting both Tony Blair and George Bush alike, raising serious question marks on their survival in their political offices. Bush is facing an election in November 2004 and Blair is expected to face it sometime in mid-2005. Both of them have now publicly conceded that Saddam Hussain's WMD may never be found in Iraq. In a recent election, their staunch supporter in Spain, Jose Maria Aznar, has been shown the door by the Spanish electorate. In Italy, Prime Minister Silvio Berlusconi, another supporter, is faced with a constant survival battle. All those who supported Bush in waging the war against Iraq are found running for cover as the invaders could not sustain the myth that Saddam Hussain possessed WMDs. At the end of the day, it is clear that the US war on Iraq was a pre-meditated act of aggression, driven by many undisclosed selfish motives, which the WMD figleaf was too small to cover. A few days prior to the massive anti-Iraq War demonstration in February 2003 in Hyde Park, London, I told candidly to the International Secretary of the British Labour Party, in London, that Tony Blair's approach to Iraq war would alienate the British voters and may cost the Labour Party dearly unless the Party brought about a change in its leadership before the next General Election. Predictably, he was unhappy to hear that candid observation from me as early as January 2003. But, the by-election results in Britain in constituencies like Leicester South and Brent East (London), and the recent UK local elections, all have conveyed the same message most eloquently. George Bush tried to justify his pre-meditated attack on Iraq by playing up another false story that Saddam Hussain was a supporter of Al Qaeda. The US Commission chaired by Thomas Kean could not find any evidence to that effect. However, Tony Blair's credibility among the British electorate has taken a steep decline after his support for Iraq invasion. 55 percent of voters in Britain believes that Blair lied to them on WMD in Iraq.[2]

It may be noted that of all the western powers involved in the 2003 war in Iraq, Britain is the only country which has the longest connection with Iraq – of about two centuries. As early as 1800 Britain established a residency in Basra and opened an office of the East India Company there. Two years later, in 1802, London opened a Consulate also in Baghdad. Following the defeat of the Ottoman Empire in the First World War, in 1920 the League of Nations made Iraq a mandated territory of Britain. Two treaties Britain concluded with Iraq during that period – a 20-year Anglo-Iraqi Treaty of 1922 and a treaty of alliance between them signed in 1930, which gave Britain the right to use some air bases in Iraq – governed their relationship at that time. But, Britain's mandate in Iraq ended in 1932 when Iraq joined the League of Nations as a full member. In the post-war period, in 1955 Britain and Iraq became members of the Baghdad Pact (CENTO). But Iraq left that Pact in 1959 and terminated also its special agreement with Britain. Following this, in the same year Britain vacated the Iraqi bases also.

Significantly, all along, Baghdad staked its claim over Kuwait as an integral part of Iraq. But, Britain never conceded that claim of Iraq for Kuwait. Therefore, anticipating future troubles from Iraq, prior to the grant of independence to Kuwait in 1961, in 1960 the British cabinet decided to protect Kuwait's independence, if necessary by use of force. As oil became a strategic material in the 1960s and 1970s, due to its heavy deposits in the region, Iraq, Kuwait and other OPEC countries in the middle east and the Gulf became more important for the developed countries of the west. Significantly, Iraq and Kuwait alone accounted for 40 per cent of the world's oil resources. Therefore, unification of the two countries even peacefully was not politically acceptable to the west since it would give Iraq a commanding position in the global oil market.

Therefore, when Iraq invaded Kuwait in 1990-91, that was foiled by a concert of other powers, including the United States and Britain. Simultaneously, to prevent the recurrence of such invasion, they took measures to cripple Iraq both economically and militarily. Accordingly, in 1991, the United Nations imposed sanctions against Iraq, while the United States continued its war with Iraq over Kuwait until 1998, when the United States and Britain rained cruise missiles on Baghdad against Saddam Hussain. Indeed, the UN sanctions and the prolonged US war had together weakened Iraq considerably. As UN sanctions restricted Iraq's oil sales substantially, the Iraqi treasury became increasingly hollow. It destroyed Iraq's education system, which was rated the best in West Asia. It had other implications too. In 1994, Baghdad effected a 50 percent cut in food rations of the people, which had led to widespread malnutrition. In addition, in 2002, the size of Iraq's armed forces was cut down to about one-third of what it was in 1991. Therefore, cumulatively, by 2002 Iraq was reduced to a weak and insignificant power. It was such a weak country that Bush and Blair had chosen to paint, with the help of doctored intelligence reports, as a source of imminent threat to the security of their countries. However, in tune with the UN resolution, Baghdad, until 1998, cooperated with the UN weapon inspectors in Iraq. But Iraq expelled the weapon inspectors in 1998, following the information that the United States was using those weapon inspectors for espionage in Iraq.

George Bush's election to the US Presidency was a turning point for Iraq. According to a former US Treasury Secretary, Paul O' Neill, ever since he became President, Bush has been gunning for Iraqi President Saddam Hussain and was looking for some excuse to eliminate him and occupy Iraq, and to establish a firm control over its oil wealth.[3] Pertinently, in a speech in Texas in September 2002, Bush charaterised Saddam Hussain as 'the guy who tried to kill my dad'[4]. He saw in the Al Qaeda attacks on the World Trade Centre in New York on 11 September 2001 an opportunity to link the name of Saddam Hussain and Iraq to it and called Iraq a partner in the 'axis of evil' which exported terror. Initially, Bush openly argued that Saddam Hussain had links with 9/11 attacks and with Osama Bin Laden and the Al Qaeda. But, when these linkage could not be established, Bush changed the track and accused Saddam Hussain, without any evidence, that he had failed to fulfil the UN mandated disarmament obligations and was in possession of the WMDs. Obviously, Bush was itching for a clash with Saddam Hussain and was preparing the ground for it by making baseless allegations.

It may be recalled that Bush's accusation that Saddam Hussain had plotted 'to kill my dad' had emanated from a contrived, but 'disrupted' plot to assassinate the father Bush, then US President, during his visit to Kuwait in 1993. Seymur Hersh, well known American journalist, after verifying the evidence provided by the White House with experts, came to the conclusion, published in an article in the *New Yorker*, that the so-called 'disrupted' plot was a fake construct.[5] But, the other accusation that Iraq possessed WMD in violation of UN resolutions was iterated and reiterated from the White

House and 10 Downing Street, under the cloak of secrecy of top US and UK intelligence sources, to mislead the world that Saddam Hussain and Iraq had posed an imminent danger to the world. In this clever hoodwinking exercise George Bush and Tony Blair had worked as teamsters.

However, there seems to be certain unstated US motives behind the removal of Saddam Hussain and the occupation of Iraq. One of the key motives was the preservation of the dollar monopoly in oil trade. For about four decades US dollar enjoyed the monopoly as the sole currency of petroleum trade in the world which had immensely helped the United States to build its strong economy. But, after the launch of the Euro by the European Union in 1999, France has persuaded Saddam Hussain to agree to trade Iraq's petroleum against euro also. Thus a significant beginning was made in Iraq to end the dollar monopoly in the petroleum trade. Other OPEC countries were also began to follow the Iraqi example and showed their inclination to trade their oil against euro also. In the circumstances, the US wanted to force Iraq to return to its oil trade against the US dollar, and restore the dollar's position as the exclusive currency of oil trade. But Washington did not succeed in that venture. Therefore, it appears that placement of Iraq, the second largest source of oil in the world, under the US control was the solution Washington envisaged to ensure oil trade in dollar. Through such a measure, complemented by the removal of Saddam Hussain from power in Iraq, President Bush wanted to nip in the bud the new trend among the OPEC countries to trade oil against euro, and send a clear warning to all other OPEC leaders that if they followed Saddam Hussain's example, their fate also would not be different. Therefore, the American war in Iraq in 2003 was the inaugural war between the dollar and the euro for dominance in the global currency market.[6] By occupying Iraq and by stationing its army there, the US wanted to intimidate all other oil rich middle east countries to act according to the

American wish. Indeed, hawks in the White House had argued that US must unseat Saddam Hussain to send a message across the middle east and elsewhere that US would destroy its opponents wherever they are. And would do so whether the Europeans and the international community like it or not.[7]

However, the reiteration of the United States and Britain that Iraq possessed weapons of mass destruction in violation of UN resolutions led to the return of a new team of UN weapon inspectors to Iraq under the leaderships of Hans Blix and Mohamad El Baradei. Iraq allowed the weapon inspectors to inspect all the sites they wanted in Iraq. But. they could not find any WMD anywhere in Iraq. Yet, Bush and Blair continued to insist that they had clear evidence that Iraq had WMDs and planned to attack Iraq without waiting for the weapon inspection route for disarming Iraq. President Bush made it clear that if the UN route failed to disarm Iraq, America would disarm Iraq through unilateral action. Instantly, he shifted his objective from disarmament to regime change in Iraq as a prelude to his 'liberation' of the middle east. He became impatient with the UN WMD inspection process to disarm Iraq. Tony Blair parroted George Bush when he said: 'I passionately believe, we must disarm Iraq of weapons of mass destruction. Saddam should take the peaceful route and disarm. If he does not, he will be disarmed by force.'[8]

When the United States and Britain failed to get a second resolution from the UN Security Council, authorizing them to use force in Iraq, they said that 'the UNSC has failed in its responsibilities, but we will rise to ours', and took authorization from their respective national legislatures to disarm Iraq. After giving a 48 hour ultimatum to Saddam Hussain, on 17 March 2003, to quit power, the United States and Britain invaded Iraq on 20 March 2003. So, clearly, the US~UK invasion of Iraq was pre-meditated, and basically unconnected with the question whether Iraq possessed

WMDs or not. In tune with that approach, the US strategists had repeatedly indicated that they were preparing for a prolonged occupation of Iraq. They were boisterous to cite the example of Europe where US forces remain stay put for more than half a century after the Second World War, and said that they can remain in Iraq also for another 50 years. So, obviously it did not matter much for the American establishment whether they had the UN mandate or not, or whether their action was in conformity with international law or not.

The international community was sharply divided on the question of use of force against Iraq without exhausting the UN weapon inspection route to disarm Iraq. For example, countries like France, Russia, Germany and China wanted that the UN weapon inspectors should be given more time to complete their task to disarm Iraq. They firmly supported a UN solution to the question of Iraq's WMD. But, US and UK firmly opposed it, probably because they knew very well that since Iraq did not have WMDs, the UN inspectors would never find any WMD there.

Opposition to US-UK plan to invade Iraq was quite widespread. Many questioned the premises on which US and UK wanted to attack Iraq. They argued that in 2003 Iraq did not pose any threat either to US or to UK since Iraq's military capability was severely crippled since 1991 after the imposition of the UN sanctions, and that its armed forces in 2002 was only one-third of what it was in 1991. Also they pointed out that the UN weapon inspectors did not find any WMD in Iraq. Similarly, no evidence has also been produced to show any linkage between Al Qaeda and Saddam Hussain or to establish any Iraqi role in the attack on the World Trade Centre on 11 September 2001. On the contrary, the overwhelming evidence was that Osama bin Laden intensely hated Saddam Hussain. Moreover, Iraq did not have any long-range missile to deliver any WMD either to US or UK or even to Israel. Therefore, critics viewed the American action as part of a show of jingoism of President Bush to impress upon his countrymen that he can teach lessons to his targets, and chose, with the skill and intution of a low calibre police man, a soft target – a weak Iraq – to show it.

By February 2003, opposition to the US and the British moves to use force in Iraq was mounting across the world. There was consensus among important powers like Russia, France, China and Germany that they would not consent US-UK invasion of Iraq.[9] In the NATO meeting on 10 February 2003, France, Germany and Belgium vetoed a Turkish move to invoke Article 4 of the North Atlantic Treaty to defend Turkey in the event of war against Iraq, through the deployment of AWACS surveilance planes, Patriot missiles and anti-chemical and anti-biological warfare teams in Turkey. They vetoed the move on the ground that it would be construed as sanctioning military action against Iraq.[10] On 14 February 2003 UN weapon inspectors, Hans Blix and Mohamed El Baradei, had submitted their new report to the UN Security Council to the effect that they did not find any weapons of mass destruction in Iraq. On 15 February 2003, millions of people across the world joined protest marches against waging a war against Iraq. In Hyde Park, in London, though the organizers had expected only half-a-million turn out for demonstration, the actual turnout was one-and-a-half million demonstrators, indicating how the British public in London got worked up against launching a war on Iraq.

Yet, America and Britain had launched their invasion of Iraq on 20 March 2003, without the UN sanction and in violation of international law. The US occupation of Iraq was complete by 9 April 2003. Baghdad fell to US forces without Iraqi resistence even from the Republican Guards who were allegedly bribed heavily by the US forces to make their way to Baghdad without resistence. Once occupied, the US soldiers also joined the looters in plundering away priceless artefacts from Iraq's national museum. Everything, other than oil establishments, was allowed to be destroyed in the mayhem. After occupying Iraq, the United States sent its own team of 1000 weapon inspectors to search for WMDs in Iraq. Many apprehended that US might plant evidences of WMDs in Iraq. But, a watchful media kept up its vigilance against such moves. Soon after the US occupation of Iraq in April 2003, the *New York Times* reported that America had intended to stay in Iraq for several years.[11] It showed that the so-called transfer of power in Iraq in June 2004 would be a sham exercise and the installation of a puppet regime in Baghdad would not end the US and UK occupation of Iraq. Saddam Hussain was taken prisoner in December 2003, and was subsequently killed after a bogus trial at a Kangaroo Court.

II

What was the British role in an essentially US war in Iraq? What shaped the British attitude towards it? Why did Britain join US in the invasion of Iraq? Answer to these questions are very much intertwined with Britain's long-standing special relationship with the United States, nurtured during the post-war period. It has been widely recognized that the high point of that special relationship was marked during the Thatcher-Reagan administrations in the 1980s. Dr. Nimmi Kurian, Associate Professor of the Centre for Policy Research in New Delhi, has published a book recently, focusing on this facet of Thatcher-Reagan relationship under the title *The High Noon*.[12] That book tells us vividly how the two leaders of Britain and the United States had risked their interests to support each other in critical times, as was manifested during the Falklands War of 1982 and the Libyan Crisis of 1986. The book also underlined that though the two leaders worked very closely together, the relationship Margaret Thatcher and Ronald Reagan maintained as British Prime Minister and US President all through was a respectable and healthy one, and not 'poodle-like', with sufficient room for disagreements.[13]

But, that was not the healthy framework that was adopted by the present British Prime Minister Tony Blair and the US President George Bush in the conduct of their bilateral relationship. It appears that in his eagerness to outshine Margaret Thatcher of the Thatcher-Reagan era of Anglo-American special relationship, and establish more closeness with the US President, Britain's Labour Prime Minister Tony Blair has repeatedly displayed a poodle-like characteristic of abject servility to the US Republican President George Bush. In his determination to remain closer to Bush at all costs, Blair chose oven to ignore the British public opinion, opinion of his own Parliamentary Labour Party, and opinion of senior colleagues of his own Council of Ministers. He appeared more concerned about his standing in White House than his standing among the British public. The pattern Blair followed was that the US President would take the decision and the British Prime Minister would follow him like his coat-tail. That was how Tony Blair behaved through out the Iraqi crisis in 2002-2004.

Ever since President George Bush made public, in January 2002, the road map of his war against terrorism and named Iraq, besides Iran and North Korea, in his axis of evil, Tony Blair became his mouth-piece of that perception. He blindly supported all the arguments Bush had advanced against Iraq and Saddam Hussain. In many press conferences Tony Blair sounded more hawkish than even Bush. Blair told the House of Commons, in March 2002, that Iraq breached the UN Security Council resolutions regarding the weapons of mass destruction. In April 2002 he emphasized: 'We know that he (Saddam Hussain) has stockpiles of major amounts of chemical and biological weapons', and that the Iraqi leader was trying 'to acquire nuclear capability' and 'ballistic missile capability of a longer range'. He said candidly: 'Let's be in no doubt whatever, Saddam Hussain has acquired weapons of mass destruction over a long period of time.'[14]

To reinforce President Bush's arguments against Iraq and Saddam Hussain, in March 2002 Tony Blair initiated an exercise to gather intelligence information to prepare a dossier of evidence against Iraq, giving more precise information about Iraq's weapon programmes. He wanted to take that dossier with him when he was going to meet George Bush in Texas on 5 April 2002. But Blair could not take that dossier with him to Bush at that time since he could not gather any credible evidence against Iraq on WMD to support a military action against Baghdad. So, the 6-page dossier, which was prepared by the British Cabinet Office for publication was withdrawn for want of evidence against Iraq's WMD programme in it. The expert speculations which formed part of that dossier could hardly be treated as credible evidence to justify an invasion against Iraq. So, Blair's dossier had conclusively failed to provide any credible evidence to the effect that after the departure of the UN weapon inspectors from Iraq in December 1998 Iraq had developed any WMD. But, many months later, in February 2003, Blair's government published a dossier on Iraq's WMD which was crafted with the help of plagiarized portions of a 12-year old Ph.D thesis on 1991 Gulf War, written by Abraham al-Marashi of Monterey, California, which was presented as information drawn from classified intelligence report.[15] The US Secretaty of State, Colin Powell, naively commended it as the 'new intelligence material' and the 'exquisite detail of Iraqi deception activities.'

However, during his meeting with George Bush at Texas in April 2002, Tony Blair endorced Bush's new agenda of 'regime change' in Iraq, in place of disarming Iraq. There they decided to launch a joint military attack on Iraq with the objective of 'regime change' in Iraq. At a joint press conference after their meeting on 5 April 2002 President Bush said: 'I explained the Prime Minister that the policy of my government is the removal of Saddam Hussain and that all options are open.' Blair accepted the new Bush agenda publicly at that press conference. Subsequently, on several occasions, Bush continued to flaunt that he was targetting

Saddam Hussain personally. In June 2002, he ordered also the assassination of Saddam Hussain, in a manner circumventing a US Congressional ban on assassination of Heads of States.[16] Pertinently, the US allegedly tried to assassinate Saddam Hussain in 1991 also, when the-father Bush (Senior) was the US President.

The Bush agenda of military action to effect a regime change in Iraq and Blair's support for it was widely criticized in Britain. People in Britain vehemently opposed a blind military action against Iraq without credible evidence. 58 percent of the British public was clearly opposed to military action against Iraq. This popular opposition to British support for US war in Iraq took the form of a mass upsurge. Many Labour Party leaders, Labour MPs and former Labour Ministers had openly opposed Blair's approach. Disquiet was discernible in Blair's Council of Ministers also. They said that there was no convincing evidence against Iraq which warranted a military attack on that country.

In the House of Commons, 125 Labour MPs signed a motion to support the return of UN weapon inspectors in Iraq to achieve disarmament of Iraq without a war. Even some cabinet ministers were opposed to Blair's support to US war in Iraq. Robin Cook, Leader of the House of Commons and former Foreign Secretary, Claire Short, International Development Minister, David Blunket, Home Secretary, and so on were among those who opposed Britain's joining the US war in Iraq without clear evidence against Baghdad on WMD. They demanded clear evidence on that count. They were emphatic that all diplomatic solutions must be explored before contemplating any military action.

Many in Britain questioned the legality of the war against Iraq since it violated international law, and was not authorized by the UN Security Council either.[17] Blair government's legal experts recommended the British government to take a new UN Security Council resolution to settle the legality of the military action. They advised the government that joining an attack on Iraq without a UN mandate would be illegal. A former Chief of Defence Staff, Field Marshal Lord Bramall, told Blair candidly: 'You are supposed to get UN backing. Some lawyers will say you have that, as Saddam has defied UN resolutions. But I think the moral question is not open and shut'.[18] Similarly, the British military was quite unenthusiastic about joining the Iraq war, the legality of which they had serious doubts. Therefore. the military leaders in Britain wanted legal advice in the matter. Pertinently, two US soldiers decided to desert the US army and sought asylum in Canada, arguing that the US war on Iraq was illegal under international law and that they have 'a right not to choose to participate.'[19]

But, Tony Blair's priorities were different. In the Iraq crisis he saw an opportunity to strengthen his personal relationship with President Bush. He took a hawkish position on Iraq and supported the President's approach to use force to remove Saddam Hussain. He accepted Bush's assertion that Saddam Hussain was involved in Al Qaeda's terrorist attacks on the World Trade Centre in New York on 11 September 2001, although the Russian President V1adimir Putin made it very clear that Iraq was not a supporter of Taliban.

According to Jane's defence weekly, Britain started its preparations for Iraq war from November 2002 onwards when it enhanced its military sea lift capability to transport its main battle tank to Iraq. Simultaneously, it also began the preparations to send troops to the Gulf for war against Iraq. In January 2003, Tony Blair told Saddam Hussain to give up chemical, biological and nuclear weapons, which, obviously, Saddam Hussain did not have. Britain sent its aircraft carrier *HMS Ark Royal* and 15 other naval vessals to the Gulf. They included a helicopter carrier, 3 destroyers, and a nuclear submarine, carrying about 3000 royal marines. In all Britain despatched 45,000 troops to Gulf for action against Iraq. In addition, Britain deployed 14 fighter jets in Jordan. Blair did all these when a majority, 58 percent, of the British people believed that war with Iraq was not justifiable. Only 13 percent of British people said that they would support the British troop involvement in Iraq war without the UN authorization.[20]

From February 2003 onwards opposition to Blair's support for US war in Iraq began to mount in Britain. On 15 February 2003, London, Glasgow, and 250 other British cities witnessed largest public demonstrations in their history opposing war against Iraq. Indeed, London witnessed a mass upsurge that day. As mentioned earlier, although the organizers had expected only a half-a-million turn out at the Hyde Park, the actual turn out was 1.5 million people despite the suspension of London's public transport system that day. Anthony Wedgewood Benn, who met Saddam Hussain earlier and got first hand information from the Iraqi President that Iraq did not possess WMD, led the demonstration in the Hyde Park.

Fissures in the British government and in the Parliamentary Labour Party against Blair's support for US war on Iraq began to appear in early March 2003. On 10 March 2003 a Cabinet Minister, Clare Short, International Development Secretary, publicly criticised Tony Blair for his support for US war in Iraq and characterised his move an 'extraordinarily-reckless' and 'indefensible'. Andrew Reed, another government functionary (Parliamentary Private Secretary) submitted his resignation from the government in protest. When Tony Blair presented his case in the House of Commons, on 10 March 2003, for sending British troops to Iraq, there was a major revolt in the British Parliamentary Labour Party. 121 Labour MPs defied the Party whip and voted for an amendment which said that the case for war in Iraq had remained unproven. It was reported that about 160 to 170 Labour MPs were opposed to war in Iraq. Robin Cook, Leader of the House of Commons and former Foreign Secretary, also disapproved the British support for US war in Iraq. He resigned from the government on 17 March 2003.[21]

In an article Robin Cook wrote: 'I already had my fill of this bloody and unnecessary war.'[22] Blair's two other ministers, Lord Philip Hunt and John Denham, had also resigned from the government on this issue. In all 10 members of Blair's government had resigned in protest against Blair's support for US war on Iraq, of whom Robin Cook was the highest ranking personality. Despite all these developments in the home front, Blair was ready to stand by Bush at all costs. As a former Labour minister said. Blair had more sympathy for wishes of Washington on Iraq than what he did have for his own party.[23] That was seen in Britain an act of abject servility. Similarly, the British trade unions, the main support base of the Labour Party, also expressed their disapproval of Blair's line of action in Iraq. Bill Morris, General Secretary of the large Transport and General Workers' Union, said that the bond between Blair, Labour Party, and the British public had been broken. [24]

Tony Blair's woes pertaining to Iraq war began to surface after he and President Bush had completed their agenda of occupying Iraq and unseating Saddam Hussain from power in April 2003. Soon after, Blair was accused of misleading the Parliament and the public regarding Iraq's WMD. In May 2003, the BBC reported an incident of 'sexing up' of an MI6 intelligence dossier on Iraq at Prime Minister's Office to the effect that Iraq had possessed weapons of mass destruction in order to win public and political support for military action in Iraq. It was revealed that the intelligence dossier was doctored in Blair's office by his officials to mislead Britain and the world.[25] The BBC correspondent cited a senior intelligence official as his source of information that the Prime Minister's communication chief, Alastair Campbell, had doctored the dossier to the effect that Saddam Hussain had possessed the ability to deploy chemical and biological weapons 'within 45 minutes'. Such a reference was not there in the original MI6 intelligence dossier, but was inserted in the Report at No. 10 Downing Street. [26] Therefore, obviously, this insertion in the dossier was made not on the basis of any fact but out of political expediency to show that there existed an imminent threat from Saddam Hussain and Iraq.[27]

The suicide of David Kelly, a former British UN weapon inspector in Iraq, the main source of the BBC Report, two days after he deposed before the British Parliament's Foreign Affairs Select Committee, which inquired the 'sexed up' case, gave sharper focus on this moral issue. Indeeed, the "sex up" was a deliberate act of perfidy is clear from the fact that though more than a year has passed after US and UK occupied Iraq, they could not produce any evidence to prove that Iraq possessed WMD when they invaded that country in March 2003. It may be noted that after the occupation US had sent its own team of 1000 weapon inspectors, under David Kay, to search Iraq for WMD, and offered $ 250,000 reward for information on WMD. Yet, even the US weapon inspection team could not trace any WMD in Iraq, the figleaf under which US and UK waged the illegal war on Iraq on 20 March 2003. The spuriousness of the WMD charge on Iraq was further confirmed by the resignation of David Kay, the Chief of the US weapon inspection team, who, after resignation in January 2004, stated categorically that no WMD would be found in Iraq. He said: 'I don't think they existed. What everyone was talking about is stockpiles produced after the end of the last (1991) Gulf War; and I don't think there was a large scale production programme in the 1990s.'[28] However, the fact is that by mid-1990s, Iraq's WMD ceased to exist. In a recent study on WMD in Iraq, the Washington based think tank, Carnegie Endowment for International Peace, has concluded that there was no convincing evidence that Iraq had reconstituted its nuclear programme, and that the Bush administration officials had 'systematically' misrepresented Iraq's WMD programmes.[29] Besides, it said categorically that there was no evidence that Baghdad did possess WMD when US and UK invaded it in 2003. Pertinently, it may be recalled that the doctored British

Intelligence dossier on Iraq's WMD, published in September 2002, had come up with a sensational revelation that Saddam Hussain had WMD ready for launching against UK and US with 45 minutes notice! But in January 2004 Tony Blair himself admitted that he did not know whether WMD would ever be found in Iraq.[30] *Times of India* wrote: 'From Hans Blix to El Baradei to David Kelly to now David Kay, every known authority on WMD has all but rubbished the weapons story that the Bush-Blair duo spun out to go into Iraq. Kay, who led a 1000 strong inspection team into Iraq, in fact resigned last week saying, the weapons did not exist. In other words, Iraq was attacked and Saddam Hussain was humiliated and captured for a complete non-reason.' [31] All these facts have negated the main justification put forth by Bush and Blair for US-UK invasion of Iraq.

It may also be noted that President Bush also had his share of deceit. In his State of the Union address in January 2003 at the US Congress, Bush asserted that Iraq had sought nuclear material from Africa. But, after six months, and after occupying Iraq, the White House admitted that that accusation was misplaced, and put the blame conveniently on the CIA.

The point is that the 'sex up' of the British intelligence dossier, Kay's statement, the findings of all known UN Weapon Inspectors like Hans Blix, El Baradei, David Kelly, and so on, make it absolutely clear that Iraq did not have prohibited weapons, nor did it violate UN resolutions. It also reveals that Tony Blair and George Bush had lied all the way through to their countrymen and the world to win support for their illegal invasion of Iraq. It has brought out clearly that the US-UK invasion of Iraq had nothing to do with WMD or terrorism, but was an unabashed act of imposition to control and steal the oil wealth of Iraq with the mindset of predatory imperialist. It also proves that US and Britain waged an illegal war on Iraq, destroyed that country, humiliated its President Saddam Hussain, captured him from his country for no reason and killed him finally. They invaded Iraq on fictitious grounds simply to destroy a sovereign country and grab its oil wealth. However, Bush has indicated that removal of Saddam Hussain would be the beginning of the liberation of the middle east. But, the larger question is: who will liberate the middle east from this self-appointed liberator? Another pertinent question is: since the US-UK war on Iraq was illegal, and the grounds on which the war was waged have been proved fictitious, who should be held responsible for all the destruction and damage that have been caused by it in Iraq? And who should pay the cost of the reconstruction of Iraq and restore the *status quo ante*? Undoubtedly, America and Britain should squarely be held responsible for all the destruction there, and they should be made to pay the full cost of Iraq's reconstruction. The death and destruction that took place in Iraq during this war, and thereafter, should be declared as crimes against humanity.

In March 2004, voters of Spain have shown the door to their Prime Minister Jose Maria Aznar for supporting the illegal US war on Iraq. Pertinently, Aznar sent a contingent of Spanish troops also to Iraq to support US. The new Socialist Prime Minister Jose Luis Rodriguez Zapatero has now decided to withdraw those Spanish troops from Iraq. That seems to be a new beginning for Bush's chore-boys during the Iraq war. Now the test is for George Bush and Tony Blair. In US, Bush is facing a Presidential election in November 2004. Blair will be facing a general election sometime in late 2005. The big moral question before the American and the British electorates is whether they should continue to repose their confidence on these two leaders who lied to them from the White House and from No.10 Downing Street.[32] With their popularity curve showing a steady decline since the Iraq war, both these leaders are in the throes of their struggle for political survival. Generally, foreign policy issues seldom play any decisive role in the general elections of both the United States or Britain. But, contrary to that general trend, in the forthcoming general elections in both US and UK a foreign policy issue — their war on Iraq — is likely to play a decisive role. Peace, stability and prosperity of the world will be safe if powerful nations of the world are headed by wise men. Higher the power of a nation, wiser should be its leader.

Contrary to the expectations of US and UK establishments, Saddam Hussain's arrest by the US forces in December 2003 had ignited an upsurge of nationalism throughout Iraq, which found its expression in the form of violent actions against US occupation forces and their allies. It appeared that the country got more united against the US-British occupation. An Indian newspaper commented that 'the Iraqis have risen *en masse* against the neo-colonial occupation of their country by the United States and its smattering of allies.' [33] For them. forcing a withdrawal of US and UK forces is the first pre-requisite of the restoration of Iraqi freedom. It is becoming increasingly obvious that the Iraqi Governing Council, composed mainly of Quislings, is fastly losing its control over Iraq.

III

Clearly, the US-UK war on Iraq was a pre-meditated action motivated by secret unstated objectives. The Bush-Blair insistance that Iraq had WMD was a deliberate ploy to justify the start of the invasion of Iraq. They assumed that once inside Iraq, even if this falsehood got exposed, through various manoeuvrings in UN and outside, they can stay put in Iraq indefinitely, under one pretext or another, and keep Iraq's oil wealth under their full control. This deep desire to grab the oil wealth of Iraq first, and then, eventually, of other middle east countries has the potential to prove the nemesis of today's lone super power in due course. This US desire, born out of arrogance, is reminiscent of similar desires hotly pursued by Napoleon Bonaparte and Adolf Hitler to conquer Russia and bring Moscow under their thumb, which ultimately led to their nemesis. If we look back to the history of mankind, the downfall of apparently invincible great powers has been kicked off by one critical mistake of an unwise ruler. The deep desire of George Bush to forcibly occupy Iraq and grab its oil wealth by hook or by crook can prove as decisive as Napoleon's and Hitler's decision to attack Moscow. It may prove a turning point in America's history, the beginning of its decline and fall. Change of leadership in Washington is the only way US can retrieve itself from its present quagmire in Iraq and prevent its crashing. Iraq in not Vietnam. There is no exit route there for the US except acceptance of its failure. The US transfer of power to its puppet regime in Baghdad in June 2004 was a sham exercise since the US and UK would continue to keep their occupation armies (120,000 US soldiers and 10,000 British soldiers) inside Iraq, mainly around Iraq's oil establishments. US and UK military presence in Iraq is a provocation. Iraqis are angry about it which they express every day, by sending more body bags to the United States.[34]

War on Iraq will also have to be viewed in the context of the sea change the international situation has undergone during the last 15 years.With the disintegration of the Soviet Union, the bipolar system which had provided certain level of stability and balance in the international system during the post-war period has given way to a dangerous unipolar system, commandeered by the United States. This has totally upset the global balance of power. In the new situation, the United States is upstaging the world scene like a Frankenstein, and an arrogant international bully, challenging the rest of the world, with a warning that nobody should stand in the way of US in its pursuit of national ambitions. From its present behaviour and the prevalent thinking in Washington, it is clear that America, under Bush, is harbouring an ambition to become the hegemon of the world. In the pursuit of that ambition, Washington has shown readiness to bypass international law and international organizations like the United Nations. American leaders have openly decried the United Nations in recent times when they found that the world body was not cooperating fully with the American agenda. Apparently. the US agenda seems to revolve around the objective of establishing a firm control over the world's strategic resources which legitimately belong to other sovereign nations. At the same time it seeks regime changes in countries which show resistance to the US hegemonic approach. It openly orders arrests and assassinations of personalities who give leadership to such resistance, by putting into practice the dictum that might is right. America's war on Iraq in 2003 epitomised all these features of the new US approach to world politics under George Bush. Therefore, international relations is faced with a dangerous situation. Through its action in Iraq, the Bush administration was testing waters for crafting America's future global strategy and policy.

However, the British policy towards the US war on Iraq was not really 'British' but of Blair's since a vast majority of the British people was vocally against the policy pursued by the Prime Minister. The British electorate used the opportunity provided by the local government elections in Britain, in June 2004, to give a resounding 'no' to Blair's policy, by rejecting an unusually large number of Labour Party candidates, the worst performance of the Party since mid-1970s. In the share of votes the Labour fell to third, with 26 percent, leaving the first and second positions to the Conservatives and Liberal Democrats with 38 percent and 29 percent respectively.[35] Clare Short, former UK International Development Secretary, has urged Blair to step aside. She said: 'I think that the electorate is sending a message to Tony Blair because the Labour Party is incapable of correcting him. What he did in Iraq has brought disgrace and dishonour on Britain around the world'. She said: 'As Tony Blair won't change the policy, the only way to make correction is for him to step aside from the leadership'.[36] Certainly, the Iraq fiasco has cast a shadow over his leadership of the British Labour Party.

Blair's support for Bush during the Iraq war may have further strengthened Britain's special relationship with the United States, but the spectre it presented was one of abject servility of Britain to the United States, a spectre that was not discernible even in the 'High Noon' of that relationship marked during the Thatcher-Reagan period. The enthusiastic imitation of Bush's hawkish pronouncements by Blair was clearly a pointer to that reality. However, people of Iraq seem less hostile to Britain than what they are towards the US since they seem to make a clear distinction between the attitudes of the Blair establishment in Whitehall and of the British people who held unprecedented anti-Iraq war demonstration all over the country. What it means is that a leadership change in Britain can quickly heal the wounds caused by the chore-boy behaviour of Blair towards the Bush establishment. Wedgewood Benn's meeting with Saddam Hussain in early February 2003 and the anti-Iraq war demonstrations he led in UK have made a strong impact on the minds of Iraqis that they recognize that the people of Britain overwhelmingly opposed Blair's support for Bush on war in Iraq. Leadership change in US and UK can expedite the process of restoration of normal relationship between Iraq and other West Asian countries on the one hand and US and UK on the other.

NOTES

This paper was presented at a Seminar in Bombay long before the US Presidential Election in 2004 and the British Parliamentary Elections in 2005.

1. *The Hindu* (Madras), 16 July 2004.
2. *The Hindu*, 21 July 2004.
3. *Times of India* (Bombay), 13 January 2004.
4. *Times of India*, 17 April 2003.
5. See Milan Rai, *War Plan Iraq : Ten Reasons Against War on Iraq* (London. Verso. 2002), p. 132.
6. B. Vivekanandan,'European Union and the Emerging Global System'. See Chapter 2.
7. *International Herald Tribune* (Paris), 14 April 2002.
8. *Times of India*, 14 January 2003.

9. *Indian Express* (New Delhi), 14 February 2003.
10. *Times of India,* 11 February 2003.
11. *New York Times,* 23 April 2003.
12. Nimmi Kurian, *The High Noon : Anglo-American Special Relationship Under Thatcher and Reagan* (New Delhi. Lancer's Books, 2001).
13. Ibid. Also see the Chapter 'Anglo-American Special Relationship', in B. Vivekanandan, *In Retrospect : Reflections On Select Issues in World Prolitics, 1975-2000* (New Delhi, Lancer's Books, 2001), pp. 300-325.
14. *The Times* (London), 12 March 2002.
15. *The Pioneer* (New Delhi), 6 June 2003.
16. *The Guardian* (London), 17 June 2002.
17. *The Economist* wrote in January 2002 that America did not have a legal mandate for serious military intervention in Iraq. *The Economist* (London), 26 January 2002. p. 59.
18. *Daily Mirror* (London), 30 July and 5 August 2002.
19. *The Hindu,* 14 April 2004.
20. *Times of India,* 14 January 2003.
21. *Times of India,* 18 March 2003.
22. *Times of India,* 1 April 2003.
23. See the statement of Britain's former Northern Ireland Minister, Mo Mowlam. *Financial Times* (London), 25 March 2002.
24. *Times of India,* 18 March 2003.
25. *Times of India,* 4 June 2003.
26. *The Pioneer,* 25 July 2003.
27. In July 2004. Tony Blair accepted 'full responsibility' for the intelligence mistakes made in the run up to the Iraq war. *The Hindu,* 16 July 2004.
28. *Times of India,* 25 January 2004.
29. *Indian Express,* 9 January 2004.
30. *Times of India,* 13 January 2004.
31. 'Weapons of Deceit', *Times of India,* 27 January 2004.
32. 55 per cent of British voters believed that Blair 'lied' over Iraq. *The Hindu,* 21 July 2004.
33. 'A Mass Uprising'. *The Hindu,* 14 April 2004.
34. Though US official casualty figures are 900 soldiers, a Russian source said that 'the real number of US losses may be as high as 2000 casualties and upto 12,000 wounded'. *The Hindu,*24 July 2004.
35. *The Hindu,* 13 June 2004 and 17 July 2004.
36. *Ibid.*

5

UN Reforms in Perspective

It is Time for A New Treaty, A New Charter and A New UN

Renovation of the United Nations is imperative to restore its credibility and effectiveness. The unipolar system, and the unilateralism of the lone super power, have pushed the UN to the margins, and reduced its space as the arbiter of international peace and security. Its obsolete power structure has added to its inadequacies. Cumulatively, they have considerably whittled down the esteem and credibility of the UN. This is particularly so during the last one-and-a-half decades. Therefore, it is natural that when an international organization gets slighted by its progenitors, on matters assigned to it, it tries to revamp itself to show its continued relevance, sometimes successfully and sometimes unsuccessfully. The United Nations is at that point now. Increasingly, signals are being given out to the effect that the UN today is not central to the global security system, though it still pretends to be so. Powerful countries have systematically undercut the credibility of the UN by quietly appropriating its role and by acting on their own without its consent. However, if extreme selfishness of any veto-wielding permanent member of the Security Council prevents meaningful reform needed to meet the demands of the 21st century, other member states will have to initiate moves to reconstitute the UN under a new international treaty and a new Charter.

Demands for Reform

The need to reform the UN was felt soon after the end of the cold war to attune it to the realities of our times. In furtherance of it, in a report in 1992, entitled the *Agenda for Peace*, the UN Secretary General Boutros Boutros-Ghali proposed that the UN Security Council should have a peace enforcement unit — a UN army of 5000 military personnel – which could be deployed instantly, on its own, to areas of conflict. He proposed also that the Security Council should, on its own, take cognizance of a developing critical situation and take coercive action, on its own, without waiting for a formal complaint from a member state. Logically, it meant that the Security Council should be given the power of initiative, and make preventive action as part of peace-keeping. But, these ideas for reforming the UN could not elicit much support from the world capitals.

Subsequently, in 1995, the UN General Assembly called for the restructuring of the UN to meet the challenges of the new millennium. In tune with that demand, a more serious proposal for comprehensive reform of the UN was made in a recent report of a 16-member panel, appointed by the UN Secretary General, Kofi Annan. The Panel examined both security and development issues. The security threats which the panel noted included economic and social threats, inter-state conflicts, internal conflicts, genocide and large-scale atrocities, terrorism, weapons of mass destruction, and so on. Among the questions which the panel examined were: How the UN can take effective measures to prevent and remove threats to peace and security, and how it can strengthen international cooperation. The panel recommended, *inter alia*, major structural changes in the UN by way of expanding the membership of the Security Council from 15 to 24 to enable it to become broad based, credible, and equitable, and to make it more representative of the global community. At the same time, the panel recommended a new dual-class structure for the permanent members of the Security Council – some with veto power and others without it. Therefore, though the panel made important recommendations they were couched in a framework of inequality among the same category of members, a framework which belongs to a bygone era and which has generated acrimonious debates the world over. The panel's recommendations have been further revised and refined at the secretariat of the General Assembly President for presenting them as draft proposals for the consideration of a UN summit, to be held in September 2005. However, a key element of UN reform is the structural changes needed in the composition of the Security Council because it is the hub of real power in the UN system.

UN Record : A Mixed Bag

The UN was established in 1945, with the stated objective of securing peace and 'save succeeding generations from the scourge of war.' In the words of a former UN Secretary General, Dag Hammarskjoeld: 'the purpose of UN is not to bring humanity to heaven, but to save it from hell.' However, at the time of UN's establishment, the hope was that all major powers in it would sincerely cooperate with one another to prevent the eruption of another world war. With sixty years behind, the UN record today is a mixed bag. Although the world has been spared of a single war of the Second World War magnitude, the death, destruction and suffering caused by numerous inter-state and regional wars during the last six decades clearly surpass the death, destruction and suffering caused by the Second World War. During the last sixty years, there took place more than 100 regional/inter-state wars and conflicts, in which the UN has undertaken more than 50 peace keeping missions. However, if there was no major war of intercontinental dimension during the last six decades, with the direct involvement of big powers as belligerents, it was much more due to the nuclear deterrence than due to the presence and activities of the United Nations. That apart, besides dealing with issues pertaining to peace and security, the UN has also undertaken tasks like developmental assistance, public health and child welfare, and made notable contributions towards the advancement of public health and child welfare through bodies like the WHO and the UNICEF.

The Overestimation

In the early years of the UN, and in the wake of the euphoria it had generated at that time, many world leaders overestimated its efficacy and impartiality in the execution of the tasks assigned to it under the UN Charter. But, soon, such naïve leaders came to the realization that the UN labyrinth was also a hub of political manipulations, and that it was not the simple merit of a case that mattered, but how to promote national advantage by taking a particular stand on an issue in hand at the Security Council meeting. India was the first country to learn that lesson through the hard way. India's first Prime Minister, Jawaharlal Nehru, was among those who had overestimated the efficacy and impartiality of the UN Security Council as an instrument to vacate aggressions. Owing to a skimpy understanding of the UN labyrinth, Prime Minister Nehru rushed to the Security Council with a complaint against the Pakistani aggression of Jammu and Kashmir, in 1948, to get the aggressor out from the occupied territory, which the Indian army, if allowed to do so, could have easily accomplished in five days at that time. But, instead of forcing the aggressor out immediately, the Security Council dilly-dallied. The manipulative politics in the Security Council helped Pakistan to stabilize its aggression in Jammu and Kashmir, by rephrasing that 'aggression' as an international 'dispute' between India and Pakistan. Certainly, that hand-in-glove response of the Security Council at that time has, since then, caused irreparable losses to India and Pakistan in terms of resources and human lives. The purpose of that twist seems to be to drive a wedge permanently between India and Pakistan and bleed them perennially, and prevent or delay India's rise as a great power in the world.

However, barring the lone case of Kuwait in 1991, the UN record of vacating the aggressor from the occupied territories is dismal. Generally, the methodology UN followed favoured the aggressor. When aggression takes place in small states, the UN Security Council calls for a cease-fire, which generally helps the aggressor to consolidate its position there as the cease-fire put the aggressor and the victim on the same plane, and the issue gets lingered on indefinitely. This type of the operation of the UN Collective Security system jettisons the principles of justice and international law under the cloak of political expediency. Therefore, generally, the UN collective security system has not worked the way it was envisaged in 1945.

The Veto Power

From the very beginning, the UN Security Council has been a hub of power politics. In 1945, it created five veto-wielding powers – Britain, United States, Soviet Union, France and China – as permanent members of the Security Council, a new apex body, the equivalent of which was not there in the League of Nations. In the context of 1945, these five countries were either credible powers or, as imperial powers, controlled large territories and populations. France and China were made permanent members of the Security Council at the behest of Britain and the United States respectively. It may be recalled that even at the UN's founding conference in 1944, at San Francisco, the question of bestowing veto power on a few member states had generated acrimonious controversies, which had taken that conference even to the brink of its derailment. But, in the end, the powerful trio – Britain, United States and the Soviet Union – closed their ranks and carried the day and kept intact the veto power of the permanent members of the Security Council. However, as far as the value of the veto power is concerned, it must be recognized that much more than the actual exercise of the veto power, the right of veto in the Security Council itself gives tremendous leverage for the veto wielding countries in the world of diplomacy. In today's context, veto power in the Security Council is an effective symbol of power politics. That fact cannot be wished away.

Yet, there are commentators who berate the veto power of the permanent members of the Security Council, obviously to dissuade the potential new permanent members of the Council from insisting on it. Generally, they argue that in the post-cold war period the P-5 countries have exercised less number of vetoes, compared to the ones exercised during the cold war period. This argument is quite misplaced. It may be seen that a large number of vetoes in the Security Council, by the veto powers, has been exercised either to advance their narrow national or sectarian interests, or to support their friends and allies for political reasons or on ideological considerations, rather that in the interests of peace and security in the world.

Record of Dealing with Interventions

It may be noted that, over the years, the big powers have constantly tried to use the UN as an instrument to legitimate their interventions. But, whenever the Security Council refused to oblige them, or whenever they suspected of its disapproval, they ignored it and acted on their own, or in alliance with willing partners, to advance their interests. During the cold war, under the bipolar system, the Soviet Union and the United States had functioned as restraints on each other's reckless behaviour. In South Korea, UN was able to intervene against the North Korean aggression because the Soviet Union boycotted the Security Council meeting, and the Chinese seat in the Council was occupied by Taiwan, an ally of the United States. Therefore, though technically the UN could intervene in Korea legitimately under the UN Charter, soon the whole issue had moved in the direction of a super power confrontation as the United States firmly supported South Korea, where as the Soviet Union and the People's Republic of China supported North Korea. The outcome was the armistice, which created the 38th parallel as the dividing line between North Korea and South Korea. But, at another flashpoint of super power confrontation, during the Cuban missile crisis of 1962, the world body could do little when the United States and the Soviet Union came face to face to the brink of a third world war. The sagacity and good sense of the Soviet leader, Nikita Khrushchev, saved the situation and a war between the two super powers was averted. There are other notable failures too. The UN could do little when the Soviet Union militarily intervened in Hungary in 1956 and in Czechoslovakia in 1968, under the garb of defending the communist system in those countries, and in Afghanistan in 1979, under the Brezhnev doctrine. Similarly the UN could do little when the United States militarily intervened in Grenada in 1983, in Panama in 1989, and when America and Britain launched attacks, on their own, on Libya in 1986, and in Iraq in 2003. The main reason for this UN failure was that the culprits in all these cases were veto-wielding Security Council members. Off and on, they did what they wanted to do under the nose of the UN while the world body watched their illegalities helplessly.

Misuse of Self-defense

The UN Charter clearly prohibits the use of force without the authorization of the Security Council, except in self-defense under Article 51 of the UN Charter. But, some powerful countries have thoroughly misused this Article on self-defense. In the Balkans, the United States and NATO unilaterally intervened on their own and used force under the cover of Article 51 of the Charter for self-defense. The Security Council never authorized them to use force in Yugoslavia. Notably, they did so without even claiming that they were under threat from Yugoslavia. The Bush administration has cited President Clinton's action in the Balkans as a precedent to justify the launching of a unilateral attack on Iraq without the expressed UN sanction. When the US Secretary of State Colin Powell was asked, prior to the US invasion of Iraq, whether the United States would seek specific UN Security Council approval for launching attack on Iraq, he affirmed that the President had the authority to do so, as the US did in Kosovo in the company of like-minded countries. In Afghanistan, in the aftermath of the 9/11 terrorist attack, the US-led alliance invaded that country, toppled its government and searched for the Al Qaeda activists in the mountain caves under the guise of self-defense. Though UN has subsequently approved a multinational stabilization force and a peace-building mission, the US-led 'Operation Enduring Freedom' continues indefinitely, searching for Al Qaeda terrorists in Afghanistan in a self-defense exercise to defend the United States! Similarly, no sensible person believed that in 2003 Iraq posed any threat to the security of the United States, to make Washington to justify its attack on Iraq under the cover of self-defense. The fact that Iraq was under severe UN sanctions for the preceding 12 years had reduced Baghdad, in 2003, to a mere shadow of what it was in 1991. To portray such an emaciated country, with 'no fly zones' even inside, as a threat to US or UK required false and fictitious evidence, which only the CIA and MI6 could concoct at the cost of their own reputation. Of late, some powerful countries want to bring pre-emptive strikes and hot pursuits also under the ambit of right to self-defense. In the past this right was claimed and unilaterally practiced only by Israel against Arabs, under the protective umbrella of the United States. But, countries like US also want to make them an integral part of self-defense.

If this demand is legitimized, it will have disastrous consequences. It will generate more hegemons in the world.

Record in the Post-Cold War Period

In its sixty years of existence, the UN has witnessed the beginning and the end of the cold war, and, in between, it has undertaken many peace-keeping operations, which were mainly in the form of supervision of cease-fire agreements between countries which stopped fighting. From the Korean crisis of 1950-51 up to the restoration of the sovereignty of Kuwait in 1990-91, the UN could contain or defuse many tensions in the world. However, the restraint the bipolar world had applied on competing powers has practically disappeared, following the collapse of the Soviet Union, and the birth of a unipolar world led by the lone super power – the United States. As America has accumulated enormous power and started to display its arrogance of power through unilateral actions, the UN Security Council got increasingly marginalized since then in the decision-making pertaining to peace and war.

UN's failures in the post-cold war period are marked by developments in Bosnia-Herzogovina, Somalia, Rwanda and Iraq. At the same time there are success stories too, like the ones in Namibia, Cambodia, South Africa, El-Salvador, Guatimala, Mozambique, and Kuwait. In South Africa the UN supervised democratic elections after ending apartheid. In Angola it could defuse a confrontation between MPLA and UNITA and save that country from a major bloodbath, although a civil war still continued there for about a decade. Similarly, it restored peace in conflict-ridden countries like Mozambique and Guatimala, and restored democracies in Guatimala and Kampuchea. But, on balance, the failures outweigh the successes. For example, in Rwanda the Belgian UN peace keepers simply watched a genocide raging there in 1994, following the shooting down of a plane presidents of Rwanda and Burundi were travelling, on 6 April 1994, near the Kigali airport. That carnage continued for more than three months in which the Hutu gangs, backed by the Hutu army, massacred about 800,000 Tutsis and moderate Hutus. What was the UN's on-the-spot response to this genocide? Five days after the start of the massacre, the UN troops were ordered to withdraw to their airport. Ten days later, on 21 April, barring 270 soldiers, they were all withdrawn from Rwanda while the genocide was still in full swing. The indifference the UN had shown in Rwanda in 1994, when 800,000 people were butchered in three months, is an inglorious chapter in the history of the UN. In Somalia, the US troops led the 'humanitarian' intervention under the UN flag. But, soon, under the impact of their typical GI style of 'humanitarian' operations, many Somalians were either killed or wounded in battles with the UN(US) forces. It turned the people of Somalia hostile to the UN forces. Similarly, Israel continues to occupy territories it occupied since 1967, except from Gaza strip and Sinai, despite many UN resolutions to end that occupation. Israel still occupies most of the West Bank and Jerusalem. The UN failure to stop the US-UK attack on Iraq in 2003 was a crowning failure in a series of its failures. For the UN it was, indeed, a disaster. That illegal war has raised serious question marks about the future of the UN.

Arms Trade: An Impediment

Since mid-1970s, the UN could not function on expected lines partly because powerful countries have developed new avenues to enhance their national income, by stimulating demands for war material across the world. Major arms producing countries have made promotion of arms trade as an integral part of their international agenda, which militates against the peace and security objectives of the UN. Arms trade has stirred up wars and conflicts and promoted poverty in the developing countries. Indeed, from 1970s onwards arms lobbies are very active in influencing state policies to promote their business interests worldwide. To stimulate stable demands for their arms, they needed prolonged tensions and conflicts between countries, so that both sides are sucked into a state of permanent arms race. The deterrence doctrine, which countries have adopted uncritically as their security doctrine in the post-war period, has given the philosophical support to this nefarious game. It means that stirring up tensions and wars between nations have also become a matter of state policy of arms trading countries. If we study the history of tensions and wars during the last 35 years, this fact becomes quite clear.

After oil has become a critical strategic material for the developed countries, many of these countries have chosen the path of arming the rich OPEC countries as a methodology to plough back the petro-dollars to them after supplying junks of arms to these underdeveloped countries. As a result, during the last 30 years, the middle-east and the Gulf have been transformed into a veritable powder keg as a strategy to rob the region's newly generated resources. Arms race between major oil producing countries has been promoted systematically so that they exchanged their petro-dollars for the unproductive and obsolete junks of arms from the oil importing developed countries. By pumping in arms to both belligerents, they sadistically prolonged the mutual bleeding of countries like Iran and Iraq during the Iran-Iraq war in the 1980s, for example, to promote the business of arms lobbies of big powers. Indeed these arms lobbies are known to have a big say in the external policies of important countries like the United States, and in making them to put profit above everything. Therefore, it is imperative to curb the influence of these arms trading countries on the UN Security Council.

Big Powers Slight UN

A severe blow to the UN, as an institution, came from the calculated slight of it by the big powers and their venture to usurp its authority and role, and act as arbiters of peace and security. It may be noted that until 1990s, on issues pertaining to conflict management or in undertaking peace-keeping missions, the UN acted only under Chapters VI and VII of the UN Charter, when a state or a group of states drew the attention of the Security Council to a pertinent situation. The UN did not involve in it automatically or unilaterally, and the question of its intervention was decided by the Security Council. It never intervened, on such situations, on the prodding of any single power, which had decided outside the UN mechanism, to intervene. But that position was altered at the behest of the United States when, in 1998, it unilaterally launched missile attacks on Afghanistan and Sudan, without the authorization of the Security Council. Besides, a new pattern of unilateral intervention was set in motion after the US-led NATO forces unilaterally used force in Yugoslavia in 1999 without the approval of the UN Security Council, and subsequently foisted on the UN a unilateral and pre-emptive role in Yugoslavia. It is said that the US and other NATO powers did not even approach the UN Security Council in the matter on the apprehension that Russia and China might veto the move if they approached the Council for approval. However, the malignancy of that US-NATO action has not been reduced even a bit by the fact that, after the conflict, the US and NATO sought the Security Council endorsement and the UN participation in the policing of Kosovo. That is how the unilateralism of the US has impacted on the role of the United Nations. It has, in a way, given credence to the unilateral use of force by powerful countries and has expanded the scope of illegal intervention.

The US-led NATO attack on Yugoslavia in 1999 assumed added importance because the lone super power and a powerful military grouping had acted on their own and usurped the authority of the UN Security Council. Here, they, not the Security Council, became the arbiters of peace and security, and used force arbitrarily and set a new pattern of international relations of a unipolar world. Certainly, NATO's creeping role as the arbiter of peace and security in the world does not augur well for international peace and security. In Yugoslavia, NATO acted outside the UN and became the main instrument of the US to marginalize the UN and reduce it to a mere peace keeping instrument.

The slight of the UN by America and Britain had reached its crescendo during the US-led invasion of Iraq in April 2003, making it a turning point for the United Nations. Indeed, in the Iraq war, the Security Council was deprived of its legitimate right to apply the rules governing the use of force. When Washington found that on Iraq the UN was not playing second fiddle to US plans, President George Bush had openly belittled the UN and scorned of its role and importance. He denounced the UN as a basket case, ignored the Security Council and unilaterally took military action against Iraq. The debates, discussions and resolutions in the UN Security Council prior to the invasion had no impact on the US-UK schedule for launching their invasion on Iraq. On the eve of the war on Iraq, President Bush stated publicly that he would go ahead with his military operations against Iraq whether the UN Security Council approved it or not. That was the level of US marginalization of the UN. The failure of UN to stop America and Britain from invading Iraq on false pretexts, and simply on personal vendetta of President Bush, born out of an unverified CIA story that a decade ago Saddam Hussein had hatched a plan to kill the father Bush (Sr), is a pointer to the credibility crisis the world body is faced with today. Indeed, after the US-UK invasion of Iraq, the credibility and prestige of the UN has plummeted to an all-time low. The Iraq war divided the Security Council, split the NATO, and made people to sit back and think how to fend against the proliferating expressions of arrogance of the US, which has become unilateralist in its approach to international peace and security.

The Biggest Threat

The biggest single threat to the UN today is the rise of the US as the lone super power, with a readiness to act alone, or in the company of willing partners, outside the UN system and international law. Washington's display of arrogance of power has threatened UN's credibility, and its unilateralism has constantly reduced the space for the UN. Pertinently, in the past, a US President ventured to send the US police to arrest the President of a neighbouring country on some charges. No finger of reproof was raised at that time against that outrage on State's sovereignty and inviolability of international borders. As US displays scant respect for the UN, the latter can hardly moderate the US hawkishness and unilateralism. A citadel of democracy, and a champion of freedom, liberty, and the rule of law at home, the US, especially under George W. Bush, has now gone militaristic, and imperialistic in its tone and tenor. In the circumstances, even London is free only to agree with Washington and not to disagree. It is the US wish that prevails.

Historically, a single super power domination of the world is dangerous. In the past, there was a strong belief that democracies, unlike dictatorships, would not pose any danger to peace and security in the world since they are viewed as respecters of the rule of law and international law. But, the pattern of behaviour the US democracy has presented in recent years is slowly disproving this belief. If democracies like America or Britain wantonly march their armies into the territories of other sovereign states for selfish reasons, under one pretext or another, we have to be cautious even about the military might of democracies. We have to revise our perception that democracies are law abiding, and are less aggressive than dictatorships even when they attain unbridled power. The US example shows that under the leadership of unwise politicians, even strong democracies can wave big sticks and lose their balance, and show off the arrogance of power to a point of threatening the security of other sovereign states. It also shows that the power factor acts independently on the psyche of immature leaders whether they lead a democracy or a dictatorship. From that angle, there is only a thin divide that separates the mindsets of the Fuhrer, Adolf Hitler, and President George W. Bush when both of them became power drunk and became conscious that they were leaders of states whose power could not be matched by any other state, or even by a combination of a few states. The US President decides which country is 'evil', and then arranges for its attack.

The international legal order is under severe attack. When Britain expressed doubts about the legality of the 2003 Iraq war, and of the US fig leaf that the UN Security Council's authorization of 1990 for the Gulf war contained the authority needed to launch the war against Iraq in 2003, the US Secretary of State, Madeline Albright, told the British Foreign Secretary, Robin Cook, that he should 'get new lawyers', obviously urging him to manipulate the legal opinion also.

The Iraq war has shown that the international rules governing the use of force have broken down completely in the full glare of an open debate in the UN and outside. A democratic country has assumed the role of a Frankenstein and sadistically displayed its overkill capacity against a country which was emaciated by 12 years of stringent UN sanctions. It also destroyed the footprints of an old civilization. However, the fact remains that the UN has failed to prevent unnecessary wars the big powers have, time and again, unilaterally imposed on small countries on some pretext. In the present unipolar world, if the lone super power acts on its own, individually or in group but without the UN authorization, on major international peace and security issues, it raises serious question marks on the survival of the United Nations as a credible organization. We should not be blind to the fact that the lone super power is seeking world domination, as Adolf Hitler sought for Germany in the 1930s.

It can lead to disastrous consequences for the UN, and for peace and stability in the world. Today we are faced with a rampant America, moving aggressively around like a Frankenstein, and ready to take on anybody who would stand in its way. If history is any guide, such behaviour can lead to a new 'coalition of the concerned', as a countervailing force, as it took place in the1930s and early 1940s in Europe against Germany. However, as countries increasingly lose their faith in UN as a guarantor of their safety and security, while they pretend that they still count on UN, they make their own arrangements and alliances for their security.

The United States often brandish its fiscal prowess to coerce the UN to toe its line. Repeatedly, Washington sought to apply direct pressure on UN by withholding its dues to the UN. Recently, a US Congressman, Henry Hyde, has proposed that America should withhold its dues to the UN as a tactic to apply pressure on the world body to agree to reforms on the lines of US thinking. He said that reforms can be pushed through by threatening a unilateral reduction in the US contribution to the UN budget, which indicates a particular mindset prevalent in US. It may be noted that US is firmly opposed to any commitment to the creation of an International Criminal Court, to Kyoto Protocol on global warming, and to devote 0.7 per cent of the GNP for development assistance. It wants to stress more on non-proliferation than on disarmament. But the US hope of applying financial pressure on UN to achieve these objectives may not yield the desired results since other countries will not be persuaded by this big stick from the United States. Pertinently, in the UN, the member states are committed to share its expenses 'as apportioned by General Assembly'.

Humanitarian Intervention

In a move to circumvent some of the UN stipulations for intervention in sovereign states, demands have been made, from powerful quarters, for the recognition of the right to 'humanitarian intervention' in sovereign states. As a corollary to it, they floated a new line of argument that sovereignty should not be a barrier to international intervention in extreme circumstances. In 1999, the UN Secretary General, Kofi Annan, favoured humanitarian intervention in states where civilian populations are at risk. He made that proposal in the context of an exceptional situation, like the carnage in Rwanda. However, if that right is conceded, it would place the right of intervention in sovereign states under a very elastic legal framework of what constituted 'humanitarian' at a given circumstance. Under the umbrella of 'humanitarian' intervention, any kind of intervention in sovereign states by use of force may get justification. To provide room for such interventions would be inimical to peace and security in the world. Therefore, to concede such intervention right in a unipolar world, practicing unilateralism, will be disastrous for the poor and weak countries, which will be ordered very often to dance to the tune of big powers. It can lead to the rule of the jungle, rather than the rule of law, in international relations, and to quickly turn the UN system irrelevant. After all, which are the likely powers which would be doing this 'humanitarian intervention'? US, NATO, UN? Though Kofi Annan proposed 'humanitarian intervention' with good intention, in the hands of powerful countries, which practice unilateralism, the application of such provisions need not necessarily be on the basis of objective situation in a given country at a given time. Therefore, the UN reform process should not dilute the respect for the state sovereignty, presently incorporated in the UN Charter. Respect for national sovereignty should remain a fundamental tenet of the reformed UN as well.

US and the League's Failure

It may be recalled that the US was the main architect of the failure of the League of Nations, the precursor of the United

Nations. From the very beginning the League was a crippled child because, although it was the brainchild of a US President, Woodrow Wilson, who made it part of his famous 14-Points at the end of the First World War, the United States refused to be its member. As a result, when the League was slighted systematically by major powers of the time on critical situations, it could do little to keep them on the track of the rule of international law. In the wake of the militarization of Germany and Japan in 1920s and 1930s, and of the unilateralist approach they followed in the conduct of their international relations, the League crashed eventually under these pressures. The international community heard its swan song when the Second World War broke out in 1939. At the end of the day, we have seen the spectacle of the signatories of the Kellog-Briand Pact of 1928, which was meant to outlaw the war, appearing themselves as important belligerents in the Second World War. Developments during the last one-and-a-half decades make one to wonder whether the UN is also slowly slipping into the path the League of Nations had gone in the 1930s. History repeats in the present epoch, though with some difference, when we find that the states whose Heads of Government were signatories of the UN Security Council statement on 31 January 1992, reiterating their adherence to international law and the UN Charter, and that they would resolve all international disputes peacefully under the provisions of the Charter, were found invading Iraq, in 2003, in violation of the UN Charter and the international law.

To a great extent, the international legal system is voluntary. States are bound by the provisions of international treaties only if they are signatories to them. But, a treaty would become a dead letter when a significant number of its signatories, particularly if they are great powers also, acts in violation of the treaty. This is mainly because in such a situation enforcement becomes difficult. However, during the post-cold war period, considerable devaluation of the

Security Council has taken place after the US and the NATO together crafted a parallel peace-enforcement machinery, outside the ambit of the UN, and manoeuvered a *post-facto* recognition of the Security Council, as evident during the Balkan crisis. Therefore, US now shows some tolerance to arguments for expansion of the Security Council after its considerable devaluation, and after demonstrating that the big powers have the right to act outside the purview of the Security Council also, when necessary. Obviously, the UN is not in a position to exercise any control over either the US or NATO if they practice unilateralism or show defiance.

Security Council Structure Obsolete

Like the League, UN was also the brainchild of a US President, Franklin D. Roosevelt. When it was established in 1945 it had 51 founder members; India was one among them. Today its membership is 191. The structuring of the UN Security Council in 1945 was conditioned by the power equations existed at that time, and was done with the main objective of preventing the outbreak of another world war. At its founding conference, held in 1944 at San Francisco, it was decided that five permanent members of the Security Council – Britain, United States, Soviet Union, China and France – would enjoy veto power on any Security Council decision. It was agreed upon, mainly to prevent the imposition of majority decision on any big power, which could ignite a major war between big powers. As a result, it was made essential that any move for uniting for peace, under the UN Charter, should have unanimous support of all permanent members of the Security Council. But, sixty years later, that structure has become obsolete and inadequate. As the power scenario in the world has undergone a sea-change, the criterion used in 1945 to select these five countries as permanent members do not hold good in 2005. Since then, Britain and France have lost their empires, and new power centres have also emerged in the world. That reality is not reflected in the present composition of the Security Council as it has become thoroughly unrepresentative. Today, four permanent members of the Security Council, out of a total of five, together represent only about 600 million people. China represents in it another billion people. But, though India represents another billion people it has been kept out of the core group of the Security Council. Therefore, it is important that the UN Security Council becomes a more representative body, reflecting the realities of the 21st century. Today, the P-5 countries which represent a small minority of the global community dictate the UN agenda for peace and security. Indeed, the fluctuating fortune of the world body is determined mainly by the oscillating attitudes of these P-5 countries – most importantly of the United States.

India's Claim

If we look at the contemporary realities, from every angle, India has the right to be in the UN Security Council as a permanent member, with all the rights enjoyed by other permanent members. Besides the fact that India represents one-sixth of the humanity, in terms of geographical spread, geo-political position, resource base, economic and scientific potential, highly skilled man power and its position as a nuclear weapon state, India is a major country in the world. It is the largest democracy which believes in the rule of law, and is a responsible military power. It is the leading maritime power of the Indian Ocean region.

India is a firm supporter of the UN system, and a major contributor to the UN peace-keeping operations. During the last half-a-century, India has participated in more than 30 UN peace-keeping missions and has contributed more than 50,000 soldiers for the purpose. During the course of these peace-keeping missions India has lost a total of 107 soldiers. Indeed, India is one of the two countries (the other is Canada) which have lost more than 100 soldiers at the altar of the UN peace-keeping missions. Other big powers like the United States and Britain have suffered much less number of casualties in this context. In addition, India's stand in the UN has been constructive and New Delhi has used the forum to promote larger causes like decolonization, advancement of human rights, and ending of racial discrimination.

Offer of a Permanent Seat

It may be recalled that as early as 1955, on the occasion of the tenth anniversary of the founding of the United Nations at San Francisco, the US proposed that India should occupy the permanent Asian seat in the UN Security Council, which was then occupied by Taiwan. But, the Indian Prime Minister, Jawaharlal Nehru, poured cold water on that proposal and declined it in favour of the People's Republic of China. As a result, today India is at the receiving end as both America and China are opposed to India's permanent membership in the UN Security Council, with veto power. Beijing has threatened that it would veto any proposal to expand the UN Security Council. Therefore, if China today opposes India's right to be in the Security Council, as a permanent member with veto power, its responsibility goes back squarely to the naivete of Jawaharlal Nehru who remained all the time, as far as his perception of China was concerned, in an artificial world of his own creation. However, it is imperative that the UN Security Council should have a fair and equitable representation. How to ensure it, as part of a comprehensive UN reform, is a key question. Similarly, without extending veto power to new permanent members, expansion of the UN Security Council will be phoney. The veto-less permanent members will be only toothless tigers there.

India should not accept any proposal which is couched in a framework of inequality among the same category of members. Not only that it would make India a second class permanent member of the Security Council, but also that in world politics and diplomacy it would make the Chinese hegemony in Asia a permanent feature, which is just not acceptable. However, discrimination among permanent members is unjustifiable; either the veto power should be discarded completely, or it should be extended uniformly to every permanent member. The best course would be to abolish the veto, rather than creating two classes of permanent members, and make the decision making truly democratic, even if it is attached with the stipulation of a two-third majority for all decisions. However, India has every right to be a permanent member of the Security Council at par with other permanent members. Certainly, UN reform is important and necessary and should be done expeditiously. But, it should be done in a just manner to strengthen the legitimacy and representative character of the Security Council. In today's world, the Security Council cannot continue to function like the erstwhile apartheid regime of South Africa, where representatives of a small minority ruled over the vast majority.

India announced its candidature for a permanent seat in the UN Security Council in 1994. Subsequently, it is enjoined by Germany, Japan and Brazil to form a G-4 group to jointly pursue the objective. On 11 July 2005, the G-4 countries have introduced a draft framework resolution in the UN General Assembly, as part of proposals for reforming the UN. The resolution calls for the expansion of the Security Council from the present 15 members to 25 members, with six new permanent seats, without veto power, and four non-permanent seats. In the resolution, the new permanent members' claim for veto power has been deferred for 15 years. The G-4 resolution was co-sponsored by 23 states, including France.

Although UN reform has many facets, the reform of the Security Council constitutes the heart of it because it pertains to the apex body which takes crucial decisions at critical times. A notable feature of the Security Council is the in-built inequality in its initial restructuring. At the time of its structuring in 1945 as a new entity, which was not there in the League of Nations, it was still largely a world of colonial powers. Though its architect, the United States, was a champion of democracy, equality and liberty at home, these principles are seldom adhered to when it came to America's foreign policy and external relations. In the realm of international relations, Washington promoted inequality as a matter of state policy, and upstaged the world as a harbinger of inequality in the world. Therefore, it is not surprising that the United States structured the UN Security Council, in 1945, with unequal membership in it – some with veto powers and others without it. Moreover, this is also the organ which has been criticized as neither representative of the UN membership nor reflects the realities of the power structure of the present epoch. This obsolete composition of the apex body of the UN does not measure up to the demands of the 21st century. Yet, it seems that Washington and Beijing want to preserve this unequal structure even in a reformed UN. Pertinently, soon after the G-4 countries introduced the draft framework resolution in the General Assembly, the United States and China have come out with statements, urging the member States of the UN to vote against the resolution. However, it is high time for them to realize that unequally composed international structures belong to a bygone age, and that they cannot endure for long in the present epoch. Notably, any change in the Charter needs the unanimous support of all veto-wielding permanent members also, besides obtaining the mandatory two-thirds majority of the total UN membership, i.e. of 128 members, for the resolution.

North-South Cooperation and Common Security

Conflict prevention is the best way to maintain peace,

and preventive diplomacy is infinitely less costlier than wars and conflicts, even if they are fought under the UN flag. But, the pertinent question is how to achieve it without giving a room for the big powers to impose their will on small powers. That requires new peace structures, based on solidarity and common destiny of the humankind. Therefore, if the UN ventures meaningful reforms, along with its present programmes of poverty eradication, health care, child welfare and so on, the new reform package should also imbibe programmes like 'North-South Cooperation', and 'Common Security' enunciated by world statesmen like Willy Brandt and Olof Palme respectively, which can constitute the bedrocks of economic justice and enduring peace, by building up stable peace structures based on solidarity around them on a global scale. It must be recognized that the collective security system, which enunciates the dictum that all for one and one for all to end aggression, has not worked well under the UN, as big powers themselves have indulged in acts of aggression. Therefore, the collective security approach should give way to a 'common security' approach, by which the States are encouraged to ensure their security by ensuring the security of their neighbours. It will engender a new type of international relations, accompanied by a progressive and multilaterally organized scaling down of offensive capabilities of states. What the world needs is organized peace and community of power, instead of the balance of power and deterrence doctrine. Indeed, a reformed UN should be an instrument to encourage all countries to move away from the deterrence doctrine and the balance of power approach and imbibe the common security approach which will revolutionize international relations for the better. Bridging the gap between the rich and the poor nations, and between the rich and poor people inside societies is imperative for a peaceful world. Therefore, the UN should promote also the construction of welfare states across the world for improving the quality of life of ordinary people.

A new concern is: how to resolve intra-state conflicts like genocide, ethnic cleansing and so on, without undermining the state sovereignty. In my view, the UN should devise ways and means to deal with them effectively through national governments, while preserving their national sovereignty, failing which, through the international action under the UN authorization. Similar are questions like how to deal with challenges like international terrorism, perpetuated by non-state actors, and so on. It is my conviction that a framework based on international solidarity can effectively contain all these new challenges.

Conclusion

If the United Nations wants to remain credible, effective and enduring, it has to change in tune with the changing times. In the new context, it cannot continue to function effectively with obsolete structures of a bygone era, and needs new structures based on principles of equality and solidarity. Since the UN Charter does not allow any restructuring without the consent of all P-5 countries, if any of the entrenched P-5 countries of the Security Council remains obstinate against any meaningful change in the present structures, other like minded states will have to seriously consider whether there is another way to manage peace and security in the world. Since the P-5 seem to be keen to keep their privileged position in the Security Council, and are not in favour of extending it with anyone else, it seems that the veto power of the P-5 will stay with the present UN. Therefore, the alternative is to reconstitute the UN under a new international treaty, and with a new Charter, bereft of veto power for the members of the Security Council. It would mean the establishment of a new UN to succeed the present one, with a new apex structure based on equality and solidarity, which can effectively meet the challenges of the 21st century. If P-5 countries do not accept the equality principle, while reforming the present Security Council, India and other like-minded countries should take the initiative to concretize a new international treaty to establish a new UN system, which upholds the principle of equality, and which reflects the realities of our times. Initiative, with a positive vision is the need of the hour.

6

Globalization and Developing Countries

For any internationalist, globalization is an enchanting proposition because it instantly inspires people to lift their sights above the neighbourhood and look beyond the frontiers of their countries, cultures and continents. It instantly takes one's thought closer to the concept of 'One World' espoused by Social Democrats. In this context, it is worth recalling what the founding fathers of the Socialist International had declared at the time of the establishment of the International in Paris in July 1889. They proclaimed that an objective of founding the International was 'the creation of a society in which all women and men, irrespective of sex or nationality will enjoy the wealth produced by the work of all workers.' It implied three fundamental principles–equality, distributive justice and solidarity. It was explicit that the wealth of the world should be equitably shared for enjoyment among all people.

In the post-war period, eminent international Social Democratic statesmen and visionaries like Willy Brandt, Bruno Kriesky, Olof Palme and Kalevi Sorsa gave new impetus to this objective in the 1970s and 1980s when they invoked the principle of international solidarity for bringing together the developed and the developing countries within a mutually beneficial cooperative framework. They envisaged concerted global action to assist the development of the developing countries. While Bruno Kriesky pleaded for a New Marshall Plan for Third World development, Willy Brandt chaired an International Commission on North-South Cooperation and made very valid recommendations for building a fruitful partnership between the developed and the developing countries on the valid ground that the development of developing countries is in the best interest of developed countries themselves. Olof Palme kept on reminding that socialism means solidarity. Kalevi Sorsa complemented these efforts but presiding over the Socialist International Disarmament Advisory Council (SIDAC) for conserving world resources for development through disarmament measures.[1] The spirit that permeated all these moves was to help to build a non-exploitative, sharing and mutually beneficial world society and harness it also through the development of the developing countries. That enlightened approach was widely welcomed in the developing world. If globalization is pursued on these lines, and within the framework of international solidarity, that would bring benefits to the whole humanity.

But a close look at the ongoing globalization, from the viewpoint of the developing countries, reveals that the enlightened approach and benign features mentioned above are conspicuous by their absence in it. Its objectives, framework, and direction belong to a different track.

A few years ago, my illustrious teacher, Prof. M.S. Rajan, made a profound observation about the behaviour pattern of states during the last 350 years. He said that despite many changes in the world, the continuing desire of a small number of powerful states to exercise hegemony over others remain central to their behaviour, although the actors kept on changing in different epochs.[2] Perhaps, the substance of this observation might help us to understand the ongoing globalization process.

Globalization, in its present form, is anchored in the bedrocks of liberalization, privatization, monetarism, free market and business nationalism, as conceived and perfected by neo-conservatives, and epitomized by Thatcherism and Reaganomics of the 1980s. Its basic character is exploitative and domination oriented and its methodology is coercive. Cumulatively, it personifies the desires of a few centers of economic and technological power to dominate the world and to reorganize the world economy to their advantage on neo-colonialist lines. It is aimed to make encroachments on the sovereignty and autonomous development of poor countries and lead them to a debt-based developmental process, which will not only undermine their self-reliance but also increase their dependence on international moneylenders. This is altogether a different track from what was being envisaged by Willy Brandt and his Social Democratic colleagues.

Therefore, essentially, the philosophical foundation of present globalization is flawed and detrimental to the development of the developing countries. It is being imposed on the developing countries by a few developed countries in tandem with their transnational corporations (TNCs), the IMF, the World Bank and the WTO. Every vulnerable point of developing countries has been ruthlessly exploited for this purpose. Its unstated objectives in the developing countries seem to be maximization of profits, capturing of third world markets, snatching of domestic markets of indigenous producers, unfettered freedom for the TNCs in the host countries, and so on.

With the help of modern technology, globalization has come to symbolize concentration of power, information, wealth and production and supply in the hands of a few rich advanced countries and their TNCs and building up of a new global exploitative structure. It is attuned to the creation of a global economic and free market system where the survival of the fittest becomes the law – with TNCs as the likely winners. Unlike in the old colonial system where the local agents of the imperial power were visible and physically present in the colony for everyone to see, today remote control systems have been established to quietly apply effective pressures on the political leaderships of developing countries to comply with the dictates of the largely invisible masters. The IMF and the World Bank also do their share of arm twisting to force the developing countries to effect structural reforms and pave the way for globalization and free market, unmindful of its harmful effects on the local population. Of late, the WTO also has joined this coercive apparatus for advancing the interests of a few rich countries and their TNCs. Indeed, it extends *de facto* assistance to the TNCs to wrest complete freedom to invest anywhere. Any government which resists gets penalized.

The liberalization of the third world economies is a pre-requisite for globalization. It means facilitating free play of market forces in both national and international economic transactions through deregulation, privatization, removal of trade barriers and free flow of foreign capital. To attain this prerequisite, the TNCs seek a reduction of customs tariffs for their export items so that their products produced by using the economy of scale can compete freely with the domestic products of the host country and edge them out and capture their markets. Similarly, they seek unfettered freedom to invest in any sector of economies of the developing countries and seek national treatment from the host country so that the latter will have little control over the operations of the TNCs. In these efforts the TNCs are actively aided by their home countries, the IMF, the World Bank and the WTO. One of the consequences will be that if the TNCs are allowed to invest in sectors which are hitherto principal sources of employment and income of the local people, such foreign investments will sound the deathknell of domestic industries of developing countries. Huge TNCs of rich countries will in no time overwhelm them and they will be forced either to fold up or to merge with a TNC. Products of small and medium industries will lose their local markets, with the disastrous consequence of rise in unemployment and the resultant social unrest in these countries.

Driving the developing countries first into the debt trap was a methodology, which seem to have been followed systematically to coerce them into the track of globalization-liberalization. Indeed, the lending policies pursued by the international money-lenders during the past two-and-a-half decades have landed many developing countries in to debt traps. And this vulnerability of the debtor countries has been liberally exploited to promote globalization and liberalization of their economies. It seems that the debt trap for the developing countries was laid way back in the 1970s when, in order to save the Western banking system from collapse, following the flooding of the world currency markets with petro-dollars, the IMF advised many developing countries to borrow. To encourage more borrowing new terms like 'Debt is not a bad thing', 'Safe borrowing' and so on have been floated to manipulate the psyche of the developing countries, and the 'Safe level' of borrowing has been constantly revised upwards to load the poor countries with heavy debts. As a result, the economies of most of the developing countries of Latin America, Asia and Africa have developed a dependency syndrome and have been virtually reduced to the level of bonded labourers of international money-lenders. Therefore, they remain weak and vulnerable as they have to struggle hard to find additional resources every year for debt servicing. In the process many of these economies are getting sunk under the weight of foreign debt.[3] It is this grave situation which has led to the massive demonstration, and submission of petitions signed by 8 million people, in Cologne, in June 1999, at the site of the G-8 meeting demanding the cancellation of the Third World debt.[4] However, the pull of the debt is such that most of the borrowers from the IMF soon returned to it for more loans for repayment of their earlier loans. Nevertheless, for the developing countries foreign debt has proved debilitating and they just cannot grow with that liability at the bottom of their economies. Indeed, in many of them the debt provided new opportunities for foreign investors to swap foreign currency debt with solid assets of the debtor countries at very low prices, which is otherwise called "debt for equity swaps".

However, in the whole globalization exercise, the role of the IMF and the World Bank deserves special attention. Deviating from the purpose for which these Bretton Woods institutions have been created, in recent decades they have become political and ideologically partisan and they seem to have taken upon themselves the onus of pursuing the goals of neo-conservatives by imposing liberalization packages on the developing countries. There are enough evidences to show how they have applied pressures on many developing countries to remove restrictions on the flow of goods and capital through measures like reduction of tariffs, permission for majority control to foreign investors and manufacturers in collaborative ventures, full convertibility of local currency on current account, and so on. Indeed, the IMF and the World Bank have pursued these measures also through their structural adjustment programme (SAP) packages which have been made a conditionality for granting loans to poor countries or for bailing out a country in severe economic crisis. These SAP packages contained not only measures like internal deregulation, privatization and import-export liberalization, but also measures such as maintenance of fiscal balance (which generally results in the curtailment of social spending) , inflation control, and high interest rates, which can have adverse impact on employment situation. According to Prof. Muchkund Dubey, India's former Foreign Secretary, the IMF and the World Bank now function as 'policemen' of the North over the South.[5] However, their loaded stipulations like export orientation, import liberalization, privatization, more foreign private investments, etc., and other packages to the developing countries seem to have been drawn in tandem with the G-7 countries and are aimed at the promotion of the interests of these countries and their TNCs. By using debt and loan, and their strategic position as international money-lenders, the IMF and the World Bank even dictate national policies of many developing countries. For example, by exploiting

India's weakness as a debtor country, they have dictated structural adjustment programme to India to change the country's economic and monetary policies. The SAP contains heavy dosages of domestic liberalization and import liberalization. In 1997, the IMF descended to much lower levels and asked India to hike prices of petroleum products and phase out fertilizer subsidies. Further it demanded reduction of civil service employment, cutting subsidies, more privatization, a flexible approach to exchange rate management, and more openings for foreign banks and foreign insurance companies. It pressed for further trade liberalization through more tariff cuts, elimination of quantitative restrictions (QRs) on consumer goods, and by phasing out small-scale sector reservations. For India, they were bitter pills to swallow.

Moreover, it has been found that in the pursuit of globalization in many developing countries of Asia, Africa and Latin America, the IMF and the World Bank have liberally used their former employees and pensioners, who still occupied key positions in their own countries, to effect major policy changes from the top on the lines prescribed by them. It is not difficult to spot such champions of globalization and liberalization in many developing countries, including in India. However, the fact remains that many developing countries which have unsuspectingly followed the advices of IMF and World Bank on SAP and other measures, including full convertibility, to harness globalization have come to grief, as has been experienced by countries of Latin America, and East and Southeast Asia. It is well known that Mexico, for example, under the leadership of President Carlos Salinas, had reoriented its economic policy under the guidance of IMF, World Bank, and the United States. In the end the whole Mexican economy got derailed. The free market system had resulted in the impoverishment of the Mexican people. The pent-up anger against those who put Mexico on such a disastrous track reached the crescendo when the opposition leaders demanded that leaders like President Carlos Salinas should be tried for treason. Experiences of other Latin American countries and countries of East and Southeast Asia are not different.

It appears that an objective of this whole exercise of globalization and liberalization is to facilitate the TNCs to capture the domestic markets of the developing countries and to systematically liquidate small and medium local enterprises there through methods like collaborations, mergers and takeovers. These borderless entities, which mostly belong to rich countries, are spread in areas like oil industry, tyre industry, chemical industry, electronics industry, electrical engineering, foodstuffs and so on, and have themselves become huge entities over which neither any national government nor any international organization has any meaningful control.[6] Pertinently, it has been found that of the largest 100 economies of the world more than 50 are TNCs. Moreover, the TNCs control about two-thirds of world trade. In many cases they have become *de facto* monopolies, dictating prices globally. Many developing countries have not yet realized the extent of empire building the TNCs have accomplished by now in the fields of production, trade and investment under the garb of globalization-liberalization-privatization and free trade. Indeed, their role in the global market today makes free trade a mockery. According to Vic Thorpe: '...the very concept of "Free trade" is made ridiculous by the knowledge that one-third of all trade across national borders is simply transfers of stock at internally managed prices between the subsidiaries of the same multinational company; at least another third is sales made by multinationals to other companies; and a good part of the remaining third is imports from smaller national contractors and resource providers to the same multinationals.' He says that, it looks like a global market but not a free market. 'We are witnessing not just the globalization, but the corporatization of trade. Now more than ever, the world has a planned economy. But it is planned in secret, behind the board room doors of the multinationals. The national political process has lost control over the real world of economics'.[7]

In order to raise hopes on globalization highly exaggerated tales of its benefits have been propagated in the developing countries. The TNCs and the FDIs have been projected as carriers of modern technology to the developing countries. But the substance of this propaganda was found phoney. Neither the TNCs nor the FDIs brought any critically needed technology with them to the developing countries. Instead, the developing countries had to face more obstacles to the transfer of high technologies to them. For example, India's efforts to obtain 'Cray' Supercomputer from the United States were repeatedly frustrated in this manner, which forced New Delhi to concentrate its scientific research to produce its own Supercomputer, *Param*. India's *Param* not only matches the U.S. 'Cray' computers, but it is highly cost effective also. Similarly, there is little R&D collaboration between the developed and developing countries. It has been found that generally the TNCs of U.S. and Japan do their R&D in their own countries. European TNCs, though sometimes do their research and development outside their countries, still do by and large within their region. However, there is little chance for collaboration between TNCs and the developing countries in the field of technology modernization. Pertinently, a recent UNCTAD report – *World Development Report* – has shown that most of the foreign direct investments came to developing countries in the form of purchase of domestic enterprises by the TNCs. In 1999, such purchases constituted 82 percent of the FDI, through which the developing countries could hardly get any new or modern technology transferred to them.

Another exaggeration was that of globalization and TNCs would bring a large number of highly paid jobs to the developing countries. It may be noted, in this context, the

TNCs preference has always been rich countries and more advanced among the developing countries to locate their investment. Professor Bruce Scott of the Harvard Business School of the United States has brought out this fact in a recent article in the New York journal *Foreign Affairs*, in which he wrote:

> The total stock of foreign direct investment did rise almost seven folds from 1980 to 1997, increasing from 4 percent to 12 percent of world GDP during that period. But very little has gone to the poorest countries. In 1997, about 70 percent went from one rich country to another, 8 developing countries have received about 20 percent, and the remainder [10 percent] was divided among more than one hundred poor nations. According to the World Bank, the truly poor countries received less than 7 percent of the foreign direct investment to all developing countries in 1992-98. At the same time the unrestricted opening up of capital markets in developing countries gives larger firms from rich countries the opportunity for takeovers that are reminiscent of colonialism. It is not accidental that rich countries insist on open markets where they have an advantage....[8]

Therefore, the number of high paid jobs these investments can generate in the developing countries cannot go beyond their minuscule level. Secondly, the TNC investments in the developing countries are mostly in job displacement areas. Their capital-intensive hi-tech investments have the effect of destruction of millions of existing and potential jobs in the developing world. Of course, it is possible that shifting some production units of a TNC to a developing country, primarily to take advantage of cheap labour or proximity of raw material or markets, might bring some new jobs. But, fuelling unemployment has been a notable feature of globalization in many developing countries.

What we witness today as a result of globalization is increasing disappearance of secure and decently-paid jobs, replaced by low paid casual workers with no job security at all. In India, for example, after globalization process got underway, there is a significant decline in employment as a result of closures and lay-offs. At the same time there is a change in the nature of jobs as well. For example, in the post-reform period, the proportion of casual labour has increased from 31. 2 percent in 1988 to 37 per cent in 1998 – indicating that the globalization process in India has pushed more workers from the organized sector to the unorganized sector, from secure to insecure jobs.[9] In addition, globalization-liberalization-privatization process in India has given rise to a network of small and medium sized sub-contractors, who function as approved middlemen exploiters of the employees. Jobs under them remain low paid and service conditions do not exist in such jobs. There are a large number of private security services which come under this category. Similar is the plight of the low paid employees of the newly mushroomed private courier services. Hiring and firing is practiced in all these sectors with impunity. This new phenomenon following globalization has intensified job insecurity and stress even among those who are already in jobs.

It is my conviction that long-term unemployment in any society – developing or developed – is socially and politically dangerous and would provide a fertile ground for extremist elements to take countries to undemocratic paths and organized crime and social unrest. Xenophobia can also grow fast in such a climate. Therefore, no sensible government anywhere in the world should go for policies which have the potential to breed unemployment and the resultant unrest in society. It is worth recalling that unemployment among the youth was the most important factor which made many parts of Europe in the 1930s a fertile ground for growth of Nazism and Fascism, which had taken the world to the final catastrophe – the Second World War.

I have no doubt that if the employment oriented small- and medium- scale enterprises of the developing countries (in India alone small-scale and cottage industries alone provide employment for 12 million people) are allowed to be edged out of production and market by the TNCs through the globalization process, the resultant unemployment will fuel tremendous social unrest which can destabilize democratic systems. History tells us that a country steeped in social unrest or civil strife can never make any progress and its energy and resources will be wasted in combating that unrest. Widespread use of modern technology at the popular level will make containment of such unrest very difficult and costly.

What does globalization mean in the life of ordinary people in a developing country, like India, is best illustrated by an Indian film maker, Anand Patwardhan, in a documentary film entitled *Fishing in the Sea of Greed*. The film depicts the hardships of India's fishermen due to the induction of huge mechanized foreign ships of big transnational fishing companies, with their 15-km long nets and onboard processing plants, for fishing which destroys the livelihood of millions of fishermen in India's 6000 kilometres long coastal bed. From posse of mechanized trawlers in the 1970s, India's poor fisherman today are faced with a large number of huge foreign ships fishing around against their small catamarans. According to Anand Patwardhan, one such ship can scoop more fish in one day than what the thousand catamarans can catch in a year. Similar illustrations exist in many other sectors of livelihood of ordinary people in the developing countries as a result of globalization-liberalization.

Potential large-scale flow of foreign capital was another pie in the sky held on before the developing countries to entice them to embrace globalization, liberalization and privatization. But this also was found phoney. The latest World Bank statistics show that there is a net capital outflow from the developing countries to the developed countries as a result of the present globalization process. According to the Bank's recent publication, *Global Development Finance*, the flow of investment from the developed countries to the developing countries in 1991 was $143 billion, and the flow in the reverse direction was $17 billion. But, in 2000, the flow from the developed to the developing countries was $ 299 billion, whereas the flow from the developing to the developed countries was $ 307 billion–which means that in net terms the developing countries have exported $ 8 billion of their capital to the developed world. Therefore, even in terms of foreign investments, globalization has not benefited the developing countries in any significant way. On the other hand, it is leading the developing countries to lose their capital to the developed countries. Already, billions of dollars (a UNDP estimate said a few years ago $ 500 billion) are flowing out from the south to the north every year in the form of trade advantages, debt servicing, royalties, profits on foreign investments, and capital flight. This massive outflow of resources is already crippling the southern economies.

Therefore, the two arguments which were advanced to support globalization – flow of additional capital and technology – have not been found strong. In the circumstances, an Indian economist has come to the conclusion that 'Globalization is neither leading to greater investment in the developing countries nor bringing in new technologies.' He wrote: 'The case for foreign investment is becoming weaker everyday. It is getting us neither capital nor technology. We should therefore focus on retaining our own capital within the country'.[10]

The promise of more choices for consumers through globalization was also phoney as the TNCs, the main agents of globalization, have systematically captured markets and effectively reduced choices by eliminating potential competitors in the market through collaboration, mergers and outright purchases of local enterprises. The TNCs, which control about two-thirds of world trade, organize production and distribution on a global basis by using the economy of scale, by extensively using the electronic media for advertisement, have been manipulating the consumers psyche worldwide to harmonize consumption patterns across the world. Cumulatively, globalization has effectively reduced consumer choices.

Another negative fallout of globalization for the developing countries is the globalization of prices without globalization of incomes, which has invariably resulted in the marginalization of the poor everywhere. What can be the impact of this lopsided feature of globalization, in practical terms for the developing countries? If we take for example the globalization of prices of life saving medicines by the pharmaceutical companies of affluent countries, accompanied by privatization of health care as a result of the IMF/World Bank dictates for Structural Adjustment Programme in the developing countries, it would simply mean death for millions of people from the poorest sections of society everywhere in the developing world who cannot afford to buy these medicines at the globalized price. It must not be forgotten that, according to the World Bank report there are 1.2 billion (one-fifth of humanity) people in the world whose per-capita income is less than $ 1 per day. In sub-Saharan Africa, 46 percent of the population come under this category.[11] Children and the aged ones from these strata of society will be the worst victims, whose mortality rate will inevitably rise as a result. A well known Indian economist, Professor Deepak Nayyar, has said recently that globalization has introduced a new dimension to the exclusion of the common man from consumption possibilities which only creates frustration and alienation.[12] Therefore there is need to look at the impact of globalization-liberalization-privatization from the angle of the poor people who are not protected by welfare state systems. Of late, even the President of the World Bank, James Wolfensohn, has realized such a need. In a 'foreword' to the recently published *World Development Report*, he wrote: 'The forces of global integration and technological advance can and must be harnessed to serve the interests of the poor people.'[13] We must also not forget the fact that 50 percent of world population which live in the poorest of the developing countries (LDCs) accounts only for 5. 6 per cent of the world's income. Similarly, the gap in the average per capita income between the rich and the poor countries remains at the ratio of 58 : 1. The present parameters and course of globalization can only further aggravate this inequality. That trend should not be encouraged. However, the price policy pertaining to internationally patented essential items like medicines should take into account these ground realities.

There is an overwhelming impression in the developing world that the on going globalization is devoid of humanitarian goals, ethics or compassion. As India's former Finance Secretary, K.P. Geethakrishnan, a supporter of globalization-liberalization in the beginning, cryptically remarked: 'In free market's policies there is no place for compassion or sympathy' for the poor.[14] Similar assessment has come from sources in Scandinavia as well. For example, Pierre Schori, Sweden's Deputy Foreign Minister, observed in 1997 that 'Globalization without a global political and ethical framework cannot be a driving force for combating poverty and creating peace, democracy and development'.[15] However, the question is: can the rich countries remain indifferent to it? No. As professor Bruce Scott has written prophetically: 'Overtime, the rich countries will be forced to pay more attention to the fortunes of the poor – if only to enjoy their own prosperity and safety.'[16]

Globalization-liberalization has not significantly enhanced the access of the developing countries to the markets of the developed world mainly because of dualism practiced by some of the votaries of globalization and free market. Many of them have been found preaching free market while practicing protectionism and try to keep products of developing countries out of their markets on one pretext or another. The Indian experience in this regard is not very encouraging. For example, India's market access in the West has not improved in any way due to globalization, as it has not found much additional space in the Western markets for its manufactures after it joined the globalization process. Not only that, in recent years some developed countries have chosen to erect many non-tariff barriers or to impose *de facto* trade sanctions against Indian exports on one pretext of another – labour standards, technical standards, sanitary standards, or by using patenting instruments like the patenting of Basmati Rice, produced only in India's northern states, to the Rice Tech in the United States. The flimsy pretext on which the Indian rayon skirts, a very popular item among the U.S. women, were pushed out of the U.S. market to favour domestic producers by saying that the skirts are not fire proof is a case in point. In Europe too, new non-tariff barriers have been erected against Indian exports. The European Union's new stipulation, effective from 1st April 1998, that the milk products should remain untouched by human beings from the stage of milching up to retailing is clearly directed against India's ambition to become a major exporter of dairy products. Strangely, the hitherto used sterilization technology has suddenly become inadequate for the EU's health standards! The dichotomy is that while the West is pushing India to open up its domestic market for their exports through globalization and liberalization, it is systematically closing its markets for Indian exports through protectionist measures.

An unsavory aspect of globalization is that it has not been harnessed through an open, rational, constructive reform process. By and large, it has been thrust on the developing countries. It is not out of conviction that the developing countries have joined the band wagon of globalization and have undertaken structural adjustment programmes to pave the way for globalization and the TNCs. They have been constantly coerced to do so by a few power centres from abroad after fully exploiting their vulnerabilities at critical times. This element of coercion indicates the current unjust exploitative part of globalization which will unravel itself in due course. That is the reason why many people in the developing countries who initially gave support for globalization-liberalization-privatization process have now turned against it.

In India more and more economists have come out in the open to publicly express their dissatisfaction on globalization.[17] But, the most significant expression of dissatisfaction over the way globalization-liberalization-privatization process has worked in India came from the President of India, K. R. Narayanan, in his Republic Day message on 25 January 2000. In a veiled warning the President said: 'The fury of the patient and long-suffering people would be unleashed if the three-way fast-lane of liberalization, privatization and globalization failed to provide "safe pedestrian crossings" for the unempowered in India.' He said: 'Many social upheavals can be traced to the neglect of the lowest tier of society, whose discontent moves towards the path of violence.'[18] However, the strongest international expression of dissatisfaction over the effects of globalization was made recently in Genoa (Italy) in front of the leaders of the G-7 countries when they met there in summit in July 2001. It was one of the strongest anti-globalization demonstrations the world has witnessed for focusing the neglect of the poor developing countries by the G-7. The demonstrators drew the attention of the G-7 leaders to how the poor people get hit instantly when low income countries are forced to adopt the market-based globalized system. As a result, for the first time the G-7 leaders were forced to acknowledge, at the summit, that globalization has to be to work for all.[19] But, they have not yet spelled out how they are going to accomplish it. However, the credibility of the G-7 statement will be tested in the coming years.

If globalization is expected to promote a balanced global interdependency, globalized social standard will have to become an integral part of that agenda. But, as of today, there is no such social agenda attached to globalization for overcoming the problems of poverty and hunger in the developing countries. It is irrational to leave human welfare at the mercy of the market forces, and does not augur well for the poor people who get marginalized everywhere at every turn towards globalization. Disparities and imbalances in the developing countries have increased after liberalization and privatization. This has occurred mainly because since globalization has been pursued through deregulation strategies, its main concerns remained limited to the promotion of free trade, profit, and the TNCs rather than the betterment of living standards of the poor people.

This situation cannot be remedied satisfactorily until meaningful empowerment of the developing countries takes place. This means, they should have an effective say in the global decision-making process. It is a fact that despite all changes in the world, the developing countries still do not have any meaningful say in the macro-economic management of the global economy. The rules of the game are decided by powerful developed countries and other international institutions like the IMF and the World Bank, in which a few powerful countries enjoy commanding positions. So long as the situation remains unchanged, the developing countries cannot hope to get their due share from globalization.

Therefore, if one looks at the course of the present globalization from the point of view of the developing countries, one is bound to feel pessimistic about it. For the developing countries it is a leap in the dark, the consequences of which remain incomprehensible. That does not mean that globalization did not have any positive effects on any developing country. Of course, growth and expansion did take place in some developing countries. But in the vast majority of them the negative effect are more conspicuous. It has perpetuated poverty, degradation and social unrest in developing countries and increased the vulnerability of the poor people. Income disparities have widened, unemployment worsened. The gap between the developed and the developing countries has also widened rapidly. Therefore, from the perspective of developing countries, the whole globalization programme today is directed to weaken their economies and to preserve the dominance of a few rich countries and their TNCs. What my professor, M.S. Rajan, said, which I mentioned in the beginning, remains valid in the current epoch too. The IMF, World Bank, the WTO and the G-7 are all seen as active partners in this globalization project. However, one cannot overlook the fact that mindless globalization has undermined many economies of Latin America, East and Southeast Asia and Africa. The current slowdown and recession across the world does not augur well for the globalized economies. Impoverishment of developing countries is not the best way to ensure peace, prosperity and stability in the world.

There should be no doubt that a globalized world that is now in the making, unless its parameters are changed drastically, will belong to a few dominant and powerful countries and their TNCs, in which TNCs, not the States, will be playing a pivotal role in every area of economic activity, accompanied by its adverse social impact. However, it is my conviction that if globalization has to become a positive force for human development, it has to adopt a more positive and enlightened approach which can raise the quality of life, everywhere across the world, to a higher level. This calls for an alternative egalitarian approach attuned to the construction of one world based on international solidarity. The parameters of globalization will have to be changed. What is needed is a more globally responsible globalization, which recognizes the rights of individuals everywhere and the need to remove inequalities in societies for accomplishing it. The pertinent ideas articulated by great international Social Democratic statesmen and visionaries like Willy Brandt, Bruno Kriesky, Olof Palme and Kalevi Sorsa will have to be brought back to the global agenda for fostering a meaningful and healthy cooperation between the developed and the developing countries. That will be in the best interests of the whole humanity. And that will also save the world economy from recurrent recessions.

REFERENCES

1. For more details see B. Vivekanandan, *International Concerns of European Social Democrats* (London, Macmillan, New York St. Martin's, 1997).
2. M. S. Rajan, 'Reforming the Sovereign State System: A Non-aligned Perspective', in Kanti P.Bajpai and Harish C. Shukul, eds., *Interpreting World Politics* (New Delhi, Sage, 1995), pp. 206-8.
3. B. Vivekanandan, n.1, pp. 48-58.
4. *Indian Express* (New Delhi), 19 June 1999.
5. Muchkund Dubey, *Globalization, Inter-dependence and Global Institutions,* Mimeo, p.12
6. B. Vivekanandan, n.1, pp. 59-62.
7. Vic Thorpe, 'Global Unionism: The Challenge', in Ronaldo Munck and Peter Waterman, eds., *Labour Worldwide in the Era of Globalization* (London, Macmillan, 1999) p. 219.
8. Bruce R. Scott, 'The Great Divide in the Global Village', *Foreign Affairs* (New York), January- February 2001, pp.160-4.
9. Ruddar Dutt, 'Hidden Dangers of Economic Reforms', *The Hindu Business Line* (New Delhi), 19 October 2000.
10. Bharat Jhunjhunwala, 'Technology Without Capital', *The Pioneer* (New Delhi), 8 May 2001.
11. Robert J. Samuelson, 'The Spirit of Capitalism', *Foreign Affairs,* January-February 2001, p. 206.
12. Prof. Deepak Nayyar's Prem Bhatia Memorial Lecture on 'Democracy and Development: The Indian Experience', delivered on 11 August 2001, in New Delhi. *The Hindu,* 12 August 2001.
13. *The Hindu,* 9 March 2001.
14. *Indian Express* (New Delhi), 9 January 1995.
15. Pierre Schori's speech at the Council meeting of the Socialist International, held in New Delhi on 10-11 November 1997.
16. Bruce R. Scott, n.8, p. 176.
17. One Indian economist, Professor Ruddar Dutt, said that import liberalisation has done a lot of harm to the Indian economy. See Ruddar

Dutt, n.9. Another economist, Vikram Chadha, said: '...on the whole, so far the process of India's global integration has worked more to its detriment than being benign to our economic growth.' See Vikram Chadha, 'Implications of India's Global Orientation During 90s: Accomplishment and Pitfalls', in P.P. Arya and B.B. Tandon, eds., *Multinationals* versus *Swadeshi Today: A Policy Framework for Economic Nationalism* (New Delhi: Deep and Deep, 1999), pp. 38-61. Yet another one said: 'Looking again at the post-1991 period, we reach the rather pessimistic conclusion that the reforms were not able, in the net, to generate favourable supply-side forces that we might have expected of them.' see Subir Gokarn, 'Economic Reforms, Growth and Inflation in India', in Subhashis Gangopadhyay and Nilima Wadhwa, eds., *Economic Reforms for the Poor* (New Delhi, Konark 2000).

18. See the text of President K.R. Narayanan's speech telecast on 25 January 2000, on the eve of India's Republic Day.
19. *The Pioneer* (New Delhi), 5 August 2001.

7

Nordic Welfare States

Viewed from India

In the history of societal reconstruction the Nordic States — Sweden, Denmark, Norway, Finland and Iceland — have made an outstanding contribution to the advancement of human civilization in the 20th century and have become a lodestar for other states. This they have achieved by capturing early the spirit of the age — the urge for equality and solidarity — and established highly advanced welfare states in the region.

When I first visited the Nordic States 16 years ago to write a book on social democracy in the region, I was deeply impressed by the way the Nordic societies have been organized — socially, economically and politically — with an uncommon sensibility to the dignity of the needy people in society and by the way they have successfully fused principles of equality and distributive justice within a dynamic framework of human solidarity. If I have given the title *Pathfinders*[1] to my book on Scandinavian Social Democrats, it was mainly due to my deep appreciation of their achievement in the construction of advanced welfare states in the region which has earned them a pride of place in the minds of socially conscious people across the world. Indeed, they have been viewed as model societies for emulation.

It must be recognized that the construction of modern welfare states in the Nordic region has an ideological dimension. Its philosophical foundation was laid on the principles of democratic socialism, as articulated by the Social Democratic Parties (SDPs) of Scandinavia. Indeed, the SDPs and the labour movements were the vanguards of the construction of Nordic welfare states. The underlying principles were equality, solidarity and distributive justice and the goal they set was the establishment of a new social order which would free people from all kinds of dependencies, and build a community whose members would cooperate with one another as free and equal citizens. They argued that in order to enjoy genuine freedom everyone must enjoy a credible sense of security. Since an individual in isolation cannot ensure such an enduring and credible security, it was imperative to follow a collective approach based on cooperation and state control.

Construction of welfare states in the Nordic region is the result of sustained efforts. It took many years for its champions — the Social Democrats — to make necessary political alliances and prepare the ground for its introduction. In order to ensure smooth passage of pertinent legislations in the national Parliaments, the Social Democrats had followed an intelligent process of consensus building through political negotiations with like minded parties and forged enduring alliances with the Agrarians and the Communists — a strategy which worked well and facilitated the establishment of modern welfare states in the Nordic. The opportunity for launching it was provided by the Great Depression of early 1930s, and its sheet anchor was a full employment policy.

It may be noted that prior to the establishment of welfare states in the Nordic, there existed a rudimentary form of social assistance, under Poor Laws, provided by the municipalities after conducting humiliating need tests. The recipients had to instantly forego their citizenship rights as well. The spirit and emphasis explicit in the Poor Law administration was how to keep the number of social assistance claimants down. The humiliating means test for social assistance and the stigma attached to its recipients had ensured that objective. But, the modern welfare state system in the Nordic has freed the welfare assistance recipients from such humiliations.

Though the initial objective of the welfare state was alleviation of poverty, the Nordic Welfare States have gone far beyond that agenda and enveloped in it larger objectives like reduction of inequality and promotion of distributive justice and human solidarity, in addition to programmes like social insurance and provision of social services to the needy people. The agenda of distributive justice was pursued both vertically and horizontally — vertically from the rich to the poor by the means of a steeply progressive taxation system, and horizontally through the establishment of a cradle-to-the-grave welfare state system for the entire population. Interwoven in it are the social security programmes like old-age pensions, insurance against sickness, accidents and industrial injuries, family allowances, child care allowances, maternity grants, unemployment insurance, educational facilities, provision for proper housing, and so on. As a result, security of everyone, including children, the aged and the disabled, irrespective of their family circumstances, is ensured everywhere in the Nordic States. Since matters touching vital interests of the people, like education, health, social insurance, employment and so on, are taken care of by the welfare state system, the popular support for it remains strong everywhere in the Nordic States despite shortcomings in the management of the system. That is one of the reasons why the allurements offered by the no-tax or low-tax parties in the region do not make any significant impact on the vast majority of the electorates in the region.

The fulcrum of the Nordic Welfare State system is a full employment policy pursued by the Nordic states which has sustained the system all along. The centrality of this policy has been recognized everywhere. It enabled the governments to raise the necessary resources to support the system and generated a new psyche among the people in favour of solidarity and sharing incomes without much heart burning. It is laudable that as early as 1930s the Nordic states have understood the dynamism of a full employment policy in the economic and societal development, which many countries have not yet well understood. Contrary to the conservative approach of keeping a reservoir of unemployed people in society as a methodology to keep the wages down and the labour organizations weak, the Nordic Social Democrats, who had championed the full employment policy in the wake of Depression in the early 1930s, were moved by a conviction that provision of jobs for every employable person is the best way to promote prosperity and uphold human dignity and equality in society. Indeed, if we view it at a micro-level, provision of a job to a person to earn his livelihood is infinitely better than doling out to him unemployment benefits. That apart, with full employment continuing year after year and incomes rising, the quality of life everywhere in the Nordic states got a sudden elevation. It also enabled the Nordic countries to introduce solidarity wages where the gap between the take-home pays of employees was brought down to an impressive level compared to countries anywhere else in the world.

It may be noted that, there has always been a co-relationship between the employment position and the revenue resources and public spending. Full employment meant higher tax revenues and less spending on social assistance. Unemployment meant shrinkage of tax revenues and higher expenditure on unemployment benefits and social assistance. Experience shows that the full employment policy pursued by the Nordic States enabled them to spend the least on account of unemployment benefits, and more on employment generation measures, job training, job mobility, education, preventive health care and industrial accident measures, family services, and so on. However, in the context of healthy socio-economic development, full employment is not just a programme of the past. It is a programme for the future as well, for all countries, which want to prevent potentially unmanageable social unrest and the disastrous consequences, which it would entail in future. Unemployment generates many avoidable social problems. If a section of society gets marginalized and idling, it has dangerous portents.

The Nordic Welfare State is built around a strong central state, which performs the twin roles of a regulator and a provider. Here, the state has a responsibility to solve social problems. This would mean the creation of space for everyone in every sector — in employment, education, housing, etc. At the same time, in the operation of the welfare state programmes, the responsibility is shared between the central government and the local governments. While the decision making is done by the national government, the implementation of those decisions remains the responsibility of the local governments or municipalities. The funding, by and large, is mobilized through taxation, following a pay-as-you-go method. But, the social benefits one is entitled from the system do not necessarily depend upon one's contributions. A steeply progressive income tax system ensured not only necessary resource mobilization, but also strengthened the egalitarian process in the region. The cooperative movement has reinforced the ethos of consensual approach of the region.

A major outcome of the establishment of welfare states in the Nordic region is the significant expansion of the citizen's social rights like social security, education, health care, employment, and so on, which are assured through various insurance schemes and state funding and contributions from the employers and the employees. And the benefits are extended to everyone in the land without discrimination, befitting a higher form of social order. They are reinforced by a co-determination process, collective bargaining and contractually binding wage agreements

Welfare State succumbed under the strains of global crisis, rising costs, high taxation, aggressive market liberalism and mass unemployment? According to him, it did not succumb because it was built on general consensus across the political spectrum. Its core elements like universalism, active employment policy, large social spending, tax revenues as the main source of welfare financing, a combination of flat rate and income based benefits, etc. still remain intact.[6] Moreover, as Dr. Nimmi Kurian said, the system worked well despite the crisis of 1990s because the system had shown sufficient resilience to absorb the shocks and adaptability to the changing requirements.[7]

The Nordic Welfare State has been a Democratic Socialist alternative to the communist system established in the Soviet Union through the means of a violent revolution. Therefore, the Nordic Welfare State system and the Soviet system found themselves on opposite sides as they represented two different methods to harness equality in society. Events in the past decade have shown that the path of democracy and reforms chosen by the Nordic States was enduring and sustainable than the path of violence chosen by the Soviet communists. But, unable to comprehend these differences, when the Soviet system collapsed in the early 1990s, many commentators had chosen to hastily conclude that socialism and what it represented, including the welfare state system, was dead. But more careful scrutiny has corrected this misperception. The Nordic Welfare State remains strong and enduring.

Yet, certain difficulties loom large in the horizon for the Nordic Welfare states, though they are not exclusive phenomena of the region. One is the demographic change that is under way in the region. A growing ageing population is complemented by a shrinking mass of young people as a result of low birth rates. From the Welfare State angle, it would mean rising social expenditure — payment of pensions and sickness insurance — for the upkeep of the ageing population against a shrinking tax base, due to smaller number of young people joining the job market, for funding the social service requirements and thus weakening the financial bases of welfare states. It is estimated that in the coming three decades the pensioners are likely to grow in big numbers. How to cope with this developing imbalance in the composition of the population and its likely impact on many facets of life in the Nordic region is a question which needs careful examination and mature response. However, keeping that in view, in order to keep the pension payments under manageable limits, cuts have already been proposed in the pension of future pensioners. Already in some countries the old age group accounts for the bulk of the social expenditure, and has even overtaken the health sector in social spending. For example, in Denmark, 40 per cent of the social expenditure in 1999 went to the old age group, where as 18 percent went for health care, 14 percent for employment, 12 percent for families with children, 11 percent for invalids and 6 percent for others.[8]

I envisage another difficulty, which may arise from the existing hiatus in the welfare policy perspectives of the European Union and the Nordic States, which have joined the European Union. The EU is yet to commit itself to a universal social security system, and Social protection at EU level remains a far cry. It seems that instead of enriching the Nordic Welfare State system, the European Union, in its vigorous pursuit of convergence of policies, market orientation and low priority for social policy, may cause steady erosion of the welfare state content of the Nordic region. Therefore, it is likely that the EU's impact on the Nordic States may not be helpful to the preservation of the Welfare State system in the region. This needs to be guarded against.

Another difficulty may arise from the indiscriminate adoption of job displacing high technology by states without carefully weighing its impact on the employment front. It must be remembered that full employment policy was a bedrock of the Nordic Welfare State system. High rate of labour market participation is an essential element of it. This policy was carried on by following an active labour market policy which was pursued through measures like job training, education, etc., to requalify the long-term unemployed to find suitable jobs in the job market. This was also a preventive social policy so that everybody earned his/her livelihood. Therefore, any dilution of that policy would prove inimical to the Welfare State system. Needless to say that a steady job killer of our times is the job displacing advanced technology which can instantly make millions of employees redundant or kill potential jobs and create a large mass of unemployed people of working age. In a market driven globalizing world where the production processes and international trade are getting increasingly concentrated in the hands of a limited number of large transnational corporations, which hardly display any social responsibility, in their drive for maximization of profits they use advanced technology as their tool for replacing human labour to the maximum extent. Taking a cue from them, even smaller enterprises too follow a similar approach and feed on the creation of an army of unemployed people all around. Since these entities, and the market as well, are generally unconcerned about the social consequences of mass unemployment, the state will have to be more active in regulating the technology adoption in the production line and in the service sector with a view to preserve maximum job opportunities for the people of the working age. Therefore, the Nordic States also will have to pay special attention to the question of technology adoption and unemployment generation. If technology adoption is not regulated, even an active labour market policy cannot have the desired results. Unemployed people, even after educational training and retraining, will still not find jobs for using their newly acquired skills. This will not be healthy for the society. Perhaps, the concept of 'appropriate technology', which is widely discussed in India may be of some relevance in this context. However, for the Nordic States the continuation of a full employment policy is still the best option for the preservation of the Welfare State system. The economic and technology policies need to be kept employment friendly and will have to be attuned to the preservation and creation of job opportunities so that more people earn their wage and remain in the rolls as taxpayers.

The Nordic Welfare States have many impressive achievements to boast of. As Joakim Palme said recently, in terms of socio-political performance, they have a good track record — poverty and inequality are low while participation is high.[9] They have not only eliminated poverty, in the classical sense, and considerably reduced inequalities in the region but also achieved distributive justice to a level which few countries can match. They have succeeded in providing generous benefits to the people of all categories following basically a universal approach. They have promoted equitable income distribution and ensured individual security, which have virtually freed people from worrying about the future security of their children. They have also made adequate provisions for education, health care, child care, and care for the aged and infants, which no market can satisfactorily ensure. Above all, they have promoted social cohesion and solidarity. Therefore, despite the difficulties the Nordic Welfare States have experienced in the early 1990s, crass individualization has not gained ground in the region to an extent which can threaten the solidarity approach. No wonder that the Welfare State system in the Nordic has been seen as a civilized alternative to both capitalist and communist state systems. It has demonstrated the success of an enlightened reformist approach, an evolutionary process where enduring social transformation is effected in a peaceful manner and an example of how wealth could be distributed in a civilized manner. Significantly, the benefits disbursed are free from any stigma and personal obligation to any individual, as resource mobilization and disbursement of benefits are done without discrimination and through regulations and public institutions.

The Nordic Welfare State is built around a strong central state enjoying complete independence for decision making on fiscal and monetary policies. And as such the state government has a pivotal role in it both as a regulator and a provider. A firm state control over the national economy is essential to discharge these responsibilities. But a globalization-liberalization process will have constraining effects on the freedom of states to take independent decisions in these regards and on the pivotal role of the nation state. Their attacks on the nation state are aimed at encouraging a process of hollowing out the state, and undermining its capacity to do any effective intervention in the socio-economic fields, particularly in providing social protection to people. European Union's monetary policy also has a similar potential. They can erode tax bases of the social security system. How to deal with these new developing situations is a challenge to the Nordic Welfare States.

In the early 1930s, eminent British socialist, R.H. Tawney, had perceived Welfare State as a strategy to harness equality in society. The Nordic countries have made that perception a reality. The basic security model in the Nordic is based on an egalitarian strategy of giving flat rate entitlements to everyone — to both rich and poor — since targeted support to the poor would have promoted only inequality. Moreover, the recipient would not be stigmatized nor would it promote social exclusion. As a result, in several sectors of life like health care, education, and caring services, inequality has been drastically eliminated. The system has been reinforced by making provisions for ensuring economic security during contingencies like unemployment, sickness, and old age. Policies they have pursued in these regards have been attuned to reduce inequality in society. This is true of income inequality in the Nordic countries as well. This is an aspect which is relevant for other countries as well since equality continues to be the spirit of our age.

The Nordic Welfare State has exercised and will continue to exercise enormous influence on societal reconstruction across the world. Its influence on the development of welfare state system in Canada is wellknown. Leonard Marsh, the author of the famous Marsh Report (1943) which formed the basis of the Canadian Welfare State, was tremendously impressed by the Nordic Welfare State initiatives which he saw during his visit to the region in the 1930s. Indeed, the recommendations of the Marsh Report had many features in common with the Welfare State system which the Nordic region had initiated at that time. Similarly, in the post-war period, many developing countries have drawn inspiration from the Nordic Welfare State model and tried to emulate it in their own limited ways, which are still at various stages of their development. The best description of that condition has come from Mr. Kalevi Sorsa, former Prime Minister of Finland, and the best internationally known Finnish statesman after Urho Kekkonen. While inaugurating an International Seminar on Social Democracy in New Delhi (India) in 1995, Mr. Sorsa said: 'Just when the welfare state has been built up in the Northern region of Western Europe to such a degree that political discussion is concerned about whether the build-up should continue or whether some parts of the edifice should actually be dismantled, the southern/ eastern region of the continent still faces the demanding task of completing the safety net'.[10] Describing the current state of Welfare States in other parts of the world he said :

> While in one region the foundation of the welfare state is just being laid, in another there may already be efforts underway to change or eliminate certain welfare services that have proven to be of minor importance. And while in one region the basement of the welfare state is just being put in place, in another

> the rooms are already being decorated for individual occupancy on the basis of equal sharing of the total welfare.[11]

No doubt, The Nordic model has played a significant role in guiding the world in this direction.

However, the most spectacular impact the Nordic Welfare State system has made in the recent past was on the erstwhile Soviet Union. The success of the Nordic system in the building up of egalitarian societies in the region was no mean a factor which had influenced the Soviet leader Mikhail Gorbachev to introduce *Perestroika* and *Glasnost* in the Soviet Union, which had also triggered a systemic change in the Soviet Union and Eastern Europe. The importance Gorbachev had attached to the success of the Nordic Welfare States could be gauged from the fact that he had sent a team of top Soviet economists to Helsinki and Stockholm to make an indepth study of the texture and working of the Welfare State system in Finland and Sweden. In fact, Gorbachev had a deep desire to pattern the Soviet system after the Nordic Welfare State model.[12]

From India, we look at the Nordic Welfare State system with great admiration. Undoubtedly, it is the largest successful human solidarity project in the world. Since its independence in 1947, India has tried to introduce the rudiments of a welfare state system. There, the welfare state programmes are pursued largely by the states, though the central government also plays a role in it. Therefore, India does not have a universal welfare programme uniformly applied in the whole country. At the same time, certain highly developed Indian states, like Kerala for example, have introduced certain features of the welfare state system, though even they are in no way near to the Nordic Welfare State system. It is true that in the aftermath of independence India had slowly moved in the direction of constructing a welfare state in the country. But, that process was petrified since early 1980s when India's economic establishment began to follow the prescriptions of the IMF and the World Bank.

Welfare State system as an agenda has been drawn basically by keeping in view the problems of the poor people in society, though subsequently its ambit was enlarged to encompass all citizens. Yet, how successful the social protection in the Nordic States is will have to be judged from the angle of the poor people in society. Pertinently, underlining the imperative need to approach problems and formulate policies from the angle of the poor people in society, a great Indian, Mahatma Gandhi, once told the Indian political leadership:

> Whenever you are in doubt or when the self becomes too much with you, apply the following test: 'Recall the face of the poorest and the weakest man whom you may have seen and ask yourself if the step you contemplate is going to be of any use to him. Will he gain anything by it? Will it restore him to a control over his own life and destiny? In other words, will it lead to Swaraj for the hungry and spiritually starving millions? Then you will find your doubts and your self melting away.[13]

I think by building up advanced welfare states, the political leaderships of the Nordic states have lived upto Mahatma Gandhi's expectations. However, in the ultimate analysis, the Nordic Welfare State is good economics, good politics and good sociology. It is a splendid example of how public spending on welfare can create general conditions for economic growth, and how preventive policies reduce potential social problems and help the development of a healthy, stress-free society. Politically, it has promoted consensus building, with greater emphasis on cooperation and conciliation, everywhere in the region which has also changed the psyche and ethos of the Nordic states. It has engendered a spirit of equality and assured an acceptable level of living standards for all in the society. The example the Nordic states have shown through the construction of Welfare States deserves emulation everywhere, transcending cultures and continents, for the benefit of mankind. Its realization requires not only political will but also a general psyche of compassion, a willingness to share without heart burning, and a commitment to human solidarity. That is the way a new world society, based on peace, democracy, equality, prosperity, distributive justice and solidarity could be constructed. I hope, some day this would become a reality.

REFERENCES

1. B. Vivekanandan, *Pathfinders: Social Democrats of Scandinavia*, Bombay, Somaiya, 1991.
2. In terms of GDP, the social expenditure of the Nordic countries in 1998 was as follows: Denmark and Norway — 30 percent; Finland — 27.2 percent; and Sweden 33.3 percent.
3. Sweden had a public deficit of 13 percent of its GDP, whereas Finland's deficit was around 8 percent of its GDP.
4. In Sweden, unemployment figures remained below 10 percent (8.2 percent in 1993) through out the period of depression, whereas in Finland the figure was close to 20 percent. In Denmark, the figure was 26.3 percent in the age group of 15-66. See J. P. Roos, 'Consequences of the Crisis of 1990s to the Nordic Welfare States: Finland and Sweden', and Peter Abrahamson, 'Welfare State System in Denmark: Development and Challenges', papers presented at the International Seminar on 'Welfare State Systems: Development and Challenges' held on 9–11 April 2001 at Jawaharlal Nehru University, New Delhi, India.
5. Nimmi Kurian, 'The Swedish Welfare State and the Challenges of the 1990s', paper presented at the International Seminar on 'Welfare State Systems: Development and Challenges' held on 9–11 April 2001 at Jawaharlal Nehru University, New Delhi.
6. J. P. Roos, n. 4.
7. Nimmi Kurian, n. 5
8. Peter Abrahamson, n. 4
9. Joakim Palme, 'The European Modernization of Social Protection in a Nordic Perspective', paper presented at the International Seminar on 'Welfare State Systems: Development and Challenges' held on 9–11 April 2001 at Jawaharlal Nehru University, New Delhi.

10. Kalevi Sorsa, 'New Challenges to an Old Movement', in B. Vivekanandan, ed., *Building on Solidarity: Social Democracy and the New Millennium*, New Delhi, Lancer's Books, 2000, p. 32.
11. *Ibid.*, p. 33.
12. For details, see B. Vivekanandan, *International Concerns of European Social Democrats*, London, Macmillan, and New York, St. Martins, 1997, pp. 179-81.
13. See Madhu Dandavate, *Gandhi's Human Touch*, New Delhi, Jayaprakash Foundation, 1997, p. 23.

8

Freedom of Tibet

The first three decades after the Second World War had witnessed freedom of almost all imperial possessions of European colonial powers in Asia, Africa and Latin America. This was achieved through a combination of concerted pressures mounted on the Western imperial powers through freedom movements inside the colonies, complemented by pressures exerted by the international community, and partly due to the realization on the part of the imperial powers that, in the long-run, holding on to the colonies any longer in the face of uprisings and revolts would prove costly for them. Therefore, they decided that it was better to gracefully quit the colonies.

It took another one-and-a-half decades for the Soviet Union to understand this lesson of history and let of the territorial acquisitions it made, using the opportunities provided by the Second World War, in the Baltic – Estonia, Lithuania and Latvia – and in Eastern Europe, besides Afghanistan which it occupied in 1979. The soviet military power, its super power status, backed by a regimented dictatorial system, could not help the Soviet Union to retain those new imperial possessions for long. Although, repeatedly, movements in these countries for freedom and democracy were suppressed with the help of tanks and machine guns – in Czechoslovakia in 1968, for example – those perceived advantages the Soviet Union enjoyed in the world proved no match for people's urge for restoration of their freedom in all these countries. Suddenly, with the speed of a lightning, the Soviet empire collapsed like a house of cards, following a series of revolts in 1989, and all the imperial possessions of the Soviet Union snatched back their freedom from the Kremlin. The Soviet Union had ended its occupation of Afghanistan also. In the end, the chain of events struck at the very survival of the Soviet Union itself and led to its final collapse, with more Soviet republics declaring their own independence.

One should have thought that there is a good lesson for China to learn from the experience of the Soviet Union *vis-a-vis* its own imperial possession of Tibet and gracefully quit Tibet and restore the freedom that country enjoyed before its occupation by China in 1950. Instead, China holds on to its occupation of Tibet, despite repeated revolts of the Tibetans, and tries to establish its grip over Tibet by effecting demographic changes in the country by inducting more and more Chinese in Tibet for settlements. That way, China has indeed put into motion a policy of cultural genocide in Tibet, denied basic human rights to the Tibetan people and has reduced certain areas of Tibet as dumping grounds of nuclear waste and other toxic materials, and, thus, further endangered the health of the Tibetans.

Tibet is clearly an independent state, presently under the Chinese occupation. The Chinese arguments against that fact hold no water. There are clear evidences that from 1911 onwards upto the Chinese occupation, on 7 October 1950, Tibet remained an independent country, exercised its powers, and dealt with other nations accordingly. Tibet participated along with China, and British India at the Simla Convention in 1914 as an equal partner. During the Second World War other powers also dealt with Tibet independently. Tibet refused its consent to China for example, in 1941 when China wanted to develop a road communication, through Tibet to Assam to facilitate supplies during the war. In 1947, Tibet participated at the Asian Relations Conference, convened in New Delhi as an independent country. Moreover, a document like the so called 17-point 'agreement' which the

Chinese produce as a justification to perpetuate their occupation of Tibet, was cooked up by the Chinese after they occupied Tibet and has no moral or legal validity as it was 'negotiated' and 'concluded' by a 'delegation' headed by Ngabo Ngawang Jigme, who himself was a prisoner in Peking and the Chinese Government, through intimidation and deceit, and without any proper consultation with the Dalai Lama, who was kept all along in the dark about the terms of negotiation at Peking or its outcome. The fact that the Dalai Lama refused to put his seal on this so-called 17-point 'agreement' of 23 May 1951 which for the first time said that Tibet was a part of China, deprives it of all moral and legal authority.

The other relevant document which needs the scrutiny of jurists is the Trade Agreement concluded between India and China in 1954 by which India agreed to the 'sovereignty' of China over Tibet. It is not clear who gave India this right to barter the sovereignty of Tibet to China without the consent of the people of Tibet. The Simla Convention of 1914, in which India, China and Tibet participated as equals, did not confer any such right to India to do so. Therefore, it appears that India had in 1954, exercised a right over Tibet which India really did not possess. Therefore, to that extent the 1954 Trade Agreement between India and China is null and void. However, it needs the scrutiny of jurists to examine whether India had any right to confer upon China sovereignty over Tibet as it referred to in the Sino-Indian Trade Agreement of 1954. If so, India should review its position and rectify this mistake publicly.

However, the point is that the international community should not give credibility to the documents, like the 17-point 'agreement' which the Chinese cite to perpetuate its occupation of Tibet. The fact remains that the Chinese activities in Tibet between 1950 and 1959, which forced the Dalai Lama to leave his country, and establish a government in exile in India, is a sordid drama of intimidation and deceit played on innocent and peace loving Tibetans to stabilize the Chinese occupation of Tibet.

During these developments in 1950s, the international community did precious little to help Tibet to protect its freedom. This was partly because as Tibet pursued a policy of peaceful isolation and had hardly any international contact, the rest of the world knew little about Tibet's international status. Tibet's only international contact was with its neighbours – India, Nepal and China, besides Britain as India's imperial power. As a result, when China turned out an aggressor on Tibet, in 1950, Tibet sought, and could expect, effective help only from India and Britain. If India exercised farsightedness at that time and if India and Britain had the will, they could have taken the initiative to mobilize world opinion against the Chinese occupation of Tibet in 1950. But Jawaharlal Nehru's romantic view of China at that time blurred his vision over the expansionist streak in the Chinese policy. Similarly Britain's view was blinkered by its eagerness, though unsuccessfully, to salvage its market in China after the Communist revolution, for which it accorded early recognition to China in 1950 itself. As a result, both India and Britain virtually turned a Nelson's eye to this aggression in 1950 and India particularly, advised Tibet to conduct negotiations with China directly on the basis of the Simla Convention. Thus from 1950, they left Tibet, and a young Dalai Lama, practically at China's mercy and endangered India's own future security. I believe, if India and Britain took the necessary initiative on time, the Truman administration of the United States, which was willing to play a role, could have been brought into the picture and Tibet's independent position could have been preserved. The fact that peace loving Tibet did not have a well trained modern army to resist the Chinese army, and other powers like India and Britain, which had the potential to mobilize adequate international support, shrugged off their shoulders, helped China to quickly annex Tibet. Therefore, the international community has a duty to undo the injustice and damage done to Tibet's freedom through their inaction in 1950.

International Reactions

From 1950 onwards, Britain reiterated that since 1911 Tibet had been an independent country. This was a correct statement of fact as there has been ample evidence to show that Tibet had functioned as an independent country since 1911 and throughout the Second World War and upto the Chinese occupation in 1950. During this period it had its own borders, concluded international treaties, Conventions, agreements and commercial settlements with other countries as an independent country.

After the Dalai Lama was forced to leave Tibet in 1959, between 1959 and 1965 the UN General Assembly passed three resolutions reiterating Tibet's right to self-determination. Britain voted for the resolutions both in 1961 and 1965.

Barring the salutary act that India granted political asylum to the Dalai Lama and about a lakh of Tibetans who accompanied him in 1959, India took hardly any initiative either to safeguard Tibet's freedom in 1950 on the basis of its obligations under the Simla Convention of 1914, or help Tibet to regain its freedom subsequently. Instead, whatever right India enjoyed in Tibet under the Simla Convention prior to the Chinese occupation in 1950, it gave away, and more, to China in 1954 under the Sino-Indian Trade Agreement and abdicated its active direct role to find a solution to the Tibetan question. This crucial folly committed between 1951 and 1954, during the negotiations between India and China on Tibet was the real cause of the Chinese aggression of India in 1962 and the continuing troubled relationship between them thereafter, as India allowed Tibet to disappear as an effective buffer state between the two countries.

Despite the best efforts of the Dalai Lama in 1970s and 1980s the cause of Tibet's freedom from occupation of China suffered grievous neglect in the international arena as a focal point. A major reason for this neglect was that many countries had pursued a policy of appeasement towards China for various politico-economic reasons. The other major reason was that in the context of the cold war politics, the main focal point of world politics remained East-West relations and the connected arms race between the power blocs. The cumulative effect was that many countries did not allow the Dalai Lama even to visit them, and whenever he could visit, the government leaders of those countries refused to meet him. I would like to draw your attention to three interesting examples in this context. As late as 1987, the Government of Thailand issued instructions to all its embassies not to issue visa to the Dalai Lama. Similarly, under the pressure of the Chinese government, the Canadian Prime Minister Brian Mulrony, refused to meet the Dalai Lama when the latter visited Canada in 1990. The Chinese warned the Canadians that any official recognition to the Dalai Lama would be considered in Peking as an unfriendly act against China. Similarly, in March 1991 when the Dalai lama visited Britain, Prime Minister John Major refused to meet him, although during this visit the Dalai Lama could meet other important British leaders, including the Opposition Leader Neil Kinnock and Prince Charles. The influential British newspaper *The Times* (London) criticized Major on this count and characterised Major's action as a 'pointless appeasement of China's vociferous protests against Dalai Lama's visit' and advised Major to meet the Dalai Lama.

Winds of Change

However, the winds of change began to blow in favour of Tibet from late 1980s onwards. Many parliamentary delegations, including ones from the Unites States, Australia,

Austria and the European Community visited Tibet in recent years on fact finding missions and appraised the world of the prevailing situation in Tibet. As a result, in 1991 the US Congress declared Tibet as a country under the Chinese occupation. Similarly, the European Parliament, in a resolution in December 1992, supported self-determination for Tibetans. In 1991, in a resolution, the UN sub-commission on Prevention of Discrimination and Protection of Minorities, expressed concern at 'continuing reports of violations of fundamental human rights and freedom which threatened the distinct cultural, religious and national identity of the Tibetan people.' In January 1993, an All Party Parliamentary Group For Tibet in Britain convened a conference, in London, of eminent jurists from all over the world to examine the facts provided by the Chinese and the Tibetans. After examining the facts, the jurists declared that 'by reason of the act of aggression and military occupation the Tibetan people's right to the exercise of self-determination has been denied. Since the military action of 1949-50, Tibet has been under the alien occupation and domination of the People's Republic of China and has been administered with the characteristics of colonial administration.'

In a parallel stream of developments, the Dalai Lama presented a 5-point Peace for Tibet before the Congressional Human Right Commission, in Washington, on 21 September 1987, which called for 'commencement of earnest negotiations on the future status of Tibet and of relations between the Tibetans and Chinese peoples'. In June 1989, The Dalai Lama was invited to address the European Parliament at Strasbourg. The Nobel Committee has invited the attention of the World Community to the subjugation of six million Tibetans by the Chinese by awarding Nobel Prize for Peace to The Dalai Lama in 1989. The Thai Government changed its attitude to the Dalai Lama and received him in September 1990. In April 1991 the American President George Bush received the Dalai Lama in Washington. In May 1991

Britain and other European countries boycotted Chinese celebrations, in Lhasa, of 40th anniversary of the Chinese rule in Tibet. In December 1991, the British Prime Minister John Major received the Dalai Lama in London. Recently, the Dalai Lama met the US President Clinton who assured the Dalai Lama all possible help. Clinton made it clear that the large-scale transfer of Chinese population to Tibet had threatened Tibet's unique identity and culture and made it clear that China should make significant progress in preserving Tibet's unique identity, or else he would effectively sever trade ties with China.

I consider these developments as positive ones, and are clear indications that Tibet's freedom from the Chinese occupation has become a focal point of international attention. However, many countries still view Tibet only as a human rights issue. But that perspective needs to be changed. The question of Tibet is basically an imperialistic/ colonial issue and it has to be dealt with accordingly. The objective should be the end of Chinese occupation of Tibet, restoration of its freedom and independence so that the Dalai Lama and a substantial number of Tibetans who took refuge in India could return to their homeland in freedom and dignity as soon as possible. Keeping this objective in view, countries should come forward to accord *de facto* and *de jure* recognition of the Tibetan Government-in-exile under the Dalai Lama's leadership and put pressure on China to open up direct negotiations between the Dalai Lama and the Chinese leadership with a view to bring an end to the Chinese occupation of Tibet peacefully. The restoration of Tibet's independence in that manner will be in the best interest of China too if it wants to avoid what happened to the Soviet Union and its empire since 1989. Despite the massacre at the Tiananmen Sqaure in June 1989, people's urge for democratization and liberation and against dictatorship is very much alive in China. Like the Soviet Union in the past, China today presents the picture of a huge unmanageable land mass, with a basically volatile population, more volatile than East Europeans and people in the Soviet Republics. Indeed, it has all the potential to fall under its own weight, if it did not shed its colonial ambitions in Tibet on time. China annexed Tibet in the same manner as Soviet Union annexed the Baltic States and the East European Countries and Afghanistan. In the same way, Tibet's freedom also is inevitable. Whether it should be with or without any serious long-term consequence for China in future is a matter for the Chinese to decide. A timely and correct response from China would save a lot of time, energy and resources of China and of the world community.

Implications for India and Asia

Freedom of Tibet is of central importance to peace in Asia as an independent Tibet would re-establish an effective buffer state between the two big Asian powers — India and China. It was the disappearance of Tibet as an independent buffer state which caused the Chinese aggression of India in 1962 as the former Indo-Tibetan border became Sino-Indian border after the Chinese occupation. It would remove the nuclear missiles that the Chinese have positioned in Tibet, targeted against India, which can facilitate India to take an early decision on its nuclear option. It can lead to the development of a balanced and healthy relationship not only between India and China but among India, Tibet and China which could constitute a keystone of peace in Asia, a necessary condition for progress in the Indian sub-continent.

In the changed world situation India should consider the question of reviewing its policy on Tibet. If India had committed an inadvertent mistake in conceding to China sovereignty over Tibet, which China never claimed before 1950, during our negotiations with China between 1951 and 1954, a right which India really did not have to do so on its own, we should frankly admit that fact and appraise the world community of the factual position so that the international community could take remedial measures. India should review the policy on Tibet and anchor it in conformity with the statement Jawaharlal Nehru made in the Parliament on 7 December, 1950. India should also consider the question of the necessary early recognition to the Tibetan government-in-exile under the Dalai Lama and encourage the rest of world also to do so. Undoubtedly, India has a lot to gain from the restoration of Tibet's independence.

9

Peace Through Power*

The Pakistan Atomic Energy Commission has announced that the atomic reactor at Islamabad splitted the atom in a sustained fission reaction on 21 December 1965. The obvious aim is to produce nuclear weapons. Thus Pakistan also is qualifying for the membership of the privileged Nuclear Club. The steady increase in the nuclear capabilities of China and Pakistan is to be underlined so far as the defence and diplomacy of a democratic country like India is concerned.

Though the late Prime Minister Lal Bahadur Shastri gave a hint favourable to the production of atomic weapons, he categorically rejected the idea later. From the calm and cool reaction of the people in the helm of affairs it appears that they still refuse to understand the gravity of the challenge to the nation's security. In this context, a perspective analysis of the subject becomes imperative.

Action and Reaction

In the modern world the defence policy of a nation is, to an extent, shaped by the policies of other nations. It is, therefore, more or less a mixture of action and reaction. Such a policy has three major components : (1) national self-interest; (2) the situational factors impinging on the State; and (3) the action taken by the State.

National self-interest is the prime criterion in terms of which a State judges situational factors, determines the relative priorities to be given to different goals and establishes and evaluates courses of action. This makes the defence policy of a nation a continuous affair. Since each nation is a

* Published in 1966.

sovereign entity, no external force has the right to dictate what its national interests should be. And each State adopts such policies as it sees best and fit, using such combinations as it seems expedient and wise.[1]

India, as the world's largest democracy is in the midst of her greatest transition, interrupted often by the obstinacy and greed of neighbouring Pakistan and China. The regimes of these two countries, after failing to provide a decent living to their countrymen, are trying to weaken the Indian economy and cut the roots of our long-range development plans. The challenge, not confined to India's territorial integrity, affects other equally important aspects like her way of life, system of Government and system of democratic planning.

National security is of supreme importance for a developing nation like India. To ensure it we have to make our defence establishment up to date and efficient enough to enable it to meet all eventualities.

Chinese Threat

Recently I read an article based on the views of a foreigner, in a Sunday magazine, discouraging India from becoming a nuclear Power. Regarding the Chinese nuclear threat to India, the article says China is not only India's adversary but also the potential adversary of the two most powerful nations, the United States and the Soviet Union. And so, ultimately, neither Russia nor America can afford to let China attack India 'in depth'. Whether they act jointly or singly, they will always possess a marked strategic advantage over China. Obviously, these are sophistications. Suppose it happens, at what cost? No Power in this world is free from pressure tactics in international politics. Therefore, when we consider these views, we have to examine the possible pressures that this country may face on such crucial occasions.

Santayana's renowned dictum, 'Those who cannot remember the past are condemned to repeat it', is a sound advice for statesmen concerned with India's defence efforts.

Experience shows that policies of nations are subject to frequent changes. When such a state of affairs prevails all over the world, to depend on other countries, especially on vital aspects like defence, is suicidal in the long run. Instances are numerous that the steps of some Heads of State, who tried to help other nations in crises, were defeated by other pressures. For instance, in the U.S., some of the efforts of the past Presidents to help foreign countries in times of crisis were defeated by Congressional Acts. The Neutrality Act of 1935 and the Ludlow Resolutions of 1938 are warnings of history. No American commentator or public figure advocated military intervention in East Asia when Japanese expansion began in 1931, though U.S. Secretary of State Henry Lawis Stimson drew thunderous applause for his declaration that America would not 'recognize' territorial gains made by conquest. Such instances of isolation, refusing to get entangled in war, are not rare in American history. Recollection of such instances makes one feel that it is yet to be seen whether substantial aid and positive help will flow into India from the U.S. in future, as it did during the Chinese aggression. It was because of the dynamic leadership of President Kennedy, who commanded the confidence of the American Congress throughout and who was a great friend of India and great admirer of Nehru, that India could secure massive military and other aids in 1962 without any strings. This personal factor was the underlying aspect of that help.

Race for Arms

The international order is entirely competitive. Nations demonstrate their progress in several ways. Militarily, no nation, big or small, refuses to subscribe to its armour though it may preach loudly about world peace and disarmament. For example, it is said that Japan, an ardent supporter of the partial test ban treaty, is making it sure that it is in a position to manufacture nuclear weapons immediately, when the occasion demands it. For most countries, the Disarmament

Conference is a cover for military preparations for the suppression of weak nationalities. To a considerable degree, the strong Powers arrange their business and settle their mutual accounts behind doors, at the expense of small and weak nations.[2]

If we consider situational factors, very few nations have such mischievous neighbours as India has now. In the light of this, it is absolutely necessary for India to develop an independent defence and a foreign policy based on the prime criterion of national self-interest. This is because even the U.S. has failed to fulfil promises given to India. We reacted violently when the U.S. declared that it would supply arms to Pakistan. We promptly raised the question whether Pakistan considered such aid as meant for resisting Communist aggression or would use it to strengthen its bargaining position *vis-à-vis* India in the dispute over Kashmir and canal waters. There is a clause in the South-East Asia Defence Treaty Organisation which specifies that the treaty would apply only to the communist aggression.[3] But during the September 1965 conflict, Pakistan used against India U.S. weapons procured on the basis of this pact. We have to see what explanation the U.S. gives to brush it aside lightly. This kind of breach of trust India cannot suffer any more. If she wants to be among the first-rate Powers of the world, she has to free her economy from the clutches of foreign aid which jeopardizes her efforts to become self-sufficient.

Age-Old Theory

Machiavelli said covenants without force are nothing but words.[4] This centuries-old theory is not obsolete even today. An impartial observer of world politics can see that strength – not tradition, population and moral principles – is the criterion of effectiveness. Indian policy-makers should not wink at the realities of pressure politics. In the interest of the nation, they should not also refuse to adjust the foreign and the defence policies to the newly-created situations. India's moral posture against the bomb does not make her great in Afro-Asian eyes. When China exploded her first atom bomb, no important non-aligned country in Asia and Africa lifted a finger of reproof. Considering this particular aspect, India must have the wisdom to foresee the probable diplomatic jam in her relations with the Asian-African countries in general and South-East Asia in particular, due to Chinese pressures.

Strength always plays a dominant role. The opinions of nations like the U.S. and the Soviet Union are held in high esteem in world politics because of the simple fact that they have enough force behind them to implement what they say. India, as the largest democracy, must also have a powerful voice on world issues and problems. How can she be a weak spectator when nationalism of her neighbours takes an aggressive turn? China and Pakistan have attacked India more than once. The memory of those who sacrificed their lives during these invasions demands a permanent deterrent. 'Deterrence', says Kissinger, 'is the attempt to keep an opponent from adopting a certain course of action by posing risks which will seem to him out of proportion to any gains to be achieved.'[5] 'There is only one way to ensure peace,' said Winston Churchill, 'and that is to be so much stronger than your enemy that he will never dare to attack you.'[6] One increases the deterrence when one magnifies the risks of destruction which the opponent incurs, and decreases the measure of destruction which he may be able to inflict.[7] It is with this objective India has to shape her defence policy.

Sword of Democles

India should be a big Power like America and Russia. Otherwise the fate of Tibet may fall upon her. The development and possession of nuclear arms alone can protect the democratic India from her aggressive neighbours. The bombs exploded by China and the attempt of Pakistan to become a nuclear Power make the task imperative.

The terrifying threat of atomic warfare is dangling like the Sword of Democles over human civilization. May be, mutual forbearance will bar the use of atomic weapons. But we, as a nation, cannot take a major risk. We have to follow a new programme, i.e., 'rely in the future primarily on our massive mobile retaliatory power which we can use at our discretion against the major source of aggression.'[8]

The most effective argument that stands in the way of the development of nuclear arms is advanced in the name of 'poor India' and her economy. Even the Government stresses this factor. They say that the economy will be strained considerably. Without strains we cannot achieve anything substantially. If the people are prepared to bear hardships and tighten their belts for the defence of their motherland – a spirit amply demonstrated at the time of the Chinese and Pakistani invasions – finance will not be a problem.

There is the example of the Soviet people. 'The people of the Soviet Union tightened their belts and starved and deprived themselves of even necessary articles, so that payments (for machinery) could be made abroad. They sent their food-stuffs abroad and, with the price obtained for them, paid for the machinery. It was a struggle against the backward conditions of Russia, against the new standard of living. Almost with full enthusiasm they put up with further sacrifices and lived a hard ascetic life; they sacrificed their present for the great future that seemed to beckon them and of which they were the proud and privileged builders.'[9] Russia's dramatic rise from economic impoverishment and diplomatic isolation to the rank of Super Power is really remarkable. The mighty and prosperous Soviet Union of today is the rich result of sacrifices. The people of India have to follow the Soviet example, and sacrifice their present pleasures for future glory.

To become an operational nuclear Power with a stock of plutonium bombs will cost crores of rupees. The tremendous cost of such a military establishment is indeed a severe drain on the country's economy. Economy is always welcome and desirable, but at what cost? Not at the cost of national security and integrity.

Disastrous Dependence

It is disastrous to rely on the assurances of friends any more, especially on vital needs like defence, food, etc. India is not a small country to live like a protectorate. She should not be allowed to be singled out from the privileged few who monopolize the nuclear arms. Big Powers oppose proliferation of the bomb technology, not mainly because the chances of irresponsible use of the atom bomb will be greater but because 'the secret of bomb technology is a diplomatic lever to keep weaker nations on the line. As long as the stockpiles of nuclear weapons are not destroyed, the countries with nuclear bombs in their possession retain an upper hand over non-nuclear countries which, in terms of international power politics, they will hate to lose.'[10] It is against this background that one has to think whether India should become a Nuclear Power or not. No doubt, every far-sighted Indian will favour the production of nuclear bombs as a deterrent against all possible threats.

It is well known that India believes in peace. India does not need military power to take what belongs to others or to compel anyone to accept its over lordship. We have no desire to annex the territory of others. But there is the possibility of force being used against us and against our interests. Military power is necessary to deter these interferences, and if they do occur, to stop them.[11]

Peace through power breeds mutual respect among nations. Russia and Americа, believe in divergent ideologies and ways of life, are now compelled to live as peaceful neighbours, not because of any basic change in thinking but because of the awareness of the destructive capacities of each other. So, for more than one reason, instead of depending on miscalculations and futile hopes, it is high time that India adopted a policy of peace through power, emerging as a Nuclear Power to keep her prestige, integrity and security—to quote Frank Moraes, to "give teeth to her Power status."

Great Opportunity

It is apt here to note the words of the Spartan King *Archidamus*: 'We Spartans... are taught to consider that the schemes of our enemies are not dissimilar to our own. ... In practice we always base our preparations against an enemy on the assumption that his plans are good; indeed it is right to rest our hopes not on a belief in his blunders, but on the soundness of our provisions. Nor ought we believe that there is much difference between man and man.'[12] India has to deal with the present situation as a great opportunity and as a great challange as well.

NOTES

1. *Charles O, Lerche, Foreign Policy of American People.*
2. *Jane Degras, Soviet Documents on Foreign Policy,* Vol. II.
3. *Stephen D. Kertz,* (Ed.). *American Diplomacy in a New Era.*
4. *Nicolo Machiavelli; The Prince.*
5. *Henry A. Kissinger; Nuclear Weapons and Foreign Policy.*
6. *Winston Churchill;* In a Statement in 1913.
7. *Dean Acheson; Power and Diplomacy.*
8. *Richard Nixon;* In a speech reported in *The New York Times,* 14 March, 1954.
9. *Jawaharlal Nehru: Glympses of World History.*
10. *Robi Chakravarti,* 'The Bomb Debate and India's Foreign Policy, *Economic Weekly,* 28 November 1964.
11. Dean Acheson, *Power and Diplomacy.*
12. King Archidamus; Reported by *Thucydides.*

10

Common Security

National security is a legitimate concern of States. But, the methodologies adopted for ensuring it varied from time to time. In the past, nations tried to ensure their security through pre-emptive wars and conquests which were primarily aimed at the annihilation of adversaries. Victory or defeat was the only language that was known to the leaders of that period. Waging war was also a power expression adopted by states during that period. But, when we look back, that methodology was undoubtedly predatory.

Prevention of war as an idea gained the attention of statesmen only in the aftermath of the First World War. Under the debris of the First World War, they wished that the world should not suffer similar devastation again. In order to prevent wars in future, they established the League of Nations. But, it did not deliver as it did not have any clear concept or instrumentality of how to prevent wars. Hitler's ambition to bring the whole of Europe under his yoke, supported by the enormous military build up, had plunged Europe once again into another devastating World War. But, in the aftermath of the Second World War, prevention of future wars became an agenda item of security experts once again.

In 1945, the United States had dropped atom bombs in Hiroshima and Nagasaki. A year later, in 1946, the American strategic expert, Bernard Brodie, published a book entitled *The Ultimate Weapon*. That gave birth to a new security doctrine – the doctrine of deterrence – for the prevention of wars.

Though the deterrence doctrine was conceived in the context of the invention of nuclear weapons, in the post-war period it became the security doctrine of countries which even had only the conventional arms. However, the quintessence of the deterrence doctrine is that a nation can deter its adversary from launching an attack on it by the display of a superior fire power. And that the nations should continue to increase the fire power and maintain the superiority in order to prevent attacks on it. In other words, it is a continuous display of the 'stick' to the opponent. On the face of it, the strategy would appear credible. Its champions have never failed to site the prolonged peace in Europe since 1945 as an achievement of the doctrine of deterrence.

But, if we critically look at the way the deterrence doctrine has worked during the last half-a-century, we will find that it has served as the locomotive of arms race in the world. Following the rationale and the logic which the deterrence doctrine has provided, nations have been chasing the mirage of the maintenance of superiority in weaponry against one another. But, in an era in which rapid change in technology is making weapons and weapon systems obsolete in quick succession – generally in about five years – this chase for superiority is obviously a futile and costly exercise. Yet, in the process, the world has accumulated weapons sufficient to destroy the humanity many times over. But, not satisfied with the advanced weapon systems positioned on earth to deter the adversary, a country like the United States has planned to position nuclear weapons in space to be fired upon earth in order to deter the adversary. Therefore, under the influence of the deterrence doctrine, every step has been taken to reduce the Earth into an ashtray revolving around the Sun.

While at the global level, the super powers and their military blocs vied with each other in a constant endeavour to maintain superiority over the other, at regional levels too, nations have followed the same deterrence strategy against their potential adversaries and became the lucrative markets of leading arms exporters of the world. The net result is that at multiple levels, every nation in the world got enmeshed in a process of arms race that has made the merchants of arms happy. Moreover, in order to upgrade the weapon systems to maintain their deterrence capability, nations had to spend more and more of their resources, sometimes even by taking loans from abroad, for the purchase of the latest weapons. This unsustainable approach has been kept up with the full realization that the money utilized for arms purchase would give no returns in productive terms, and, therefore, could take the country to bankruptcy. In other words, it is a recurring wasteful expenditure of gigantic proportion. Indeed, trapped under the deterrence doctrine, trillions of dollars worth world resources have been sent down the drain over the years, which has significantly crippled the global development process. Therefore, it may be seen that the deterrence doctrine has steadily forced a large number of countries to spend their newly generated resources for the purchase of arms, while poverty and hunger persisted in many of them. That process is still on, and will continue so long as the nations continue to put their faith on the deterrence doctrine for their national security.

Therefore, I hold the view that the deterrence doctrine has served the humanity negatively. If there is still poverty everywhere, and if the quality of life remains still low even in countries whose productivity was reasonably high, it is, to a great extent, because of the drain of resources caused by the adherence of many countries to the deterrence doctrine. Therefore, it is imperative that for the welfare of mankind the nations should rely less and less on the unsustainable doctrine of deterrence, and opt for a sustainable alternative doctrine for their national security, which would also be conducive to their economic and social development.

In the early 1980s the Social Democrats of Europe had paid attention to this critical question, with a view to find whether the same objective of the prevention of war can be achieved through a more sensible alternative to the arms race and high military spending. Following this, in 1982 they came up with a new concept, called 'Common Security' and challenged the deterrence doctrine's validity as a sustainable basis for national security.

Though the term 'Common Security' was originally coined by a German Social Democrat, Egom Bahr, the most celebrated exponent of the Common Security doctrine was Olof Palme, former Social Democratic Prime Minister of Sweden. The salient features of the Common Security doctrine he had enunciated was elaborated in the Palme Commission Report on Disarmament and Security Issues (*Common Security: A Blueprint for Survival*) which was published in 1982. What is the main message which this new Common Security doctrine conveys? The cardinal message the Common Security doctrine radiates is that the countries can survive only together, and, therefore, they should build their security in cooperation with their neighbours and adversaries and not on the insecurity of their neighbours and adversaries. And that their security must rest not on the threat of mutual destruction, but on their longing for joint survival.

The exponents of Common Security have reasoned that: in the nuclear age no nation can win a nuclear war; no nation can protect its citizens through unilateral military measures alone; in the ultimate analysis, every country, including the most powerful country, is dependent on the 'good sense and restraint' of other countries; countries should organize their security with the objective of joint survival through collective responsibility; and that it can be achieved only through dialogue and negotiations.

At the operational side, Common Security calls for a downward spiral of armaments. It stipulates that States should progressively, in mutual agreement, scale down their offensive capabilities to the minimum and rely more on their defensive structures. This stipulation is applicable not only for the nuclear weapons but also for the conventional weapons since a conventional war can also be enormously destructive.

In the application of Common Security, the approach is not based on unilateralism. Its framework has to be multilateral, and the negotiations will have to be both at regional as well as global levels.

Common Security demands that there should be an end to arms race and arms competition through negotiations, national restraint and collective responsibility. It underlines that arms race based on the deterrence doctrine is unsustainable, and is a waste of world resources which can be utilized fruitfully for human development and human welfare. It is a fact that when poor countries spend more of their resources for arms for security, they are threatened from within through social eruptions caused by poverty, deprivation and unemployment. Of course, when armaments substitute economic development, social unrest becomes inevitable.

Therefore, if the world wants to move in the direction of achieving real security, the countries must change their approach to armaments and security. Instead of getting enmeshed in an arms race, they should begin to organize their security in cooperation with one another. They should strive to promote policies of 'interlocking restraints'. In short, cooperation should replace confrontation. This is the principal message of Common Security.

I have elaborated the Common Security doctrine in my book, *International Concerns of European Social Democrats*, published from London and New York by Macmillan and St. Martin's Presses in 1997.

I may mention that when the Common Security doctrine was enunciated in 1982, the champions of deterrence doctrine viewed it initially as utopian. But, soon they began to recognize its validity. As the cost of the piling up of arms to maintain deterrence became too strenuous even for the super powers, they were forced to appreciate the logic and the rationale behind the Common Security doctrine. The Soviet President Mikhail Gorbachev was the first to grasp the significance of it. The US President Ronald Reagan quickly followed him. However, the *de facto* recognition of the Common Security doctrine by the super powers came during the Gorbachev-Reagan summit at Reykjavik in 1986 when they had discussed the question of effecting a steep reduction in their nuclear stockpiles and delivery systems. The INF Treaty of 1987 to totally dispense with two classes of missiles from their world-wide inventories was a major step they had taken on the lines stipulated by the Common Security doctrine. Similarly, the START-I (1991) and START-II (1992) had effected further cuts in nuclear arms. Similarly, the treaty on Conventional Forces in Europe (CFE) in 1993 was another step in tune with the Common Security doctrine. But these are only some small but significant beginnings which underlines the validity of Common Security as a security doctrine for the future.

What is the relevance of the Common Security doctrine for India or South Asia? As mentioned earlier, Common Security is not a national concept which can be practiced by States unilaterally. It is both a regional as well as a global concept. Therefore, for India, the area of its immediate application will have to encompass all the states of the South Asian region.

It may be noted that like many other States in the post-war period, the countries of South Asia also have anchored their defence policies on the deterrence doctrine. As a result, they have also got into the track of an arms race, though of a limited nature, to the delight of arms traders of the world. It had led to a few wars also in the region. However, that approach had drained out a substantial portion of the resources the people of the region have generated during the last 50 years. It had crippling effects on the development of the region and had kept the standard of living of the vast majority of people very low.

The fundamental question is: Should we continue with this self-defeating exercise in the region or should we make a turn around and take the South Asian region form an antagonistic, suspicion-based confrontationist frame work to a relationship based on cooperation, mutual concern and trust? If we take all aspects into account, a Common Security approach among the countries of South Asia is imperative for us in the region. It will bring immeasurable benefits to the region. Its larger Asian dimension can be thought of later at a second stage. However, it is premature to talk about it at present.

In conclusion, we must take note of the fact that on the threshold of the new millennium, countries everywhere are engaged in the exercise of re-assessing their threat perceptions. There is also an increasing realization that the old ways of ensuring national security through a narrowly based deterrence doctrine, or the one based on military alliance and bloc politics, is obsolete and unsustainable. That will not meet the requirements of the 21st century. Therefore, the need is for a more positive and increasingly synchronized approach towards national, regional and global security management. The basic objective should be to ensure national security at a substantially reduced cost, so that the new resources which people generate get channelled towards developmental purposes and welfare activities. That is possible only if the international community moves forward with a vision, which is shared by nations and peoples all over the world. No doubt, that positive vision will have the be anchored in the Common Security doctrine, enunciated by Olof Palme and other Social Democrats of Europe. This is mainly because of the following reasons. The Common Security is a security architecture which is based on positive interdependence and international solidarity. It will enhance the level of cooperation among countries and erstwhile adversaries. It is a civilized and a more sensible way of practical cooperation among all countries of various regions for the prevention of wars and conflicts and for the preservation of peace befitting the new era and the new civilizational threshold. It would create an environment where waging a war would become practically impossible for nations. It can release a lot of world resources for developmental purposes. That will also enhance the prospects of more fruitful developmental cooperation between nations.

11

India's Public Sector*

Before he was ensnared by the Indian capitalists, Jawaharlal Nehru wrote in his autobiography in 1936: 'Inevitably we are led to the only possible solution — the establishment of a socialist order, first within the national boundaries, and eventually the world as a whole, with a controlled production and distribution of wealth for public good. How this is brought about is another matter, but it is clear that the good of a nation or of mankind must not be held up because some people who profit by the existing order object to the change. If political or social institutions stand in the way of such a change, they have to be removed. To compromise with them at the cost of that desirable and practical ideal would be a gross betrayal.'

The programme of public sector in the Indian economic system is meant to blend the social ownership of the principal means of production with the social control of those which remain under private ownership. There is a purpose behind such ownership: the exercise over it of democratic control, ensuring that the concern will be managed in the public interest.

Social Necessity

The existence of a large public sector in a developing country is a social necessity, congenial to the needs and aspirations of the people at large. The social ownership is not peculiar to India alone. In Communist countries it is complete. In socialist countries it is partial. Even in a capitalist country like the United States the size of the public sector is much

* 1967

bigger than that in India. But its growth in India was subjected to a major controversy among politicians and economists, at home as well as abroad.

Capitalist countries have been highly critical of it. It would have been better if they had a better understanding of the Indian situation, about which Prof. John Kenneth Galbraith wrote (*Foreign Affairs*, July 1958): 'The commitment of the goal of a Socialist society is central in modern Indian thought. It is regularly averred by the Government and, indeed, by nearly all articulate Indians. Even the most intransigent Indian at heart.... The misunderstanding of India lies in the failure to see the unique inapplicability of the free enterprise formula – either in its pure or diluted form – to that country. As noted, the Indian commitment to the semantics of socialism is at least as deep as ours to the semantics of free enterprise.'

The crux of the problem is that in a country like India, where nearly every one is poor and where many are hungry, the choice should be whether the private monopoly, with all the corruption and insecurity it contains, or public ownership should dominate in production and distribution. One has to concede, it is the latter since it ensures more stability and security.

A striking aspect of Indian economy today is the growth of the public sector. The ideological foundation of this new development is socialism, and in political dialogues, positions are usually taken for or against it according to one's distance from socialist philosophy and egalitarianism. The public sector in India has grown through several important stages. When India won independence, State investment was confined to the classical lines reserved for such investment in other capitalist or colonial countries; that is the Railways and communications, power generation, some ordnance workshops and other units considered vital to the imperialist power, to be placed under its direct control.

The Industrial Policy Resolutions of 1948 and 1956 gave a new momentum in this direction. They clearly demarcated industrial sectors which have been reserved for development by the Government. They included projects which are highly capital-intensive and which have long gestation periods and which are of strategic importance. A notable aspect has been that the sector has been expanding mainly by way of construction and developing new units and not so much through nationalizing existing ones. At present there are more than 60 industrial and commercial undertakings under the ownership and control of the Government. In addition to that, there are some departmentalized undertakings also. Six major public sector concerns are statutory corporations, while the rest are incorporated companies.

Nationalization

Nationalization of the key and basic industries was a suggestion put forth by eminent personalities in India to enlarge the base of the public sector. The advantages of nationalizing key and basic industries and financial institutions are many. It places in the hands of the Government large financial resources of development and gives a material basis for the nation's economy. It undermines the chances of extraneous influence from sources of vested interest in the economic life of the country and creates the best pre-requisites for further broadening of the State sector by providing experienced technical personnel for the sector's undertakings. And above all it facilitates the attainment of equality and social justice in the shortest possible time without coercion.

In spite of such economic and social advantages little nationalization of existing enterprises has taken place in the country since 1947 beyond the State Bank of India, air transport, and life insurance business. Since independence the Government of India and the Indian National Congress adopted a lukewarm attitude towards the nationalization programme. This attitude became clear first in the Constituent Assembly, on 17 February, 1948. A resolution was moved by Kazi Syed Karimuddin, which said, 'This Assembly is of the opinion that the economic pattern of this country shall be socialist economy based on the principle of nationalization of key industries and co-operative and collective farming and socialization of the material resources of the country and that the Government of India shall adopt the said principle immediately.' Speaking on this resolution, Jawaharlal Nehru expressed the view that we should not waste our resources by changing the ownership from private hands to those of the State. Since then the programme of nationalization of key industries and financial institutions was completely shelved. That was a signal blow to the speedy growth of the public sector in India. The private sector is still holding a very large area of industries and financial institutions which were brought under the purview of Industrial Policy Resolutions.

Quest For Equality

The quest for equality and dignity of man is the chief objective of the economic reconstruction in India. The enlargement of public sector is considered as a stepping stone towards this objective. This aspect is very important when we look at the fact that Indian economy is not a socialist economy. It is essentially a capitalist one with an imperialist background—a hurdle in the way to the attainment of an egalitarian society. The need is to break through this capitalist set-up.

The socialist economy to which India is ideologically wedded demands the commanding position of the State in its economic affairs. Only a determined government can conceivably attach a truly anti-capitalistic significance to the management of the public sector as well as of the economy as a whole. It can do this only if the activities of the public sector are planned as a whole, with no restraint placed on public enterprise even when it threatens to undermine the position of private industry. But unfortunately in India the public sector functions as a sort of a beneficent milch cow for private capital. The straight subsidies and grants from the public exchequer and the public contracts farmed out to private industry with a guaranteed profit are examples of techniques whereby the Government has allowed the public sector to be exploited. Some of the Government-owned finance corporations like the Industrial Development Corporation and State Financial Corporations are used mainly to feed the private capitalists.

Rapid Development

State ownership in India is young and weak from the point of view of the rate and scale of accumulation; and its structure is backward. In view of the ascending trend of socialism in the country, the state enterprises demand rapid development. The policy which the Government of India has adopted at the present time, of accelerating the development of productive forces by creating heavy industries in a relatively short time, is stilted by foreign aid and the undue influence exerted by the indigenous private monopolists on the Government.

Any study on public sector will be incomplete if it overlooks the impact of the private sector and private monopoly on the nation's economy and the Government's attitude towards them. Indian economy as already stated is a capitalist one. The position and influence that private big business enjoy in this country poses a big problem. The sources of the position and power of these big business are many. One is the bigness of the concerns itself. The Tatas own 53 companies with a total assets of Rs. 417.7 crores. The Birlas own 151 companies with a total assets of Rs. 292.7 crores. They produce various commodities ranging from railway locomotives to soap and hair oil. Railway wagons, cars, cement, steel, cranes, fans, cloth, paper, jute and vanaspati are among the other items. Like them, there are at least 75 other groups of companies with assets above

Rs. 5 crores, with the total assets at Rs. 2,605.95 crores. This constitutes 46.9 percent of the assets of all non-Government and non-banking companies in India.

This dominance of these big business groups in the nation's economic affairs is detrimental to the small and medium-size producers. In many cases a single undertaking is the only supplier, or often it commands a very large portion of the market. In such cases, they are in a strategic position to dictate prices and regulate the volume of production in such a manner as to maximize the profits. There is no valid reason why they should not be brought under the ownership and control of the Government, except the fact that they are financiers of the ruling Congress Party, to give a sound base to the public sector.

Pillars of Power

The people of India are very sensitive about this problem. Jawaharlal Nehru's soft approach in dealing with these big business groups led ultimately to the concentration of economic power and wealth in the hands of a few. The strategic centres where agglomeration prevails are big industry, business and banking. These three constitutes the pillars of economic power in developing India.

In the name of a private sector, these strategic centres of economy are flourishing largely in the hands of a few, who enjoy the virtual control over them. Four business houses of India – Tata, Birla, Dalmia-Jain and Martin Burn – have 26.6 percent of the total share capital of the non-Government companies. The banks in India are at the disposal of a few families and industrial borrowers. About 650 accounts constitute two-thirds of the total advances. This indicates how dominant they are in our economic system. Now, they grow octopus like, stretching their long tentacles into every aspect of the national life, including the very functioning of the governmental machinery. In shaping Government policies, they exert a lot of influence through the ruling party bosses, members of Parliament, and above all the monopolist press they own.

Of all the means, the foremost is of the ruling Congress Party machinery. Time and again the Indian National Congress has accepted huge sums of money from big business houses for the party's expenses, election and other. Promising full protection to the big business, the party found it convenient to finance itself largely with donations from the business monopolists. The big business contribution to the election fund of the Congress Party in 1962 can be taken as an example. In fact, in the last General Elections the business houses provided 48.93 percent of the Congress funds. For the election expenses, according to the official figures, in 1962, the party received Rs. 15,56,000 from Tatas, Rs. 10,70,000 from Martin Burn (the owner of Indian Iron and Steel Ltd.), Rs. 7,78,239 from Birlas and Rs. 6,92,500 from Khatau Makanji. For other purposes in 1962 and 1963 the Party received Rs. 1,86,000 and Rs. 40,000 respectively from Tatas and Rs. 59,023 and Rs. 60,117 respectively from Birlas.

Steel the 'Backbone'

It is important to note that the biggest contributors to the Congress fund were the private owners of the backbone of our industrial development — steel. No one can conceive that these contributions to the ruling party were just because of their ideological commitment to the Congress. The Industrial Policy Resolution states that steel is a basic industry. The nationwide consensus is to nationalize the steel industry with top priority. But the big business demonstrates that through the weight of money, by way of giving ransom to the Congress Party every year not to nationalize their concerns, they can stop the Congress Government from yielding to the wishes of the nation. The balance-sheets of 144 major registered companies impending nationalization disclosed that they gave the ruling party Rs. 79,04,197 in 1961-62 to fight the General Elections and Rs. 9,81,970 and Rs. 3,02,392 in 1962-63 and 1963-64 respectively. Of the above mentioned contribution for 1961-62 Rs. 68,74,571 was from 31 business groups.

Another strong weapon they use is the chain newspapers they own as adjuncts to their business. The Birlas own the *Hindustan Times* with its financial paper *The Eastern Economist*. The Sahu-Jain group owns the *Times of India,* with its financial paper the *Economic Times*. *The Statesman* is owned by a group of industrialists including the Tatas. Through the mass media they give prompt advice to the policy makers. Many a Minister and civil servant strictly follow the 'advice' of these spokesmen of big business in framing economic policies and give sufficient safeguard to their ill-gotten profits and wealth. Using all the channels available to them, they strive to restrict expenditures of the budget mainly to the construction of State enterprises like electric power systems, railroads, automobile highways, ports, other means of communication, irrigation and other enterprises except plants and factories. This is all the more advantageous to the private business because by and large they comprise what is called the infrastructure branches of the economy. In this way, they manage to see that State orders are open to them and new territories are placed at their disposal.

Direct Challenge

These are some of the factors indirectly affecting the growth of the public sector in India. But the direct challenge comes from the pelf of the private sector itself. With the resources at their command and the economic power they enjoy, they are enabled to buy the best, but unpatriotic, brains in every field, offering high salaries which the public sector cannot afford to pay, and thus practically snatch them away from public sector some times. In order to keep a close link with the civil servants and other keymen in the Government and the ruling party, they offer high posts and fat salaries to the relatives of those concerned, irrespective of their professional competence. In many cases they take retired civil servants and ex-ministers on their Boards of Directors in order to influence their erstwhile subordinates in the ministry and the Government. In this way caught between a weak Government policy and the pressures of the private sector, the State enterprises could not help becoming subordinate to the latter.

Thus the subordination of the public sector to the interests of the private sector has been systematic in the ruling circles. In certain cases they give priority to the development of private concerns contrary to the letter and spirit of the Industrial Policy Resolutions. A recent instance of flouting the resolution was the permission given to the Indian Iron and Steel Company Ltd. for expansion from 1 million to 1.3 million tons of ingots and the permission given to the Tatas to negotiate with the World Bank (who once advised the Government of India not to go for steel production, stating that imported steel would be cheaper than that indigeneously produced) for loans to step up the production of the Tata Iron and Steel Company to 2 million ton ingots per annum. In the meantime the expansion scheme of the Rourkela Steel Plant from 1.8 million to 2.5 million tons of ingot per year is suspended for an year, apparently not because of any fault of its West German collaborators. The Congress Government is doing many things as if there is no Industrial Policy Resolution at all.

Bureaucratic Control

A focal point in criticizing the public sector is in the name of efficiency emanating from the bureaucratic control of the management and administration. There are three main forms under which the State enterprises are organized. They are departmental management, statutory corporations, and joint stock companies. Most of the concerns belong to the last category. In comparison, the departmentally-managed concerns are the worst sufferers. In the fetter of red tape and circumlocution quick decision becomes almost an impossibility, a condition which is not favourable for any healthy growth. It is in this group the interference from above is maximum. The efficient conduct of a public enterprise ultimately depends on the removal of road blocks and unnecessary interference from outside in its internal affairs. An important step to be taken in this direction is to free them from the bureaucratic set-up and ensure them freedom of action and autonomy. In the question of autonomy the statutory corporations top in the group, with enough freedom to withstand direct and indirect pressures from the representatives of the Government at various levels, combining the advantages of autonomy with accountability. The least desirable form of public sector is the joint stock companies.

A right step to boost efficiency in the management of public sector is that when they become sufficiently large, they should be brought under a machinery directly responsible to the elected Government, probably through high-level boards comprising the representatives of industry or service with elected political representatives. It can bring effective co-ordination on the one hand and have supervision, at the highest level, on the other. Also, it will enhance the position and autonomy of the concerns. The industries ripe for the establishment of such boards are iron and steel, fertilizers, heavy electricals and heavy engineering.

Civil Servants

There is a serious danger in assigning top-level managerial posts in the public sector enterprises to civil servants for shorter periods. The civil servants change their places frequently and there is a constant exchange of responsibility in their case between the Government administration and the managements of public enterprises. This arrangement thwarts the autonomy of the enterprises and prevents growth of enterprise. Since most of the managerial personnel of the public sector belong to the category of all-India services, while functioning in the enterprises as executives, they always keep an eye on New Delhi hoping to return to the Secretariat. The hope for a different line of career makes one's position vulnerable to influences from various levels of the State apparatus. This situation generally creates problems of discipline and efficiency in the public sector.

In order to provide efficiency and drive in the State-owned enterprises, India has to follow the Swedish model of bifurcating the Civil Service into Public Service and Public Enterprises Service and facilitate the growth of expertise. The establishment of a management pool of officials selected from various departments can be considered as a step in this direction. But it does not solve the problem adequately.

As a part of efficiency drive and considering the growing importance of the public sector in nation's economic development it is repeatedly suggested that a separate Ministry should be constituted to manage the day-to-day affairs of the public undertakings, so that the financial and managerial requirements can be pooled and satisfactorily managed. The managerial personnel should remain within the jurisdiction of the Ministry. This will provide a sound base for the healthy growth of the public sector.

Our expanding public sector, with a host of projects, steel mills, fertilizer plants and machine building industries, is the pride of India. Our hopes and dreams are greatly centred on it. In spite of the luke-warm attitude of the party in power to expand it through nationalization, it grew because of the economic exigencies. Every Indian can feel proud that breaking the blockades and other hurdles placed by the capitalists in India and abroad to stunt its growth, some public sector undertakings like the Hindustan Machine Tools and the Hindustan Steel, have already entered the overseas market to compete with the products of highly industrialized countries.

Unfortunately, so far, it could not make any impact on the day-to-day problems of the people at large, mainly because of its limited role in the area of consumer goods industry. Until the dominance of the State enterprise is established in this important area the common man will not feel the social benefits, emanating from the large-scale State enterprises, leading to greater equality and social justice. Already the public sector has become the symbol of the nation's fight against monopoly and exploitation. Franklin D. Roosevelt was a better spokesman of the whole concept when he said: 'The power of a few to manage the economic life of the nation must be diffused among the many or be transferred to the public and democratically controlled government.' The progressive forces in India feel the second one the fitter for the Indian conditions.

12

India's Language Problem*

As a major issue the language problem appeared first in the political arena during the time of general elections held under the Act of 1935. The main controversy at that time was between Hindi and Urdu as national language though some muffled voices were raised in favour of one or two other languages like Tamil and Bengali, for special consideration. In the excitement Gandhiji's desire of making Hidustani as the national language was side-tracked. With the introduction of provincial autonomy in 1937 the question of an inter-provincial language came to the fore. The decade that followed witnessed the fiercest controversy over the question. But no concrete result came out. The Hindi-Urdu controversy died down with the partition of India.

After independence politicians became enthusiastic for the replacement of the language of the erstwhile rulers with a suitable national language. A substantial section acclaimed Hindi as the would-be official language of the Indian Union. They wanted a similar change in the medium of instruction in the institutions of higher learning also. As a preliminary step a few books were translated into Hindi and many books were written in Hindi.

But when the initial enthusiasm subsided the linguistic situation showed signs of unexpected complexity. This started with the intensification of the hate-English campaign. And perhaps, no other problem could have roused so much emotion and controversy since independence among politicians and educationists and evoked more contradictory views from the people of the various regions of the country.

* 1967

Constituent Assembly Decision

Meanwhile, the Constituent Assembly sat down to frame the Constitution of India. And the question of the national language also came for its scrutiny. Sharp differences of opinion were expressed over the adoption of a regional language as the national language. The opposition was mainly based on the fact that if a regional language was accepted as the national language it would put the people of other regions in built-up disadvantage. However, with the barest of majorities, a decision was arrived at that Hindi written in Devanagari Script should be the 'official language of the Union', and that English should continue to be used for all the purposes for which it was used immediately before independence.

But the Constitution-makers did not envisage the possibility of any future linguistic exclusiveness and conflict joining forces with latent regionalism and fissiparous tendencies.

In 1950, when Hindi formally became the official language of the Indian Union, people in non-Hindi speaking regions, especially in Bengal and the South, registered their protest and stated that if Hindi replaced English in the all India competitive examinations for recruitment to the various services, candidates from non-Hindi speaking regions would be put at a disadvantage. This feeling was widespread and deep-seated especially in South India.

After a pause of a few years the language problem began to take a new turn. All sorts of complications, doubts, fears and suspicions began to creep into the minds of various regions of India. Opposition to the fifteen year time limit for the switch-over, and also to the introduction of Hindi as such started gaining momentum among some sections of the people. Eminent personalities of the country including lawyers, judges, educationists, scientists and other public men, irrespective of the region they hail from, also started making plea for the retention of English as the official language. At the same time supporters of Hindi also intensified their campaign for the introduction of Hindi as early as possible. Thus two opposite groups with clear-cut objects were set in. This led to the appointment of the Official Language Commission in 1955 to study the problem. The Commission submitted its report in 1956. The controversy once again started with ominous implications.

Nehru's Assurance

In Madras and Calcutta two – language conventions were held in December 1957 and March 1958 respectively. They were attended by several prominent personalities of India. The general consensus of opinion at these conventions was that English should continue indefinitely as the official language of the country and that the Constitution should be amended to that effect. At the same time, the advocates of Hindi intensified their campaign to make Hindi official language, if possible even before the expiry of fifteen years and they put 1965 as the dead line.

The linguistic reorganization of States was an important land-mark in the history of the language problem. Contrary to the expectations of those who pioneered it, instead of harmony it resulted in accentuating the spirit of linguistic rivalry. This started undermining the unity of India. Political parties like Dravida Munnetra Kazhagam emerged with the slogan of a separate Dravidastan and gained roots under the aegis of this rivalry. The new situation demanded a review of the whole language policy. In order to maintain the unity of India unhampered, many sophisticated Indians felt that the continuance of English as the *lingua franca* was a necessity. In India English, which was looked upon during the British period as an instrument of imperialism, came to be regarded as the vehicle of modern knowledge on science, technology and culture. The change in the political situation, which led to a shift in the attitude of the public towards English, ultimately paved the way for the three-language formula which it is said, represented the minimum measure of agreement between the conflicting views.

In 1959 Frank Anthony introduced a private-member resolution in Parliament to include English in the VIIIth Schedule of the Constitution. This was necessitated by the hostile altitude adopted towards English by the people in Hindi-speaking areas. They believed that unless English was first destroyed, Hindi would not make any headway in the non-Hindi speaking areas. During the monsoon session of the Parliament in 1959 Jawaharlal Nehru made a historic speech on national language. On 7 August 1959 Jawaharlal Nehru, as Prime Minister, assured the linguistic minorities that ' I would have it [English] as an alternative language as long as people require it and the decision for that I would leave not to the Hind-knowing people but to the non-Hindi knowing people.'

This statement weathered the storm. The linguistic minorities and the non-Hindi speaking states welcomed Nehru's declaration and considered that his assurance was as valid as English was included in the VIIIth Schedule of the Constitution. But the administrative blundering of some Central Ministries forfeited the confidence that was reposed in Nehru's assurance and a demand was put forth for getting a statutory guarantee for the assurance. But the champions of Hindi today are trying to find out the ways and means to scuttle the move and uproot English from the Indian soil. It is still not clear whether they have bestowed serious thoughts over the consequences of such a step.

As in the case of any other British colonies, the English language stepped unto Indian territory as a language of British imperialism. For a long time it was nurtured to fulfil the needs of the colonial regime. Many of our freedom fighters regarded it as an instrument of foreign dominance. During the time of the freedom struggle Mahatma Gandhi also spoke against English. But today we have to assess his statements in the background of the freedom struggle. Gandhiji started anti-English campaign as a strategy to strengthen the nationalist movement. If we examine some of his statements in those days it is evident that he modelled his criticism against English with much reservations. In 1921 Gandhiji wrote, 'English is a language of international discourse, it is a language of diplomacy and it contains rich literature.'

Chagla's Observation

The Eighth Schedule of the Indian Constitution enumerates various important languages recognized in India. Even a dead language like Sanskrit has found a place in that Schedule, but not English. The Schedule does not mention names of several other languages and those spoken by primitives and tribals. But while speaking over the private member resolution moved by Frank Anthony in Parliament, Jawaharlal Nehru made it explicitly clear that non-inclusion of an existing language in the Eighth Schedule did not mean that it ceased to be India's national language.

About this period M. C. Chagla, as the Chief Justice of Bombay High Court, observed that in the constitutional sense 'English is as much an Indian language today, as much recognized by the Constitution and as much entitled to protection as any other language spoken by any other section or community in this country'. The meaning of Nehru's statement as well as Chagla's judgement was that English should be regarded as a national language, though not incorporated in the Constitution.

It was at this time that Jawaharlal Nehru gave the pledge that English would continue indefinitely for all practical purposes as a parallel official language and that Hindi would not be forced on non-Hindi speaking people against their will. The assurance had almost the same effect that the passing of Anthony's Resolution would have had. The present demand for constitutional guarantee came up because some quarters in the administration began to give scant respect to those assurances.

Looking into the constitutional provision making Hindi as the official language of the Indian Union, one can see that the provision has been much watered down in the face of the volume of opposition to the adoption of Hindi as the official language, particularly from the non-Hindi speaking areas. The Constituent Assembly passed this provision in an atmosphere when the country was riding a crest of enthusiasm which came in the way of their seeing the inherent difficulties. The article declared Hindi as the official language but did not state how this article should be enforced in the states and what should be its status there. One has to suspect whether this provision will meet the fate of the Prohibition Law of the United States. The day on which the Official Language Commission was constituted to make recommendations the issue was reopened and the provision in the Constitution out-lived its utility.

Government' View

And that made the way clear to review the linguistic policy of the Government of India in view of the practical difficulties involved in implementing the constitutional provisions. It is pertinent to note here an observation made by the Official Language Commission, which said, 'English is one of the foremost languages in the world today. In international bodies and conferences, English has in the last ten years shot ahead of other languages which previously used to share the field along with it, and now English is unquestionably the foremost medium of international communication. In many countries of the world, English is being used as the first or compulsory second language in the educational system. For instance knowledge in respect of scientific advances and discoveries is on the whole more quickly available in the English language than in any other, and it is becoming necessary for scientists and technicians working in various fields in the different countries to know English in order to keep pace with the advances of research in their respective departments of study. We in India happen to have a considerable measure of linguistic competence in the English language developed over a period of a couple of centuries of British rule, and it would be wantonly foolish to throw away this language.' (Report, p. 33).

In this connection it may also be mentioned that the Constitution provides for minority protection too. This important provision, which demonstrates the democratic character of our Constitution should not be ignored. Since Anglo-Indians are recognized as a minority, their mother tongue – English – also should be given the status of an Indian language and also must be given the protection entitled to other national languages.

People who are opposing the continuance of English as official or link language always quote figures – right or wrong–to justify their stand. Inflated figures are often given even by responsible persons. Moraji Desai in order to justify his stand to introduce Hindi as the official language stated that more than 50 per cent of the population transact in Hindi. In the meantime they give deflated figures with regard to English. It is a fact that among the Indian languages, Hindi is spoken by the largest number. But there is some difficulty to get the exact number of people who speak this language. Even official documents cannot be treated as a reliable source since these were subjected to substantial distortion. Usually they give a total figure of those who speak of Hindi, Urdu, Hindustani and Punjabi altogether and give a percentage round about 40. If we exclude the speakers of other languages on the basis of approximation, the Hindi-speaking population constitutes about 33 percent.

Similarly, the number of English-knowing people in India is also kept vague. According to Prime Minister Indira Gandhi the number is about one percent. To the Deputy Prime Minister Morarji Desai, it is about two percent.

Since they use these figures with motives, I adopt a different method to calculate the number of English kowing population. In the *Eleventh Annual Report of the Registrar of Newspapers* for India it is stated that the circulation figures of the English Indian newspapers and journals in 1966 was 55.5 lakhs, that is, one-fourth of the circulation of all the newspapers in India. Here I exclude the number of foreign journals and newspapers which too have a fairly good circulation. The basic assumption is that one newspaper is read by a minimum of four persons. And if this assumption is accepted in India, there are at least 222 lakhs of people with a fairly good knowledge of English. This means that in the national average 5 percent of the total population is competent to communicate in English. This figure is far higher than that of some of the national languages included in the VIIIth Schedule of the Indian Constitution.

But these figures in general have not much significance in considering the question of the *lingua franca*. In calculating the number of those who speak in Hindi and other regional languages, the figure contains a vast multitude of illiterates. On the contrary the 5 percent English knowing people are necessarily literates and the extent of mobility is highest in this section.

Mobile Population

It is stated that there are about 350 million illiterates in India. In determining the link language this vast multitude has to be kept out of the picture since most of them are permanently stuck in their own regions. So excluding this the mobile population come from the remaining 860 lakhs. It is for them the link language matters much. It is to be noted that of the literates 25 percent are English speaking. But if we take the number of literates in Hindi it comes to about 253 lakhs. This means that in the national average it comes to about 5.3 percent.

But among the literates it comes to about 29 percent. An

important point to be put under scrutiny is the area in which these principal contenders are located. While the Hindi-speaking 29 percent is concentrated in a particular region, the English-speaking 25 percent is spread all over the country linking every nook and corner of India. Therefore, it is obvious that the link of national unity is built up by English and English alone and not by any other language.

Some people are bent upon throwing out English at all costs. But they hardly realize what is likely to fill the vacuum. The chance is not for a single national language but for a plethora of regional languages. The present situation is that in the non-Hindi speaking states of north India the effort to displace English is vigorous while the efforts to substitute it with Hindi is weak. In South India the replacement of English with Dravidian languages would definitely break the national unity psychologically as well as materially. S. Nijalingappa, as the Mysore Chief Minister, recently made a statement to that effect.

The general approach of the non-Hindi speaking states can be seen in another statement, recently made by the Kerala Chief Minister, E.M.S. Namboodiripad, in which he favoured continuance of English as an associate official language at the Centre and 'rapid transition' from English to regional languages in States. Obviously he favoured this rapid transition to fill the vacuum with regional languages and not by Hindi. According to Namboodiripad the formula of gradual transition would result only in the 'imposition of Hindi' on the non-Hindi speaking people. If this tendency gains momentum and if English is replaced by regional languages it would, no doubt, lead to a communication break-down between the elites of the various parts of the country. It appears that the present policy of the Union Education Minister takes no account of these realities. If the trend continues, in future, all India conferences will be a tower of Babel.

Translation

The Finance Minister of India, Morarji Desai, recently stated that there would be no dearth of funds for the translation of books and documents from English to Indian languages. Whether he did actually mean what he said is yet to be seen. It is a fact that the financial commitment behind this statements is quite unwieldy for Indian finance, especially when the country is desperately tapping all the sources for additional resources for economic development. However, the language problem should not be given and cannot have priority over the economic problems. Today money is badly needed to feed, clothe and educate millions of Indians. And, therefore, this extravagance in the name of translation is quite absurd and reminds one of the stories spread about Mohammed bin Tuglak. Moreover, in a fastly changing world of science and technology a book on these subjects becomes almost obsolete by the time it comes out in print. A scientist have to read hundreds of periodicals today to keep abreast of these rapid changes. In the circumstance the question of translation in our regional languages to impart new knowledge looks almost an impossibility.

Another important factor is that it will make it impossible for students from other regions and other nations to join a university in India. No university or college in India has cent per cent local students. In some of the larger institutions of cosmopolitan cities the percentage of non-regional students is as high as 40 to 45. No university can ignore these non-regional students. Sufficient room must be given to accommodate this section.

The same imbalance will be there in selecting the best in the field. Many are likely to be eliminated for posts in the name of the lack of proficiency in the regional language.

Equally important is the political implication of this policy. The all-India character of our education is fast diminishing. What is at stake is the unity of India to which education, rather than economic and political systems, gives a conscious base. If this base is undermined by creating several barriers on the cross country migration, as many had pointed out, it will give birth to chauvinistic tendencies in different linguistic regions of India. Can we have a well-knit all India service when the switch over to regional languages takes place completely? If recruitment to the all India services are made on the basis of a multi-media, will it be possible for it to retain its all India character? Similarly can we have an all India bar and judiciary in which interstate movement of advocates and judges are quite common?

Educationists' Views

Since the problem is more of an academic character the political parties and government should give due weight to the opinion of wise educationists, who, irrespective of the linguistic regions they come from, expressed their fear that the switch over to the regional languages would stunt the intellectual capacity of students. If political parties and government fail to listen to them it would do great harm to the young people, whom we expect to be the torch bearers of India's excellence.

Historical evidence would seem to support the conclusion that the student community of India is not willing to accept the switch over from English to the regional languages, unless it is thrust upon them in a dictatorial way. It is seen that if an option is given between English and the regional language to the university students, they voluntarily opt for English. This was made abundantly clear by the experiment in Madras by C. Subramaniam as the State Education Minister. He made a serious attempt to introduce Tamil as the medium of instruction in colleges, especially in arts subjects. But the response from the students was so poor that even the offer of special stipends failed to induce them to opt for the new medium. Ultimately the Government's decision to replace English by Tamil in colleges was revoked and the idea was given up.

Opinion Survey

A more recent instance was that the Academy of General Education, Manipal in Mysore State, conducted an opinion survey on the switch-over to the regional language as the medium of instruction. The survey revealed that 82 percent of the students opposed the proposed change. Similarly, of the members of the faculty, 85 percent opposed the change in the medium of instruction.

Similarly, the scheme to introduce all the fourteen Indian languages as the medium of the all-India competitive examination conducted by the Union Public Service Commission is impracticable. On the proposed 'state quotas' in the services on the basis of population, one has to fear whether these 'quota' system and other divisions on services and the like may undermine the unity of India as well as efficiency in administration. The English educated non-Hindi speaking middle class of India are skeptical about all these proposals which is likely to act to their disadvantage. They fear that they will not have a fair chance in the all-India competitive examination. Such fears are deep seated, widespread and genuine.

M.C. Chagla resigned from the Cabinet on the language question. According to him the introduction of regional languages in place of English in all the universities through a hasty process of switch-over will balkanize the intellectual life of India. No doubt, he can be considered a 'great cautioner' at a crucial moment in the nation's history. As K.M. Munshi stated, Chagla's resignation was a welcome protest against balkanization of the country. Some newspapers observed that his resignation was nothing less than 'a warning against a second partition of India.'

Pant's Warnings

As Dr. Zakir Hussain stated 'Language is meant to bring people together to join them and not to separate them or rend them asunder.' Dr. S. Radhakrishnan already had voiced concern over the proposed language policy and stated that it would affect the future of thousands of students going abroad and also a number of foreign students coming in for higher education every year, if regional languages were to become media of instruction in our universities. A recent statement of the Uttar Pradesh Law Minister, in a press conference that even inter-state correspondence would be switched over to Hindi, and that 'No English translation will be provided for Hindi correspondence' is an example of rigidity. As Pandit G. B. Pant, stated in Parliament on 2 September, 1959, that 'Artificial ways of building up a language can never succeed and perhaps our methods have been artificial till now.' Nobody is opposed to the development of regional languages.

But the urge to banish English from the curriculam of our schools and colleges is hard to understand. If regional languages become the media of higher learning, scientific education will degenerate into a study of a few out of date text books.

In hurrying up to eliminate English we should not forget the value of English in the immediate present, nor its importance in shaping our future. English today is the most powerful unifying element in our national life. It provides the key to inter-regional and international intercourse. Though the Casabiancas in Indian politics stands for the immediate banishment of English, wisdom demands that statesmen should refrain from taking any step which would lead to an intellectual vacuum, and intellectual aridity.

Azad's View

Attempts to banish English are mainly centered round the intention of transforming Hindi as the national language. But how far deliberate development of a language is possible is yet to be seen. Historical precedents are not always encouraging. As Maulana Abul Kalam Azad observed, Hindi could not blossom into a truly national language merely by doing away with English. It is an approach wrong and rash. When will politics in India become a problem-solving affair rather than a problem creating affair?

13

Whither India?*

Whither India? This is a question every patriotic Indian should ask himself when the Congress government celebrated the silver jubilee of India's independence. In view of the present appalling crisis to which the nation has been guided by 25 years of uninterrupted Congress rule, it can well be called the silver jubilee of the Congress failure.

When nations like Japan and Germany began their career from the ashes of the Second World War and made strident advances in improving the standard of living of their people and became strong and wealthy nations during the last 25 years, why this country which started its independent career 25 years ago with a strong balance of payment reserve, and with vast natural resources and manpower, is limping like this with a dependent posture? It is shameful that in average per capita income India takes the 102 nd place in the world, that too even after receiving loans and grants worth of Rs. 2,388 crores from the World Bank so far. When the highest per capita income in the world is Rs. 35,700, it is just Rs. 825 in India. Per capita income in Japan is Rs. 14,000 while in China it is Rs. 1,200. It is appalling that 60 percent of the population earns less than 50 paise per day. In the circumstances what jubilation an ordinary citizen can have in the silver jubilee year when abject poverty and insecurity haunt him everywhere?

Confession of Failure?

The nation is on the verge of a crisis, but whether the crisis would lead to a calamity or not, one will have to wait and

---

* 1973, during the Silver Jubilee of India's independence

see. Prime Minister Indira Gandhi has admitted the fact of this brewing crisis recently when she said that extremely difficult days are ahead. This admission is nothing but a confession of failure. The so called 'Indira wave', which swept the poll twice during the last two years, also has just receded and a new wave of unrest is surging all over. Undoubtedly, this crisis situation has emanated from the government's general failure in improving the lot of the people. The failure is so widespread that it is no longer possible to limit its effects to a particular front. As the economic situation turns from bad to worse, food stocks rapidly running down, prices going up, foreign trade dwindling, one cannot escape from having concern over the dark days ahead for the people, thanks to the mismanagement of the Congress Government. Obviously even an improvement of the situation is possible only through the removal of the Congress from power.

If we look at the national scene, in no period in history so much frustration was evident as it is today. The pain and misery of an average Indian is so appalling but no one in the Central Secretariat apparently has any concern for him. In fact no honest attempt has been made so far to improve the lot of the lower strata of society, especially of people below the poverty line. The benefits of whatever little progress the nation made have gone to the upper strata of society. The government's rudderless planning has created a privileged section which apes Western standards of comfort and living, unmindful of the abject poverty around them. These people, who always hover around the seats of power, manage to get priorities in planning to the needs of their luxurious living habits.

Prime Minister Indira Gandhi, in a recent article to the New York Journal *Foreign Affairs* (October 1972), claimed that India has attained self-sufficiency in cereals – a claim repeated off and on by other Central ministers also. She tried to impress upon the world that there was a green revolution in India and the country has attained self-sufficiency in food.

The fact is that the so-called 'green revolution' is either a myth or irrelevant to the common man. Statistics shows that between 1964 and 1973 the food production increased only by 1.8 percent in average. However, hardly the ink of the claim of the prime minister has dried on the paper when Indian ministers and officials were sprung all over the world in search of cereals for imports. The hollowness of this claim at the highest level is neatly exposed by the unprecedented scarcity situation prevailing all over the country. An interesting phenomenon is that on the one hand ministers go on promising in public that there is enough buffer stock of food, and, on the other, they and the Food Secretary go abroad secretly to look for purchase of food.

Shameful deal

Even though the Indira government conveniently put climatic conditions to blame for the famine situation, the responsibility rests squarely with the Congress. It is unfortunate that though India is an essentially agricultural country with plenty of cultivable land and water resources, the government has failed to utilize them properly to achieve self-sufficiency in food at least.

In the past this governmental failure was smoke-screened by large-scale food imports from abroad, quite often even after compromising the nation's self-interest and self-respect through such schemes like PL-480 which had permitted the American Embassy in New Delhi to hold large sums of money in Indian currency and spend it at its discretion. In fact the chunk of the foreign exchange reserve we inherited at the time of independence has also been spent purely on eatables. This kind of unproductive drain of foreign exchange over the years is criminal in view of the present difficult drive to earn it after providing subsidies and incentives for exporters. In 1969 India imported half-a-million tons of food for Rs. 55 crores. But it appears that this year's food imports will be on a much more larger scale, bringing in further erosion of our foreign exchange reserve. Now to import food the Government is prepared to go to the United States even under PL-480 scheme. If this is true, particularly with the Nixon Administration which had the audacity to send a task force of its Seventh Fleet to the Bay of Bengal to blackmail us during the Bangladesh crisis, it is a shameful deal which no Indian can relish.

During the last decade, instead of concentrating on enhanced production by bringing in new lands under cultivation, the Government has adopted weak-kneed and premature measures like price incentive, liberal credit, application of high-yielding variety of seeds, etc. Virtually there was no expansion of acreage. The Government's incompetence is so glaring that in States which are so vulnerable to water and food scarcity due to vagaries of weather year after year, nothing has been done effectively to prevent their recurrence. Periodical relief measures hardly touch the basic problem. Consequently, in the silver jubilee year of our independence extreme scarcity conditions prevail in States like Maharashtra, Gujarat, Mysore, Rajasthan and Madhya Pradesh. What does our planning mean if, even after four Five-Year Plans, the vast majority of the population is left at the mercy of nature's cruelties year after year? The Government has been all along callous to the plight of the permanent victims of these cruelties.

In the purely temporary outlook the Government fights shy to take long-term measures to transform India into a land of prosperity and plenty. A silver lining in the dark sky is an imaginative programme for building a 2000-mile feeder canal system linking the Ganga in the north with the Cauvery in the south. It appears that against heavy odds Dr. K. L. Rao, Irrigation Minister, is fighting a lone battle inside the government to get priority for this ambitious project envisaged to utilize the substantial monsoon flows of northern rivers, which at present go waste. This river canal system will make thousands of acres of fallow land cultivable through irrigation. Its estimated cost of Rs. 2,500 crores is worth spending in view of the vast potential of the project.

No More of This

The economic situation has turned from bad to worse. The nation is going bankrupt year after year and our apparent progress is only a hollow shell built up over huge foreign debt. The Prime Minster in a recent article 'India and the World' in *Foreign Affairs* admitted that at present more than half of the external assistance to India goes for repayments of earlier foreign debts (p. 68). This is the appalling situation. Since the Congress government failed miserably to utilize earlier foreign loans for productive purposes. Its initial calculations to clear the debt with our exports have just failed. Consequently, when the repayment schedule started we were in no position to do so. So we take new loans to clear earlier ones. What a bankrupt situation! Have the wealthy nations finally succeeded to make us their permanent dependents? For the last five years we are getting debt relief. Now we are approaching the World Bank nations again to get debt relief and reschedule India's debt repayment. Britain and Japan have already extended debt relief loans to India, The United States has agreed to reschedule the repayment of loans. What a shameful situation! For whose mistake we hang our heads in shame? Can we allow this state of affairs to continue? No more. When can we be free from this foreign debt? The debt is mounting. In fact the Congress government's habit of borrowing has a demoralizing effect on our will for self-reliance. The malady afflicting the economy is so chronic and the symptoms too prominent to escape public notice.

Domestically, our economy is plagued with an unprecedented rise in price spiral and black money. The price index of food grains had moved up from 100 in 1961 to 214 in 1969-70. During the last one year itself it has gone up by

20 percent. An average family spends more than 70 percent of the income for food necessities alone. Even though the prime minister conveniently puts the blame for the higher price spiral on the vagaries of weather like drought and flood and other alibis like stoppage of external aid, etc., the situation speaks eloquently of the Congress government's incompetence. Time and again the Congress party and the government pledge their determination to hold the price line. But with what effect? All these lip services were meant for mere public consumption. An interesting phenomenon is that while a decline in production immediately reflects in a rise in prices, an increase in production does not reflect in a corresponding decline in it. Even in capitalist countries the governments have a firm grip over the prices of essential commodities but, strangely, not in India! Hoarders and black-marketeers and monopolists have a free hand to control the marketing forces here. At least in a few instances the government itself is instrumental for the increase in the prices of essential commodities. To cite a recent instance, the government enhanced the price of levy sugar to Rs. 2 per kilogram not to the benefit of the farmer or to the consumer but to the benefit of the mill owners! In Delhi's open market the price of sugar per kilogram is Rs. 4. It is believed that three years ago the ruling party was benefited to the tune of Rs. 1 crore from mill-owners when the government decided to decontrol the sugar distribution. This kind of governmental measures are nothing but the promotion of middle man's exploitation. Obviously the government's concern is not for the consumer.

Black Money

No one has the doubt that a crucial and permanent factor in the upward spiral of prices is the inflation caused by the parallel functioning of black money in our economy. It has been estimated that in 1971, against a total white money supply of Rs. 7,341 crores there was Rs. 3,000 crores of black money. This fact gives a rough idea of the capabilities of black money. Added to this is the inflationary effect of the annual tax arrears which have jumped from Rs. 187 cores in 1952 to Rs. 840 crores in 1971. Even a senior Cabinet minister, like Jagjivan Ram, chose to keep more than Rs. 30,000 as tax arrears for more than 10 years, an offence which, in the criterion of the new public morality, was dismissed by the Prime Minister as 'simple forgetfulness'. The thorough failure of the governmental measures so far could be seen from the fact that, between 1965 and 1971, 1,200 police raids could unearth only Rs. 7 crores of black money.

Any government concerned for a stable economy cannot overlook the parallel functioning of black money which plays havoc with the social and economic fabric of our nation. For years together the government is adopting a callous attitude of indifference on this most important factor which plagues our very living. The most sensible proposal to kill the evil of black money (in currency and also counterfeit notes) at one stroke is demonetization, i.e. by issuing new currency notes and withdrawing accountable old notes over a short specific period. If that is done, black money will die automatically in its hiding places. After all the printing of roughly 3,500 million notes is not costlier than the damage black money is doing to our socio-economic set-up. But the Congress government is not prepared to do it for obvious reasons. Without black money where will it go for party funds to run the shell-like party machinery which needs annual pumping in of crores of rupees to maintain its external form? This overwhelming consideration for the Congress party's financial interests stops the government form any honest attempt to eradicate black money. Even the Wanchoo Committee's interim report, submitted in November 1970, favouring demonetization of notes of higher denomination and also ceiling on cash holdings has been rejected by the government. If it had implemented the Wanchoo

Committee's recommendations, obviously its impact on the Congress party's finances would have been severe. If that happens, how many years it will take to complete the work on its proposed headquarters 'Indira Bhavan', or from where they can collect money to spend huge amounts on every candidate during elections? When the Congress government itself thrives on black money can it take measures against it?

Widespread Unemployment

Further, the government has perpetuated inflation by deficit financing and overdrafts. A striking factor behind this monetary expansion is the increase in the net bank credit on the Government – Rs. 1,001 crores against Rs. 831 crores in 1970-71 – bridging a wide budgetary gap. It is significant that during the four Plans the government has released more than Rs. 3,000 crores in deficit financing. But there was no corresponding increase in production.

Added to this is the calamitous situation created by the widespread unemployment. Neither the Congress government nor the Congress party is honest in dealing with this problem. Even our scientific talent is not fully utilized. Unemployment among the scientists and engineers is also going up. As per the latest available information, in June 1972 unemployment figures among the educated (in thousands) stood at 497.4 in Tamil Nadu, 536.9 in Bihar, 772.4 in Uttar Pradesh, 160.6 in Kerala, 306.5 in Mysore, 360.6 in Andhra Pradesh, 216.0 in Maharashtra, 216.0 in Orissa, 23.4 in Punjab, 170.1 in Rajasthan, 341.8 in Madhya Pradesh, 119.5 in Haryana, 92.7 in Assam, 194.1 in Gujarat, 143.7 in Delhi, 13.0 in Goa and 31.4 in Tripura. It is in the face of this appalling situation that the Congress party and the government together try to befool the unemployed. Recently the Congress Working Committee asked the government to create half-a-million jobs in one year for employing the educated. This is bound to be an artificial scheme. Does this command mean anything except propaganda? Leaders promise this in public with a flourish but admit in private that this cannot be done. It is this kind of hypocrisy that governs the nation today. The under utilization of this talented man-power is a major factor in keeping the nation backward. The employed and low-paid young men are surging with discontent that they cannot make both ends meet.

Land Reforms

In a bid to give a socialist façade to its essentially capitalist character the Congress government has started talking about land reforms. It summoned the Congress Chief Ministers to explore the possibilities. But obviously the party and the government are not serious about it. Some state governments, like West Bengal, have not bothered to keep proper, up-to-date land survey records, without which no reform leading to a land ceiling is possible. This indifference about land records is because local Congress bosses are generally landlords, themselves having a vested interest in maintaining the *status quo*. However, when the report of the sub-committee on land ceiling came up before the Congress Working Committee, it expressed opposition to antedate the enforcement of land ceiling laws from September 1970. In effect they want to give landlords adequate time to manipulate in between through all sorts of shady transactions and defeat the very purpose of land reforms. Consequently, despite a formal ceiling law, there will be no surplus land available for redistribution.

This hypocritical approach of the Congress towards land reforms is also natural as the party is composed of wealthy landowners. Prominent Congress Leaders like Indira Gandhi, Fakhruddin Ali Ahmed, Y. B. Chavan and V. P. Naik are all having substantial land at their disposal. There was a furore in the Maharashtra Assembly two years ago when Chavan and Naik bought additional 12 and 14 acres of land respectively in their wives' name to escape public criticism. Naik's purchase was over and above his holding of 118 acres at that time. These are, for example, the captains of land reforms in the Congress Party! Can they do it in a fruitful way? It is reported that many Congress Chief Ministers are either lukewarm over the proposal or want land reforms watered down through a higher ceiling. Among the Chief Ministers who expressed misgivings about the proposal are Bansi Lal of Haryana, Kamalapati Tripathi of Uttar Pradesh and P. C. Sethi of Madhya Pradesh. The Congress has proved again that it cannot go against rich landlords. The Congress land reform can end only in a hoax.

Kerala's Example

The only State which made a substantial headway in implementing land reforms effectively is Kerala. Undoubtedly, it is the happy culmination of the initiative taken by the first Socialist Ministry in Kerala (then Travancore-Cochin State) headed by the late Pattom Thanu Pillai in 1954. The Socialist Land Reform Bill, which stipulated a maximum land ceiling at Rs. 3,600 annual income, was the model for future land reform bills in the country. For bringing out such a pioneer reform bill in agrarian relations in the State the Congress and the Communists joined together and ousted that minority Praja Socialist Party Ministry. Though the Socialists were penalized for it, they created a situation that subsequent Ministries had to give top priority to land reforms. Therefore, the Socialists have a pride of place in the history of land reforms in this country.

Promotion of monopoly houses has been the major achievement of the Congress Government all these years. All of them have expanded their empires beyond recognition. Therefore, for them Silver Jubilee has a great meaning. As a matter of fact the Congress government was always subservient to monopoly houses like the Tatas and the Birlas. This is probably because the entire Congress hierarchy now belongs to be the heir-apparents of earlier Congress leaders like Jawaharlal Nehru who were carrying blank cheques of these business houses during the freedom struggle – Birla himself stated this some years ago. Even today the Congress and its leaders owes so much to these monopoly houses in maintaining the party machinery. In the circumstances the Congress government cannot but protect these vested interests. The soft corner for monopolists is evident from the fact that contrary to the Monopoly Enquiry Commission's recommendations, the Government continues to give licences to monopoly houses for the manufacture of fertilisers and steel. It was reported that between 1969 and 1971 the Birlas got 14 new licences, the Tatas 13, the Sarabhai group 8, the Mafatlals 7, the Goenkas 4, Thapars 5, Shri Ram 4, Singhania 5, and Bangur 3. Apart from this, most of the monopoly houses have been recently permitted to increase production in certain industries up to double their licenced capacity. Not satisfied with what the Government has done over the years for them, Sidhartha Shankar Ray, the West Bengal Chief Minister who was in the Central cabinet till recently, openly pleads that the expansion of monopoly houses needs sympathetic consideration. Ray, unlike others, was honest about it at least to speak out about what the government is doing inside the Secretariat in the name of socialism. This shows that concentration of wealth in a few hands is deliberately helped by the Congress administration. The government's special love for monopoly houses has attracted criticism even from some Congress leaders like Chandrasekhar and Kishan Kant, both Young Turks. In Parliament they accused the government of non-implementation of anti-monopoly legislation.

Callous Indifference

The government's special love for monopoly houses and the private sector has resulted in callous indifference to the growth and efficiency of public sector undertakings. The way in which these undertakings are managed in this country is apt to bring discredit to the concept of public sector itself. What more the government can do to discredit the socialist concept! As a matter of fact none of the public sector plants – steel, power, fertilizer, etc.– works to capacity. The widespread deterioration in the affairs of the public sector undertakings caught the attention of the public recently when it was disclosed that 19 public sector undertakings were functioning without Chairmen or Managing Directors. In September 1972 the Government admitted in Parliament that in all 34 top posts were vacant in these undertakings. Of these the most disturbing fact was that in the Fertiliser Corporation alone as many as nine posts of General Managers of projects were vacant. Of these eight had been vacant for over two years. This simple instance can give one adequate insight into the apathy of the Government towards public sector undertakings.

And a Future Ford

Corruption and nepotism have become the hallmark of the new public morality. The most glaring instance of nepotism perpetuated at the highest level is the various moves connected with the establishment of a factory by Sanjay Gandhi, son of the Prime Minister, to produce small cars at a rate of 50,000 a year. What is most shocking in this shady deal is the reversal of pronounced State policies for personal ends. The Nehru Government had declared that as a matter of public policy small cars would be produced in the public sector only. This policy was thrown into the dustbin when the present Prime Minister's son returned from the United Kingdom after attending a sandwich course on motor mechanism. (For anybody else this qualification would be just good enough to get the job of a mechanic in a car factory). When the appropriate moment arrived, the Prime Minister took over the portfolio of Industrial Licensing herself to pass the orders, with her seal and signature, to issue licence to her son to produce the small car in the private sector. Subsequently, in August 1972, the Indira Government finally came out with the verdict that the small car project in the public sector is not feasible. This reveals the hidden outlook of the Prime Minister, her integrity to the concept of public sector, and her vision of a future socialist society. She wants her son to be a future Ford of this country, and not an ordinary citizen of a future socialist society, nor an employee of a public sector car-manufacturing company. This is the future design of Congress socialism.

Custodians of wealth are picked from different corners of the country as Directors of the new small-car factory 'Maruti Ltd.', of which the Prime Minister's son Sanjay Gandhi is the Managing Director and V.R. Mohan of Lucknow, M.A. Chitambaram of Madras, S. N. Kapadia of Bombay and Raunaq Singh of Delhi are all Directors. Apart from them, public finance institutions are lined up behind this private company to provide adequate funds for its development. Strangely, the Industrial Finance Corporation's biggest loan for 1972-73 has been given to 'Maruti' in a record time of one week! What efficiency is IFC's functioning! The Bansi Lal Government of Haryana extended special help by way of giving 296 acres of land in Gurgaon, near New Delhi, to establish the factory, at the rate of Rs.11,000 per acre – that too with a special favour to make the payment on 18 annual instalments – when the prevailing price in the locality is Rs. 60,000. All these preliminary things to start a Rs. 17 crore project are done by Sanjay Gandhi whose declared bank balance in 1972 was Rs. 748! Will another young man with similar bank balance be provided with equal facilities for doing a similar job? In simple terms this is political corruption at the highest level.

Related to this is the disposal of serious corruption charges levelled against Bansi Lal, the Haryana Chief Minister, who gave land to Prime Minister's son to establish the car factory at a concessional price. Even though the memorandum containing serious corruption charges against Bansi Lal was submitted by 125 MPs and MLAs to the President of India, no enquiry has been ordered. After completing the ritual of a formal examination by some Cabinet ministers, the prime minister came out with the announcement that Bansi Lal has been cleared of the corruption charges. Obviously the decision was not based on the merit of the charges. If it were so, instead of Central Ministers, an impartial Commission would have been appointed to go through them. Probably, in passing the verdict on the case without referring it to an impartial Commission, the prime minister could not overlook the special favour the accused has done to her son. If the fence itself eats up the crop, who can help? When this is the position at the Centre, needless to speak about the States. In general the public morality of the Congress leaders has gone descended to such a low level that it does not attach any stigma to the leaders indulging in corruption or practicing nepotism. When will we attain the British standard and purity in public life where recently Reginald Maudling, Britain's Home Secretary, resigned following an allegation that he had a business tie with a bankrupt architect. If such standards are maintained here, from Prime Minister downwards, how many would be eligible to remain in the Central Cabinet?

Credibility Gap

The credibility gap of the Congress and the government is constantly widening. Over the years there has been no co-relationship between words and deeds. AICC meetings have become a gigantic farce to hoodwink the masses. Between the propaganda and policy falls the shadow. This has always been true for the last 25 years. Even some Congressmen are bitter over this credibility gap. Chandrasekhar recently stated that the Congress leadership is not serious in implementing the pledges made in the election manifesto. The slogan 'Garibi Hatao' is nothing but empty words uttered to catch the poor man's vote. Today the slogan 'Garibi Hatao' stands out as the symbol of deceit. Knowing full well that there is no oasis in sight, the Congress and the Prime Minister are engaged in creating a mirage. The party is thriving with the rich man's money and the poor man's vote. But this situation cannot last long.

Impending Calamity

The widespread student unrest, the frustration among the youth, and the deep discontent among the workers are disquieting symptoms of the impending calamity. If rational distribution of the nation's wealth is not made in the near future, the bleak outlook might compel this surging humanity to take extraordinary measures to share the fortunes. They are well informed of the glaring disparities in income and the standard of living existing today. However, having failed to cope up with the new situation, the Government has started blaming external elements like the CIA for the failures. The Prime Minister made public statements blaming the CIA for the present waves of unrest. The Congress Chief Ministers of Assam, Madhya Pradesh, Orissa and Kashmir and Congress President S.D. Sharma have all spoken about it. But nobody has any evidence to place before the public. When the Prime Minister was asked recently for the proof of her allegation against the CIA, her reply was: 'It is not for us to prove that this agency is working in our country. It is for the CIA to prove that it is not active in India.' A State Governor, B.K. Nehru, said that there is no proof. This exploded the myth built up around CIA.

Authoritarian Tedency

The most alarming feature of the present situation is the authoritarian tendency explicit in the Congress government. As Jayaprakash Narayan said recently, India has only a shell of parliamentary democracy but not the substance. There is a constant attempt to smother the freedom of expression. Recently the freedom of the press was threatened by the Government. But the Supreme Court came to its rescue. However, our newspapers are still fighting shy to expose the misdeeds of those in power. If we had a journalist of Jack Anderson's calibre he would have told us the real story, and the leading characters, behind the State Bank of India fraud case and Nagarwala's subsequent death in prison.

As a feature of the growing authoritarianism, the States are put in constant dependence on the Central Government. Their financial position has been kept bankrupt. All expanding taxes like excise duty, income tax, etc., are kept by the Centre and all contracting taxes like land tax are given to the States. Moreover, at least in four States the Congress legislators were recently deprived of their right to have a leader of their choice. They got puppet Chief Ministers 'appointed' by the Centre. West Bengal, Madhya Pradesh, Gujarat and Orissa are all having Chief Ministers inducted like that. This shows that, apart from the Governors, the Centre virtually appoints the Chief Ministers also. Siddartha Shankar Ray, P. C. Sethi, Ganshyam Oza and Nandini Satpathy were all Central Ministers before they were imposed upon their respective States. That is how Indira Gandhi is building up a cadre of her chore-boys in the States. This is a dangerous trend which needs to be nipped in the bud.

Personality Cult

Personality cult is officially promoted. These days we see a flush of Prime Minister's name everywhere whether for new institutions or trade marks. We have a number of them now like Indira Giri, Indira Dock, Indu Film, Indira University, etc. Such proposals are encouraged by the Prime Minister to develop a personality cult. In certain cases she herself went to inaugurate them. No leader in a parliamentary democracy does like this when he or she remains in the office of Prime Minister. Moreover, State-owned mass media like the all India Radio and television are geared up to promote it. The Opposition parties' unanimous bid to make AIR an autonomous public corporation like BBC is constantly rejected by the Congress Government to promote its partisan ends. The cult has been sufficiently developed in the Congress party. Therefore, power is concentrated not only in a single party but in a single individual, Smt. Indira Gandhi. It is one woman's wishes that govern the system. As a result, it threatens individual liberty, independence of the judiciary and the impartiality of the administrator at various levels. In the circumstances, public opinion receives no attention. There is no respect for the Opposition both in Parliament and outside. Elections are rigged and the Congress party gives the lead to invade polling booths and snatch ballot boxes. Those who express opposite view are harassed and victimized. Of late, University campuses have been transformed into police cantonments and the young boys and girls of many universities are subjected to police atrocities and humiliation for ventilating genuine grievances.

In Russia's Orbit

In our external relationship, two outstanding recent steps of the Indira Government have done incalculable damage to our long-term national interest – the Indo-Soviet Treaty of 1971 and the Simla Accord between India and Pakistan. The Indo-Soviet treaty has not only blown up our traditional policy of non-alignment in international relationship but has brought in considerable suspicion in the minds of other nations of the free world. They genuinely feel that the treaty has deprived India of its traditional and respectable position of an independent, non-aligned nation capable enough to look at world issues on merits. The fact that India carried out this independent role under a bi-polar system in the past does not minimize its importance under the emerging multi-polar system. But by aligning ourselves with the Soviet Union we have allowed this role to slip out of our hands. India is now in the Soviet orbit, a satellite of the Kremlin. Whatever the interpretation by official circles in New Delhi, this treaty has reduced India's status in world politics from that of a non-aligned nation to that of an ally of Moscow.

By a foolish act the government has unnecessarily erected a barrier between India and other non-communist friendly nations. The benefits we derive out of this treaty are so negligible, but the long-term damage is incalculable. Others will look at us with distrust. It appears that the government is already feeling it. That is why time and again members of the government, from Indira Gandhi downwards, shout at the top of their voice that India is still non-aligned and so on, which nobody believes. In an effort to convince others on this point Finance Minister Y B Chavan went up to Washington in September 1972 to express India's willingness to sign a treaty with the United States similar to the Indo-Soviet Treaty. Obviously to hide one mistake the government is prepared to commit more mistakes. After all, why is this over-enthusiasm about it unless the Indo-Soviet Treaty pricks the conscience of the people in power? This is the contribution of the pro-Moscow Kashmiri Cabal who are deeply entrenched in the decision-making apparatus after the Congress split three years ago. Patriotic Indians will not allow this blot to remain on India's face for long. Undoubtedly, the Indo-Soviet Treaty is clearly against our national interest, and it stands out as the monument of the Indira Government's folly in international relationship.

Supreme Blunder

Probably, the Simla Agreement is the supreme blunder Indira Gandhi has committed. Obviously, in signing this accord, our Prime Minister and her aides were hoodwinked by Zulfikar Ali Bhutto with his excellent diplomatic skill. Bhutto came to Simla to get 5,000 square miles of Pakistani territory vacated by the Indian soldiers without clubbing the issue with the solution to the 24-year-old Kashmir problem. He succeeded remarkably in his main objective. Mr. Bhutto could restore 5,000 square miles, lost in war, to Pakistan by a simple customary promise. The troops withdrawal has also been completed. But one simple question still remains: Where do we stand vis-à-vis Pakistan? Confrontation again? Friendship? Even Indira Gandhi is not sure.

The Simla Accord is the result of an attempt to save the skin of an enthusiastic Prime Minister who wants to project herself as the champion of peace. It was not in the best interest of this country. It was the second blunder within a year in our relationship with Pakistan. During the December 1971 war we got a unique opportunity to settle the Kashmir problem once and for all by forcing Pakistan to vacate the occupied areas of Kashmir and forcing it to agree to a final demarcation of the international boundary. Surrender of the Pakistani army in Dacca had a tremendous demoralizing effect on it in the western front. But the untimely cease-fire declaration by the Prime Minister prevented the Indian Army from availing itself of the unique opportunity to solve the Kashmir problem. As Major-General E. D'souza, who was operating on the Kashmir front said on 23 December, 1971, if the war had continued for another 48 hours our forces would have thrown the Pakistan forces out of the occupied areas of Kashmir between Uri-Poonch and the Pippa Valley. But Indira Gandhi was not keen to settle the Kashmir problem. The Simla Accord was the final proof of it.

The present widespread discontent is the cumulative effect of the general failure of the Congress Government during the last 25 years in India's internal and external affairs. The nation is ill and suffering from an agricultural and industrial depression. The upward spiral of inflation and prices makes it extremely difficult for even the fixed-income groups like the middle class and the white-collar employees to make both ends meet. Despite four Five-Year Plans the vast majority of the population are living in sub-human conditions. The responsibility for this explosive situation rests squarely on the Congress Government which has ruled this country ever since Independence. Therefore, the sooner the Congress is dislodged from power the better for the nation. When this will happen would depend upon the ability and vision of the Opposition parties and other patriotic Indians and how soon they will be able to transform the prevalent discontent and unrest through agitations and hartals, into a massive movement against the Congress government.

United Challenge

Socialist forces in India have special responsibility in guiding the people in this direction. They should realize that division among socialist forces is a boon for the Congress to continue in power. It is now obvious that the people want a democratic socialist society in this country. Of late they have realized that this is not possible through the gimmicks of the Indira regime which has proved itself incapable and unreliable. Undoubtedly Indira Gandhi's Government is less than and worse than a routine government. Our apparent progress is an illusion. In the circumstances, it is the task of the Socialists to provide a viable alternative to the Congress, for which unification of socialist forces is necessary. In bringing out this unity the Socialist Party should provide the initiative and the platform.

Also by Prof. B. Vivekanandan

International Concerns of European Social Democrats (London, Macmillan & New York, St. Martin's, 1997).

Welfare States and the Future (London & New York, Palgrave Macmillan, 2005).

Pathfinders: Social Democrats of Scandinavia (Bombay, Somaiya, 1991).

Building on Solidarity : Social Democracy and the New Millennium (New Delhi, Lancer's Books, 2000).

Contemporary Socialism: An Analysis (New Delhi, Harman, 1992)

In Retrospect: Reflections on Select Issues in World Politics, 1975-2000 (New Delhi, Lancer's Books, 2001).

The Shrinking Circle: The Commonwealth in British Foreign Policy, 1945 - 1974 (Bombay, Somaiya, 1983).

The Modern Commonwealth (Introduction) (New Delhi, Arnold-Heinemann, 1984).

Welfare State System in Scandinavia (Bombay, CISDS, 2002).

India Looks Ahead : Jayaprakash Narayan Memorial Lectures, 1990 – 2001 (New Delhi, Lancer's Books, 2002).

The Issues of Our Times (Bombay, Somaiya, 1991).

As The Mind Unfolds: Issues and Personalities (Madhu Dandavate) (New Delhi, Shipra, 1993).

Echoes in Parliament: Madhu Dandavate's Speeches, 1971 - 1990 (New Delhi, Allied, 1995).

Contemporary Europe and South Asia (New Delhi, Concept, 2001).

Why Social Democracy? (Calcutta, Jadavpur University, 2007).

Index